Search Engines
Information Retrieval in Practice

Search Engines
Information Retrieval in Practice

W. BRUCE CROFT
University of Massachusetts, Amherst

DONALD METZLER
Yahoo! Research

TREVOR STROHMAN
Google Inc.

Boston Columbus Indianapolis New York San Francisco Upper Saddle River
Amsterdam Cape Town Dubai London Madrid Milan Munich Paris Montreal Toronto
Delhi Mexico City Sao Paulo Sydney Hong Kong Seoul Singapore Taipei Tokyo

Editor-in-Chief	Michael Hirsch
Acquisitions Editor	Matt Goldstein
Editorial Assistant	Sarah Milmore
Managing Editor	Jeff Holcomb
Online Product Manager	Bethany Tidd
Director of Marketing	Margaret Waples
Marketing Manager	Erin Davis
Marketing Coordinator	Kathryn Ferranti
Senior Manufacturing Buyer	Carol Melville
Text Design, Composition, and Illustrations	W. Bruce Croft, Donald Metzler, and Trevor Strohman
Cover Design	Jodi Notowitz

1 2 3 4 5 6 7 8 9 10—RRDH—13 12 11 10 09

ISBN-13: 978-0-13-136489-9
ISBN-10: 0-13-136489-8

Preface

This book provides an overview of the important issues in information retrieval, and how those issues affect the design and implementation of search engines. Not every topic is covered at the same level of detail. We focus instead on what we consider to be the most important alternatives to implementing search engine components and the information retrieval models underlying them. Web search engines are obviously a major topic, and we base our coverage primarily on the technology we all use on the Web,[1] but search engines are also used in many other applications. That is the reason for the strong emphasis on the information retrieval theories and concepts that underlie all search engines.

The target audience for the book is primarily undergraduates in computer science or computer engineering, but graduate students should also find this useful. We also consider the book to be suitable for most students in information science programs. Finally, practicing search engineers should benefit from the book, whatever their background. There is mathematics in the book, but nothing too esoteric. There are also code and programming exercises in the book, but nothing beyond the capabilities of someone who has taken some basic computer science and programming classes.

The exercises at the end of each chapter make extensive use of a Java™-based open source search engine called Galago. Galago was designed both for this book and to incorporate lessons learned from experience with the Lemur and Indri projects. In other words, this is a fully functional search engine that can be used to support real applications. Many of the programming exercises require the use, modification, and extension of Galago components.

---

[1] In keeping with common usage, most uses of the word "web" in this book are not capitalized, except when we refer to the World Wide Web as a separate entity.

Contents

In the first chapter, we provide a high-level review of the field of information retrieval and its relationship to search engines. In the second chapter, we describe the architecture of a search engine. This is done to introduce the entire range of search engine components without getting stuck in the details of any particular aspect. In Chapter 3, we focus on crawling, document feeds, and other techniques for acquiring the information that will be searched. Chapter 4 describes the statistical nature of text and the techniques that are used to process it, recognize important features, and prepare it for indexing. Chapter 5 describes how to create indexes for efficient search and how those indexes are used to process queries. In Chapter 6, we describe the techniques that are used to process queries and transform them into better representations of the user's information need.

Ranking algorithms and the retrieval models they are based on are covered in Chapter 7. This chapter also includes an overview of machine learning techniques and how they relate to information retrieval and search engines. Chapter 8 describes the evaluation and performance metrics that are used to compare and tune search engines. Chapter 9 covers the important classes of techniques used for classification, filtering, clustering, and dealing with spam. Social search is a term used to describe search applications that involve communities of people in tagging content or answering questions. Search techniques for these applications and peer-to-peer search are described in Chapter 10. Finally, in Chapter 11, we give an overview of advanced techniques that capture more of the content of documents than simple word-based approaches. This includes techniques that use linguistic features, the document structure, and the content of nontextual media, such as images or music.

Information retrieval theory and the design, implementation, evaluation, and use of search engines cover too many topics to describe them all in depth in one book. We have tried to focus on the most important topics while giving some coverage to all aspects of this challenging and rewarding subject.

Supplements

A range of supplementary material is provided for the book. This material is designed both for those taking a course based on the book and for those giving the course. Specifically, this includes:

- Extensive lecture slides (in PDF and PPT format)

- Solutions to selected end–of–chapter problems (instructors only)
- Test collections for exercises
- Galago search engine

The supplements are available at www.search-engines-book.com, or at www.aw.com.

Acknowledgments

First and foremost, this book would not have happened without the tremendous support and encouragement from our wives, Pam Aselton, Anne-Marie Strohman, and Shelley Wang. The University of Massachusetts Amherst provided material support for the preparation of the book and awarded a Conti Faculty Fellowship to Croft, which sped up our progress significantly. The staff at the Center for Intelligent Information Retrieval (Jean Joyce, Kate Moruzzi, Glenn Stowell, and Andre Gauthier) made our lives easier in many ways, and our colleagues and students in the Center provided the stimulating environment that makes working in this area so rewarding. A number of people reviewed parts of the book and we appreciated their comments. Finally, we have to mention our children, Doug, Eric, Evan, and Natalie, or they would never forgive us.

BRUCE CROFT
DON METZLER
TREVOR STROHMAN

Contents

List of Figures

List of Tables

1

Search Engines and Information Retrieval

"Mr. Helpmann, I'm keen to get into
Information Retrieval."

Sam Lowry, *Brazil*

1.1 What Is Information Retrieval?

This book is designed to help people understand search engines, evaluate and
compare them, and modify them for specific applications. Searching for information on the Web is, for most people, a daily activity. Search and communication are by far the most popular uses of the computer. Not surprisingly, many
people in companies and universities are trying to improve search by coming up
with easier and faster ways to find the right information. These people, whether
they call themselves computer scientists, software engineers, information scientists, search engine optimizers, or something else, are working in the field of *Information Retrieval*.[1] So, before we launch into a detailed journey through the
internals of search engines, we will take a few pages to provide a context for the
rest of the book.

Gerard Salton, a pioneer in information retrieval and one of the leading figures
from the 1960s to the 1990s, proposed the following definition in his classic 1968
textbook (Salton, 1968):

> Information retrieval is a field concerned with the structure, analysis, or-
> ganization, storage, searching, and retrieval of information.

Despite the huge advances in the understanding and technology of search in the
past 40 years, this definition is still appropriate and accurate. The term "informa-

---

[1] Information retrieval is often abbreviated as IR. In this book, we mostly use the full
term. This has nothing to do with the fact that many people think IR means "infrared"
or something else.

tion" is very general, and information retrieval includes work on a wide range of types of information and a variety of applications related to search.

The primary focus of the field since the 1950s has been on text and text *documents*. Web pages, email, scholarly papers, books, and news stories are just a few of the many examples of documents. All of these documents have some amount of structure, such as the title, author, date, and abstract information associated with the content of papers that appear in scientific journals. The elements of this structure are called attributes, or fields, when referring to database records. The important distinction between a document and a typical database record, such as a bank account record or a flight reservation, is that most of the information in the document is in the form of text, which is relatively unstructured.

To illustrate this difference, consider the information contained in two typical attributes of an account record, the account number and current balance. Both are very well defined, both in terms of their format (for example, a six-digit integer for an account number and a real number with two decimal places for balance) and their meaning. It is very easy to compare values of these attributes, and consequently it is straightforward to implement algorithms to identify the records that satisfy queries such as "Find account number 321456" or "Find accounts with balances greater than $50,000.00".

Now consider a news story about the merger of two banks. The story will have some attributes, such as the headline and source of the story, but the primary content is the story itself. In a database system, this critical piece of information would typically be stored as a single large attribute with no internal structure. Most of the queries submitted to a web search engine such as Google[2] that relate to this story will be of the form "bank merger" or "bank takeover". To do this search, we must design algorithms that can compare the text of the queries with the text of the story and decide whether the story contains the information that is being sought. Defining the meaning of a word, a sentence, a paragraph, or a whole news story is much more difficult than defining an account number, and consequently comparing text is not easy. Understanding and modeling how people compare texts, and designing computer algorithms to accurately perform this comparison, is at the core of information retrieval.

Increasingly, applications of information retrieval involve multimedia documents with structure, significant text content, and other media. Popular information media include pictures, video, and audio, including music and speech. In

---

[2] http://www.google.com

some applications, such as in legal support, scanned document images are also important. These media have content that, like text, is difficult to describe and compare. The current technology for searching non-text documents relies on text descriptions of their content rather than the contents themselves, but progress is being made on techniques for direct comparison of images, for example.

In addition to a range of media, information retrieval involves a range of tasks and applications. The usual search scenario involves someone typing in a query to a search engine and receiving answers in the form of a list of documents in ranked order. Although searching the World Wide Web (*web search*) is by far the most common application involving information retrieval, search is also a crucial part of applications in corporations, government, and many other domains. *Vertical search* is a specialized form of web search where the domain of the search is restricted to a particular topic. *Enterprise search* involves finding the required information in the huge variety of computer files scattered across a corporate intranet. Web pages are certainly a part of that distributed information store, but most information will be found in sources such as email, reports, presentations, spreadsheets, and structured data in corporate databases. *Desktop search* is the personal version of enterprise search, where the information sources are the files stored on an individual computer, including email messages and web pages that have recently been browsed. *Peer-to-peer search* involves finding information in networks of nodes or computers without any centralized control. This type of search began as a file sharing tool for music but can be used in any community based on shared interests, or even shared locality in the case of mobile devices. Search and related information retrieval techniques are used for advertising, for intelligence analysis, for scientific discovery, for health care, for customer support, for real estate, and so on. Any application that involves a *collection*[3] of text or other unstructured information will need to organize and search that information.

Search based on a user query (sometimes called *ad hoc search* because the range of possible queries is huge and not prespecified) is not the only text-based task that is studied in information retrieval. Other tasks include *filtering*, *classification*, and *question answering*. Filtering or tracking involves detecting stories of interest based on a person's interests and providing an alert using email or some other mechanism. Classification or categorization uses a defined set of labels or classes

---

[3] The term *database* is often used to refer to a collection of either structured or unstructured data. To avoid confusion, we mostly use the term *document collection* (or just *collection*) for text. However, the terms *web database* and *search engine database* are so common that we occasionally use them in this book.

(such as the categories listed in the Yahoo! Directory[4]) and automatically assigns those labels to documents. Question answering is similar to search but is aimed at more specific questions, such as "What is the height of Mt. Everest?". The goal of question answering is to return a specific answer found in the text, rather than a list of documents. Table 1.1 summarizes some of these aspects or dimensions of the field of information retrieval.

Examples of Content	Examples of Applications	Examples of Tasks
Text	Web search	Ad hoc search
Images	Vertical search	Filtering
Video	Enterprise search	Classification
Scanned documents	Desktop search	Question answering
Audio	Peer-to-peer search	
Music		

Table 1.1. Some dimensions of information retrieval

1.2 The Big Issues

Information retrieval researchers have focused on a few key issues that remain just as important in the era of commercial web search engines working with billions of web pages as they were when tests were done in the 1960s on document collections containing about 1.5 megabytes of text. One of these issues is *relevance*. Relevance is a fundamental concept in information retrieval. Loosely speaking, a relevant document contains the information that a person was looking for when she submitted a query to the search engine. Although this sounds simple, there are many factors that go into a person's decision as to whether a particular document is relevant. These factors must be taken into account when designing algorithms for comparing text and ranking documents. Simply comparing the text of a query with the text of a document and looking for an exact match, as might be done in a database system or using the grep utility in Unix, produces very poor results in terms of relevance. One obvious reason for this is that language can be used to ex-

---

[4] http://dir.yahoo.com/

press the same concepts in many different ways, often with very different words. This is referred to as the *vocabulary mismatch problem* in information retrieval.

It is also important to distinguish between *topical relevance* and *user relevance*. A text document is topically relevant to a query if it is on the same topic. For example, a news story about a tornado in Kansas would be topically relevant to the query "severe weather events". The person who asked the question (often called the user) may not consider the story relevant, however, if she has seen that story before, or if the story is five years old, or if the story is in Chinese from a Chinese news agency. User relevance takes these additional features of the story into account.

To address the issue of relevance, researchers propose *retrieval models* and test how well they work. A retrieval model is a formal representation of the process of matching a query and a document. It is the basis of the *ranking algorithm* that is used in a search engine to produce the ranked list of documents. A good retrieval model will find documents that are likely to be considered relevant by the person who submitted the query. Some retrieval models focus on topical relevance, but a search engine deployed in a real environment must use ranking algorithms that incorporate user relevance.

An interesting feature of the retrieval models used in information retrieval is that they typically model the statistical properties of text rather than the linguistic structure. This means, for example, that the ranking algorithms are typically far more concerned with the counts of word occurrences than whether the word is a noun or an adjective. More advanced models do incorporate linguistic features, but they tend to be of secondary importance. The use of word frequency information to represent text started with another information retrieval pioneer, H.P. Luhn, in the 1950s. This view of text did not become popular in other fields of computer science, such as natural language processing, until the 1990s.

Another core issue for information retrieval is *evaluation*. Since the quality of a document ranking depends on how well it matches a person's expectations, it was necessary early on to develop evaluation measures and experimental procedures for acquiring this data and using it to compare ranking algorithms. Cyril Cleverdon led the way in developing evaluation methods in the early 1960s, and two of the measures he used, *precision* and *recall*, are still popular. Precision is a very intuitive measure, and is the proportion of retrieved documents that are relevant. Recall is the proportion of relevant documents that are retrieved. When the recall measure is used, there is an assumption that all the relevant documents for a given query are known. Such an assumption is clearly problematic in a web search environment, but with smaller *test collections* of documents, this measure can be useful. A test collection[5] for information retrieval experiments consists of a collection of text documents, a sample of typical queries, and a list of relevant documents for each query (the *relevance judgments*). The best-known test collections are those associated with the TREC[6] evaluation forum.

Evaluation of retrieval models and search engines is a very active area, with much of the current focus on using large volumes of log data from user interactions, such as *clickthrough* data, which records the documents that were clicked on during a search session. Clickthrough and other log data is strongly correlated with relevance so it can be used to evaluate search, but search engine companies still use relevance judgments in addition to log data to ensure the validity of their results.

The third core issue for information retrieval is the emphasis on users and their *information needs*. This should be clear given that the evaluation of search is user-centered. That is, the users of a search engine are the ultimate judges of quality. This has led to numerous studies on how people interact with search engines and, in particular, to the development of techniques to help people express their information needs. An information need is the underlying cause of the query that a person submits to a search engine. In contrast to a request to a database system, such as for the balance of a bank account, text queries are often poor descriptions of what the user actually wants. A one-word query such as "cats" could be a request for information on where to buy cats or for a description of the Broadway musical. Despite their lack of specificity, however, one-word queries are very common in web search. Techniques such as *query suggestion*, *query expansion*, and *relevance feedback* use interaction and context to refine the initial query in order to produce better ranked lists.

These issues will come up throughout this book, and will be discussed in considerably more detail. We now have sufficient background to start talking about the main product of research in information retrieval—namely, search engines.

1.3 Search Engines

A search engine is the practical application of information retrieval techniques to large-scale text collections. A web search engine is the obvious example, but as

---

[5] Also known as an evaluation *corpus* (plural *corpora*).

[6] Text REtrieval Conference—http://trec.nist.gov/

has been mentioned, search engines can be found in many different applications, such as desktop search or enterprise search. Search engines have been around for many years. For example, MEDLINE, the online medical literature search system, started in the 1970s. The term "search engine" was originally used to refer to specialized hardware for text search. From the mid-1980s onward, however, it gradually came to be used in preference to "information retrieval system" as the name for the software system that compares queries to documents and produces ranked result lists of documents. There is much more to a search engine than the ranking algorithm, of course, and we will discuss the general architecture of these systems in the next chapter.

Search engines come in a number of configurations that reflect the applications they are designed for. Web search engines, such as Google and Yahoo!,[7] must be able to capture, or *crawl*, many terabytes of data, and then provide subsecond response times to millions of queries submitted every day from around the world. Enterprise search engines—for example, Autonomy[8]—must be able to process the large variety of information sources in a company and use company-specific knowledge as part of search and related tasks, such as *data mining*. Data mining refers to the automatic discovery of interesting structure in data and includes techniques such as *clustering*. Desktop search engines, such as the Microsoft Vista™ search feature, must be able to rapidly incorporate new documents, web pages, and email as the person creates or looks at them, as well as provide an intuitive interface for searching this very heterogeneous mix of information. There is overlap between these categories with systems such as Google, for example, which is available in configurations for enterprise and desktop search.

Open source search engines are another important class of systems that have somewhat different design goals than the commercial search engines. There are a number of these systems, and the Wikipedia page for information retrieval[9] provides links to many of them. Three systems of particular interest are Lucene,[10] Lemur,[11] and the system provided with this book, Galago.[12] Lucene is a popular Java-based search engine that has been used for a wide range of commercial applications. The information retrieval techniques that it uses are relatively simple.

[7] http://www.yahoo.com

[8] http://www.autonomy.com

[9] http://en.wikipedia.org/wiki/Information_retrieval

[10] http://lucene.apache.org

[11] http://www.lemurproject.org

[12] http://www.search-engines-book.com

Lemur is an open source toolkit that includes the Indri C++-based search engine. Lemur has primarily been used by information retrieval researchers to compare advanced search techniques. Galago is a Java-based search engine that is based on the Lemur and Indri projects. The assignments in this book make extensive use of Galago. It is designed to be fast, adaptable, and easy to understand, and incorporates very effective information retrieval techniques.

The "big issues" in the design of search engines include the ones identified for information retrieval: effective ranking algorithms, evaluation, and user interaction. There are, however, a number of additional critical features of search engines that result from their deployment in large-scale, operational environments. Foremost among these features is the *performance* of the search engine in terms of measures such as *response time*, *query throughput*, and *indexing speed*. Response time is the delay between submitting a query and receiving the result list, throughput measures the number of queries that can be processed in a given time, and indexing speed is the rate at which text documents can be transformed into indexes for searching. An *index* is a data structure that improves the speed of search. The design of indexes for search engines is one of the major topics in this book.

Another important performance measure is how fast new data can be incorporated into the indexes. Search applications typically deal with dynamic, constantly changing information. *Coverage* measures how much of the existing information in, say, a corporate information environment has been indexed and stored in the search engine, and *recency* or *freshness* measures the "age" of the stored information.

Search engines can be used with small collections, such as a few hundred emails and documents on a desktop, or extremely large collections, such as the entire Web. There may be only a few users of a given application, or many thousands. *Scalability* is clearly an important issue for search engine design. Designs that work for a given application should continue to work as the amount of data and the number of users grow. In section 1.1, we described how search engines are used in many applications and for many tasks. To do this, they have to be *customizable* or *adaptable*. This means that many different aspects of the search engine, such as the ranking algorithm, the interface, or the indexing strategy, must be able to be tuned and adapted to the requirements of the application.

Practical issues that impact search engine design also occur for specific applications. The best example of this is *spam* in web search. Spam is generally thought of as unwanted email, but more generally it could be defined as misleading, inappropriate, or non-relevant information in a document that is designed for some commercial benefit. There are many kinds of spam, but one type that search engines must deal with is spam words put into a document to cause it to be retrieved in response to popular queries. The practice of "spamdexing" can significantly degrade the quality of a search engine's ranking, and web search engine designers have to develop techniques to identify the spam and remove those documents. Figure 1.1 summarizes the major issues involved in search engine design.

Information Retrieval   **Search Engines**

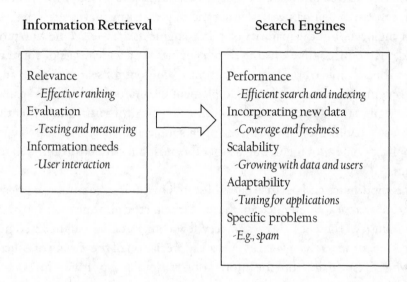

Relevance
   -Effective ranking
Evaluation
   -Testing and measuring
Information needs
   -User interaction

Performance
   -Efficient search and indexing
Incorporating new data
   -Coverage and freshness
Scalability
   -Growing with data and users
Adaptability
   -Tuning for applications
Specific problems
   -E.g., spam

Fig. 1.1. Search engine design and the core information retrieval issues

Based on this discussion of the relationship between information retrieval and search engines, we now consider what roles computer scientists and others play in the design and use of search engines.

1.4 Search Engineers

Information retrieval research involves the development of mathematical models of text and language, large-scale experiments with test collections or users, and a lot of scholarly paper writing. For these reasons, it tends to be done by academics or people in research laboratories. These people are primarily trained in computer science, although information science, mathematics, and, occasionally, social science and computational linguistics are also represented. So who works with search engines? To a large extent, it is the same sort of people but with a more practical emphasis. The computing industry has started to use the term *search engineer* to describe this type of person. Search engineers are primarily people trained in computer science, mostly with a systems or database background. Surprisingly few of them have training in information retrieval, which is one of the major motivations for this book.

What is the role of a search engineer? Certainly the people who work in the major web search companies designing and implementing new search engines are search engineers, but the majority of search engineers are the people who modify, extend, maintain, or tune existing search engines for a wide range of commercial applications. People who design or "optimize" content for search engines are also search engineers, as are people who implement techniques to deal with spam. The search engines that search engineers work with cover the entire range mentioned in the last section: they primarily use open source and enterprise search engines for application development, but also get the most out of desktop and web search engines.

The importance and pervasiveness of search in modern computer applications has meant that search engineering has become a crucial profession in the computer industry. There are, however, very few courses being taught in computer science departments that give students an appreciation of the variety of issues that are involved, especially from the information retrieval perspective. This book is intended to give potential search engineers the understanding and tools they need.

References and Further Reading

In each chapter, we provide some pointers to papers and books that give more detail on the topics that have been covered. This additional reading should not be necessary to understand material that has been presented, but instead will give more background, more depth in some cases, and, for advanced topics, will describe techniques and research results that are not covered in this book.

The classic references on information retrieval, in our opinion, are the books by Salton (1968; 1983) and van Rijsbergen (1979). Van Rijsbergen's book remains popular, since it is available on the Web.[13] All three books provide excellent descriptions of the research done in the early years of information retrieval, up to the late 1970s. Salton's early book was particularly important in terms of defining the field of information retrieval for computer science. More recent books include Baeza-Yates and Ribeiro-Neto (1999) and Manning et al. (2008).

Research papers on all the topics covered in this book can be found in the Proceedings of the Association for Computing Machinery (ACM) Special Interest Group on Information Retrieval (SIGIR) Conference. These proceedings are available on the Web as part of the ACM Digital Library.[14] Good papers on information retrieval and search also appear in the European Conference on Information Retrieval (ECIR), the Conference on Information and Knowledge Management (CIKM), and the Web Search and Data Mining Conference (WSDM). The WSDM conference is a spin-off of the World Wide Web Conference (WWW), which has included some important papers on web search. The proceedings from the TREC workshops are available online and contain useful descriptions of new research techniques from many different academic and industry groups. An overview of the TREC experiments can be found in Voorhees and Harman (2005). An increasing number of search-related papers are beginning to appear in database conferences, such as VLDB and SIGMOD. Occasional papers also show up in language technology conferences, such as ACL and HLT (Association for Computational Linguistics and Human Language Technologies), machine learning conferences, and others.

---

[13] http://www.dcs.gla.ac.uk/Keith/Preface.html

[14] http://www.acm.org/dl

Exercises

1.1. Think up and write down a small number of queries for a web search engine. Make sure that the queries vary in length (i.e., they are not all one word). Try to specify exactly what information you are looking for in some of the queries. Run these queries on two commercial web search engines and compare the top 10 results for each query by doing relevance judgments. Write a report that answers at least the following questions: What is the precision of the results? What is the overlap between the results for the two search engines? Is one search engine clearly better than the other? If so, by how much? How do short queries perform compared to long queries?

1.2. *Site search* is another common application of search engines. In this case, search is restricted to the web pages at a given website. Compare site search to web search, vertical search, and enterprise search.

1.3. List five web services or sites that you use that appear to use search, *not* including web search engines. Describe the role of search for that service. Also describe whether the search is based on a database or grep style of matching, or if the search is using some type of ranking.

1.4. Use the Web to find as many examples as you can of open source search engines, information retrieval systems, or related technology. Give a brief description of each search engine and summarize the similarities and differences between them.

2

Architecture of a Search Engine

> "While your first question may be the most pertinent, you may or may not realize it is also the most irrelevant."
>
> The Architect, *Matrix Reloaded*

2.1 What Is an Architecture?

In this chapter, we describe the basic software architecture of a search engine. Although there is no universal agreement on the definition, a software architecture generally consists of software components, the interfaces provided by those components, and the relationships between them. An architecture is used to describe a system at a particular level of abstraction. An example of an architecture used to provide a standard for integrating search and related language technology components is UIMA (Unstructured Information Management Architecture).[1] UIMA defines interfaces for components in order to simplify the addition of new technologies into systems that handle text and other unstructured data.

Our search engine architecture is used to present high-level descriptions of the important components of the system and the relationships between them. It is not a code-level description, although some of the components do correspond to software modules in the Galago search engine and other systems. We use this architecture in this chapter and throughout the book to provide context to the discussion of specific techniques.

An architecture is designed to ensure that a system will satisfy the application requirements or goals. The two primary goals of a search engine are:

- Effectiveness (quality): We want to be able to retrieve the most relevant set of documents possible for a query.
- Efficiency (speed): We want to process queries from users as quickly as possible.

---

[1] http://www.research.ibm.com/UIMA

We may have more specific goals, too, but usually these fall into the categories of effectiveness or efficiency (or both). For instance, the collection of documents we want to search may be changing; making sure that the search engine immediately reacts to changes in documents is both an effectiveness issue and an efficiency issue.

The architecture of a search engine is determined by these two requirements. Because we want an efficient system, search engines employ specialized data structures that are optimized for fast retrieval. Because we want high-quality results, search engines carefully process text and store text statistics that help improve the relevance of results.

Many of the components we discuss in the following sections have been used for decades, and this general design has been shown to be a useful compromise between the competing goals of effective and efficient retrieval. In later chapters, we will discuss these components in more detail.

2.2 Basic Building Blocks

Search engine components support two major functions, which we call the *indexing process* and the *query process*. The indexing process builds the structures that enable searching, and the query process uses those structures and a person's query to produce a ranked list of documents. Figure 2.1 shows the high-level "building blocks" of the indexing process. These major components are *text acquisition*, *text transformation*, and *index creation*.

The task of the text acquisition component is to identify and make available the documents that will be searched. Although in some cases this will involve simply using an existing collection, text acquisition will more often require building a collection by *crawling* or scanning the Web, a corporate intranet, a desktop, or other sources of information. In addition to passing documents to the next component in the indexing process, the text acquisition component creates a document data store, which contains the text and *metadata* for all the documents. Metadata is information about a document that is not part of the text content, such the document type (e.g., email or web page), document structure, and other features, such as document length.

The text transformation component transforms documents into *index terms* or *features*. Index terms, as the name implies, are the parts of a document that are stored in the index and used in searching. The simplest index term is a word, but not every word may be used for searching. A "feature" is more often used in

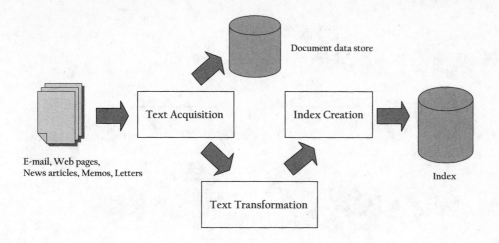

Fig. 2.1. The indexing process

the field of machine learning to refer to a part of a text document that is used to represent its content, which also describes an index term. Examples of other types of index terms or features are phrases, names of people, dates, and links in a web page. Index terms are sometimes simply referred to as "terms." The set of all the terms that are indexed for a document collection is called the *index vocabulary*.

The index creation component takes the output of the text transformation component and creates the indexes or data structures that enable fast searching. Given the large number of documents in many search applications, index creation must be efficient, both in terms of time and space. Indexes must also be able to be efficiently *updated* when new documents are acquired. *Inverted indexes*, or sometimes *inverted files*, are by far the most common form of index used by search engines. An inverted index, very simply, contains a list for every index term of the documents that contain that index term. It is inverted in the sense of being the opposite of a document file that lists, for every document, the index terms they contain. There are many variations of inverted indexes, and the particular form of index used is one of the most important aspects of a search engine.

Figure 2.2 shows the building blocks of the query process. The major components are *user interaction*, *ranking*, and *evaluation*.

The user interaction component provides the interface between the person doing the searching and the search engine. One task for this component is accepting the user's query and transforming it into index terms. Another task is to take

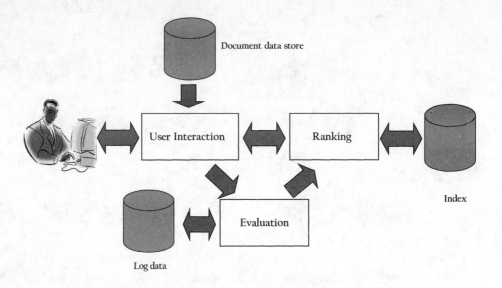

Fig. 2.2. The query process

the ranked list of documents from the search engine and organize it into the results shown to the user. This includes, for example, generating the *snippets* used to summarize documents. The document data store is one of the sources of information used in generating the results. Finally, this component also provides a range of techniques for refining the query so that it better represents the information need.

The ranking component is the core of the search engine. It takes the transformed query from the user interaction component and generates a ranked list of documents using scores based on a retrieval model. Ranking must be both efficient, since many queries may need to be processed in a short time, and effective, since the quality of the ranking determines whether the search engine accomplishes the goal of finding relevant information. The efficiency of ranking depends on the indexes, and the effectiveness depends on the retrieval model.

The task of the evaluation component is to measure and monitor effectiveness and efficiency. An important part of that is to record and analyze user behavior using *log data*. The results of evaluation are used to tune and improve the ranking component. Most of the evaluation component is not part of the online search engine, apart from logging user and system data. Evaluation is primarily an offline activity, but it is a critical part of any search application.

2.3 Breaking It Down

We now look in more detail at the components of each of the basic building blocks. Not all of these components will be part of every search engine, but together they cover what we consider to be the most important functions for a broad range of search applications.

2.3.1 Text Acquisition

Crawler

In many applications, the *crawler* component has the primary responsibility for identifying and acquiring documents for the search engine. There are a number of different types of crawlers, but the most common is the general web crawler. A web crawler is designed to follow the links on web pages to discover and download new pages. Although this sounds deceptively simple, there are significant challenges in designing a web crawler that can efficiently handle the huge volume of new pages on the Web, while at the same time ensuring that pages that may have changed since the last time a crawler visited a site are kept "fresh" for the search engine. A web crawler can be restricted to a single site, such as a university, as the basis for *site search*. *Focused*, or *topical*, web crawlers use classification techniques to restrict the pages that are visited to those that are likely to be about a specific topic. This type of crawler may be used by a *vertical* or *topical* search application, such as a search engine that provides access to medical information on web pages.

> Text Acquisition
>
> Crawler
> Feeds
> Conversion
> Document data store

For enterprise search, the crawler is adapted to discover and update all documents and web pages related to a company's operation. An enterprise *document crawler* follows links to discover both external and internal (i.e., restricted to the corporate intranet) pages, but also must scan both corporate and personal directories to identify email, word processing documents, presentations, database records, and other company information. Document crawlers are also used for desktop search, although in this case only the user's personal directories need to be scanned.

Feeds

Document feeds are a mechanism for accessing a real-time stream of documents. For example, a news feed is a constant stream of news stories and updates. In contrast to a crawler, which must discover new documents, a search engine acquires new documents from a feed simply by monitoring it. *RSS*[2] is a common standard used for web feeds for content such as news, blogs, or video. An RSS "reader" is used to subscribe to RSS feeds, which are formatted using *XML*.[3] XML is a language for describing data formats, similar to HTML.[4] The reader monitors those feeds and provides new content when it arrives. Radio and television feeds are also used in some search applications, where the "documents" contain automatically segmented audio and video streams, together with associated text from closed captions or speech recognition.

Conversion

The documents found by a crawler or provided by a feed are rarely in plain text. Instead, they come in a variety of formats, such as HTML, XML, Adobe PDF, Microsoft Word™, Microsoft PowerPoint®, and so on. Most search engines require that these documents be converted into a consistent text plus metadata format. In this conversion, the control sequences and non-content data associated with a particular format are either removed or recorded as metadata. In the case of HTML and XML, much of this process can be described as part of the text transformation component. For other formats, the conversion process is a basic step that prepares the document for further processing. PDF documents, for example, must be converted to text. Various utilities are available that perform this conversion, with varying degrees of accuracy. Similarly, utilities are available to convert the various Microsoft Office® formats into text.

Another common conversion problem comes from the way text is *encoded* in a document. ASCII[5] is a common standard single-byte character encoding scheme used for text. ASCII uses either 7 or 8 bits (extended ASCII) to represent either 128 or 256 possible characters. Some languages, however, such as Chinese, have many more characters than English and use a number of other encoding schemes. Unicode is a standard encoding scheme that uses 16 bits (typically) to represent most of the world's languages. Any application that deals with documents in different languages has to ensure that they are converted into a consistent encoding scheme before further processing.

---

[2] RSS actually refers to a family of standards with similar names (and the same initials), such as Really Simple Syndication or Rich Site Summary.

[3] eXtensible Markup Language

[4] HyperText Markup Language

[5] American Standard Code for Information Interchange

Document data store

The document data store is a database used to manage large numbers of documents and the structured data that is associated with them. The document contents are typically stored in compressed form for efficiency. The structured data consists of document metadata and other information extracted from the documents, such as links and *anchor text* (the text associated with a link). A *relational database system* can be used to store the documents and metadata. Some applications, however, use a simpler, more efficient storage system to provide very fast retrieval times for very large document stores.

Although the original documents are available on the Web, in the enterprise database, the document data store is necessary to provide fast access to the document contents for a range of search engine components. Generating summaries of retrieved documents, for example, would take far too long if the search engine had to access the original documents and reprocess them.

2.3.2 Text Transformation

Parser

The parsing component is responsible for processing the sequence of text *tokens* in the document to recognize structural elements such as titles, figures, links, and headings. *Tokenizing* the text is an important first step in this process. In many cases, tokens are the same as words. Both document and query text must be transformed into tokens in the same manner so that they can be easily compared. There are a number of decisions that potentially affect retrieval that make tokenizing non-trivial. For example, a simple definition for tokens could be strings of alphanumeric characters that are separated by spaces. This does not tell us, however, how to deal with special characters such as capital letters, hyphens, and apostrophes. Should we treat "apple" the same as "Apple"? Is "on-line" two words or one word? Should the apostrophe in "O'Connor" be treated the same as the one in "owner's"? In some languages, tokenizing gets even more interesting. Chinese, for example, has no obvious word separator like a space in English.

Text Transformation
Parser
Stopping
Stemming
Link Analysis
Information Extraction
Classifier

Document structure is often specified by a markup language such as HTML or XML. HTML is the default language used for specifying the structure of web pages. XML has much more flexibility and is used as a data interchange format for many applications. The document parser uses knowledge of the *syntax* of the markup language to identify the structure.

Both HTML and XML use *tags* to define document *elements*. For example, <h2> Search </h2> defines "Search" as a second-level heading in HTML. Tags and other control sequences must be treated appropriately when tokenizing. Other types of documents, such as email and presentations, have a specific syntax and methods for specifying structure, but much of this may be be removed or simplified by the conversion component.

Stopping

The stopping component has the simple task of removing common words from the stream of tokens that become index terms. The most common words are typically *function* words that help form sentence structure but contribute little on their own to the description of the topics covered by the text. Examples are "the", "of", "to", and "for". Because they are so common, removing them can reduce the size of the indexes considerably. Depending on the retrieval model that is used as the basis of the ranking, removing these words usually has no impact on the search engine's effectiveness, and may even improve it somewhat. Despite these potential advantages, it can be difficult to decide how many words to include on the *stopword list*. Some stopword lists used in research contain hundreds of words. The problem with using such lists is that it becomes impossible to search with queries like "to be or not to be" or "down under". To avoid this, search applications may use very small stopword lists (perhaps just containing "the") when processing document text, but then use longer lists for the default processing of query text.

Stemming

Stemming is another word-level transformation. The task of the stemming component (or *stemmer*) is to group words that are derived from a common *stem*. Grouping "fish", "fishes", and "fishing" is one example. By replacing each member of a group with one designated word (for example, the shortest, which in this case is "fish"), we increase the likelihood that words used in queries and documents will match. Stemming, in fact, generally produces small improvements in ranking effectiveness. Similar to stopping, stemming can be done aggressively, conservatively, or not at all. Aggressive stemming can cause search problems. It may not be appropriate, for example, to retrieve documents about different varieties of fish in response to the query "fishing". Some search applications use more conservative stemming, such as simply identifying plural forms using the letter "s", or they may do no stemming when processing document text and focus on adding appropriate word variants to the query.

Some languages, such as Arabic, have more complicated *morphology* than English, and stemming is consequently more important. An effective stemming component in Arabic has a huge impact on search effectiveness. In contrast, there is little word variation in other languages, such as Chinese, and for these languages stemming is not effective.

Link extraction and analysis

Links and the corresponding anchor text in web pages can readily be identified and extracted during document parsing. Extraction means that this information is recorded in the document data store, and can be indexed separately from the general text content. Web search engines make extensive use of this information through *link analysis* algorithms such as PageRank (Brin & Page, 1998). Link analysis provides the search engine with a rating of the popularity, and to some extent, the *authority* of a page (in other words, how important it is). *Anchor text*, which is the clickable text of a web link, can be used to enhance the text content of a page that the link points to. These two factors can significantly improve the effectiveness of web search for some types of queries.

Information extraction

Information extraction is used to identify index terms that are more complex than single words. This may be as simple as words in bold or words in headings, but in general may require significant additional computation. Extracting syntactic features such as noun phrases, for example, requires some form of syntactic analysis or *part-of-speech tagging*. Research in this area has focused on techniques for extracting features with specific semantic content, such as *named entity* recognizers, which can reliably identify information such as person names, company names, dates, and locations.

Classifier

The classifier component identifies class-related metadata for documents or parts of documents. This covers a range of functions that are often described separately. Classification techniques assign predefined class labels to documents. These labels typically represent topical categories such as "sports", "politics", or "business". Two important examples of other types of classification are identifying documents as spam, and identifying the non-content parts of documents, such as advertising. Clustering techniques are used to group related documents without predefined categories. These document groups can be used in a variety of ways during ranking or user interaction.

2.3.3 Index Creation

Document statistics

The task of the document statistics component is simply to gather and record statistical information about words, features, and documents. This information is used by the ranking component to compute scores for documents. The types of data generally required are the counts of index term occurrences (both words and more complex features) in individual documents, the positions in the documents where the index terms occurred, the counts of occurrences over groups of documents (such as all documents labeled "sports" or the entire collection of documents), and the lengths of documents in terms of the number of tokens. The actual data required is determined by the retrieval model and associated ranking algorithm. The document statistics are stored in *lookup tables*, which are data structures designed for fast retrieval.

Weighting

Index term *weights* reflect the relative importance of words in documents, and are used in computing scores for ranking. The specific form of a weight is determined by the retrieval model. The weighting component calculates weights using the document statistics and stores them in lookup tables. Weights could be calculated as part of the query process, and some types of weights require information about the query, but by doing as much calculation as possible during the indexing process, the efficiency of the query process will be improved.

One of the most common types used in older retrieval models is known as *tf.idf* weighting. There are many variations of these weights, but they are all based on a combination of the frequency or count of index term occurrences in a document (the *term frequency*, or *tf*) and the frequency of index term occurrence over the entire collection of documents (*inverse document frequency*, or *idf*). The *idf* weight is called inverse document frequency because it gives high weights to terms that occur in very few documents. A typical formula for *idf* is $\log N/n$, where N is the total number of documents indexed by the search engine and n is the number of documents that contain a particular term.

Inversion

The *inversion* component is the core of the indexing process. Its task is to change the stream of document-term information coming from the text transformation component into term-document information for the creation of inverted indexes. The challenge is to do this efficiently, not only for large numbers of documents when the inverted indexes are initially created, but also when the indexes are updated with new documents from feeds or crawls. The format of the inverted indexes is designed for fast query processing and depends to some extent on the ranking algorithm used. The indexes are also compressed to further enhance efficiency.

Index distribution

The index distribution component distributes indexes across multiple computers and potentially across multiple sites on a network. Distribution is essential for efficient performance with web search engines. By distributing the indexes for a subset of the documents (*document distribution*), both indexing and query processing can be done in *parallel*. Distributing the indexes for a subset of terms (*term distribution*) can also support parallel processing of queries. *Replication* is a form of distribution where copies of indexes or parts of indexes are stored in multiple sites so that query processing can be made more efficient by reducing communication delays. Peer-to-peer search involves a less organized form of distribution where each node in a network maintains its own indexes and collection of documents.

2.3.4 User Interaction

Query input

The query input component provides an interface and a parser for a *query language*. The simplest query languages, such as those used in most web search interfaces, have only a small number of *operators*. An operator is a command in the query language that is used to indicate text that should be treated in a special way. In general, operators help to clarify the meaning of the query by constraining how

> User Interaction
>
> Query input
> Query transformation
> Results Output

text in the document can match text in the query. An example of an operator in a simple query language is the use of quotes to indicate that the enclosed words should occur as a phrase in the document, rather than as individual words with no relationship. A typical web query, however, consists of a small number of *keywords* with no operators. A keyword is simply a word that is important for specifying the topic of a query. Because the ranking algorithms for most web search engines are designed for keyword queries, longer queries that may contain a lower proportion of keywords typically do not work well. For example, the query "search engines" may produce a better result with a web search engine than the query "what are typical implementation techniques and data structures used in search engines". One of the challenges for search engine design is to give good results for a range of queries, and better results for more specific queries.

More complex query languages are available, either for people who want to have a lot of control over the search results or for applications using a search engine. In the same way that the SQL query language (Elmasri & Navathe, 2006) is not designed for the typical user of a database application (the *end user*), these query languages are not designed for the end users of search applications. *Boolean* query languages have a long history in information retrieval. The operators in this language include Boolean **AND, OR,** and **NOT,** and some form of *proximity* operator that specifies that words must occur together within a specific distance (usually in terms of word count). Other query languages include these and other operators in a probabilistic framework designed to allow specification of features related to both document structure and content.

Query transformation

The query transformation component includes a range of techniques that are designed to improve the initial query, both before and after producing a document ranking. The simplest processing involves some of the same text transformation techniques used on document text. Tokenizing, stopping, and stemming must be done on the query text to produce index terms that are comparable to the document terms.

Spell checking and *query suggestion* are query transformation techniques that produce similar output. In both cases, the user is presented with alternatives to the initial query that are likely to either correct spelling errors or be more specific descriptions of their information needs. These techniques often leverage the extensive *query logs* collected for web applications. *Query expansion* techniques also suggest or add additional terms to the query, but usually based on an analysis of term occurrences in documents. This analysis may use different sources of information, such as the whole document collection, the retrieved documents, or documents on the user's computer. *Relevance feedback* is a technique that expands queries based on term occurrences in documents that are identified as relevant by the user.

Results output

The results output component is responsible for constructing the display of ranked documents coming from the ranking component. This may include tasks such as generating *snippets* to summarize the retrieved documents, *highlighting* important words and passages in documents, clustering the output to identify related groups of documents, and finding appropriate advertising to add to the results display. In applications that involve documents in multiple languages, the results may be translated into a common language.

Ranking

Scoring
Optimization
Distribution

2.3.5 Ranking

Scoring

The scoring component, also called *query processing*, calculates scores for documents using the ranking algorithm, which is based on a retrieval model. The designers of some search engines explicitly state the retrieval model they use. For other search engines, only the ranking algorithm is discussed (if any details at all are revealed), but all ranking algorithms are based implicitly on a retrieval model. The features and weights used in a ranking algorithm, which may have been derived *empirically* (by testing and evaluation), must be related to topical and user relevance, or the search engine would not work.

Many different retrieval models and methods of deriving ranking algorithms have been proposed. The basic form of the document score calculated by many of these models is

$$\sum_i q_i.d_i$$

where the summation is over all of the terms in the vocabulary of the collection, q_i is the query term weight of the ith term, and d_i is the document term weight. The term weights depend on the particular retrieval model being used, but are generally similar to *tf.idf* weights. In Chapter 7, we discuss the ranking algorithms based on the *BM25* and *query likelihood* retrieval models (as well as others) in more detail.

The document scores must be calculated and compared very rapidly in order to determine the ranked order of the documents that are given to the results output component. This is the task of the performance optimization component.

Performance optimization

Performance optimization involves the design of ranking algorithms and the associated indexes to decrease response time and increase query throughput. Given a particular form of document scoring, there are a number of ways to calculate those scores and produce the ranked document output. For example, scores can be computed by accessing the index for a query term, computing the contribution for that term to a document's score, adding this contribution to a score accumulator, and then accessing the next index. This is referred to as *term-at-a-time* scoring. Another alternative is to access all the indexes for the query terms simultaneously, and compute scores by moving pointers through the indexes to find the terms present in a document. In this *document-at-a-time* scoring, the final document score is calculated immediately instead of being accumulated one term at a time. In both cases, further optimizations are possible that significantly decrease the time required to compute the top-ranked documents. *Safe* optimizations guarantee that the scores calculated will be the same as the scores without optimization. *Unsafe* optimizations, which do not have this property, can in some cases be faster, so it is important to carefully evaluate the impact of the optimization.

Distribution

Given some form of index distribution, ranking can also be distributed. A *query broker* decides how to allocate queries to processors in a network and is responsible for assembling the final ranked list for the query. The operation of the broker depends on the form of index distribution. *Caching* is another form of distribution where indexes or even ranked document lists from previous queries are left in local memory. If the query or index term is popular, there is a significant chance that this information can be reused with substantial time savings.

2.3.6 Evaluation

Logging

Logs of the users' queries and their interactions with the search engine are one of the most valuable sources of information for tuning and improving search effectiveness and efficiency. Query logs can be used for spell checking, query suggestions, query caching, and other tasks, such as helping to match advertising to searches. Documents in a result list that are clicked on and browsed tend to be relevant. This means that logs of user clicks on documents (clickthrough data) and information such as the *dwell time* (time spent looking at a document) can be used to evaluate and train ranking algorithms.

> Evaluation
>
> Logging
> Ranking Analysis
> Performance Analysis

Ranking analysis

Given either log data or explicit relevance judgments for a large number of (query, document) pairs, the effectiveness of a ranking algorithm can be measured and compared to alternatives. This is a critical part of improving a search engine and selecting values for parameters that are appropriate for the application. A variety of evaluation measures are commonly used, and these should also be selected to measure outcomes that make sense for the application. Measures that emphasize the quality of the top-ranked documents, rather than the whole list, for example, are appropriate for many types of web queries.

Performance analysis

The performance analysis component involves monitoring and improving overall system performance, in the same way that the ranking analysis component monitors effectiveness. A variety of performance measures are used, such as response time and throughput, but the measures used also depend on the application. For example, a distributed search application should monitor network usage and efficiency in addition to other measures. For ranking analysis, test collections are often used to provide a controlled experimental environment. The equivalent for performance analysis is *simulations*, where actual networks, processors, storage devices, and data are replaced with mathematical models that can be adjusted using parameters.

2.4 How Does It *Really* Work?

Now you know the names and the basic functions of the components of a search engine, but we haven't said much yet about how these components actually perform these functions. That's what the rest of the book is about. Each chapter describes, in depth, how one or more components work. If you still don't understand a component after finishing the appropriate chapter, you can study the Galago code, which is one implementation of the ideas presented, or the references described at the end of each chapter.

References and Further Reading

Detailed references on the techniques and models mentioned in the component descriptions will be given in the appropriate chapters. There are a few general references for search architectures. A database textbook, such as Elmasri and Navathe (2006), provides descriptions of database system architecture and the associated query languages that are interesting to compare with the search engine architecture discussed here. There are some similarities at the high level, but database systems focus on structured data and exact match rather than on text and ranking, so most of the components are very different.

The classic research paper on web search engine architecture, which gives an overview of an early version of Google, is Brin and Page (1998). Another system overview for an earlier general-purpose search engine (Inquery) is found in Callan et al. (1992). A comprehensive description of the Lucene architecture and components can be found in Hatcher and Gospodnetic (2004).

Exercises

2.1. Find some examples of the search engine components described in this chapter in the Galago code.

2.2. Document filtering is an application that stores a large number of queries or user profiles and compares these profiles to every incoming document on a feed. Documents that are sufficiently similar to the profile are forwarded to that person via email or some other mechanism. Describe the architecture of a filtering engine and how it may differ from a search engine.

2.3. A *more-like-this* query occurs when the user can click on a particular document in the result list and tell the search engine to find documents that are similar to this one. Describe which low-level components are used to answer this type of query and the sequence in which they are used.

3

Crawls and Feeds

"You've stuck your webs into my business for the last time."

Doc Ock, *Spider Man 2*

3.1 Deciding What to Search

This book is about the details of building a search engine, from the mathematics behind ranking to the algorithms of query processing. Although we focus heavily on the technology that makes search engines work, and great technology can make a good search engine even better, it is the information in the document collection that makes search engines useful. In other words, if the right documents are not stored in the search engine, no search technique will be able to find relevant information.

The title of this section implies the question, "What should we search?" The simple answer is *everything you possibly can*. Every document answers at least one question (i.e., "Now where was that document again?"), although the best documents answer many more. Every time a search engine adds another document, the number of questions it can answer increases. On the other hand, adding many poor-quality documents increases the burden on the ranking process to find only the best documents to show to the user. Web search engines, however, show how successful search engines can be, even when they contain billions of low-quality documents with little useful content.

Even useful documents can become less useful over time. This is especially true of news and financial information where, for example, many people want to know about today's stock market report, but only a few care about what happened yesterday. The frustration of finding out-of-date web pages and links in a search result list is, unfortunately, a common experience. Search engines are most effective when they contain the most recent information in addition to archives of older material.

This chapter introduces techniques for finding documents to search, whether on the Web, on a file server, on a computer's hard disk, or in an email program. We will discuss strategies for storing documents and keeping those documents up-to-date. Along the way, we will discuss how to pull data out of files, navigating through issues of character encodings, obsolete file formats, duplicate documents, and textual noise. By the end of this chapter you will have a solid grasp on how to get document data into a search engine, ready to be indexed.

3.2 Crawling the Web

To build a search engine that searches web pages, you first need a copy of the pages that you want to search. Unlike some of the other sources of text we will consider later, web pages are particularly easy to copy, since they are meant to be retrieved over the Internet by browsers. This instantly solves one of the major problems of getting information to search, which is how to get the data from the place it is stored to the search engine.

Finding and downloading web pages automatically is called *crawling*, and a program that downloads pages is called a *web crawler*.[1] There are some unique challenges to crawling web pages. The biggest problem is the sheer scale of the Web. There are at least tens of billions of pages on the Internet. The "at least" in the last sentence is there because nobody is sure how many pages there are. Even if the number of pages in existence today could be measured exactly, that number would be immediately wrong, because pages are constantly being created. Every time a user adds a new blog post or uploads a photo, another web page is created. Most organizations do not have enough storage space to store even a large fraction of the Web, but web search providers with plenty of resources must still constantly download new content to keep their collections current.

Another problem is that web pages are usually not under the control of the people building the search engine database. Even if you know that you want to copy all the pages from **www.company.com**, there is no easy way to find out how many pages there are on the site. The owners of that site may not want you to copy some of the data, and will probably be angry if you try to copy it too quickly or too frequently. Some of the data you want to copy may be available only by typing a request into a form, which is a difficult process to automate.

---

[1] Crawling is also occasionally referred to as *spidering*, and a crawler is sometimes called a *spider*.

3.2.1 Retrieving Web Pages

Each web page on the Internet has its own unique *uniform resource locator*, or *URL*. Any URL used to describe a web page has three parts: the scheme, the hostname, and the resource name (Figure 3.1). Web pages are stored on *web servers*, which use a protocol called *Hypertext Transfer Protocol*, or *HTTP*, to exchange information with client software. Therefore, most URLs used on the Web start with the scheme `http`, indicating that the URL represents a resource that can be retrieved using HTTP. The *hostname* follows, which is the name of the computer that is running the web server that holds this web page. In the figure, the computer's name is `www.cs.umass.edu`, which is a computer in the University of Massachusetts Computer Science department. This URL refers to a page on that computer called `/csinfo/people.html`.

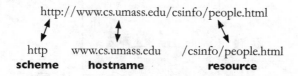

Fig. 3.1. A uniform resource locator (URL), split into three parts

Web browsers and web crawlers are two different kinds of web clients, but both fetch web pages in the same way. First, the client program connects to a *domain name system* (DNS) server. The DNS server translates the hostname into an *internet protocol* (IP) address. This IP address is a number that is typically 32 bits long, but some networks now use 128-bit IP addresses. The program then attempts to connect to a server computer with that IP address. Since that server might have many different programs running on it, with each one listening to the network for new connections, each program listens on a different *port*. A port is just a 16-bit number that identifies a particular service. By convention, requests for web pages are sent to port 80 unless specified otherwise in the URL.

Once the connection is established, the client program sends an HTTP request to the web server to request a page. The most common HTTP request type is a GET request, for example:

```
GET /csinfo/people.html HTTP/1.0
```

This simple request asks the server to send the page called `/csinfo/people.html` back to the client, using version 1.0 of the HTTP protocol specification. After sending a short header, the server sends the contents of that file back to the client. If the client wants more pages, it can send additional requests; otherwise, the client closes the connection.

A client can also fetch web pages using POST requests. A POST request is like a GET request, except that it can send additional request information to the server. By convention, GET requests are used for retrieving data that already exists on the server, whereas POST requests are used to tell the server something. A POST request might be used when you click a button to purchase something or to edit a web page. This convention is useful if you are running a web crawler, since sending only GET requests helps make sure your crawler does not inadvertently order a product.

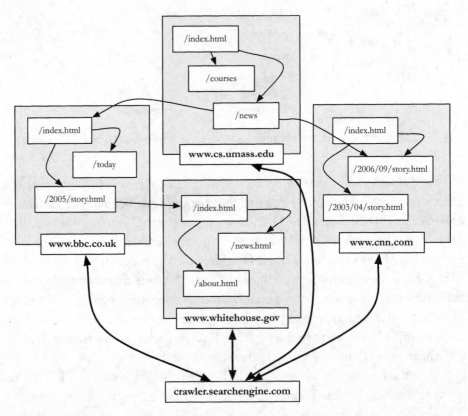

Fig. 3.2. Crawling the Web. The web crawler connects to web servers to find pages. Pages may link to other pages on the same server or on different servers.

3.2.2 The Web Crawler

Figure 3.2 shows a diagram of the Web from a simple web crawler's perspective. The web crawler has two jobs: downloading pages and finding URLs.

The crawler starts with a set of *seeds*, which are a set of URLs given to it as parameters. These seeds are added to a URL request queue. The crawler starts fetching pages from the request queue. Once a page is downloaded, it is parsed to find link tags that might contain other useful URLs to fetch. If the crawler finds a new URL that it has not seen before, it is added to the crawler's request queue, or *frontier*. The frontier may be a standard queue, or it may be ordered so that important pages move to the front of the list. This process continues until the crawler either runs out of disk space to store pages or runs out of useful links to add to the request queue.

If a crawler used only a single thread, it would not be very efficient. Notice that the web crawler spends a lot of its time waiting for responses: it waits for the DNS server response, then it waits for the connection to the web server to be acknowledged, and then it waits for the web page data to be sent from the server. During this waiting time, the CPU of the web crawler machine is idle and the network connection is unused. To reduce this inefficiency, web crawlers use threads and fetch hundreds of pages at once.

Fetching hundreds of pages at once is good for the person running the web crawler, but not necessarily good for the person running the web server on the other end. Just imagine how the request queue works in practice. When a web page like www.company.com is fetched, it is parsed and all of the links on that page are added to the request queue. The crawler will then attempt to fetch all of those pages at once. If the web server for www.company.com is not very powerful, it might spend all of its time handling requests from the crawler instead of handling requests from real users. This kind of behavior from web crawlers tends to make web server administrators very angry.

To avoid this problem, web crawlers use *politeness policies*. Reasonable web crawlers do not fetch more than one page at a time from a particular web server. In addition, web crawlers wait at least a few seconds, and sometimes minutes, between requests to the same web server. This allows web servers to spend the bulk of their time processing real user requests. To support this, the request queue is logically split into a single queue per web server. At any one time, most of these per-server queues are off-limits for crawling, because the crawler has fetched a page from that server recently. The crawler is free to read page requests only from queues that haven't been accessed within the specified politeness window.

When using a politeness window, the request queue must be very large in order to achieve good performance. Suppose a web crawler can fetch 100 pages each second, and that its politeness policy dictates that it cannot fetch more than one page each 30 seconds from a particular web server. The web crawler needs to have URLs from at least 3,000 different web servers in its request queue in order to achieve high throughput. Since many URLs will come from the same servers, the request queue needs to have tens of thousands of URLs in it before a crawler can reach its peak throughput.

```
User-agent:  *
Disallow:  /private/
Disallow:  /confidential/
Disallow:  /other/
Allow:  /other/public/

User-agent:  FavoredCrawler
Disallow:

Sitemap:  http://mysite.com/sitemap.xml.gz
```

Fig. 3.3. An example robots.txt file

Even crawling a site slowly will anger some web server administrators who object to any copying of their data. Web server administrators who feel this way can store a file called /robots.txt on their web servers. Figure 3.3 contains an example robots.txt file. The file is split into blocks of commands that start with a User-agent: specification. The User-agent: line identifies a crawler, or group of crawlers, affected by the following rules. Following this line are Allow and Disallow rules that dictate which resources the crawler is allowed to access. In the figure, the first block indicates that all crawlers need to ignore resources that begin with /private/, /confidential/, or /other/, except for those that begin with /other/public/. The second block indicates that a crawler named FavoredCrawler gets its own set of rules: it is allowed to copy everything.

The final block of the example is an optional Sitemap: directive, which will be discussed later in this section.

Figure 3.4 shows an implementation of a crawling thread, using the crawler building blocks we have seen so far. Assume that the frontier has been initialized

```
procedure CRAWLERTHREAD(frontier)
    while not frontier.done() do
        website ← frontier.nextSite()
        url ← website.nextURL()
        if website.permitsCrawl(url) then
            text ← retrieveURL(url)
            storeDocument(url, text)
            for each url in parse(text) do
                frontier.addURL(url)
            end for
        end if
        frontier.releaseSite(website)
    end while
end procedure
```

Fig. 3.4. A simple crawling thread implementation

with a few URLs that act as seeds for the crawl. The crawling thread first retrieves a website from the frontier. The crawler then identifies the next URL in the website's queue. In permitsCrawl, the crawler checks to see if the URL is okay to crawl according to the website's robots.txt file. If it can be crawled, the crawler uses retrieveURL to fetch the document contents. This is the most expensive part of the loop, and the crawler thread may block here for many seconds. Once the text has been retrieved, storeDocument stores the document text in a document database (discussed later in this chapter). The document text is then parsed so that other URLs can be found. These URLs are added to the frontier, which adds them to the appropriate website queues. When all this is finished, the website object is returned to the frontier, which takes care to enforce its politeness policy by not giving the website to another crawler thread until an appropriate amount of time has passed. In a real crawler, the timer would start immediately after the document was retrieved, since parsing and storing the document could take a long time.

3.2.3 Freshness

Web pages are constantly being added, deleted, and modified. To keep an accurate view of the Web, a web crawler must continually revisit pages it has already crawled to see if they have changed in order to maintain the *freshness* of the document collection. The opposite of a fresh copy is a *stale* copy, which means a copy that no longer reflects the real content of the web page.

Client request:
```
HEAD /csinfo/people.html HTTP/1.1
Host: www.cs.umass.edu
```

Server response:
```
HTTP/1.1 200 OK
Date: Thu, 03 Apr 2008 05:17:54 GMT
Server: Apache/2.0.52 (CentOS)
Last-Modified: Fri, 04 Jan 2008 15:28:39 GMT
ETag: "239c33-2576-2a2837c0"
Accept-Ranges: bytes
Content-Length: 9590
Connection: close
Content-Type: text/html; charset=ISO-8859-1
```

Fig. 3.5. An HTTP HEAD request and server response

The HTTP protocol has a special request type called HEAD that makes it easy to check for page changes. The HEAD request returns only header information about the page, but not the page itself. Figure 3.5 contains an example HEAD request and response. The Last-Modified value indicates the last time the page content was changed. Notice that the date is also sent along with the response, as well as in response to a GET request. This allows the web crawler to compare the date it received from a previous GET request with the Last-Modified value from a HEAD request.

A HEAD request reduces the cost of checking on a page, but does not eliminate it. It simply is not possible to check every page every minute. Not only would that attract more negative reactions from web server administrators, but it would cause enormous load on the web crawler and the incoming network connection.

Thankfully, most web pages are not updated every few minutes. Some of them, like news websites, do change frequently. Others, like a person's home page, change much less often. Even within a page type there can be huge variations in the modification rate. For example, some blogs are updated many times a day, whereas others go months between updates. It does little good to continuously check sites that are rarely updated. Therefore, one of the crawler's jobs is to measure the rate at which each page changes. Over time, this data can be used to estimate how frequently each page changes.

Given that a web crawler can't update every page immediately as it changes, the crawler needs to have some metric for measuring crawl freshness. In this chapter, we've used freshness as a general term, but freshness is also the name of a metric.

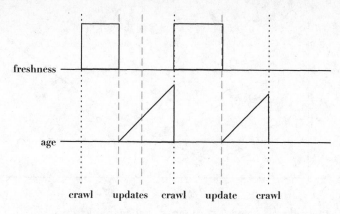

Fig. 3.6. Age and freshness of a single page over time

Under the *freshness* metric, a page is *fresh* if the crawl has the most recent copy of a web page, but *stale* otherwise. Freshness is then the fraction of the crawled pages that are currently fresh.

Keeping freshness high seems like exactly what you'd want to do, but optimizing for freshness can have unintended consequences. Suppose that http://www.example.com is a popular website that changes its front page slightly every minute. Unless your crawler continually polls http://www.example.com, you will almost always have a stale copy of that page. Notice that if you want to optimize for freshness, the appropriate strategy is to stop crawling this site completely! If it will never be fresh, it can't help your freshness value. Instead, you should allocate your crawler's resources to pages that change less frequently.

Of course, users will revolt if you decide to optimize your crawler for freshness. They will look at http://www.example.com and wonder why your indexed copy is months out of date.

Age is a better metric to use. You can see the difference between age and freshness in Figure 3.6. In the top part of the figure, you can see that pages become fresh immediately when they are crawled, but once the page changes, the crawled page becomes stale. Under the age metric, the page has age 0 until it is changed, and then its age grows until the page is crawled again.

Suppose we have a page with change frequency λ, meaning that we expect it to change λ times in a one-day period. We can calculate the expected age of a page t days after it was last crawled:

$$\text{Age}(\lambda, t) = \int_0^t P(\text{page changed at time } x)(t - x)dx$$

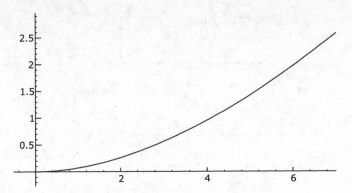

Fig. 3.7. Expected age of a page with mean change frequency $\lambda = 1/7$ (one week)

The $(t - x)$ expression is an age: we assume the page is crawled at time t, but that it changed at time x. We multiply that by the probability that the page actually changed at time x. Studies have shown that, on average, web page updates follow the Poisson distribution, meaning that the time until the next update is governed by an exponential distribution (Cho & Garcia-Molina, 2003). This gives us a formula to plug into the $P(\text{page changed at time } x)$ expression:

$$\text{Age}(\lambda, t) = \int_0^t \lambda e^{-\lambda x}(t - x)dx$$

Figure 3.7 shows the result of plotting this expression for a fixed $\lambda = 1/7$, indicating roughly one change a week. Notice how the expected age starts at zero, and rises slowly at first. This is because the page is unlikely to have changed in the first day. As the days go by, the probability that the page has changed increases. By the end of the week, the expected age of the page is about 2.6 days. This means that if your crawler crawls each page once a week, and each page in your collection has a mean update time of once a week, the pages in your index will be 2.6 days old on average just before the crawler runs again.

Notice that the second derivative of the Age function is always positive. That is, the graph is not only increasing, but its rate of increase is always increasing. This positive second derivative means that the older a page gets, the more it costs you to not crawl it. Optimizing this metric will never result in the conclusion that optimizing for freshness does, where sometimes it is economical to not crawl a page at all.

3.2.4 Focused Crawling

Some users would like a search engine that focuses on a specific topic of information. For instance, at a website about movies, users might want access to a search engine that leads to more information about movies. If built correctly, this type of *vertical search* can provide higher accuracy than general search because of the lack of extraneous information in the document collection. The computational cost of running a vertical search will also be much less than a full web search, simply because the collection will be much smaller.

The most accurate way to get web pages for this kind of engine would be to crawl a full copy of the Web and then throw out all unrelated pages. This strategy requires a huge amount of disk space and bandwidth, and most of the web pages will be discarded at the end.

A less expensive approach is *focused*, or *topical*, crawling. A focused crawler attempts to download only those pages that are about a particular topic. Focused crawlers rely on the fact that pages about a topic tend to have links to other pages on the same topic. If this were perfectly true, it would be possible to start a crawl at one on-topic page, then crawl all pages on that topic just by following links from a single root page. In practice, a number of popular pages for a specific topic are typically used as seeds.

Focused crawlers require some automatic means for determining whether a page is about a particular topic. Chapter 9 will introduce text classifiers, which are tools that can make this kind of distinction. Once a page is downloaded, the crawler uses the classifier to decide whether the page is on topic. If it is, the page is kept, and links from the page are used to find other related sites. The anchor text in the outgoing links is an important clue of topicality. Also, some pages have more on-topic links than others. As links from a particular web page are visited, the crawler can keep track of the topicality of the downloaded pages and use this to determine whether to download other similar pages. Anchor text data and page link topicality data can be combined together in order to determine which pages should be crawled next.

3.2.5 Deep Web

Not all parts of the Web are easy for a crawler to navigate. Sites that are difficult for a crawler to find are collectively referred to as the *deep Web* (also called the *hidden Web*). Some studies have estimated that the deep Web is over a hundred times larger than the traditionally indexed Web, although it is very difficult to measure this accurately.

Most sites that are a part of the deep Web fall into three broad categories:

- *Private sites* are intentionally private. They may have no incoming links, or may require you to log in with a valid account before using the rest of the site. These sites generally want to block access from crawlers, although some news publishers may still want their content indexed by major search engines.

- *Form results* are sites that can be reached only after entering some data into a form. For example, websites selling airline tickets typically ask for trip information on the site's entry page. You are shown flight information only after submitting this trip information. Even though you might want to use a search engine to find flight timetables, most crawlers will not be able to get through this form to get to the timetable information.

- *Scripted pages* are pages that use JavaScript™, Flash®, or another client-side language in the web page. If a link is not in the raw HTML source of the web page, but is instead generated by JavaScript code running on the browser, the crawler will need to execute the JavaScript on the page in order to find the link. Although this is technically possible, executing JavaScript can slow down the crawler significantly and adds complexity to the system.

Sometimes people make a distinction between *static pages* and *dynamic pages*. Static pages are files stored on a web server and displayed in a web browser unmodified, whereas dynamic pages may be the result of code executing on the web server or the client. Typically it is assumed that static pages are easy to crawl, while dynamic pages are hard. This is not quite true, however. Many websites have dynamically generated web pages that are easy to crawl; wikis are a good example of this. Other websites have static pages that are impossible to crawl because they can be accessed only through web forms.

Web administrators of sites with form results and scripted pages often want their sites to be indexed, unlike the owners of private sites. Of these two categories, scripted pages are easiest to deal with. The site owner can usually modify the pages slightly so that links are generated by code on the server instead of by code in the browser. The crawler can also run page JavaScript, or perhaps Flash as well, although these can take a lot of time.

The most difficult problems come with form results. Usually these sites are repositories of changing data, and the form submits a query to a database system. In the case where the database contains millions of records, the site would need to expose millions of links to a search engine's crawler. Adding a million links to the front page of such a site is clearly infeasible. Another option is to let the crawler guess what to enter into forms, but it is difficult to choose good form input. Even with good guesses, this approach is unlikely to expose all of the hidden data.

3.2.6 Sitemaps

As you can see from the last two sections, the biggest problems in crawling arise because site owners cannot adequately tell crawlers about their sites. In section 3.2.3, we saw how crawlers have to make guesses about when pages will be updated because polling is costly. In section 3.2.5, we saw that site owners sometimes have data that they would like to expose to a search engine, but they can't because there is no reasonable place to store the links. *Sitemaps* solve both of these problems.

```
<?xml version="1.0" encoding="UTF-8"?>
<urlset xmlns="http://www.sitemaps.org/schemas/sitemap/0.9">
  <url>
    <loc>http://www.company.com/</loc>
    <lastmod>2008-01-15</lastmod>
    <changefreq>monthly</changefreq>
    <priority>0.7</priority>
  </url>
  <url>
    <loc>http://www.company.com/items?item=truck</loc>
    <changefreq>weekly</changefreq>
  </url>
  <url>
    <loc>http://www.company.com/items?item=bicycle</loc>
    <changefreq>daily</changefreq>
  </url>
</urlset>
```

Fig. 3.8. An example sitemap file

A robots.txt file can contain a reference to a sitemap, like the one shown in Figure 3.8. A sitemap contains a list of URLs and data about those URLs, such as modification time and modification frequency.

There are three URL entries shown in the example sitemap. Each one contains a URL in a `loc` tag. The `changefreq` tag indicates how often this resource is likely to change. The first entry includes a `lastmod` tag, which indicates the last time it was changed. The first entry also includes a `priority` tag with a value of 0.7, which is higher than the default of 0.5. This tells crawlers that this page is more important than other pages on this site.

Why would a web server administrator go to the trouble to create a sitemap? One reason is that it tells search engines about pages it might not otherwise find. Look at the second and third URLs in the sitemap. Suppose these are two product pages. There may not be any links on the website to these pages; instead, the user may have to use a search form to get to them. A simple web crawler will not attempt to enter anything into a form (although some advanced crawlers do), and so these pages would be invisible to search engines. A sitemap allows crawlers to find this hidden content.

The sitemap also exposes modification times. In the discussion of page freshness, we mentioned that a crawler usually has to guess when pages are likely to change. The `changefreq` tag gives the crawler a hint about when to check a page again for changes, and the `lastmod` tag tells the crawler when a page has changed. This helps reduce the number of requests that the crawler sends to a website without sacrificing page freshness.

3.2.7 Distributed Crawling

For crawling individual websites, a single computer is sufficient. However, crawling the entire Web requires many computers devoted to crawling. Why would a single crawling computer not be enough? We will consider three reasons.

One reason to use multiple computers is to put the crawler *closer to the sites it crawls*. Long-distance network connections tend to have lower throughput (fewer bytes copied per second) and higher latency (bytes take longer to cross the network). Decreased throughput and increased latency work together to make each page request take longer. As throughput drops and latency rises, the crawler has to open more connections to copy pages at the same rate.

For example, suppose a crawler has a network connection that can transfer 1MB each second. With an average web page size of 20K, it can copy 50 pages each second. If the sites that are being crawled are close, the data transfer rate from them may be 1MB a second. However, it can take 80ms for the site to start sending data, because there is some transmission delay in opening the connection and sending the request. Let's assume each request takes 100ms (80ms of latency and 20ms of data transfer). Multiplying 50 by 100ms, we see that there is 5 seconds of waiting involved in transferring 50 pages. This means that five connections will be needed to transfer 50 pages in one second. If the sites are farther away, with an average throughput of 100K per second and 500ms of latency, then each request would now take 600ms. Since 50×600ms = 30 seconds, the crawler would need to keep 30 connections open to transfer pages at the same rate.

Another reason for multiple crawling computers is to reduce the *number of sites the crawler has to remember*. A crawler has to remember all of the URLs it has already crawled, and all of the URLs that it has queued to crawl. These URLs must be easy to access, because every page that is crawled contains new links that need to be added to the crawl queue. Since the crawler's queue should not contain duplicates or sites that have already been crawled, each new URL must be checked against everything in the queue and everything that has been crawled. The data structure for this lookup needs to be in RAM; otherwise, the computer's crawl speed will be severely limited. Spreading crawling duties among many computers reduces this bookkeeping load.

Yet another reason is that crawling can use a lot of *computing resources*, including CPU resources for parsing and network bandwidth for crawling pages. Crawling a large portion of the Web is too much work for a single computer to handle.

A distributed crawler is much like a crawler on a single computer, except instead of a single queue of URLs, there are many queues. The distributed crawler uses a hash function to assign URLs to crawling computers. When a crawler sees a new URL, it computes a hash function on that URL to decide which crawling computer is responsible for it. These URLs are gathered in batches, then sent periodically to reduce the network overhead of sending a single URL at a time.

The hash function should be computed on just the host part of each URL. This assigns all the URLs for a particular host to a single crawler. Although this may promote imbalance since some hosts have more pages than others, politeness rules require a time delay between URL fetches to the same host. It is easier to maintain that kind of delay by using the same crawling computers for all URLs for the same host. In addition, we would expect that sites from domain.com will have lots of links to other pages on domain.com. By assigning domain.com to a single crawl host, we minimize the number of URLs that need to be exchanged between crawling computers.

3.3 Crawling Documents and Email

Even though the Web is a tremendous information resource, a huge amount of digital information is not stored on websites. In this section, we will consider information that you might find on a normal desktop computer, such as email, word processing documents, presentations, or spreadsheets. This information can be searched using a *desktop search* tool. In companies and organizations, *enterprise search* will make use of documents on file servers, or even on employee desktop computers, in addition to local web pages.

Many of the problems of web crawling change when we look at desktop data. In web crawling, just finding the data can be a struggle. On a desktop computer, the interesting data is stored in a file system with familiar semantics. Finding all the files on a hard disk is not particularly difficult, since file systems have directories that are easy to discover. In some ways, a file system is like a web server, but with an automatically generated sitemap.

There are unique challenges in crawling desktop data, however. The first concerns update speed. In desktop search applications, users demand search results based on the current content of their files. This means, for example, being able to search for an email the instant it is received, and being able to search for a document as soon as it has been saved. Notice that this is a much different expectation than with web search, where users can tolerate crawling delays of hours or days. Crawling the file system every second is impractical, but modern file systems can send change notifications directly to the crawler process so that it can copy new files immediately. Remote file systems from file servers usually do not provide this kind of change notification, and so they must be crawled just like a web server.

Disk space is another concern. With a web crawler, we assume that we need to keep a copy of every document that is found. This is less true on a desktop system, where the documents are already stored locally, and where users will be unhappy if a large proportion of the hard disk is taken by the indexer. A desktop crawler instead may need to read documents into memory and send them directly to the indexer. We will discuss indexing more in Chapter 5.

Since websites are meant to be viewed with web browsers, most web content is stored in HTML. On the other hand, each desktop program—the word processor, presentation tool, email program, etc.—has its own file format. So, just finding these files is not enough; eventually they will need to be converted into a format that the indexer can understand. In section 3.5 we will revisit this conversion issue.

Finally, and perhaps most importantly, crawling desktop data requires a focus on data privacy. Desktop systems can have multiple users with different accounts, and user A should not be able to find emails from user B's account through the search feature. This is especially important when we consider crawling shared network file systems, as in a corporate network. The file access permissions of each file must be recorded along with the crawled data, and must be kept up-to-date.

3.4 Document Feeds

In general Web or desktop crawling, we assume that any document can be created or modified at any time. However, many documents are *published*, meaning that they are created at a fixed time and rarely updated again. News articles, blog posts, press releases, and email are some of the documents that fit this publishing model. Most information that is time-sensitive is published.

Since each published document has an associated time, published documents from a single source can be ordered in a sequence called a *document feed*. A document feed is particularly interesting for crawlers, since the crawler can easily find all the new documents by examining only the end of the feed.

We can distinguish two kinds of document feeds, *push* and *pull*. A *push* feed alerts the subscriber to new documents. This is like a telephone, which alerts you to an incoming phone call; you don't need to continually check the phone to see if someone is calling. A *pull* feed requires the subscriber to check periodically for new documents; this is like checking your mailbox for new mail to arrive. News feeds from commercial news agencies are often push feeds, but pull feeds are overwhelmingly popular for free services. We will focus primarily on pull feeds in this section.

The most common format for pull feeds is called *RSS*. RSS has at least three definitions: Really Simple Syndication, RDF Site Summary, or Rich Site Summary. Not surprisingly, RSS also has a number of slightly incompatible implementations, and a similar competing format exists called the *Atom Syndication Format*. The proliferation of standards is the result of an idea that gained popularity too quickly for developers to agree on a single standard.

Figure 3.9 shows an RSS 2.0 feed from an example site called http://www.search-engine-news.org. This feed contains two articles: one is about an upcoming SIGIR conference, and the other is about a textbook. Notice that each entry contains a time indicating when it was published. In addition, near the top of the RSS feed there is an tag named ttl, which means *time to live*, measured in minutes. This

```
<?xml version="1.0"?>
<rss version="2.0">
  <channel>
    <title>Search Engine News</title>
    <link>http://www.search-engine-news.org/</link>
   <description>News about search engines.</description>
    <language>en-us</language>
    <pubDate>Tue, 19 Jun 2008 05:17:00 GMT</pubDate>
    <ttl>60</ttl>

    <item>
      <title>Upcoming SIGIR Conference</title>
      <link>http://www.sigir.org/conference</link>
     <description>The annual SIGIR conference is coming!
        Mark your calendars and check for cheap
        flights.</description>
      <pubDate>Tue, 05 Jun 2008 09:50:11 GMT</pubDate>
      <guid>http://search-engine-news.org#500</guid>
    </item>

    <item>
      <title>New Search Engine Textbook</title>
      <link>http://www.cs.umass.edu/search-book</link>
      <description>A new textbook about search engines
        will be published soon.</description>
      <pubDate>Tue, 05 Jun 2008 09:33:01 GMT</pubDate>
      <guid>http://search-engine-news.org#499</guid>
    </item>
  </channel>
</rss>
```

Fig. 3.9. An example RSS 2.0 feed

feed states that its contents should be cached only for 60 minutes, and information more than an hour old should be considered stale. This gives a crawler an indication of how often this feed file should be crawled.

RSS feeds are accessed just like a traditional web page, using HTTP GET requests to web servers that host them. Therefore, some of the crawling techniques we discussed before apply here as well, such as using HTTP HEAD requests to detect when RSS feeds change.

From a crawling perspective, document feeds have a number of advantages over traditional pages. Feeds give a natural structure to data; even more than with a sitemap, a web feed implies some relationship between the data items. Feeds are easy to parse and contain detailed time information, like a sitemap, but also include a description field about each page (and this description field sometimes contains the entire text of the page referenced in the URL). Most importantly, like a sitemap, feeds provide a single location to look for new data, instead of having to crawl an entire site to find a few new documents.

3.5 The Conversion Problem

Search engines are built to search through text. Unfortunately, text is stored on computers in hundreds of incompatible file formats. Standard text file formats include raw text, RTF, HTML, XML, Microsoft Word, ODF (Open Document Format) and PDF (Portable Document Format). There are tens of other less common word processors with their own file formats. But text documents aren't the only kind of document that needs to be searched; other kinds of files also contain important text, such as PowerPoint slides and Excel® spreadsheets. In addition to all of these formats, people often want to search old documents, which means that search engines may need to support obsolete file formats. It is not uncommon for a commercial search engine to support more than a hundred file types.

The most common way to handle a new file format is to use a conversion tool that converts the document content into a tagged text format such as HTML or XML. These formats are easy to parse, and they retain some of the important formatting information (font size, for example). You can see this on any major web search engine. Search for a PDF document, but then click on the "Cached" link at the bottom of a search result. You will be taken to the search engine's view of the page, which is usually an HTML rendition of the original document. For some document types, such as PowerPoint, this cached version can be nearly unreadable. Fortunately, readability isn't the primary concern of the search engine.

The point is to copy this data into the search engine so that it can be indexed and retrieved. However, translating the data into HTML has an advantage: the user does not need to have an application that can read the document's file format in order to view it. This is critical for obsolete file formats.

Documents could be converted to plain text instead of HTML or XML. However, doing this would strip the file of important information about headings and font sizes that could be useful to the indexer. As we will see later, headings and bold text tend to contain words that describe the document content well, so we want to give these words preferential treatment during scoring. Accurate conversion of formatting information allows the indexer to extract these important features.

3.5.1 Character Encodings

Even HTML files are not necessarily compatible with each other because of *character encoding* issues. The text that you see on this page is a series of little pictures we call *letters* or *glyphs*. Of course, a computer file is a stream of bits, not a collection of pictures. A character encoding is a mapping between bits and glyphs. For English, the basic character encoding that has been around since 1963 is ASCII. ASCII encodes 128 letters, numbers, special characters, and control characters in 7 bits, extended with an extra bit for storage in bytes. This scheme is fine for the English alphabet of 26 letters, but there are many other languages, and some of those have many more glyphs. The Chinese language, for example, has more than 40,000 characters, with over 3,000 in common use. For the CJK (Chinese-Japanese-Korean) family of East Asian languages, this led to the development of a number of different 2-byte standards. Other languages, such as Hindi or Arabic, also have a range of different encodings. Note that not all encodings even agree on English. The EBCDIC encoding used on mainframes, for example, is completely different than the ASCII encoding used by personal computers.

The computer industry has moved slowly in handling complicated character sets such as Chinese and Arabic. Until recently, the typical approach was to use different language-specific encodings, sometimes called *code pages*. The first 128 values of each encoding are reserved for typical English characters, punctuation, and numbers. Numbers above 128 are mapped to glyphs in the target language, from Hebrew to Arabic. However, if you use a different encoding for each language, you can't write in Hebrew and Japanese in the same document. Additionally, the text itself is no longer self-describing. It's not enough to just store data in a text file; you must also record what encoding was used.

To solve this mess of encoding issues, *Unicode* was developed. Unicode is a single mapping from numbers to glyphs that attempts to include all glyphs in common use in all known languages. This solves the problem of using multiple languages in a single file. Unfortunately, it does not fully solve the problems of binary encodings, because Unicode is a mapping between numbers and glyphs, not bits and glyphs. It turns out that there are many ways to translate Unicode numbers to glyphs! Some of the most popular include UTF-8, UTF-16, UTF-32, and UCS-2 (which is deprecated).

The proliferation of encodings comes from a need for compatibility and to save space. Encoding English text in UTF-8 is identical to the ASCII encoding. Each ASCII letter requires just one byte. However, some traditional Chinese characters can require as many as 4 bytes. The trade-off for compactness for Western languages is that each character requires a variable number of bytes, which makes it difficult to quickly compute the number of characters in a string or to jump to a random location in a string. By contrast, UTF-32 (also known as UCS-4) uses exactly 4 bytes for every character. Jumping to the twentieth character in a UTF-32 string is easy: just jump to the eightieth byte and start reading. Unfortunately, UTF-32 strings are incompatible with all old ASCII software, and UTF-32 files require four times as much space as UTF-8. Because of this, many applications use UTF-32 as their internal text encoding (where random access is important), but use UTF-8 to store text on disk.

Decimal	Hexadecimal	Encoding
0–127	0–7F	`0xxxxxxx`
128–2047	80–7FF	`110xxxxx 10xxxxxx`
2048–55295	800–D7FF	`1110xxxx 10xxxxxx 10xxxxxx`
55296–57343	D800–DFFF	Undefined
57344–65535	E000–FFFF	`1110xxxx 10xxxxxx 10xxxxxx`
65536–1114111	10000–10FFFF	`11110xxx 10xxxxxx 10xxxxxx 10xxxxxx`

Table 3.1. UTF-8 encoding

Table 3.1 shows an encoding table for UTF-8. The left columns represent ranges of decimal values, and the rightmost column shows how these values are encoded in binary. The `x` characters represent binary digits. For example, the Greek letter pi (π) is Unicode symbol number 960. In binary, that number is `00000011 11000000` (3C0 in hexadecimal). The second row of the table tells us that this letter will require 2 bytes to encode in UTF-8. The high 5 bits of the character go in the first byte, and the next 6 bits go in the second byte. The final encoding is **11001111 10000000** (CF80 in hexadecimal). The bold binary digits are the same as the digits from the table, while the x letters from the table have been filled in by binary digits from the Unicode number.

3.6 Storing the Documents

After documents have been converted to some common format, they need to be stored in preparation for indexing. The simplest document storage is no document storage, and for some applications this is preferable. In desktop search, for example, the documents are already stored in the file system and do not need to be copied elsewhere. As the crawling process runs, it can send converted documents immediately to an indexing process. By not storing the intermediate converted documents, desktop search systems can save disk space and improve indexing latency.

Most other kinds of search engines need to store documents somewhere. Fast access to the document text is required in order to build document snippets[2] for each search result. These snippets of text give the user an idea of what is inside the retrieved document without actually needing to click on a link.

Even if snippets are not necessary, there are other reasons to keep a copy of each document. Crawling for documents can be expensive in terms of both CPU and network load. It makes sense to keep copies of the documents around instead of trying to fetch them again the next time you want to build an index. Keeping old documents allows you to use HEAD requests in your crawler to save on bandwidth, or to crawl only a subset of the pages in your index.

Finally, document storage systems can be a starting point for information extraction (described in Chapter 4). The most pervasive kind of information extraction happens in web search engines, which extract anchor text from links to store with target web documents. Other kinds of extraction are possible, such as identifying names of people or places in documents. Notice that if information extraction is used in the search application, the document storage system should support modification of the document data.

We now discuss some of the basic requirements for a document storage system, including random access, compression, and updating, and consider the relative

---

[2] We discuss snippet generation in Chapter 6.

benefits of using a database system or a customized storage system such as Google's BigTable.

3.6.1 Using a Database System

If you have used a relational database before, you might be thinking that a database would be a good place to store document data. For many applications, in fact, a database is an excellent place to store documents. A database takes care of the difficult details of storing small pieces of data, such as web pages, and makes it easy to update them later. Most databases also run as a network server, so that the documents are easily available on the network. This could support, for example, a single computer serving documents for snippets while many other computers handle queries. Databases also tend to come with useful import and analysis tools that can make it easier to manage the document collection.

Many companies that run web search engines are reluctant to talk about their internal technologies. However, it appears that few, if any, of the major search engines use conventional relational databases to store documents. One problem is the sheer volume of document data, which can overwhelm traditional database systems. Database vendors also tend to expect that database servers will use the most expensive disk systems, which is impractical given the collection size. We discuss an alternative to a relational database at the end of this section that addresses some of these concerns.

3.6.2 Random Access

To retrieve documents quickly in order to compute a snippet for a search result, the document store needs to support random access. Compared to a full relational database, however, only a relatively simple lookup criterion is needed. We want a data store such that we can request the content of a document based on its URL.

The easiest way to handle this kind of lookup is with hashing. Using a hash function on the URL gives us a number we can use to find the data. For small installations, the hash function can tell us which file contains the document. For larger installations, the hash function tells us which server contains the document. Once the document location has been narrowed down to a single file, a B-Tree or sorted data structure can be used to find the offset of the document data within the file.

3.6.3 Compression and Large Files

Regardless of whether the application requires random access to documents, the document storage system should make use of large files and compression.

Even a document that seems long to a person is small by modern computer standards. For example, this chapter is approximately 10,000 words, and those words require about 70K of disk space to store. That is far bigger than the average web page, but a modern hard disk can transfer 70K of data in about a millisecond. However, the hard disk might require 10 milliseconds to seek to that file in order to start reading. This is why storing each document in its own file is not a very good idea; reading these small files requires a substantial overhead to open them. A better solution is to store many documents in a single file, and for that file to be large enough that transferring the file contents takes much more time than seeking to the beginning. A good size choice might be in the hundreds of megabytes. By storing documents close together, the indexer can spend most of its time reading data instead of seeking for it.

The Galago search engine includes parsers for three compound document formats: ARC, TREC Text, and TREC Web. In each format, many text documents are stored in the same file, with short regions of document metadata separating the documents. Figure 3.10 shows an example of the TREC Web format. Notice that each document block begins with a <DOC> tag and ends with a </DOC> tag. At the beginning of the document, the <DOCHDR> tag marks a section containing the information about the page request, such as its URL, the date it was crawled, and the HTTP headers returned by the web server. Each document record also contains a <DOCNO> field that includes a unique identifier for the document.

Even though large files make sense for data transfer from disk, reducing the total storage requirements for document collections has obvious advantages. Fortunately, text written by people is highly redundant. For instance, the letter q is almost always followed by the letter u. Shannon (1951) showed that native English speakers are able to guess the next letter of a passage of English text with 69% accuracy. HTML and XML tags are even more redundant. *Compression* techniques exploit this redundancy to make files smaller without losing any of the content. We will cover compression as it is used for document indexing in Chapter 5, in part because compression for indexing is rather specialized. While research continues into text compression, popular algorithms like DEFLATE (Deutsch, 1996) and LZW (Welch, 1984) can compress HTML and XML text by 80%. This space savings reduces the cost of storing a lot of documents, and also reduces

```
<DOC>
<DOCNO>WTX001-B01-10</DOCNO>
<DOCHDR>
http://www.example.com/test.html 204.244.59.33 19970101013145 text/html 440
HTTP/1.0 200 OK
Date: Wed, 01 Jan 1997 01:21:13 GMT
Server: Apache/1.0.3
Content-type: text/html
Content-length: 270
Last-modified: Mon, 25 Nov 1996 05:31:24 GMT
</DOCHDR>
<HTML>
<TITLE>Tropical Fish Store</TITLE>
Coming soon!
</HTML>
</DOC>
<DOC>
<DOCNO>WTX001-B01-109</DOCNO>
<DOCHDR>
http://www.example.com/fish.html 204.244.59.33 19970101013149 text/html 440
HTTP/1.0 200 OK
Date: Wed, 01 Jan 1997 01:21:19 GMT
Server: Apache/1.0.3
Content-type: text/html
Content-length: 270
Last-modified: Mon, 25 Nov 1996 05:31:24 GMT
</DOCHDR>
<HTML>
<TITLE>Fish Information</TITLE>
This page will soon contain interesting
information about tropical fish.
</HTML>
</DOC>
```

Fig. 3.10. An example of text in the TREC Web compound document format

the amount of time it takes to read a document from the disk since there are fewer bytes to read.

Compression works best with large blocks of data, which makes it a good fit for big files with many documents in them. However, it is not necessarily a good idea to compress the entire file as a single block. Most compression methods do not allow random access, so each block can only be decompressed sequentially. If you want random access to the data, it is better to consider compressing in smaller blocks, perhaps one block per document, or one block for a few documents. Small blocks reduce compression ratios (the amount of space saved) but improve request latency.

3.6.4 Update

As new versions of documents come in from the crawler, it makes sense to update the document store. The alternative is to create an entirely new document store by merging the new, changed documents from the crawler with document data from the old document store for documents that did not change. If the document data does not change very much, this merging process will be much more expensive than updating the data in place.

```
<a href="http: //example.com" >Example website</a>
```

Fig. 3.11. An example link with anchor text

Another important reason to support update is to handle anchor text. Figure 3.11 shows an example of anchor text in an HTML link tag. The HTML code in the figure will render in the web browser as a link, with the text Example website that, when clicked, will direct the user to http://example.com. Anchor text is an important feature because it provides a concise summary of what the target page is about. If the link comes from a different website, we may also believe that the summary is unbiased, which also helps us rank documents (see Chapters 4 and 7).

Collecting anchor text properly is difficult because the anchor text needs to be associated with the target page. A simple way to approach this is to use a data store that supports update. When a document is found that contains anchor text, we find the record for the target page and update the anchor text portion of the record. When it is time to index the document, the anchor text is all together and ready for indexing.

3.6.5 BigTable

Although a database can perform the duties of a document data store, the very largest document collections demand custom document storage systems. BigTable is the most well known of these systems (Chang et al., 2006). BigTable is a working system in use internally at Google, although at least two open source projects are taking a similar approach. In the next few paragraphs, we will look at the BigTable architecture to see how the problem of document storage influenced its design.

BigTable is a distributed database system originally built for the task of storing web pages. A BigTable instance really is a *big* table; it can be over a petabyte in size, but each database contains only one table. The table is split into small pieces, called *tablets*, which are served by thousands of machines (Figure 3.12).

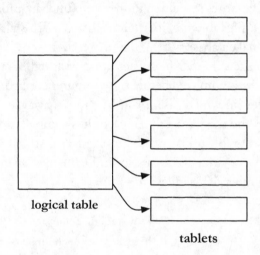

Fig. 3.12. BigTable stores data in a single logical table, which is split into many smaller tablets

If you are familiar with relational databases, you will have encountered SQL (Structured Query Language). SQL allows users to write complex and computationally expensive queries, and one of the tasks of the database system is to optimize the processing of these queries to make them as fast as possible. Because some of these queries could take a very long time to complete, a large relational database requires a complex locking system to ensure that the many users of the database do not corrupt it by reading or writing data simultaneously. Isolating users from each other is a difficult job, and many papers and books have been written about how to do it well.

The BigTable approach is quite different. There is no query language, and therefore no complex queries, and it includes only row-level transactions, which would be considered rather simple by relational database standards. However, the simplicity of the model allows BigTable to scale up to very large database sizes while using inexpensive computers, even though they may be prone to failure.

Most of the engineering in BigTable involves failure recovery. The tablets, which are the small sections of the table, are stored in a replicated file system that is accessible by all BigTable tablet servers. Any changes to a BigTable tablet are recorded to a transaction log, which is also stored in a shared file system. If any tablet server crashes, another server can immediately read the tablet data and transaction log from the file system and take over.

Most relational databases store their data in files that are constantly modified. In contrast, BigTable stores its data in immutable (unchangeable) files. Once file data is written to a BigTable file, it is never changed. This also helps in failure recovery. In relational database systems, failure recovery requires a complex series of operations to make sure that files were not corrupted because only some of the outstanding writes completed before the computer crashed. In BigTable, a file is either incomplete (in which case it can be thrown away and re-created from other BigTable files and the transaction log), or it is complete and therefore is not corrupt. To allow for table updates, the newest data is stored in RAM, whereas older data is stored in a series of files. Periodically the files are merged together to reduce the total number of disk files.

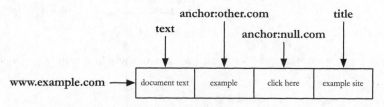

Fig. 3.13. A BigTable row

BigTables are logically organized by rows (Figure 3.13). In the figure, the row stores the data for a single web page. The URL, www.example.com, is the row key, which can be used to find this row. The row has many columns, each with a unique name. Each column can have many different timestamps, although that is not shown in the figure. The combination of a row key, a column key, and a timestamp point to a single *cell* in the row. The cell holds a series of bytes, which might be a number, a string, or some other kind of data.

In the figure, notice that there is a text column for the full text of the document as well as a title column, which makes it easy to quickly find the document title without parsing the full document text. There are two columns for anchor text. One, called anchor:other.com, includes anchor text from a link from the site other.com to example.com; the text of the link is "example", as shown in the cell. The anchor:null.com describes a link from null.com to example.com with anchor text "click here". Both of these columns are in the anchor *column group*. Other columns could be added to this column group to add information about more links.

BigTable can have a huge number of columns per row, and while all rows have the same column groups, not all rows have the same columns. This is a major departure from traditional database systems, but this flexibility is important, in part because of the lack of tables. In a relational database system, the anchor columns would be stored in one table and the document text in another. Because BigTable has just one table, all the anchor information needs to be packed into a single record. With all the anchor data stored together, only a single disk read is necessary to read all of the document data. In a two-table relational database, at least two reads would be necessary to retrieve this data.

Rows are partitioned into tablets based on their row keys. For instance, all URLs beginning with a could be located in one tablet, while all those starting with b could be in another tablet. Using this kind of range-based partitioning makes it easy for a client of BigTable to determine which server is serving each row. To look up a particular row, the client consults a list of row key ranges to determine which tablet would hold the desired row. The client then contacts the appropriate tablet server to fetch the row. The row key ranges are cached in the client, so that most of the network traffic is between clients and tablet servers.

BigTable's architecture is designed for speed and scale through massive numbers of servers, and for economy by using inexpensive computers that are expected to fail. In order to achieve these goals, BigTable sacrifices some key relational database features, such as a complex query language and multiple-table databases. However, this architecture is well suited for the task of storing and finding web pages, where the primary task is efficient lookups and updates on individual rows.

3.7 Detecting Duplicates

Duplicate and *near-duplicate* documents occur in many situations. Making copies and creating new versions of documents is a constant activity in offices, and keeping track of these is an important part of information management. On the Web, however, the situation is more extreme. In addition to the normal sources of duplication, *plagiarism* and *spam* are common, and the use of multiple URLs to point to the same web page and *mirror sites* can cause a crawler to generate large numbers of duplicate pages. Studies have shown that about 30% of the web pages in a large crawl are exact or near duplicates of pages in the other 70% (e.g., Fetterly et al., 2003).

Documents with very similar content generally provide little or no new information to the user, but consume significant resources during crawling, indexing, and search. In response to this problem, algorithms for detecting duplicate documents have been developed so that they can be removed or treated as a group during indexing and ranking.

Detecting exact duplicates is a relatively simple task that can be done using *checksumming* techniques. A checksum is a value that is computed based on the content of the document. The most straightforward checksum is a sum of the bytes in the document file. For example, the checksum for a file containing the text "Tropical fish" would be computed as follows (in hex):

T	r	o	p	i	c	a	l		f	i	s	h	*Sum*
54	72	6F	70	69	63	61	6C	20	66	69	73	68	508

Any document file containing the same text would have the same checksum. Of course, any document file containing text that happened to have the same checksum would also be treated as a duplicate. A file containing the same characters in a different order would have the same checksum, for example. More sophisticated functions, such as a *cyclic redundancy check* (CRC), have been developed that consider the positions of the bytes.

The detection of near-duplicate documents is more difficult. Even defining a near-duplicate is challenging. Web pages, for example, could have the same text content but differ in the advertisements, dates, or formatting. Other pages could have small differences in their content from revisions or updates. In general, a near-duplicate is defined using a threshold value for some similarity measure between pairs of documents. For example, a document D_1 could be defined as a near-duplicate of document D_2 if more than 90% of the words in the documents were the same.

There are two scenarios for near-duplicate detection. One is the *search* scenario, where the goal is to find near-duplicates of a given document D. This, like all search problems, conceptually involves the comparison of the query document to all other documents. For a collection containing N documents, the number of comparisons required will be $\mathcal{O}(N)$. The other scenario, *discovery*, involves finding all pairs of near-duplicate documents in the collection. This process requires $\mathcal{O}(N^2)$ comparisons. Although information retrieval techniques that measure similarity using word-based representations of documents have been shown to be effective for identifying near-duplicates in the search scenario, the computational requirements of the discovery scenario have meant that new techniques have been developed for deriving compact representations of documents. These compact representations are known as *fingerprints*.

The basic process of generating fingerprints is as follows:

1. The document is parsed into words. Non-word content, such as punctuation, HTML tags, and additional whitespace, is removed (see section 4.3).
2. The words are grouped into contiguous *n-grams* for some n. These are usually overlapping sequences of words (see section 4.3.5), although some techniques use non-overlapping sequences.
3. Some of the n-grams are selected to represent the document.
4. The selected n-grams are hashed to improve retrieval efficiency and further reduce the size of the representation.
5. The hash values are stored, typically in an inverted index.

There are a number of fingerprinting algorithms that use this general approach, and they differ mainly in how subsets of the n-grams are selected. Selecting a fixed number of n-grams at random does not lead to good performance in terms of finding near-duplicates. Consider two near-identical documents, D_1 and D_2. The fingerprints generated from n-grams selected randomly from document D_1 are unlikely to have a high overlap with the fingerprints generated from a different set of n-grams selected randomly from D_2. A more effective technique uses pre-specified combinations of characters, and selects n-grams that begin with those characters. Another popular technique, called *0 mod p*, is to select all n-grams whose hash value *modulo* p is zero, where p is a parameter.

Figure 3.14 illustrates the fingerprinting process using overlapping 3-grams, hypothetical hash values, and the *0 mod p* selection method with a p value of 4. Note that after the selection process, the document (or sentence in this case) is represented by fingerprints for the n-grams "fish include fish", "found in tropical",

Tropical fish include fish found in tropical environments around the world, including both freshwater and salt water species.

(a) Original text

tropical fish include, fish include fish, include fish found, fish found in, found in tropical, in tropical environments, tropical environments around, environments around the, around the world, the world including, world including both, including both freshwater, both freshwater and, freshwater and salt, and salt water, salt water species

(b) 3-grams

938 664 463 822 492 798 78 969 143 236 913 908 694 553 870 779

(c) Hash values

664 492 236 908

(d) Selected hash values using *0 mod 4*

Fig. 3.14. Example of fingerprinting process

"the world including", and "including both freshwater". In large-scale applications, such as finding near-duplicates on the Web, the n-grams are typically 5–10 words long and the hash values are 64 bits.[3]

Near-duplicate documents are found by comparing the fingerprints that represent them. Near-duplicate pairs are defined by the number of shared fingerprints or the ratio of shared fingerprints to the total number of fingerprints used to represent the pair of documents. Fingerprints do not capture all of the information in the document, however, and consequently this leads to errors in the detection of near-duplicates. Appropriate selection techniques can reduce these errors, but not eliminate them. As we mentioned, evaluations have shown that comparing word-based representations using a similarity measure such as the cosine correlation (see section 7.1.2) is generally significantly more effective than fingerprinting methods for finding near-duplicates. The problem with these methods is their efficiency.

---

[3] The hash values are usually generated using *Rabin fingerprinting* (Broder et al., 1997), named after the Israeli computer scientist Michael Rabin.

A recently developed fingerprinting technique called simhash (Charikar, 2002) combines the advantages of the word-based similarity measures with the efficiency of fingerprints based on hashing. It has the unusual property for a hashing function that similar documents have similar hash values. More precisely, the similarity of two pages as measured by the cosine correlation measure is proportional to the number of bits that are the same in the fingerprints generated by simhash.

The procedure for calculating a simhash fingerprint is as follows:

1. Process the document into a set of features with associated weights. We will assume the simple case where the features are words weighted by their frequency. Other weighting schemes are discussed in Chapter 7.
2. Generate a hash value with b bits (the desired size of the fingerprint) for each word. The hash value should be unique for each word.
3. In b-dimensional vector V, update the components of the vector by adding the weight for a word to every component for which the corresponding bit in the word's hash value is 1, and subtracting the weight if the value is 0.
4. After all words have been processed, generate a b-bit fingerprint by setting the ith bit to 1 if the ith component of V is positive, or 0 otherwise.

Figure 3.15 shows an example of this process for an 8-bit fingerprint. Note that common words (stopwords) are removed as part of the text processing. In practice, much larger values of b are used. Henzinger (2006) describes a large-scale Web-based evaluation where the fingerprints had 384 bits. A web page is defined as a near-duplicate of another page if the simhash fingerprints agree on more than 372 bits. This study showed significant effectiveness advantages for the simhash approach compared to fingerprints based on n-grams.

3.8 Removing Noise

Many web pages contain text, links, and pictures that are not directly related to the main content of the page. For example, Figure 3.16 shows a web page containing a news story. The main content of the page (the story) is outlined in black. This *content block* takes up less than 20% of the display area of the page, and the rest is made up of banners, advertisements, images, general navigation links, services (such as search and alerts), and miscellaneous information, such as copyright. From the perspective of the search engine, this additional material in the web page is mostly *noise* that could negatively affect the ranking of the page. A major component of the representation of a page used in a search engine is based

Tropical fish include fish found in tropical environments around the world,
including both freshwater and salt water species.

(a) Original text

tropical 2 fish 2 include 1 found 1 environments 1 around 1 world 1
including 1 both 1 freshwater 1 salt 1 water 1 species 1

(b) Words with weights

tropical	01100001	fish	10101011	include	11100110
found	00011110	environments	00101101	around	10001011
world	00101010	including	11000000	both	10101110
freshwater	00111111	salt	10110101	water	00100101
species	11101110				

(c) 8 bit hash values

1 -5 9 -9 3 1 3 3

(d) Vector V formed by summing weights

1 0 1 0 1 1 1 1

(e) 8-bit fingerprint formed from V

Fig. 3.15. Example of simhash fingerprinting process

on word counts, and the presence of a large number of words unrelated to the
main topic can be a problem. For this reason, techniques have been developed to
detect the content blocks in a web page and either ignore the other material or
reduce its importance in the indexing process.

Finn et al. (2001) describe a relatively simple technique based on the observation that there are less HTML tags in the text of the main content of typical
web pages than there is in the additional material. Figure 3.17 (also known as a
document slope curve) shows the cumulative distribution of tags in the example
web page from Figure 3.16, as a function of the total number of tokens (words or
other non-tag strings) in the page. The main text content of the page corresponds
to the "plateau" in the middle of the distribution. This flat area is relatively small
because of the large amount of formatting and presentation information in the
HTML source for the page.

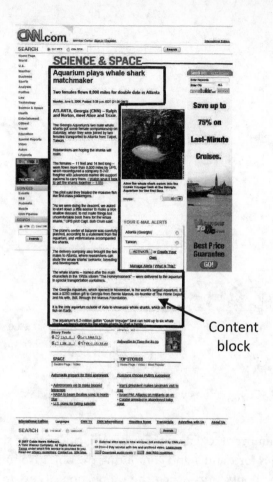

Content block

Fig. 3.16. Main content block in a web page

One way to detect the largest flat area of the distribution is to represent a web page as a sequence of bits, where $b_n = 1$ indicates that the nth token is a tag, and $b_n = 0$ otherwise. Certain tags that are mostly used to format text, such as font changes, headings, and table tags, are ignored (i.e., are represented by a 0 bit). The detection of the main content can then be viewed as an optimization problem where we find values of i and j to maximize both the number of tags below i and above j and the number of non-tag tokens between i and j. This corresponds to maximizing the corresponding objective function:

$$\sum_{n=0}^{i-1} b_n + \sum_{n=i}^{j} (1 - b_n) + \sum_{n=j+1}^{N-1} b_n$$

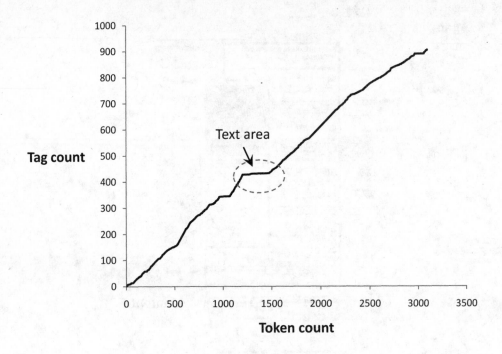

Fig. 3.17. Tag counts used to identify text blocks in a web page

where N is the number of tokens in the page. This can be done simply by scanning the possible values for i and j and computing the objective function. Note that this procedure will only work when the proportion of text tokens in the non-content section is lower than the proportion of tags, which is not the case for the web page in Figure 3.17. Pinto et al. (2002) modified this approach to use a text window to search for low-slope sections of the document slope curve.

The structure of the web page can also be used more directly to identify the content blocks in the page. To display a web page using a browser, an HTML parser interprets the structure of the page specified using the tags, and creates a Document Object Model (DOM) representation. The tree-like structure represented by the DOM can be used to identify the major components of the web page. Figure 3.18 shows part of the DOM structure[4] for the example web page in Figure 3.16. The part of the structure that contains the text of the story is indicated by the comment cnnArticleContent. Gupta et al. (2003) describe an approach that

---

[4] This was generated using the DOM Inspector tool in the Firefox browser.

navigates the DOM tree recursively, using a variety of filtering techniques to remove and modify nodes in the tree and leave only content. HTML elements such as images and scripts are removed by simple filters. More complex filters remove advertisements, lists of links, and tables that do not have "substantive" content.

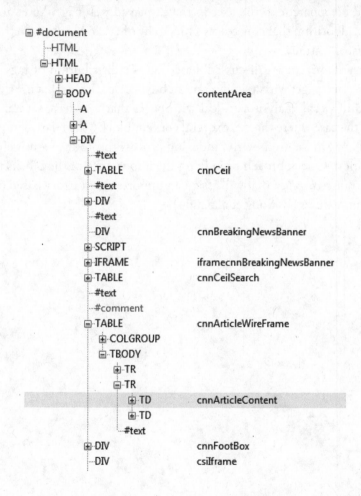

Fig. 3.18. Part of the DOM structure for the example web page

The DOM structure provides useful information about the components of a web page, but it is complex and is a mixture of logical and layout components. In Figure 3.18, for example, the content of the article is buried in a table cell (**TD** tag) in a row (**TR** tag) of an HTML table (**TABLE** tag). The table is being used in this case to specify layout rather than semantically related data. Another approach to identifying the content blocks in a page focuses on the layout and presentation of the web page. In other words, visual features—such as the position of the block, the size of the font used, the background and font colors, and the presence of separators (such as lines and spaces)—are used to define blocks of information that would be apparent to the user in the displayed web page. Yu et al. (2003) describe an algorithm that constructs a hierarchy of visual blocks from the DOM tree and visual features.

The first algorithm we discussed, based on the distribution of tags, is quite effective for web pages with a single content block. Algorithms that use the DOM structure and visual analysis can deal with pages that may have several content blocks. In the case where there are several content blocks, the relative importance of each block can be used by the indexing process to produce a more effective representation. One approach to judging the importance of the blocks in a web page is to train a *classifier* that will assign an importance category based on visual and content features (R. Song et al., 2004).

References and Further Reading

Cho and Garcia-Molina (2002, 2003) wrote a series of influential papers on web crawler design. Our discussion of page refresh policies is based heavily on Cho and Garcia-Molina (2003), and section 3.2.7 draws from Cho and Garcia-Molina (2002).

There are many open source web crawlers. The Heritrix crawler,[5] developed for the Internet Archive project, is a capable and scalable example. The system is developed in modules that are highly configurable at runtime, making it particularly suitable for experimentation.

Focused crawling attracted much attention in the early days of web search. Menczer and Belew (1998) and Chakrabarti et al. (1999) wrote two of the most influential papers. Menczer and Belew (1998) envision a focused crawler made of autonomous software agents, principally for a single user. The user enters a list of both URLs and keywords. The agent then attempts to find web pages that would be useful to the user, and the user can rate those pages to give feedback to the system. Chakrabarti et al. (1999) focus on crawling for specialized topical indexes. Their crawler uses a classifier to determine the topicality of crawled pages, as well as a distiller, which judges the quality of a page as a source of links to other topical pages. They evaluate their system against a traditional, unfocused crawler to show that an unfocused crawler seeded with topical links is not sufficient to achieve a topical crawl. The broad link structure of the Web causes the unfocused crawler to quickly drift to other topics, while the focused crawler successfully stays on topic.

The Unicode specification is an incredibly detailed work, covering tens of thousands of characters (Unicode Consortium, 2006). Because of the nature of some non-Western scripts, many glyphs are formed from grouping a number of Unicode characters together, so the specification must detail not just what the characters are, but how they can be joined together. Characters are still being added to Unicode periodically.

Bergman (2001) is an extensive study of the deep Web. Even though this study is old by web standards, it shows how sampling through search engines can be used to help estimate the amount of unindexed content on the Web. This study estimated that 550 billion web pages existed in the deep Web, compared to 1 billion in the accessible Web. He et al. (2007) describe a more recent survey that shows that the deep Web has continued to expand rapidly in recent years. An example

---

[5] http://crawler.archive.org

of a technique for generating searchable representations of deep Web databases, called query probing, is described by Ipeirotis and Gravano (2004).

Sitemaps, robots.txt files, RSS feeds, and Atom feeds each have their own specifications, which are available on the Web.[6] These formats show that successful web standards are often quite simple.

As we mentioned, database systems can be used to store documents from a web crawl for some applications. Our discussion of database systems was, however, limited mostly to a comparison with BigTable. There are a number of textbooks, such as Garcia-Molina et al. (2008), that provide much more information on how databases work, including details about important features such as query languages, locking, and recovery. BigTable, which we referenced frequently, was described in Chang et al. (2006). Other large Internet companies have built their own database systems with similar goals: large-scale distribution and high throughput, but without an expressive query language or detailed transaction support. The Dynamo system from Amazon has low latency guarantees (DeCandia et al., 2007), and Yahoo! uses their UDB system to store large datasets (Baeza-Yates & Ramakrishnan, 2008).

We mentioned DEFLATE (Deutsch, 1996) and LZW (Welch, 1984) as specific document compression algorithms in the text. DEFLATE is the basis for the popular Zip, gzip, and zlib compression tools. LZW is the basis of the Unix compress command, and is also found in file formats such as GIF, PostScript, and PDF. The text by Witten et al. (1999) provides detailed discussions about text and image compression algorithms.

Hoad and Zobel (2003) provide both a review of fingerprinting techniques and a comparison to word-based similarity measures for near-duplicate detection. Their evaluation focused on finding versions of documents and plagiarized documents. Bernstein and Zobel (2006) describe a technique for using full fingerprinting (no selection) for the task of finding *co-derivatives*, which are documents derived from the same source. Bernstein and Zobel (2005) examined the impact of duplication on evaluations of retrieval effectiveness. They showed that about 15% of the relevant documents for one of the TREC tracks were redundant, which could significantly affect the impact of the results from a user's perspective.

---

[6] http://www.sitemaps.org
http://www.robotstxt.org
http://www.rssboard.org/rss-specification
http://www.rfc-editor.org/rfc/rfc5023.txt

Henzinger (2006) describes a large-scale evaluation of near-duplicate detection on the Web. The two techniques compared were a version of Broder's "shingling" algorithm (Broder et al., 1997; Fetterly et al., 2003) and simhash (Charikar, 2002). Henzinger's study, which used 1.6 billion pages, showed that neither method worked well for detecting redundant documents *on the same site* because of the frequent use of "boilerplate" text that makes different pages look similar. For pages on different sites, the simhash algorithm achieved a precision of 50% (meaning that of those pages that were declared "near-duplicate" based on the similarity threshold, 50% were correct), whereas the Broder algorithm produced a precision of 38%.

A number of papers have been written about techniques for extracting content from web pages. Yu et al. (2003) and Gupta et al. (2003) are good sources for references to these papers.

Exercises

3.1. Suppose you have two collections of documents. The smaller collection is full of useful, accurate, high-quality information. The larger collection contains a few high-quality documents, but also contains lower-quality text that is old, out-of-date, or poorly written. What are some reasons for building a search engine for only the small collection? What are some reasons for building a search engine that covers both collections?

3.2. Suppose you have a network connection that can transfer 10MB per second. If each web page is 10K and requires 500 milliseconds to transfer, how many threads does your web crawler need to fully utilize the network connection? If your crawler needs to wait 10 seconds between requests to the same web server, what is the minimum number of distinct web servers the system needs to contact each minute to keep the network connection fully utilized?

3.3. Why do crawlers not use POST requests?

3.4. What is the advantage of using HEAD requests instead of GET requests during crawling? When would a crawler use a GET request instead of a HEAD request?

3.5. Name the three types of sites mentioned in the chapter that compose the deep Web.

3.6. How would you design a system to automatically enter data into web forms in order to crawl deep Web pages? What measures would you use to make sure your crawler's actions were not destructive (for instance, so that it doesn't add random blog comments).

3.7. Write a program that can create a valid sitemap based on the contents of a directory on your computer's hard disk. Assume that the files are accessible from a website at the URL http://www.example.com. For instance, if there is a file in your directory called homework.pdf, this would be available at http://www.example.com/homework.pdf. Use the real modification date on the file as the last modified time in the sitemap, and to help estimate the change frequency.

3.8. Write a simple single-threaded web crawler. Starting from a single input URL (perhaps a professor's web page), the crawler should download a page and then wait at least five seconds before downloading the next page. Your program should find other pages to crawl by parsing link tags found in previously crawled documents.

3.9. Suppose that, in an effort to crawl web pages faster, you set up two crawling machines with different starting seed URLs. Is this an effective strategy for distributed crawling? Why or why not?

3.10. UTF-16 is used in Java and Windows®. Compare it to UTF-8.

3.11. How does BigTable handle hardware failure?

3.12. Design a compression algorithm that compresses HTML tags. Your algorithm should detect tags in an HTML file and replace them with a code of your own design that is smaller than the tag itself. Write an encoder and decoder program.

3.13. Generate checksums for a document by adding the bytes of the document and by using the Unix command cksum. Edit the document and see if both checksums change. Can you change the document so that the simple checksum does not change?

3.14. Write a program to generate simhash fingerprints for documents. You can use any reasonable hash function for the words. Use the program to detect duplicates on your home computer. Report on the accuracy of the detection. How does the detection accuracy vary with fingerprint size?

3.15. Plot the document slope curves for a sample of web pages. The sample should include at least one page containing a news article. Test the accuracy of the simple optimization algorithm for detecting the main content block. Write your own program or use the code from http://www.aidanf.net/software/bte-body-text-extraction. Describe the cases where the algorithm fails. Would an algorithm that searched explicitly for low-slope areas of the document slope curve be successful in these cases?

3.16. Give a high-level outline of an algorithm that would use the DOM structure to identify content information in a web page. In particular, describe heuristics you would use to identify content and non-content elements of the structure.

4

Processing Text

"I was trying to comprehend the meaning of the words."

Spock, *Star Trek: The Final Frontier*

4.1 From Words to Terms

After gathering the text we want to search, the next step is to decide whether it should be modified or restructured in some way to simplify searching. The types of changes that are made at this stage are called *text transformation* or, more often, *text processing*. The goal of text processing is to convert the many forms in which words can occur into more consistent *index terms*. Index terms are the representation of the content of a document that are used for searching.

The simplest decision about text processing would be to not do it at all. A good example of this is the "find" feature in your favorite word processor. By the time you use the find command, the text you wish to search has already been gathered: it's on the screen. After you type the word you want to find, the word processor scans the document and tries to find the exact sequence of letters that you just typed. This feature is extremely useful, and nearly every text editing program can do this because users demand it.

The trouble is that exact text search is rather restrictive. The most annoying restriction is case-sensitivity: suppose you want to find "computer hardware", and there is a sentence in the document that begins with "Computer hardware". Your search query does not exactly match the text in the sentence, because the first letter of the sentence is capitalized. Fortunately, most word processors have an option for ignoring case during searches. You can think of this as a very rudimentary form of online text processing. Like most text processing techniques, ignoring case increases the probability that you will find a match for your query in the document.

Many search engines do not distinguish between uppercase and lowercase letters. However, they go much further. As we will see in this chapter, search engines can strip punctuation from words to make them easier to find. Words are split apart in a process called *tokenization*. Some words may be ignored entirely in order to make query processing more effective and efficient; this is called *stopping*. The system may use *stemming* to allow similar words (like "run" and "running") to match each other. Some documents, such as web pages, may have formatting changes (like bold or large text), or explicit *structure* (like titles, chapters, and captions) that can also be used by the system. Web pages also contain *links* to other web pages, which can be used to improve document ranking. All of these techniques are discussed in this chapter.

These text processing techniques are fairly simple, even though their effects on search results can be profound. None of these techniques involves the computer doing any kind of complex reasoning or understanding of the text. Search engines work because much of the meaning of text is captured by counts of word occurrences and co-occurrences,[1] especially when that data is gathered from the huge text collections available on the Web. Understanding the statistical nature of text is fundamental to understanding retrieval models and ranking algorithms, so we begin this chapter with a discussion of *text statistics*. More sophisticated techniques for *natural language processing* that involve syntactic and semantic analysis of text have been studied for decades, including their application to information retrieval, but to date have had little impact on ranking algorithms for search engines. These techniques are, however, being used for the task of question answering, which is described in Chapter 11. In addition, techniques involving more complex text processing are being used to identify additional index terms or features for search. *Information extraction* techniques for identifying people's names, organization names, addresses, and many other special types of features are discussed here, and *classification*, which can be used to identify semantic categories, is discussed in Chapter 9.

Finally, even though this book focuses on retrieving English documents, information retrieval techniques can be used with text in many different languages. In this chapter, we show how different languages require different types of text representation and processing.

---

[1] Word co-occurrence measures the number of times groups of words (usually pairs) occur together in documents. A *collocation* is the name given to a pair, group, or sequence of words that occur together more often than would be expected by chance. The *term association measures* that are used to find collocations are discussed in Chapter 6.

4.2 Text Statistics

Although language is incredibly rich and varied, it is also very predictable. There are many ways to describe a particular topic or event, but if the words that occur in many descriptions of an event are counted, then some words will occur much more frequently than others. Some of these frequent words, such as "and" or "the," will be common in the description of any event, but others will be characteristic of that particular event. This was observed as early as 1958 by Luhn, when he proposed that the significance of a word depended on its frequency in the document. Statistical models of word occurrences are very important in information retrieval, and are used in many of the core components of search engines, such as the ranking algorithms, query transformation, and indexing techniques. These models will be discussed in later chapters, but we start here with some of the basic models of word occurrence.

One of the most obvious features of text from a statistical point of view is that the distribution of word frequencies is very *skewed*. There are a few words that have very high frequencies and many words that have low frequencies. In fact, the two most frequent words in English ("the" and "of") account for about 10% of all word occurrences. The most frequent six words account for 20% of occurrences, and the most frequent 50 words are about 40% of all text! On the other hand, given a large sample of text, typically about one half of all the unique words in that sample occur only once. This distribution is described by *Zipf's law*,[2] which states that the frequency of the rth most common word is inversely proportional to r or, alternatively, the *rank* of a word times its frequency (f) is approximately a constant (k):

$$r \cdot f = k$$

We often want to talk about the probability of occurrence of a word, which is just the frequency of the word divided by the total number of word occurrences in the text. In this case, Zipf's law is:

$$r \cdot P_r = c$$

where P_r is the probability of occurrence for the rth ranked word, and c is a constant. For English, $c \approx 0.1$. Figure 4.1 shows the graph of Zipf's law with this constant. This clearly shows how the frequency of word occurrence falls rapidly after the first few most common words.

---

[2] Named after the American linguist George Kingsley Zipf.

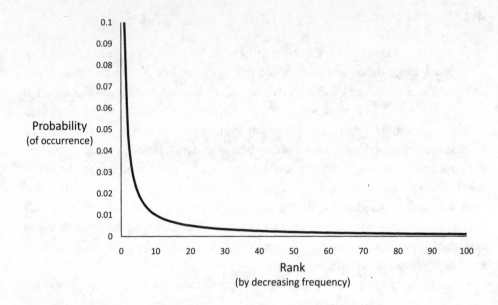

Fig. 4.1. Rank versus probability of occurrence for words assuming Zipf's law (rank × probability = 0.1)

To see how well Zipf's law predicts word occurrences in actual text collections, we will use the Associated Press collection of news stories from 1989 (called AP89) as an example. This collection was used in TREC evaluations for several years. Table 4.1 shows some statistics for the word occurrences in AP89. The vocabulary size is the number of unique words in the collection. Even in this relatively small collection, the vocabulary size is quite large (nearly 200,000 unique words). A large proportion of these words (70,000) occur only once. Words that occur once in a text corpus or book have long been regarded as important in text analysis, and have been given the special name of *Hapax Legomena*.[3]

Table 4.2 shows the 50 most frequent words from the AP89 collection, together with their frequencies, ranks, probability of occurrence (converted to a percentage of total occurrences), and the $r.P_r$ value. From this table, we can see

---

[3] The name was created by scholars studying the Bible. Since the 13th century, people have studied the word occurrences in the Bible and, of particular interest, created *concordances*, which are indexes of where words occur in the text. Concordances are the ancestors of the inverted files that are used in modern search engines. The first concordance was said to have required 500 monks to create.

Total documents	84,678
Total word occurrences	39,749,179
Vocabulary size	198,763
Words occurring > 1000 times	4,169
Words occurring once	70,064

Table 4.1. Statistics for the AP89 collection

that Zipf's law is quite accurate, in that the value of $r.P_r$ is approximately constant, and close to 0.1. The biggest variations are for some of the most frequent words. In fact, it is generally observed that Zipf's law is inaccurate for low and high ranks (high-frequency and low-frequency words). Table 4.3 gives some examples for lower-frequency words from AP89.

Figure 4.2 shows a log-log plot[4] of the $r.P_r$ values for all words in the AP89 collection. Zipf's law is shown as a straight line on this graph since $\log P_r = \log(c \cdot r^{-1}) = \log c - \log r$. This figure clearly shows how the predicted relationship breaks down at high ranks (approximately rank 10,000 and above). A number of modifications to Zipf's law have been proposed,[5] some of which have interesting connections to cognitive models of language.

It is possible to derive a simple formula for predicting the proportion of words with a given frequency from Zipf's law. A word that occurs n times has rank $r_n = k/n$. In general, more than one word may have the same frequency. We assume that the rank r_n is associated with the *last* of the group of words with the same frequency. In that case, the number of words with the same frequency n will be given by $r_n - r_{n+1}$, which is the rank of the last word in the group minus the rank of the last word of the previous group of words with a higher frequency (remember that higher-frequency words have lower ranks). For example, Table 4.4 has an example of a ranking of words in decreasing order of their frequency. The number of words with frequency 5,099 is the rank of the last member of that

---

[4] The x and y axes of a log-log plot show the logarithm of the values of x and y, not the values themselves.

[5] The most well-known is the derivation by the mathematician Benoit Mandelbrot (the same person who developed fractal geometry), which is $(r + \beta)^\alpha \cdot P_r = \gamma$, where β, α, and γ are parameters that can be tuned for a particular text. In the case of the AP89 collection, however, the fit for the frequency data is not noticeably better than the Zipf distribution.

Word	Freq.	r	P_r(%)	$r.P_r$	Word	Freq	r	P_r(%)	$r.P_r$
the	2,420,778	1	6.49	0.065	has	136,007	26	0.37	0.095
of	1,045,733	2	2.80	0.056	are	130,322	27	0.35	0.094
to	968,882	3	2.60	0.078	not	127,493	28	0.34	0.096
a	892,429	4	2.39	0.096	who	116,364	29	0.31	0.090
and	865,644	5	2.32	0.120	they	111,024	30	0.30	0.089
in	847,825	6	2.27	0.140	its	111,021	31	0.30	0.092
said	504,593	7	1.35	0.095	had	103,943	32	0.28	0.089
for	363,865	8	0.98	0.078	will	102,949	33	0.28	0.091
that	347,072	9	0.93	0.084	would	99,503	34	0.27	0.091
was	293,027	10	0.79	0.079	about	92,983	35	0.25	0.087
on	291,947	11	0.78	0.086	i	92,005	36	0.25	0.089
he	250,919	12	0.67	0.081	been	88,786	37	0.24	0.088
is	245,843	13	0.65	0.086	this	87,286	38	0.23	0.089
with	223,846	14	0.60	0.084	their	84,638	39	0.23	0.089
at	210,064	15	0.56	0.085	new	83,449	40	0.22	0.090
by	209,586	16	0.56	0.090	or	81,796	41	0.22	0.090
it	195,621	17	0.52	0.089	which	80,385	42	0.22	0.091
from	189,451	18	0.51	0.091	we	80,245	43	0.22	0.093
as	181,714	19	0.49	0.093	more	76,388	44	0.21	0.090
be	157,300	20	0.42	0.084	after	75,165	45	0.20	0.091
were	153,913	21	0.41	0.087	us	72,045	46	0.19	0.089
an	152,576	22	0.41	0.090	percent	71,956	47	0.19	0.091
have	149,749	23	0.40	0.092	up	71,082	48	0.19	0.092
his	142,285	24	0.38	0.092	one	70,266	49	0.19	0.092
but	140,880	25	0.38	0.094	people	68,988	50	0.19	0.093

Table 4.2. Most frequent 50 words from AP89

Word	Freq.	r	P_r(%)	$r.P_r$
assistant	5,095	1,021	.013	0.13
sewers	100	17,110	.000256	0.04
toothbrush	10	51,555	.000025	0.01
hazmat	1	166,945	.000002	0.04

Table 4.3. Low-frequency words from AP89

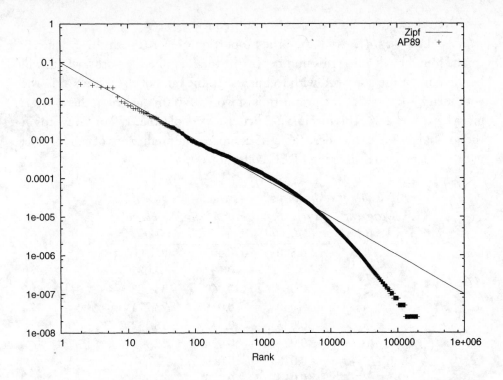

Fig. 4.2. A log-log plot of Zipf's law compared to real data from AP89. The predicted relationship between probability of occurrence and rank breaks down badly at high ranks.

group ("chemical") minus the rank of the last member of the previous group with higher frequency ("summit"), which is $1006 - 1002 = 4$.

Rank	Word	Frequency
1000	concern	5,100
1001	spoke	5,100
1002	summit	5,100
1003	bring	5,099
1004	star	5,099
1005	immediate	5,099
1006	chemical	5,099
1007	african	5,098

Table 4.4. Example word frequency ranking

Given that the number of words with frequency n is $r_n - r_{n+1} = k/n - k/(n+1) = k/n(n+1)$, then the proportion of words with this frequency can be found by dividing this number by the total number of words, which will be the rank of the last word with frequency 1. The rank of the last word in the vocabulary is $k/1 = k$. The proportion of words with frequency n, therefore, is given by $1/n(n+1)$. This formula predicts, for example, that $1/2$ of the words in the vocabulary will occur once. Table 4.5 compares the predictions of this formula with real data from a different TREC collection.

Number of Occurrences (n)	Predicted Proportion (1/n(n+1))	Actual Proportion	Actual Number of Words
1	0.500	0.402	204,357
2	0.167	0.132	67,082
3	0.083	0.069	35,083
4	0.050	0.046	23,271
5	0.033	0.032	16,332
6	0.024	0.024	12,421
7	0.018	0.019	9,766
8	0.014	0.016	8,200
9	0.011	0.014	6,907
10	0.009	0.012	5,893

Table 4.5. Proportions of words occurring n times in 336,310 documents from the TREC Volume 3 corpus. The total vocabulary size (number of unique words) is 508,209.

4.2.1 Vocabulary Growth

Another useful prediction related to word occurrence is *vocabulary growth*. As the size of the corpus grows, new words occur. Based on the assumption of a Zipf distribution for words, we would expect that the number of new words that occur in a given amount of new text would decrease as the size of the corpus increases. New words will, however, always occur due to sources such as invented words (think of all those drug names and start-up company names), spelling errors, product numbers, people's names, email addresses, and many others. The relationship between the size of the corpus and the size of the vocabulary was found empirically by Heaps (1978) to be:

$$v = k \cdot n^\beta$$

where v is the vocabulary size for a corpus of size n words, and k and β are parameters that vary for each collection. This is sometimes referred to as *Heaps' law*. Typical values for k and β are often stated to be $10 \leq k \leq 100$ and $\beta \approx 0.5$. Heaps' law predicts that the number of new words will increase very rapidly when the corpus is small and will continue to increase indefinitely, but at a slower rate for larger corpora. Figure 4.3 shows a plot of vocabulary growth for the AP89 collection compared to a graph of Heaps' law with $k = 62.95$ and $\beta = 0.455$. Clearly, Heaps' law is a good fit. The parameter values are similar for many of the other TREC news collections. As an example of the accuracy of this prediction, if the first 10,879,522 words of the AP89 collection are scanned, Heaps' law predicts that the number of unique words will be 100,151, whereas the actual value is 100,024. Predictions are much less accurate for small numbers of words ($< 1,000$).

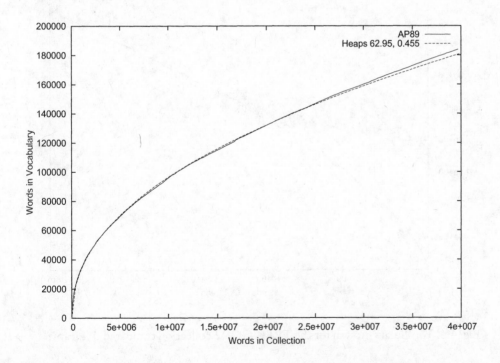

Fig. 4.3. Vocabulary growth for the TREC AP89 collection compared to Heaps' law

Web-scale collections are considerably larger than the AP89 collection. The AP89 collection contains about 40 million words, but the (relatively small) TREC Web collection GOV2[6] contains more than 20 *billion* words. With that many words, it seems likely that the number of new words would eventually drop to near zero and Heaps' law would not be applicable. It turns out this is not the case. Figure 4.4 shows a plot of vocabulary growth for GOV2 together with a graph of Heaps' law with $k = 7.34$ and $\beta = 0.648$. This data indicates that the number of unique words continues to grow steadily even after reaching 30 million. This has significant implications for the design of search engines, which will be discussed in Chapter 5. Heaps' law provides a good fit for this data, although the parameter values are very different than those for other TREC collections and outside the boundaries established as typical with these and other smaller collections.

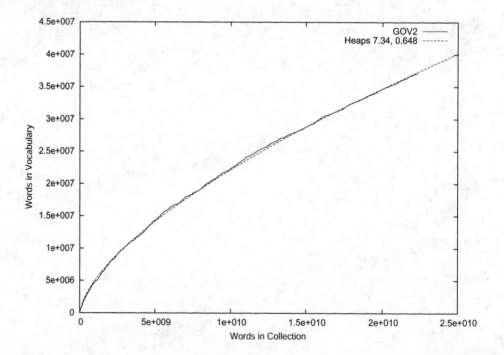

Fig. 4.4. Vocabulary growth for the TREC GOV2 collection compared to Heaps' law

---

[6] Web pages crawled from websites in the **.gov** domain during early 2004. See section 8.2 for more details.

4.2.2 Estimating Collection and Result Set Sizes

Word occurrence statistics can also be used to estimate the size of the results from a web search. All web search engines have some version of the query interface shown in Figure 4.5, where immediately after the query ("tropical fish aquarium" in this case) and before the ranked list of results, an estimate of the total number of results is given. This is typically a very large number, and descriptions of these systems always point out that it is just an estimate. Nevertheless, it is always included.

| tropical fish aquarium | Search |

Web results Page 1 of 3,880,000 results

Fig. 4.5. Result size estimate for web search

To estimate the size of a result set, we first need to define "results." For the purposes of this estimation, a result is any document (or web page) that contains *all* of the query words. Some search applications will rank documents that do not contain all the query words, but given the huge size of the Web, this is usually not necessary. If we assume that words occur *independently* of each other, then the probability of a document containing all the words in the query is simply the product of the probabilities of the individual words occurring in a document. For example, if there are three query words a, b, and c, then:

$$P(a \cap b \cap c) = P(a) \cdot P(b) \cdot P(c)$$

where $P(a \cap b \cap c)$ is the joint probability, or the probability that all three words occur in a document, and $P(a)$, $P(b)$, and $P(c)$ are the probabilities of each word occurring in a document. A search engine will always have access to the number of documents that a word occurs in (f_a, f_b, and f_c),[7] and the number of documents in the collection (N), so these probabilities can easily be estimated as $P(a) = f_a/N$, $P(b) = f_b/N$, and $P(c) = f_c/N$. This gives us

$$f_{abc} = N \cdot f_a/N \cdot f_b/N \cdot f_c/N = (f_a \cdot f_b \cdot f_c)/N^2$$

where f_{abc} is the estimated size of the result set.

---

[7] Note that these are *document occurrence frequencies*, not the total number of word occurrences (there may be many occurrences of a word in a document).

Word(s)	Document Frequency	Estimated Frequency
tropical	120,990	
fish	1,131,855	
aquarium	26,480	
breeding	81,885	
tropical fish	18,472	5,433
tropical aquarium	1,921	127
tropical breeding	5,510	393
fish aquarium	9,722	1,189
fish breeding	36,427	3,677
aquarium breeding	1,848	86
tropical fish aquarium	1,529	6
tropical fish breeding	3,629	18

Table 4.6. Document frequencies and estimated frequencies for word combinations (assuming independence) in the GOV2 Web collection. Collection size (N) is 25,205,179.

Table 4.6 gives document occurrence frequencies for the words "tropical", "fish", "aquarium", and "breeding", and for combinations of those words in the TREC GOV2 Web collection. It also gives the estimated size of the frequencies of the combinations based on the independence assumption. Clearly, this assumption does not lead to good estimates for result size, especially for combinations of three words. The problem is that the words in these combinations do not occur independently of each other. If we see the word "fish" in a document, for example, then the word "aquarium" is more likely to occur in this document than in one that does not contain "fish".

Better estimates are possible if word co-occurrence information is also available from the search engine. Obviously, this would give exact answers for two-word queries. For longer queries, we can improve the estimate by not assuming independence. In general, for three words

$$P(a \cap b \cap c) = P(a \cap b) \cdot P(c|(a \cap b))$$

where $P(a \cap b)$ is the probability that the words a and b co-occur in a document, and $P(c|(a \cap b))$ is the probability that the word c occurs in a document *given* that the words a and b occur in the document.[8] If we have co-occurrence information,

---

[8] This is called a *conditional* probability.

we can approximate this probability using either $P(c|a)$ or $P(c|b)$, whichever is the largest. For the example query "tropical fish aquarium" in Table 4.6, this means we estimate the result set size by multiplying the number of documents containing both "tropical" and "aquarium" by the probability that a document contains "fish" given that it contains "aquarium", or:

$$f_{tropical \cap fish \cap aquarium} = f_{tropical \cap aquarium} \cdot f_{fish \cap aquarium} / f_{aquarium}$$
$$= 1921 \cdot 9722/26480 = 705$$

Similarly, for the query "tropical fish breeding":

$$f_{tropical \cap fish \cap breeding} = f_{tropical \cap breeding} \cdot f_{fish \cap breeeding} / f_{breeding}$$
$$= 5510 \cdot 36427/81885 = 2451$$

These estimates are much better than the ones produced assuming independence, but they are still too low. Rather than storing even more information, such as the number of occurrences of word triples, it turns out that reasonable estimates of result size can be made using just word frequency and the size of the *current* result set. Search engines estimate the result size because they do not rank all the documents that contain the query words. Instead, they rank a much smaller subset of the documents that are likely to be the most relevant. If we know the proportion of the total documents that have been ranked (s) and the number of documents found that contain all the query words (C), we can simply estimate the result size as C/s, which assumes that the documents containing all the words are distributed uniformly.[9] The proportion of documents processed is measured by the proportion of the documents containing the least frequent word that have been processed, since all results must contain that word.

For example, if the query "tropical fish aquarium" is used to rank GOV2 documents in the Galago search engine, after processing 3,000 out of the 26,480 documents that contain "aquarium", the number of documents containing all three words is 258. This gives a result size estimate of $258/(3,000 \div 26,480) = 2,277$. After processing just over 20% of the documents, the estimate is 1,778 (compared to the actual figure of 1,529). For the query "tropical fish breeding", the estimates after processing 10% and 20% of the documents that contain "breeding" are 4,076

---

[9] We are also assuming *document-at-a-time* processing, where the inverted lists for all query words are processed at the same time, giving complete document scores (see Chapter 5).

and 3,762 (compared to 3,629). These estimates, as well as being quite accurate, do not require knowledge of the total number of documents in the collection.

Estimating the total number of documents stored in a search engine is, in fact, of significant interest to both academia (how big is the Web?) and business (which search engine has better coverage of the Web?). A number of papers have been written about techniques to do this, and one of these is based on the concept of word independence that we used before. If a and b are two words that occur independently, then

$$f_{ab}/N = f_a/N \cdot f_b/N$$

and

$$N = (f_a \cdot f_b)/f_{ab}$$

To get a reasonable estimate of N, the two words should be independent and, as we have seen from the examples in Table 4.6, this is often not the case. We can be more careful about the choice of query words, however. For example, if we use the word "lincoln" (document frequency 771,326 in GOV2), we would expect the words in the query "tropical lincoln" to be more independent than the word pairs in Table 4.6 (since the former are less semantically related). The document frequency of "tropical lincoln" in GOV2 is 3,018, which means we can estimate the size of the collection as $N = (120{,}990 \cdot 771{,}326)/3{,}018 = 30{,}922{,}045$. This is quite close to the actual number of 25,205,179.

4.3 Document Parsing

4.3.1 Overview

Document parsing involves the recognition of the content and structure of text documents. The primary content of most documents is the words that we were counting and modeling using the Zipf distribution in the previous section. Recognizing each word occurrence in the sequence of characters in a document is called *tokenizing* or *lexical analysis*. Apart from these words, there can be many other types of content in a document, such as metadata, images, graphics, code, and tables. As mentioned in Chapter 2, metadata is information about a document that is not part of the text content. Metadata content includes document attributes such as date and author, and, most importantly, the *tags* that are used by *markup languages* to identify document components. The most popular markup languages are HTML (Hypertext Markup Language) and XML (Extensible Markup Language).

The parser uses the tags and other metadata recognized in the document to interpret the document's structure based on the syntax of the markup language (*syntactic analysis*) and to produce a representation of the document that includes both the structure and content. For example, an HTML parser interprets the structure of a web page as specified using HTML tags, and creates a Document Object Model (DOM) representation of the page that is used by a web browser. In a search engine, the output of a document parser is a representation of the content and structure that will be used for creating indexes. Since it is important for a search index to represent every document in a collection, a document parser for a search engine is often more tolerant of syntax errors than parsers used in other applications.

In the first part of our discussion of document parsing, we focus on the recognition of the tokens, words, and phrases that make up the content of the documents. In later sections, we discuss separately the important topics related to document structure, namely markup, links, and extraction of structure from the text content.

4.3.2 Tokenizing

Tokenizing is the process of forming words from the sequence of characters in a document. In English text, this appears to be simple. In many early systems, a "word" was defined as any sequence of alphanumeric characters of length 3 or more, terminated by a space or other special character. All uppercase letters were also converted to lowercase.[10] This means, for example, that the text

Bigcorp's 2007 bi-annual report showed profits rose 10%.

would produce the following sequence of tokens:

bigcorp 2007 annual report showed profits rose

Although this simple tokenizing process was adequate for experiments with small test collections, it does not seem appropriate for most search applications or even experiments with TREC collections, because too much information is discarded. Some examples of issues involving tokenizing that can have significant impact on the effectiveness of search are:

---

[10] This is sometimes referred to as *case folding*, *case normalization*, or *downcasing*.

- Small words (one or two characters) can be important in some queries, usually in combinations with other words. For example, xp, ma, pm, ben e king, el paso, master p, gm, j lo, world war II.[11]
- Both hyphenated and non-hyphenated forms of many words are common. In some cases the hyphen is not needed. For example, e-bay, wal-mart, active-x, cd-rom, t-shirts. At other times, hyphens should be considered either as part of the word or a word separator. For example, winston-salem, mazda rx-7, e-cards, pre-diabetes, t-mobile, spanish-speaking.
- Special characters are an important part of the tags, URLs, code, and other important parts of documents that must be correctly tokenized.
- Capitalized words can have different meaning from lowercase words. For example, "Bush" and "Apple".
- Apostrophes can be a part of a word, a part of a possessive, or just a mistake. For example, rosie o'donnell, can't, don't, 80's, 1890's, men's straw hats, master's degree, england's ten largest cities, shriner's.
- Numbers can be important, including decimals. For example, nokia 3250, top 10 courses, united 93, quicktime 6.5 pro, 92.3 the beat, 288358 (yes, this was a real query; it's a patent number).
- Periods can occur in numbers, abbreviations (e.g., "I.B.M.", "Ph.D."), URLs, ends of sentences, and other situations.

From these examples, tokenizing seems more complicated than it first appears. The fact that these examples come from queries also emphasizes that the text processing for queries *must* be the same as that used for documents. If different tokenizing processes are used for queries and documents, many of the index terms used for documents will simply not match the corresponding terms from queries. Mistakes in tokenizing become obvious very quickly through retrieval failures.

To be able to incorporate the range of language processing required to make matching effective, the tokenizing process should be both simple and flexible. One approach to doing this is for the first pass of tokenizing to focus entirely on identifying markup or tags in the document. This could be done using a tokenizer and parser designed for the specific markup language used (e.g., HTML), but it should accommodate syntax errors in the structure, as mentioned previously. A second pass of tokenizing can then be done on the appropriate parts of the document structure. Some parts that are not used for searching, such as those containing HTML code, will be ignored in this pass.

---

[11] These and other examples were taken from a small sample of web queries.

Given that nearly everything in the text of a document can be important for some query, the tokenizing rules have to convert most of the content to searchable tokens. Instead of trying to do everything in the tokenizer, some of the more difficult issues, such as identifying word variants or recognizing that a string is a name or a date, can be handled by separate processes, including stemming, information extraction, and query transformation. Information extraction usually requires the full form of the text as input, including capitalization and punctuation, so this information must be retained until extraction has been done. Apart from this restriction, capitalization is rarely important for searching, and text can be reduced to lowercase for indexing. This does not mean that capitalized words are not used in queries. They are, in fact, used quite often, but in queries where the capitalization does not reduce ambiguity and so does not impact effectiveness. Words such as "Apple" that are often used in examples (but not so often in real queries) can be handled by query reformulation techniques (Chapter 6) or simply by relying on the most popular pages (section 4.5).

If we take the view that complicated issues are handled by other processes, the most general strategy for hyphens, apostrophes, and periods would be to treat them as word terminators (like spaces). It is important that all the tokens produced are indexed, including single characters such as "s" and "o". This will mean, for example, that the query[12] "o'connor" is equivalent to "o connor", "bob's" is equivalent to "bob s", and "rx-7" is equivalent to "rx 7". Note that this will also mean that a word such as "rx7" will be a different token than "rx-7" and therefore will be indexed separately. The task of relating the queries rx 7, rx7, and rx-7 will then be handled by the query transformation component of the search engine.

On the other hand, if we rely entirely on the query transformation component to make the appropriate connections or inferences between words, there is the risk that effectiveness could be lowered, particularly in applications where there is not enough data for reliable query expansion. In these cases, more rules can be incorporated into the tokenizer to ensure that the tokens produced by the query text will match the tokens produced from document text. For example, in the case of TREC collections, a rule that tokenizes all words containing apostrophes by the string without the apostrophe is very effective. With this rule, "O'Connor" would be tokenized as "oconnor" and "Bob's" would produce the token "bobs". Another effective rule for TREC collections is to tokenize all abbreviations con-

---

[12] We assume the common syntax for web queries where "<words>" means match exactly the phrase contained in the quotes.

taining periods as the string without periods. An abbreviation in this case is any string of alphabetic single characters separated by periods. This rule would tokenize "I.B.M." as "ibm", but "Ph.D." would still be tokenized as "ph d".

In summary, the most general tokenizing process will involve first identifying the document structure and then identifying words in text as any sequence of alphanumeric characters, terminated by a space or special character, with everything converted to lowercase. This is not much more complicated than the simple process we described at the start of the section, but it relies on information extraction and query transformation to handle the difficult issues. In many cases, additional rules are added to the tokenizer to handle some of the special characters, to ensure that query and document tokens will match.

4.3.3 Stopping

Human language is filled with function words: words that have little meaning apart from other words. The most popular—"the," "a," "an," "that," and "those"—are *determiners*. These words are part of how we describe nouns in text, and express concepts like location or quantity. Prepositions, such as "over," "under," "above," and "below," represent relative position between two nouns.

Two properties of these function words cause us to want to treat them in a special way in text processing. First, these function words are extremely common. Table 4.2 shows that nearly all of the most frequent words in the AP89 collection fall into this category. Keeping track of the quantity of these words in each document requires a lot of disk space. Second, both because of their commonness and their function, these words rarely indicate anything about document relevance on their own. If we are considering individual words in the retrieval process and not phrases, these function words will help us very little.

In information retrieval, these function words have a second name: *stopwords*. We call them stopwords because text processing stops when one is seen, and they are thrown out. Throwing out these words decreases index size, increases retrieval efficiency, and generally improves retrieval effectiveness.

Constructing a stopword list must be done with caution. Removing too many words will hurt retrieval effectiveness in particularly frustrating ways for the user. For instance, the query "to be or not to be" consists entirely of words that are usually considered stopwords. Although not removing stopwords may cause some problems in ranking, removing stopwords can cause perfectly valid queries to return no results.

A stopword list can be constructed by simply using the top n (e.g., 50) most frequent words in a collection. This can, however, lead to words being included that are important for some queries. More typically, either a standard stopword list is used,[13] or a list of frequent words and standard stopwords is manually edited to remove any words that may be significant for a particular application. It is also possible to create stopword lists that are customized for specific parts of the document structure (also called *fields*). For example, the words "click", "here", and "privacy" may be reasonable stopwords to use when processing anchor text.

If storage space requirements allow, it is best to at least index all words in the documents. If stopping is required, the stopwords can always be removed from queries. By keeping the stopwords in the index, there will be a number of possible ways to execute a query with stopwords in it. For instance, many systems will remove stopwords from a query unless the word is preceded by a plus sign (+). If keeping stopwords in an index is not possible because of space requirements, as few as possible should be removed in order to maintain maximum flexibility.

4.3.4 Stemming

Part of the expressiveness of natural language comes from the huge number of ways to convey a single idea. This can be a problem for search engines, which rely on matching words to find relevant documents. Instead of restricting matches to words that are identical, a number of techniques have been developed to allow a search engine to match words that are semantically related. *Stemming*, also called *conflation*, is a component of text processing that captures the relationships between different variations of a word. More precisely, stemming reduces the different forms of a word that occur because of *inflection* (e.g., plurals, tenses) or *derivation* (e.g., making a verb into a noun by adding the suffix -ation) to a common stem.

Suppose you want to search for news articles about Mark Spitz's Olympic swimming career. You might type "mark spitz swimming" into a search engine. However, many news articles are usually summaries of events that have already happened, so they are likely to contain the word "swam" instead of "swimming." It is the job of the stemmer to reduce "swimming" and "swam" to the same stem (probably "swim") and thereby allow the search engine to determine that there is a match between these two words.

---

[13] Such as the one distributed with the Lemur toolkit and included with Galago.

In general, using a stemmer for search applications with English text produces a small but noticeable improvement in the quality of results. In applications involving highly inflected languages, such as Arabic or Russian, stemming is a crucial part of effective search.

There are two basic types of stemmers: *algorithmic* and *dictionary-based*. An algorithmic stemmer uses a small program to decide whether two words are related, usually based on knowledge of word suffixes for a particular language. By contrast, a dictionary-based stemmer has no logic of its own, but instead relies on pre-created dictionaries of related terms to store term relationships.

The simplest kind of English algorithmic stemmer is the *suffix-s* stemmer. This kind of stemmer assumes that any word ending in the letter "s" is plural, so cakes → cake, dogs → dog. Of course, this rule is not perfect. It cannot detect many plural relationships, like "century" and "centuries". In very rare cases, it detects a relationship where it does not exist, such as with "I" and "is". The first kind of error is called a *false negative*, and the second kind of error is called a *false positive*.[14]

More complicated algorithmic stemmers reduce the number of false negatives by considering more kinds of suffixes, such as -ing or -ed. By handling more suffix types, the stemmer can find more term relationships; in other words, the false negative rate is reduced. However, the false positive rate (finding a relationship where none exists) generally increases.

The most popular algorithmic stemmer is the *Porter stemmer*.[15] This has been used in many information retrieval experiments and systems since the 1970s, and a number of implementations are available. The stemmer consists of a number of steps, each containing a set of rules for removing suffixes. At each step, the rule for the longest applicable suffix is executed. Some of the rules are obvious, whereas others require some thought to work out what they are doing. As an example, here are the first two parts of step 1 (of 5 steps):

Step 1a:
- Replace *sses* by *ss* (e.g., stresses → stress).
- Delete *s* if the preceding word part contains a vowel not immediately before the *s* (e.g., gaps → gap but gas → gas).
- Replace *ied* or *ies* by *i* if preceded by more than one letter, otherwise by *ie* (e.g., ties → tie, cries → cri).

---

[14] These terms are used in any binary decision process to describe the two types of errors. This includes evaluation (Chapter 8) and classification (Chapter 9).

[15] http://tartarus.org/martin/PorterStemmer/

- If suffix is *us* or *ss* do nothing (e.g., stress → stress).

Step 1b:

- Replace *eed*, *eedly* by *ee* if it is in the part of the word after the first non-vowel following a vowel (e.g., agreed → agree, feed → feed).
- Delete *ed*, *edly*, *ing*, *ingly* if the preceding word part contains a vowel, and then if the word ends in *at*, *bl*, or *iz* add *e* (e.g., fished → fish, pirating → pirate), or if the word ends with a double letter that is not *ll*, *ss*, or *zz*, remove the last letter (e.g., falling→ fall, dripping → drip), or if the word is short, add *e* (e.g., hoping → hope).
- Whew!

The Porter stemmer has been shown to be effective in a number of TREC evaluations and search applications. It is difficult, however, to capture all the subtleties of a language in a relatively simple algorithm. The original version of the Porter stemmer made a number of errors, both false positives and false negatives. Table 4.7 shows some of these errors. It is easy to imagine how confusing "execute" with "executive" or "organization" with "organ" could cause significant problems in the ranking. A more recent form of the stemmer (called Porter2)[16] fixes some of these problems and provides a mechanism to specify exceptions.

False positives	False negatives
organization/organ	european/europe
generalization/generic	cylinder/cylindrical
numerical/numerous	matrices/matrix
policy/police	urgency/urgent
university/universe	create/creation
addition/additive	analysis/analyses
negligible/negligent	useful/usefully
execute/executive	noise/noisy
past/paste	decompose/decomposition
ignore/ignorant	sparse/sparsity
special/specialized	resolve/resolution
head/heading	triangle/triangular

Table 4.7. Examples of errors made by the original Porter stemmer. False positives are pairs of words that have the same stem. False negatives are pairs that have different stems.

---

[16] http://snowball.tartarus.org

A dictionary-based stemmer provides a different approach to the problem of stemming errors. Instead of trying to detect word relationships from letter patterns, we can store lists of related words in a large dictionary. Since these word lists can be created by humans, we can expect that the false positive rate will be very low for these words. Related words do not even need to look similar; a dictionary stemmer can recognize that "is," "be," and "was" are all forms of the same verb. Unfortunately, the dictionary cannot be infinitely long, so it cannot react automatically to new words. This is an important problem since language is constantly evolving. It is possible to build stem dictionaries automatically by statistical analysis of a text corpus. Since this is particularly useful when stemming is used for query expansion, we discuss this technique in section 6.2.1.

Another strategy is to combine an algorithmic stemmer with a dictionary-based stemmer. Typically, irregular words such as the verb "to be" are the oldest in the language, while new words follow more regular grammatical conventions. This means that newly invented words are likely to work well with an algorithmic stemmer. A dictionary can be used to detect relationships between common words, and the algorithmic stemmer can be used for unrecognized words.

A well-known example of this hybrid approach is the *Krovetz stemmer* (Krovetz, 1993). This stemmer makes constant use of a dictionary to check whether the word is valid. The dictionary in the Krovetz stemmer is based on a general English dictionary but also uses exceptions that are generated manually. Before being stemmed, the dictionary is checked to see whether a word is present; if it is, it is either left alone (if it is in the general dictionary) or stemmed based on the exception entry. If the word is not in the dictionary, it is checked for a list of common inflectional and derivational suffixes. If one is found, it is removed and the dictionary is again checked to see whether the word is present. If it is not found, the ending of the word may be modified based on the ending that was removed. For example, if the ending -ies is found, it is replaced by -ie and checked in the dictionary. If it is found in the dictionary, the stem is accepted; otherwise the ending is replaced by y. This will result in calories → calorie, for example. The suffixes are checked in a sequence (for example, plurals before -ion endings), so multiple suffixes may be removed.

The Krovetz stemmer has a lower false positive rate than the Porter stemmer, but also tends to have a higher false negative rate, depending on the size of the exception dictionaries. Overall, the effectiveness of the two stemmers is comparable when used in search evaluations. The Krovetz stemmer has the additional advantage of producing stems that, in most cases, are full words, whereas the Porter

Original text:
Document will describe marketing strategies carried out by U.S. companies for their agricultural chemicals, report predictions for market share of such chemicals, or report market statistics for agrochemicals, pesticide, herbicide, fungicide, insecticide, fertilizer, predicted sales, market share, stimulate demand, price cut, volume of sales.

Porter stemmer:
document describ market strategi carri compani agricultur chemic report predict market share chemic report market statist agrochem pesticid herbicid fungicid insecticid fertil predict sale market share stimul demand price cut volum sale

Krovetz stemmer:
document describe marketing strategy carry company agriculture chemical report prediction market share chemical report market statistic agrochemic pesticide herbicide fungicide insecticide fertilizer predict sale stimulate demand price cut volume sale

Fig. 4.6. Comparison of stemmer output for a TREC query. Stopwords have also been removed.

stemmer often produces stems that are word fragments. This is a concern if the stems are used in the search interface.

Figure 4.6 compares the output of the Porter and Krovetz stemmers on the text of a TREC query. The output of the Krovetz stemmer is similar in terms of which words are reduced to the same stems, although "marketing" is not reduced to "market" because it was in the dictionary. The stems produced by the Krovetz stemmer are mostly words. The exception is the stem "agrochemic", which occurred because "agrochemical" was not in the dictionary. Note that text processing in this example has removed stopwords, including single characters. This resulted in the removal of "U.S." from the text, which could have significant consequences for some queries. This can be handled by better tokenization or information extraction, as we discuss in section 4.6.

As in the case of stopwords, the search engine will have more flexibility to answer a broad range of queries if the document words are not stemmed but instead are indexed in their original form. Stemming can then be done as a type of query expansion, as explained in section 6.2.1. In some applications, both the full words and their stems are indexed, in order to provide both flexibility and efficient query processing times.

We mentioned earlier that stemming can be particularly important for some languages, and have virtually no impact in others. Incorporating language-specific stemming algorithms is one of the most important aspects of customizing, or *internationalizing*, a search engine for multiple languages. We discuss other aspects of internationalization in section 4.7, but focus on the stemming issues here.

As an example, Table 4.8 shows some of the Arabic words derived from the same root. A stemming algorithm that reduced Arabic words to their roots would clearly not work (there are less than 2,000 roots in Arabic), but a broad range of prefixes and suffixes must be considered. Highly inflectional languages like Arabic have many word variants, and stemming can make a large difference in the accuracy of the ranking. An Arabic search engine with high-quality stemming can be more than 50% more effective, on average, at finding relevant documents than a system without stemming. In contrast, improvements for an English search engine vary from less than 5% on average for large collections to about 10% for small, domain-specific collections.

kitab	*a book*
kitabi	*my book*
alkitab	*the book*
kitabuki	*your book* (f)
kitabuka	*your book (m)*
kitabuhu	*his book*
kataba	*to write*
maktaba	*library, bookstore*
maktab	*office*

Table 4.8. Examples of words with the Arabic root **ktb**

Fortunately, stemmers for a number of languages have already been developed and are available as open source software. For example, the Porter stemmer is available in French, Spanish, Portuguese, Italian, Romanian, German, Dutch, Swedish, Norwegian, Danish, Russian, Finnish, Hungarian, and Turkish.[17] In addition, the statistical approach to building a stemmer that is described in section 6.2.1 can be used when only a text corpus is available.

---

[17] http://snowball.tartarus.org/

4.3.5 Phrases and N-grams

Phrases are clearly important in information retrieval. Many of the two- and three-word queries submitted to search engines are phrases, and finding documents that contain those phrases will be part of any effective ranking algorithm. For example, given the query "black sea", documents that contain that phrase are much more likely to be relevant than documents containing text such as "the sea turned black". Phrases are more precise than single words as topic descriptions (e.g., "tropical fish" versus "fish") and usually less ambiguous (e.g., "rotten apple" versus "apple"). The impact of phrases on retrieval can be complex, however. Given a query such as "fishing supplies", should the retrieved documents contain exactly that phrase, or should they get credit for containing the words "fish", "fishing", and "supplies" in the same paragraph, or even the same document? The details of how phrases affect ranking will depend on the specific retrieval model that is incorporated into the search engine, so we will defer this discussion until Chapter 7. From the perspective of text processing, the issue is whether phrases should be identified at the same time as tokenizing and stemming, so that they can be indexed for faster query processing.

There are a number of possible definitions of a phrase, and most of them have been studied in retrieval experiments over the years. Since a phrase has a grammatical definition, it seems reasonable to identify phrases using the syntactic structure of sentences. The definition that has been used most frequently in information retrieval research is that a phrase is equivalent to a simple *noun phrase*. This is often restricted even further to include just sequences of nouns, or adjectives followed by nouns. Phrases defined by these criteria can be identified using a *part-of-speech (POS) tagger*. A POS tagger marks the words in a text with labels corresponding to the part-of-speech of the word in that context. Taggers are based on statistical or rule-based approaches and are trained using large corpora that have been manually labeled. Typical tags that are used to label the words include NN (singular noun), NNS (plural noun), VB (verb), VBD (verb, past tense), VBN (verb, past participle), IN (preposition), JJ (adjective), CC (conjunction, e.g., "and", "or"), PRP (pronoun), and MD (modal auxiliary, e.g., "can", "will").

Figure 4.7 shows the output of a POS tagger for the TREC query text used in Figure 4.6. This example shows that the tagger can identify phrases that are sequences of nouns, such as "marketing/NN strategies/NNS", or adjectives followed by nouns, such as "agricultural/JJ chemicals/NNS". Taggers do, however, make mistakes. The words "predicted/VBN sales/NNS" would not be identified as a noun phrase, because "predicted" is tagged as a verb.

Original text:
Document will describe marketing strategies carried out by U.S. companies for their agricultural chemicals, report predictions for market share of such chemicals, or report market statistics for agrochemicals, pesticide, herbicide, fungicide, insecticide, fertilizer, predicted sales, market share, stimulate demand, price cut, volume of sales.

Brill tagger:
Document/NN will/MD describe/VB marketing/NN strategies/NNS carried/VBD out/IN by/IN U.S./NNP companies/NNS for/IN their/PRP agricultural/JJ chemicals/NNS ,/, report/NN predictions/NNS for/IN market/NN share/NN of/IN such/JJ chemicals/NNS ,/, or/CC report/NN market/NN statistics/NNS for/IN agrochemicals/NNS ,/, pesticide/NN ,/, herbicide/NN ,/, fungicide/NN ,/, insecticide/NN ,/, fertilizer/NN ,/, predicted/VBN sales/NNS ,/, market/NN share/NN ,/, stimulate/VB demand/NN ,/, price/NN cut/NN ,/, volume/NN of/IN sales/NNS ./.

Fig. 4.7. Output of a POS tagger for a TREC query

Table 4.9 shows the high-frequency simple noun phrases from a TREC corpus consisting mainly of news stories and a corpus of comparable size consisting of all the 1996 patents issued by the United States Patent and Trademark Office (PTO). The phrases were identified by POS tagging. The frequencies of the example phrases indicate that phrases are used more frequently in the PTO collection, because patents are written in a formal, legal style with considerable repetition. There were 1,100,000 phrases in the TREC collection that occurred more than five times, and 3,700,000 phrases in the PTO collection. Many of the TREC phrases are proper nouns, such as "los angeles" or "european union", or are topics that will be important for retrieval, such as "peace process" and "human rights". Two phrases are associated with the format of the documents ("article type", "end recording"). On the other hand, most of the high-frequency phrases in the PTO collection are standard terms used to describe all patents, such as "present invention" and "preferred embodiment", and relatively few are related to the content of the patents, such as "carbon atoms" and "ethyl acetate". One of the phrases, "group consisting", was the result of a frequent tagging error.

Although POS tagging produces reasonable phrases and is used in a number of applications, in general it is too slow to be used as the basis for phrase indexing of large collections. There are simpler and faster alternatives that are just as effective. One approach is to store word position information in the indexes and use this information to identify phrases only when a query is processed. This provides considerable flexibility in that phrases can be identified by the user or by using POS tagging on the query, and they are not restricted to adjacent groups of

TREC data		Patent data	
Frequency	*Phrase*	*Frequency*	*Phrase*
65824	united states	975362	present invention
61327	article type	191625	u.s. pat
33864	los angeles	147352	preferred embodiment
18062	hong kong	95097	carbon atoms
17788	north korea	87903	group consisting
17308	new york	81809	room temperature
15513	san diego	78458	seq id
15009	orange county	75850	brief description
12869	prime minister	66407	prior art
12799	first time	59828	perspective view
12067	soviet union	58724	first embodiment
10811	russian federation	56715	reaction mixture
9912	united nations	54619	detailed description
8127	southern california	54117	ethyl acetate
7640	south korea	52195	example 1
7620	end recording	52003	block diagram
7524	european union	46299	second embodiment
7436	south africa	41694	accompanying drawings
7362	san francisco	40554	output signal
7086	news conference	37911	first end
6792	city council	35827	second end
6348	middle east	34881	appended claims
6157	peace process	33947	distal end
5955	human rights	32338	cross-sectional view
5837	white house	30193	outer surface

Table 4.9. High-frequency noun phrases from a TREC collection and U.S. patents from 1996

words. The identification of syntactic phrases is replaced by testing word proximity constraints, such as whether two words occur within a specified text window. We describe position indexing in Chapter 5 and retrieval models that exploit word proximity in Chapter 7.

In applications with large collections and tight constraints on response time, such as web search, testing word proximities at query time is also likely to be too slow. In that case, we can go back to identifying phrases in the documents during text processing, but use a much simpler definition of a phrase: any sequence of n words. This is also known as an *n-gram*. Sequences of two words are called *bigrams*, and sequences of three words are called *trigrams*. Single words are called *unigrams*. N-grams have been used in many text applications and we will mention them again frequently in this book, particularly in association with *language models* (section 7.3). In this discussion, we are focusing on *word* n-grams, but *character* n-grams are also used in applications such as OCR, where the text is "noisy" and word matching can be difficult (section 11.6). Character n-grams are also used for indexing languages such as Chinese that have no word breaks (section 4.7). N-grams, both character and word, are generated by choosing a particular value for n and then moving that "window" forward one unit (character or word) at a time. In other words, n-grams *overlap*. For example, the word "tropical" contains the following character bigrams: tr, ro, op, pi, ic, ca, and al. Indexes based on n-grams are obviously larger than word indexes.

The more frequently a word n-gram occurs, the more likely it is to correspond to a meaningful phrase in the language. N-grams of all lengths form a Zipf distribution, with a few common phrases occurring very frequently and a large number occurring with frequency 1. In fact, the rank-frequency data for n-grams (which includes single words) fits the Zipf distribution better than words alone. Some of the most common n-grams will be made up of stopwords (e.g., "and the", "there is") and could be ignored, although as with words, we should be cautious about discarding information. Our previous example query "to be or not to be" could certainly make use of n-grams. We could potentially index all n-grams in a document text up to a specific length and make them available to the ranking algorithm. This would seem to be an extravagant use of indexing time and disk space because of the large number of possible n-grams. A document containing 1,000 words, for example, would contain 3,990 instances of word n-grams of length $2 \leq n \leq 5$. Many web search engines, however, use n-gram indexing because it provides a fast method of incorporating phrase features in the ranking.

Google recently made available a file of n-grams derived from web pages.[18] The statistics for this sample are shown in Table 4.10. An analysis of n-grams on the Web (Yang et al., 2007) found that "all rights reserved" was the most frequent trigram in English, whereas "limited liability corporation" was the most frequent in Chinese. In both cases, this was due to the large number of corporate sites, but

---

[18] http://googleresearch.blogspot.com/2006/08/all-our-n-gram-are-belong-to-you.html

it also indicates that n-grams are not dominated by common patterns of speech such as "and will be".

Number of tokens:	1,024,908,267,229
Number of sentences:	95,119,665,584
Number of unigrams:	13,588,391
Number of bigrams:	314,843,401
Number of trigrams:	977,069,902
Number of fourgrams:	1,313,818,354
Number of fivegrams:	1,176,470,663

Table 4.10. Statistics for the Google n-gram sample

4.4 Document Structure and Markup

In database applications, the fields or attributes of database records are a critical part of searching. Queries are specified in terms of the required values of these fields. In some text applications, such as email or literature search, fields such as *author* and *date* will have similar importance and will be part of the query specification. In the case of web search, queries usually do not refer to document structure or fields, but that does not mean that this structure is unimportant. Some parts of the structure of web pages, indicated by HTML markup, are very significant features used by the ranking algorithm. The document parser must recognize this structure and make it available for indexing.

As an example, Figure 4.8 shows part of a web page for a Wikipedia[19] entry. The page has some obvious structure that could be used in a ranking algorithm. The main heading for the page, "tropical fish", indicates that this phrase is particularly important. The same phrase is also in bold and italics in the body of the text, which is further evidence of its importance. Other words and phrases are used as the *anchor text* for links and are likely to be good terms to represent the content of the page.

The HTML source for this web page (Figure 4.9) shows that there is even more structure that should be represented for search. Each field or *element* in HTML is indicated by a start tag (such as `<h1>`) and an optional end tag (e.g.,

---

[19] The Web encyclopedia, http://en.wikipedia.org/.

Tropical fish

From Wikipedia, the free encyclopedia

Tropical fish include <u>fish</u> found in <u>tropical</u> environments around the world, including both <u>freshwater</u> and <u>salt water</u> species. <u>Fishkeepers</u> often use the term *tropical fish* to refer only those requiring fresh water, with saltwater tropical fish referred to as <u>*marine fish*</u>.

Tropical fish are popular <u>aquarium</u> fish , due to their often bright coloration. In freshwater fish, this coloration typically derives from <u>iridescence</u>, while salt water fish are generally <u>pigmented</u>.

Fig. 4.8. Part of a web page from Wikipedia

</h1>).[20] Elements can also have attributes (with values), given by attribute_name = "value" pairs. The <head> element of an HTML document contains metadata that is not displayed by a browser. The metadata element for keywords (<meta name="keywords") gives a list of words and phrases that can be used as additional content terms for the page. In this case, these are the titles of other Wikipedia pages. The <title> metadata element gives the title for the page (which is different from the main heading).

The <body> element of the document contains the content that is displayed. The main heading is indicated by the <h1> tag. Other headings, of different sizes and potentially different importance, would be indicated by <h2> through <h6> tags. Terms that should be displayed in bold or italic are indicated by <b> and <i> tags. Unlike typical database fields, these tags are primarily used for formatting and can occur many times in a document. They can also, as we have said, be interpreted as a tag indicating a word or phrase of some importance.

Links, such as <a href="/wiki/Fish" title="Fish">fish</a>, are very common. They are the basis of link analysis algorithms such as PageRank (Brin & Page, 1998), but also define the anchor text. Links and anchor text are of particular importance to web search and will be described in the next section. The title attribute for a link is used to provide extra information about that link, although in our example it is the words in the last part of the URL for the associated Wikipedia page. Web search engines also make use of the URL of a page as a source of additional metadata. The URL for this page is:

http://en.wikipedia.org/wiki/Tropical_fish

---

[20] In XML the end tag is not optional.

The fact that the words "tropical" and "fish" occur in the URL will increase the importance of those words for this page. The depth of a URL (i.e., the number of directories deep the page is) can also be important. For example, the URL www.ibm.com is more likely to be the home page for IBM than a page with the URL:

www.pcworld.com/businesscenter/article/698/ibm_buys_apt!

```
<html>
<head>
<meta name="keywords" content="Tropical fish, Airstone, Albinism, Algae eater,
Aquarium, Aquarium fish feeder, Aquarium furniture, Aquascaping, Bath treatment
(fishkeeping),Berlin Method, Biotope" />
...
<title>Tropical fish - Wikipedia, the free encyclopedia</title>
</head>
<body>
 ...
<h1 class="firstHeading">Tropical fish</h1>
...
<p><b>Tropical fish</b> include <a href="/wiki/Fish" title="Fish">fish</a> found in <a
href="/wiki/Tropics" title="Tropics">tropical</a> environments around the world,
including both <a href="/wiki/Fresh_water" title="Fresh water">freshwater</a> and <a
href="/wiki/Sea_water" title="Sea water">salt water</a> species. <a
href="/wiki/Fishkeeping" title="Fishkeeping">Fishkeepers</a> often use the term
<i>tropical fish</i> to refer only those requiring fresh water, with saltwater tropical fish
referred to as <i><a href="/wiki/List_of_marine_aquarium_fish_species" title="List of
marine aquarium fish species">marine fish</a></i>.</p>
<p>Tropical fish are popular <a href="/wiki/Aquarium" title="Aquarium">aquarium</a>
fish , due to their often bright coloration. In freshwater fish, this coloration typically
derives from <a href="/wiki/Iridescence" title="Iridescence">iridescence</a>, while salt
water fish are generally <a href="/wiki/Pigment" title="Pigment">pigmented</a>.</p>
...
</body></html>
```

Fig. 4.9. HTML source for example Wikipedia page

In HTML, the element types are predefined and are the same for all documents. XML, in contrast, allows each application to define what the element types are and what tags are used to represent them. XML documents can be described by a *schema*, similar to a database schema. XML elements, consequently, are more closely tied to the semantics of the data than HTML elements. Search applications often use XML to record *semantic annotations* in the documents that are produced by information extraction techniques, as described in section 4.6. A document parser for these applications would record the annotations, along with the other document structure, and make them available for indexing.

The query language XQuery[21] has been defined by the database community for searching structured data described using XML. XQuery supports queries that specify both structural and content constraints, which raises the issue of whether a database or information retrieval approach is better for building a search engine for XML data. We discuss this topic in more detail in section 11.4, but the general answer is that it will depend on the data, the application, and the user needs. For XML data that contains a substantial proportion of text, the information retrieval approach is superior. In Chapter 7, we will describe retrieval models that are designed for text documents that contain both structure and metadata.

4.5 Link Analysis

Links connecting pages are a key component of the Web. Links are a powerful navigational aid for people browsing the Web, but they also help search engines understand the relationships between the pages. These detected relationships help search engines rank web pages more effectively. It should be remembered, however, that many document collections used in search applications such as desktop or enterprise search either do not have links or have very little link structure. For these collections, link analysis will have no impact on search performance.

As we saw in the last section, a link in a web page is encoded in HTML with a statement such as:

```
For more information on this topic, please go to <a
href="http://www.somewhere.com">the somewhere page</a>.
```

When this page appears in your web browser, the words "the somewhere page" will be displayed differently than regular text, usually underlined or in a different color (or both). When you click on that link, your browser will then load the web page http://www.somewhere.com. In this link, "the somewhere page" is called the *anchor text*, and http://www.somewhere.com is the *destination*. Both components are useful in the ranking process.

---

[21] http://www.w3.org/XML/Query/

4.5.1 Anchor Text

Anchor text has two properties that make it particularly useful for ranking web pages. First, it tends to be very short, perhaps two or three words, and those words often succinctly describe the topic of the linked page. For instance, links to www.ebay.com are highly likely to contain the word "eBay" in the anchor text. Many queries are very similar to anchor text in that they are also short topical descriptions of web pages. This suggests a very simple algorithm for ranking pages: search through all links in the collection, looking for anchor text that is an exact match for the user's query. Each time there is a match, add 1 to the score of the destination page. Pages would then be ranked in decreasing order of this score. This algorithm has some glaring faults, not the least of which is how to handle the query "click here". More generally, the collection of all the anchor text in links pointing to a page can be used as an additional text field for that page, and incorporated into the ranking algorithm.

Anchor text is usually written by people who are not the authors of the destination page. This means that the anchor text can describe a destination page from a different perspective, or emphasize the most important aspect of the page from a community viewpoint. The fact that the link exists at all is a vote of importance for the destination page. Although anchor text is not mentioned as often as link analysis algorithms (for example, PageRank) in discussions of web search engines, TREC evaluations have shown that it is the most important part of the representation of a page for some types of web search. In particular, it is essential for searches where the user is trying to find a home page for a particular topic, person, or organization.

4.5.2 PageRank

There are tens of billions of web pages, but most of them are not very interesting. Many of those pages are spam and contain no useful content at all. Other pages are personal blogs, wedding announcements, or family picture albums. These pages are interesting to a small audience, but probably not broadly. On the other hand, there are a few pages that are popular and useful to many people, including news sites and the websites of popular companies.

The huge size of the Web makes this a difficult problem for search engines. Suppose a friend had told you to visit the site for eBay, and you didn't know that www.ebay.com was the URL to use. You could type "eBay" into a search engine, but there are millions of web pages that contain the word "eBay". How can the search engine choose the most popular (and probably the correct) one? One very effective approach is to use the links between web pages as a way to measure popularity. The most obvious measure is to count the number of *inlinks* (links pointing to a page) for each page and use this as a feature or piece of evidence in the ranking algorithm. Although this has been shown to be quite effective, it is very susceptible to spam. Measures based on link analysis algorithms are designed to provide more reliable ratings of web pages. Of these measures, PageRank, which is associated with the Google search engine, is most often mentioned.

PageRank is based on the idea of a *random surfer* (as in web surfer). Imagine a person named Alice who is using her web browser. Alice is extremely bored, so she wanders aimlessly between web pages. Her browser has a special "surprise me" button at the top that will jump to a random web page when she clicks it. Each time a web page loads, she chooses whether to click the "surprise me" button or whether to click one of the links on the web page. If she clicks a link on the page, she has no preference for any particular link; instead, she just picks one randomly. Alice is sufficiently bored that she intends to keep browsing the Web like this forever.[22]

To put this in a more structured form, Alice browses the Web using this algorithm:

1. Choose a random number r between 0 and 1.
2. If $r < \lambda$:
   - Click the "surprise me" button.
3. If $r \geq \lambda$:
   - Click a link at random on the current page.
4. Start again.

Typically we assume that λ is fairly small, so Alice is much more likely to click a link than to pick the "surprise me" button. Even though Alice's path through the web pages is random, Alice will still see popular pages more often than unpopular ones. That's because Alice often follows links, and links tend to point to popular pages. So, we expect that Alice will end up at a university website, for example, more often than a personal website, but less often than the CNN website.

---

[22] The PageRank calculation corresponds to finding what is known as the stationary probability distribution of a *random walk* on the graph of the Web. A random walk is a special case of a *Markov chain* in which the next state (the next page visited) depends solely on the current state (current page). The transitions that are allowed between states are all equally probable and are given by the links.

Suppose that CNN has posted a story that contains a link to a professor's web page. Alice now becomes much more likely to visit that professor's page, because Alice visits the CNN website frequently. A single link at CNN might influence Alice's activity more than hundreds of links at less popular sites, because Alice visits CNN far more often than those less popular sites.

Because of Alice's special "surprise me" button, we can be guaranteed that eventually she will reach every page on the Internet.[23] Since she plans to browse the Web for a very long time, and since the number of web pages is finite, she will visit every page a very large number of times. It is likely, however, that she will visit a popular site thousands of times more often than an unpopular one. Note that if she did not have the "surprise me" button, she would get stuck on pages that did not have links, pages whose links no longer pointed to any page, or pages that formed a loop. Links that point to the first two types of pages, or pages that have not yet been crawled, are called *dangling links*.

Now suppose that while Alice is browsing, you happened to walk into her room and glance at the web page on her screen. What is the probability that she will be looking at the CNN web page when you walk in? That probability is CNN's PageRank. Every web page on the Internet has a PageRank, and it is uniquely determined by the link structure of web pages. As this example shows, PageRank has the ability to distinguish between popular pages (those with many incoming links, or those that have links from popular pages) and unpopular ones. The PageRank value can help search engines sift through the millions of pages that contain the word "eBay" to find the one that is most popular (www.ebay.com).

Alice would have to click on many billions of links in order for us to get a reasonable estimate of PageRank, so we can't expect to compute it by using actual people. Fortunately, we can compute PageRank in a much more efficient way.

Suppose for the moment that the Web consists of just three pages, A, B, and C. We will suppose that page A links to pages B and C, page B links to page C, and page C links to page A, as shown in Figure 4.10.

The PageRank of page C, which is the probability that Alice will be looking at this page, will depend on the PageRank of pages A and B. Since Alice chooses randomly between links on a given page, if she starts in page A, there is a 50% chance that she will go to page C (because there are two outgoing links). Another way of saying this is that the PageRank for a page is divided evenly between all the

---

[23] The "surprise button" makes the random surfer model an *ergodic* Markov chain, which guarantees that the iterative calculation of PageRank will converge.

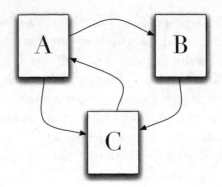

Fig. 4.10. A sample "Internet" consisting of just three web pages. The arrows denote links between the pages.

outgoing links. If we ignore the "surprise me" button, this means that the Page-Rank of page C, represented as $PR(C)$, can be calculated as:

$$PR(C) = \frac{PR(A)}{2} + \frac{PR(B)}{1}$$

More generally, we could calculate the PageRank for any page u as:

$$PR(u) = \sum_{v \in B_u} \frac{PR(v)}{L_v}$$

where B_u is the set of pages that point to u, and L_v is the number of outgoing links from page v (not counting duplicate links).

There is an obvious problem here: we don't know the PageRank values for the pages, because that is what we are trying to calculate. If we start by assuming that the PageRank values for all pages are the same (1/3 in this case), then it is easy to see that we could perform multiple iterations of the calculation. For example, in the first iteration, $PR(C) = 0.33/2 + 0.33 = 0.5$, $PR(A) = 0.33$, and $PR(B)$ = 0.17. In the next iteration, $PR(C) = 0.33/2 + 0.17 = 0.33$, $PR(A) = 0.5$, and $PR(B) = 0.17$. In the third iteration, $PR(C) = 0.42$, $PR(A) = 0.33$, and $PR(B) = 0.25$. After a few more iterations, the PageRank values converge to the final values of $PR(C) = 0.4$, $PR(A) = 0.4$, and $PR(B) = 0.2$.

If we take the "surprise me" button into account, part of the PageRank for page C will be due to the probability of coming to that page by pushing the button. Given that there is a 1/3 chance of going to any page when the button is pushed, the contribution to the PageRank for C for the button will be $\lambda/3$. This means that the total PageRank for C is now:

$$PR(C) = \frac{\lambda}{3} + (1 - \lambda) \cdot \left(\frac{PR(A)}{2} + \frac{PR(B)}{1}\right)$$

Similarly, the general formula for PageRank is:

$$PR(u) = \frac{\lambda}{N} + (1 - \lambda) \cdot \sum_{v \in B_u} \frac{PR(v)}{L_v}$$

where N is the number of pages being considered. The typical value for λ is 0.15. This can also be expressed as a matrix equation:

$$\mathbf{R} = \mathbf{TR}$$

where $\mathbf{R}$ is the vector of PageRank values and $\mathbf{T}$ is the matrix representing the transition probabilities for the random surfer model. The element $\mathbf{T}_{ij}$ represents the probability of going from page i to page j, and:

$$\mathbf{T}_{ij} = \frac{\lambda}{N} + (1 - \lambda)\frac{1}{L_i}$$

Those of you familiar with linear algebra may recognize that the solution $\mathbf{R}$ is an *eigenvector* of the matrix $\mathbf{T}$.

Figure 4.11 shows some pseudocode for computing PageRank. The algorithm takes a graph G as input. Graphs are composed of vertices and edges, so $G = (V, E)$. In this case, the vertices are web pages and the edges are links, so the pseudocode uses the letters P and L instead. A link is represented as a pair (p, q), where p and q are the source and destination pages. Dangling links, which are links where the page q does not exist, are assumed to be removed. Pages with no outbound links are *rank sinks*, in that they accumulate PageRank but do not distribute it. In this algorithm, we assume that these pages link to all other pages in the collection.

The first step is to make a guess at the PageRank value for each page. Without any better information, we assume that the PageRank is the same for each page. Since PageRank values need to sum to 1 for all pages, we assign a PageRank of $1/|P|$ to each page in the input vector I. An alternative that may produce faster convergence would be to use a value based on the number of inlinks.

```
1: procedure PAGERANK(G)
2:                              ▷ G is the web graph, consisting of vertices (pages) and edges (links).
3:     (P, L) ← G                                    ▷ Split graph into pages and links
4:     I ← a vector of length |P|                    ▷ The current PageRank estimate
5:     R ← a vector of length |P|                    ▷ The resulting better PageRank estimate
6:     for all entries Iᵢ ∈ I do
7:         Iᵢ ← 1/|P|                                 ▷ Start with each page being equally likely
8:     end for
9:     while R has not converged do
10:        for all entries Rᵢ ∈ R do
11:            Rᵢ ← λ/|P|          ▷ Each page has a λ/|P| chance of random selection
12:        end for
13:        for all pages p ∈ P do
14:            Q ← the set of pages p such that (p, q) ∈ L and q ∈ P
15:            if |Q| > 0 then
16:                for all pages q ∈ Q do
17:                    R_q ← R_q + (1 − λ)I_p/|Q| ▷ Probability I_p of being at page p
18:                end for
19:            else
20:                for all pages q ∈ P do
21:                    R_p ← R_q + (1 − λ)I_p/|P|
22:                end for
23:            end if
24:            I ← R                                  ▷ Update our current PageRank estimate
25:        end for
26:    end while
27:    return R
28: end procedure
```

Fig. 4.11. Pseudocode for the iterative PageRank algorithm

In each iteration, we start by creating a result vector, R, and storing $\lambda/|P|$ in each entry. This is the probability of landing at any particular page because of a random jump. The next step is to compute the probability of landing on a page because of a clicked link. We do that by iterating over each web page in P. At each page, we retrieve the estimated probability of being at that page, I_p. From that page, the user has a λ chance of jumping randomly, or $1 - \lambda$ of clicking on a link. There are $|Q|$ links to choose from, so the probability of jumping to a page $q \in Q$ is $(1 - \lambda)I_p/|Q|$. We add this quantity to each entry R_q. In the event that there are no usable outgoing links, we assume that the user jumps randomly, and therefore the probability $(1 - \lambda)I_p$ is spread evenly among all $|P|$ pages.

To summarize, PageRank is an important example of query-independent metadata that can improve ranking for web search. Web pages have the same PageRank value regardless of what query is being processed. Search engines that use Page-Rank will prefer pages with high PageRank values instead of assuming that all web pages are equally likely to satisfy a query. PageRank is not, however, as important in web search as the conventional wisdom holds. It is just one of many features used in ranking. It does, however, tend to have the most impact on popular queries, which is a useful property.

The *HITS*[24] algorithm (Kleinberg, 1999) for link analysis was developed at about the same time as PageRank and has also been very influential. This algorithm estimates the value of the content of a page (the *authority* value) and the value of the links to other pages (the *hub* value). Both values are computed using an iterative algorithm based solely on the link structure, similar to PageRank. The HITS algorithm, unlike PageRank, calculates authority and hub values for a subset of pages retrieved by a given query.[25] This can be an advantage in terms of the impact of the HITS metadata on ranking, but may be computationally infeasible for search engines with high query traffic. In Chapter 10, we discuss the application of the HITS algorithm to finding web communities.

4.5.3 Link Quality

It is well known that techniques such as PageRank and anchor text extraction are used in commercial search engines, so unscrupulous web page designers may try to create useless links just to improve the search engine placement of one of their web pages. This is called *link spam*. Even typical users, however, can unwittingly fool simple search engine techniques. A good example of this is with blogs.

Many blog posts are comments about other blog posts. Suppose author A reads a post called b in author B's blog. Author A might write a new blog post, called a, which contains a link to post b. In the process of posting, author A may post a *trackback* to post b in author B's blog. A trackback is a special kind of comment that alerts author B that a reply has been posted in author A's blog.

---

[24] Hypertext Induced Topic Search
[25] Query-independent versions of HITS and topic-dependent versions of PageRank have also been defined.

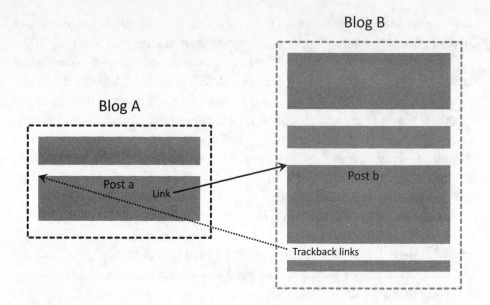

Fig. 4.12. Trackback links in blog postings

As Figure 4.12 shows, a cycle has developed between post a and post b. Post a links to post b, and post b contains a trackback link to post a. Intuitively we would say that post b is influential, because author A has decided to write about it. However, from the PageRank perspective, a and b have links to each other, and therefore neither is more influential than the other. The trouble here is that a trackback is a fundamentally different kind of link than one that appears in a post.

The comments section of a blog can also be a source of link spam. Page authors may try to promote their own websites by posting links to them in the comments section of popular blogs. Based on our discussion of PageRank, we know that a link from a popular website can make another website seem much more important. Therefore, this comments section is an attractive target for spammers.

In this case, one solution is for search engine companies to automatically detect these comment sections and effectively ignore the links during indexing. An even easier way to do this is to ask website owners to alter the unimportant links so that search engines can detect them. This is the purpose behind the rel=nofollow link attribute.

Most blog software is now designed to modify any link in a blog comment to contain the rel=nofollow attribute. Therefore, a post like this:

```
Come visit my <a href="http://www.page.com">web page</a>.
```

becomes something like this:

```
Come visit my <a rel=nofollow href="http://www.page.com">web page</a>.
```

The link still appears on the blog, but search engines are designed to ignore all links marked rel=nofollow. This helps preserve the integrity of PageRank calculation and anchor text harvesting.

4.6 Information Extraction

Information extraction is a language technology that focuses on extracting structure from text. Information extraction is used in a number of applications, and particularly for *text data mining*. For search applications, the primary use of information extraction is to identify features that can be used by the search engine to improve ranking. Some people have speculated that information extraction techniques could eventually transform text search into a database problem by extracting all of the important information from text and storing it in structured form, but current applications of these techniques are a very long way from achieving that goal.

Some of the text processing steps we have already discussed could be considered information extraction. Identifying noun phrases, titles, or even bolded text are examples. In each of these cases, a part of the text has been recognized as having some special property, and that property can be described using a markup language, such as XML. If a document is already described using HTML or XML, the recognition of some of the structural features (such as titles) is straightforward, but others, such as phrases, require additional processing before the feature can be *annotated* using the markup language. In some applications, such as when the documents in the collection are input through OCR, the document has no markup and even simple structures such as titles must be recognized and annotated.

These types of features are very general, but most of the recent research in information extraction has been concerned with features that have specific semantic content, such as *named entities*, *relationships*, and *events*. Although all of these features contain important information, *named entity recognition* has been used most often in search applications. A named entity is a word or sequence of words that is used to refer to something of interest in a particular application. The most common examples are people's names, company or organization names, locations, time and date expressions, quantities, and monetary values. It is easy to come up with other "entities" that would be important for specific applications. For an e-commerce application, for example, the recognition of product names and model numbers in web pages and reviews would be essential. In a pharmaceutical application, the recognition of drug names, dosages, and medical conditions may be important. Given the more specific nature of these features, the process of recognizing them and tagging them in text is sometimes called *semantic annotation*. Some of these recognized entities would be incorporated directly into the search using, for example, *facets* (see Chapter 6), whereas others may be used as part of browsing the search results. An example of the latter is the search engine feature that recognizes addresses in pages and provides links to the appropriate map.

Fred Smith, who lives at 10 Water Street, Springfield, MA, is a long-time collector of **tropical fish.**

<p ><PersonName><GivenName>Fred</GivenName> <Sn>Smith</Sn> </PersonName>, who lives at <address><Street >10 Water Street</Street>, <City>Springfield</City>, <State>MA</State></address>, is a long-time collector of <b>tropical fish.</b></p>

Fig. 4.13. Text tagged by information extraction

Figure 4.13 shows a sentence and the corresponding XML markup after using information extraction. In this case, the extraction was done by a well-known word processing program.[26] In addition to the usual structure markup (**<p>** and **<b>**), a number of tags have been added that indicate which words are part of named entities. It shows, for example, that an address consisting of a street ("10 Water Street"), a city ("Springfield"), and a state ("MA") was recognized in the text.

Two main approaches have been used to build named entity recognizers: rule-based and statistical. A rule-based recognizer uses one or more *lexicons* (lists of words and phrases) that categorize names. Some example categories would be locations (e.g., towns, cities, states, countries, places of interest), people's names (given names, family names), and organizations (e.g., companies, government

---

[26] Microsoft Word

agencies, international groups). If these lists are sufficiently comprehensive, much of the extraction can be done simply by lookup. In many cases, however, rules or patterns are used to verify an entity name or to find new entities that are not in the lists. For example, a pattern such as "<number> <word> street" could be used to identify street addresses. Patterns such as "<street address>, <city>" or "in <city>" could be used to verify that the name found in the location lexicon as a city was indeed a city. Similarly, a pattern such as "<street address>, <city>, <state>" could also be used to identify new cities or towns that were not in the lexicon. New person names could be recognized by rules such as "<title> <name>", where <title> would include words such as "President", "Mr.", and "CEO". Names are generally easier to extract in mixed-case text, because capitalization often indicates a name, but many patterns will apply to all lower- or uppercase text as well. Rules incorporating patterns are developed manually, often by trial and error, although an initial set of rules can also be used as *seeds* in an automated learning process that can discover new rules.[27]

A statistical entity recognizer uses a probabilistic model of the words in and around an entity. A number of different approaches have been used to build these models, but because of its importance, we will briefly describe the *Hidden Markov Model* (HMM) approach. HMMs are used for many applications in speech and language. For example, POS taggers can be implemented using this approach.

4.6.1 Hidden Markov Models for Extraction

One of the most difficult parts of entity extraction is that words can have many different meanings. The word "Bush", for example, can describe a plant or a person. Similarly, "Marathon" could be the name of a race or a location in Greece. People tell the difference between these different meanings based on the *context* of the word, meaning the words that surround it. For instance, if "Marathon" is preceded by "Boston", the text is almost certainly describing a race. We can describe the context of a word mathematically by modeling the *generation*[28] of the sequence of words in a text as a process with the *Markov property*, meaning that the next word in the sequence depends on only a small number of the previous words.

---

[27] GATE (http://gate.ac.uk) is an example of an open source toolkit that provides both an information extraction component and an environment for customizing extraction for a specific application.

[28] We discuss *generative models* in more detail in Chapter 7.

More formally, a *Markov Model* describes a process as a collection of *states* with *transitions* between them. Each of the transitions has an associated probability. The next state in the process depends solely on the current state and the transition probabilities. In a Hidden Markov Model, each state has a set of possible outputs that can be generated. As with the transitions, each output also has a probability associated with it.

Figure 4.14 shows a *state diagram* representing a very simple model for sentence generation that could be used by a named entity recognizer. In this model, the words in a sentence are assumed to be either part of an entity name (in this case, either a person, organization, or location) or not part of one. Each of these entity categories is represented by a state, and after every word the system may stay in that state (represented by the arrow loops) or transition to another state. There are two special states representing the start and end of the sentence. Associated with each state representing an entity category, there is a probability distribution of the likely sequences of words for that category.

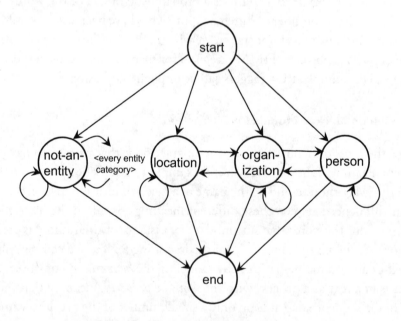

Fig. 4.14. Sentence model for statistical entity extractor

One possible use of this model is to construct new sentences. Suppose that we begin in the start state, and then the next state is randomly chosen according to the start state's transition probability table. For example, we may transition to the person state. Once we have entered the person state, we complete the transition by choosing an output according to the person state's output probability distribution. An example output may be the word "Thomas". This process would continue, with a new state being transitioned to and an output being generated during each step of the process. The final result is a set of states and their associated outputs.

Although such models can be used to generate new sentences, they are more commonly used to recognize entities in a sentence. To do this for a given sentence, a sequence of entity categories is found that gives the highest probability for the words in that sentence. Only the outputs generated by state transitions are visible (i.e., can be observed); the underlying states are "hidden." For the sentence in Figure 4.13, for example, the recognizer would find the sequence of states

<start><name><not-an-entity><location><not-an-entity><end>

to have the highest probability for that model. The words that were associated with the entity categories in this sequence would then be tagged. The problem of finding the most likely sequence of states in an HMM is solved by the *Viterbi algorithm*,[29] which is a *dynamic programming* algorithm.

The key aspect of this approach to entity recognition is that the probabilities in the sentence model must be estimated from training data. To estimate the transition and output probabilities, we generate training data that consists of text manually annotated with the correct entity tags. From this training data, we can directly estimate the probability of words associated with a given category (i.e., output probabilities), and the probability of transitions between categories. To build a more accurate recognizer, features that are highly associated with named entities, such as capitalized words and words that are all digits, would be included in the model. In addition, the transition probabilities could depend on the previous word as well as the previous category.[30] For example, the occurrence of the word "Mr." increases the probability that the next category is **Person**.

Although such training data can be useful for constructing accurate HMMs, collecting it requires a great deal of human effort. To generate approximately one million words of annotated text, which is the approximate size of training data required for accurate estimates, people would have to annotate the equivalent of

---

[29] Named after the electrical engineer Andrew Viterbi.

[30] Bikel et al. (1997) describe one of the first named entity recognizers based on the HMM approach.

more than 1,500 news stories. This may require considerably more effort than developing rules for a simple set of features. Both the rule-based and statistical approaches have recognition effectiveness of about 90%[31] for entities such as name, organization, and location, although the statistical recognizers are generally the best. Other entity categories, such as product names, are considerably more difficult. The choice of which entity recognition approach to use will depend on the application, the availability of software, and the availability of annotators.

Interestingly, there is little evidence that named entities are useful features for general search applications. Named entity recognition is a critical part of question-answering systems (section 11.5), and can be important in domain-specific or vertical search engines for accurately recognizing and indexing domain terms. Named entity recognition can also be useful for query analysis in applications such as local search, and as a tool for understanding and browsing search results.

4.7 Internationalization

The Web is used all over the world, and not just by English speakers. Although 65–70% of the Web is written in English, that percentage is continuing to decrease. More than half of the people who use the Web, and therefore search the Web, do not use English as their primary language. Other search applications, such as desktop search and corporate search, are being used in many different languages every day. Even an application designed for an environment that has mostly English-speaking users can have many non-English documents in the collection. Try using "poissons tropicaux" (tropical fish) as a query for your favorite web search engine and see how many French web pages are retrieved.[32]

A *monolingual* search engine is, as the name suggests, a search engine designed for a particular language.[33] Many of the indexing techniques and retrieval models we discuss in this book work well for any language. The differences between languages that have the most impact on search engine design are related to the text processing steps that produce the index terms for searching.

---

[31] By this we mean that about 9 out of 10 of the entities found are accurately identified, and 9 out of 10 of the existing entities are found. See Chapter 8 for details on evaluation measures.

[32] You would find many more French web pages, of course, if you used a French version of the search engine, such as http://fr.yahoo.com.

[33] We discuss *cross-language* search engines in section 6.4.

As we mentioned in the previous chapter, character encoding is a crucial issue for search engines dealing with non-English languages, and Unicode has become the predominant character encoding standard for the internationalization of software.

Other text processing steps also need to be customized for different languages. The importance of stemming for highly inflected languages has already been mentioned, but each language requires a customized stemmer. Tokenizing is also important for many languages, especially for the CJK family of languages. For these languages, the key problem is *word segmentation*, where the breaks corresponding to words or index terms must be identified in the continuous sequence of characters (spaces are generally not used). One alternative to segmenting is to index overlapping character bigrams (pairs of characters, see section 4.3.5). Figure 4.15 shows word segmentation and bigrams for the text "impact of droughts in China". Although the ranking effectiveness of search based on bigrams is quite good, word segmentation is preferred in many applications because many of the bigrams do not correspond to actual words. A segmentation technique can be implemented based on statistical approaches, such as a Hidden Markov Model, with sufficient training data. Segmentation can also be an issue in other languages. German, for example, has many compound words (such as "fischzuchttechniken" for "fish farming techniques") that should be segmented for indexing.

1. Original text
旱灾在中国造成的影响
(the impact of droughts in China)

2. Word segmentation
旱灾　在　中国　造成　的　影响
drought at   china   make   impact

3. Bigrams
旱灾　灾在　在中　中国　国造
造成　成的　的影　影响

Fig. 4.15. Chinese segmentation and bigrams

In general, given the tools that are available, it is not difficult to build a search engine for the major languages. The same statement holds for any language that has a significant amount of online text available on the Web, since this can be used as a resource to build and test the search engine components. There are, however, a large number of other so-called "low-density" languages that may have many speakers but few online resources. Building effective search engines for these languages is more of a challenge.

References and Further Reading

The properties and statistics of text and document collections has been studied for some time under the heading of *bibliometrics*, which is part of the field of *library and information science*. Information science journals such as the *Journal of the American Society of Information Science and Technology* (JASIST) or *Information Processing and Management* (IPM) contain many papers in this general area. Information retrieval has, from the beginning, emphasized a statistical view of text, and researchers from IR and information science have always worked closely together. Belew (2000) contains a good discussion of the cognitive aspects of Zipf's law and other properties of text in relationship to IR. With the shift to statistical methods in the 1990s, *natural language processing* researchers also became interested in studying the statistical properties of text. Manning and Schütze (1999) is a good summary of text statistics from this perspective. Ha et al. (2002) give an interesting result showing that phrases (or n-grams) also generally follow Zipf's law, and that combining the phrases and words results in better predictions for frequencies at low ranks.

The paper by Anagnostopoulos et al. (2005) describes a technique for estimating query result size and also points to much of the relevant literature in this area. Similarly, Broder et al. (2006) show how to estimate corpus size and compare their estimation with previous techniques.

Not much is written about tokenizing or stopping. Both are considered sufficiently "well known" that they are hardly mentioned in papers. As we have pointed out, however, getting these basic steps right is crucial for the overall system's effectiveness. For many years, researchers used the stopword list published in van Rijsbergen (1979). When it became clear that this was not sufficient for the larger TREC collections, a stopword list developed at the University of Massachusetts and distributed with the Lemur toolkit has frequently been used. As mentioned previously, this list contains over 400 words, which will be too long for many applications.

The original paper describing the Porter stemmer was written in 1979, but was reprinted in Porter (1997). The paper by Krovetz (1993) describes his stemming algorithm but also takes a more detailed approach to studying the role of morphology in a stemmer.[34] The Krovetz stemmer is available on the Lemur website. Stemmers for other languages are available from various websites (including the

---

[34] Morphology is the study of the internal structure of words, and stemming is a form of *morphological processing*.

Lemur website and the Porter stemmer website). A description of Arabic stemming techniques can be found in Larkey et al. (2002).

Research on the use of phrases in searching has a long history. Croft et al. (1991) describe retrieval experiments with phrases derived by both syntactic and statistical processing of the query, and showed that effectiveness was similar to phrases selected manually. Many groups that have participated in the TREC evaluations have used phrases as part of their search algorithms (Voorhees & Harman, 2005).

Church (1988) described an approach to building a statistical (or *stochastic*) part-of-speech tagger that is the basis for many current taggers. This approach uses manually tagged training data to train a probabilistic model of sequences of parts of speech, as well as the probability of a part of speech for a specific word. For a given sentence, the part-of-speech tagging that gives the highest probability for the whole sentence is used. This method is essentially the same as that used by a statistical entity extractor, with the states being parts of speech instead of entity categories. The Brill tagger (Brill, 1994) is a popular alternative approach that uses rules that are learned automatically from tagged data. Manning and Schütze (1999) provide a good overview of part-of-speech tagging methods.

Many variations of PageRank can be found in the literature. Many of these variations are designed to be more efficient to compute or are used in different applications. The topic-dependent version of PageRank is described in Haveliwala (2002). Both PageRank and HITS have their roots in the citation analysis algorithms developed in the field of bibliometrics.

The idea of enhancing the representation of a hypertext document (i.e., a web page) using the content of the documents that point to it has been around for some time. For example, Croft and Turtle (1989) describe a retrieval model based on incorporating text from related hypertext documents, and Dunlop and van Rijsbergen (1993) describe how documents with little text content (such as those containing images) could be retrieved using the text in linked documents. Restricting the text that is incorporated to the anchor text associated with inlinks was first mentioned by McBryan (1994). Anchor text has been shown to be essential for some categories of web search in TREC evaluations, such as in Ogilvie and Callan (2003).

Techniques have been developed for applying link analysis in collections without explicit link structure (Kurland & Lee, 2005). In this case, the links are based on similarities between the content of the documents, calculated by a similarity measure such as the cosine correlation (see Chapter 7).

Information extraction techniques were developed primarily in research programs such as TIPSTER and MUC (Cowie & Lehnert, 1996). Using named entity extraction to provide additional features for search was also studied early in the TREC evaluations (Callan et al., 1992, 1995). One of the best-known rule-based information extraction systems is FASTUS (Hobbs et al., 1997). The BBN system Identifinder (Bikel et al., 1999), which is based on an HMM, has been used in many projects.

A detailed description of HMMs and the Viterbi algorithm can be found in Manning and Schütze (1999). McCallum (2005) provides an overview of information extraction, with references to more recent advances in the field. Statistical models that incorporate more complex features than HMMs, such as *conditional random fields*, have become increasingly popular for extraction (Sutton & McCallum, 2007).

Detailed descriptions of all the major encoding schemes can be found in Wikipedia. Fujii and Croft (1993) was one of the early papers that discussed the problems of text processing for search with CJK languages. An entire journal, *ACM Transactions on Asian Language Information Processing*,[35] has now been devoted to this issue. Peng et al. (2004) describe a statistical model for Chinese word segmentation and give references to other approaches.

Exercises

4.1. Plot rank-frequency curves (using a log-log graph) for words and bigrams in the Wikipedia collection available through the book website (http://www.search-engines-book.com). Plot a curve for the combination of the two. What are the best values for the parameter c for each curve?

4.2. Plot vocabulary growth for the Wikipedia collection and estimate the parameters for Heaps' law. Should the order in which the documents are processed make any difference?

4.3. Try to estimate the number of web pages indexed by two different search engines using the technique described in this chapter. Compare the size estimates from a range of queries and discuss the consistency (or lack of it) of these estimates.

---

[35] http://talip.acm.org/

4.4. Modify the Galago tokenizer to handle apostrophes or periods in a different way. Describe the new rules your tokenizer implements. Give examples of where the new tokenizer does a better job (in your opinion) and examples where it does not.

4.5. Examine the Lemur stopword list and list 10 words that you think would cause problems for some queries. Give examples of these problems.

4.6. Process five Wikipedia documents using the Porter stemmer and the Krovetz stemmer. Compare the number of stems produced and find 10 examples of differences in the stemming that could have an impact on ranking.

4.7. Use the GATE POS tagger to tag a Wikipedia document. Define a rule or rules to identify phrases and show the top 10 most frequent phrases. Now use the POS tagger on the Wikipedia queries. Are there any problems with the phrases identified?

4.8. Find the 10 Wikipedia documents with the most inlinks. Show the collection of anchor text for those pages.

4.9. Figure 4.11 shows an algorithm for computing PageRank. Prove that the entries of the vector I sum to 1 every time the algorithm enters the loop on line 9.

4.10. Compute PageRank for the 10 Wikipedia documents found in Exercise 4.8. List the 20 documents with the highest PageRank values together with the values.

4.11. Implement a rule-based recognizer for cities (you can choose a subset of cities to make this easier). Create a test collection that you can scan manually to find cities mentioned in the text and evaluate your recognizer. Summarize the performance of the recognizer and discuss examples of failures.

4.12. Create a small test collection in some non-English language using web pages. Do the basic text processing steps of tokenizing, stemming, and stopping using tools from the book website and from other websites. Show examples of the index term representation of the documents.

5

Ranking with Indexes

"Must go faster."

David Levinson, *Independence Day*

5.1 Overview

As this is a fairly technical book, if you have read this far, you probably understand something about *data structures* and how they are used in programs. If you want to store a list of items, linked lists and arrays are good choices. If you want to quickly find an item based on an attribute, a hash table is a better choice. More complicated tasks require more complicated structures, such as B-trees or priority queues.

Why are all these data structures necessary? Strictly speaking, they aren't. Most things you want to do with a computer can be done with arrays alone. However, arrays have drawbacks: unsorted arrays are slow to search, and sorted arrays are slow at insertion. By contrast, hash tables and trees are fast for both search and insertion. These structures are more complicated than arrays, but the speed difference is compelling.

Text search is very different from traditional computing tasks, so it calls for its own kind of data structure, the *inverted index*. The name "inverted index" is really an umbrella term for many different kinds of structures that share the same general philosophy. As you will see shortly, the specific kind of data structure used depends on the ranking function. However, since the ranking functions that rank documents well have a similar form, the most useful kinds of inverted indexes are found in nearly every search engine.

This chapter is about how search engine queries are actually processed by a computer, so this whole chapter could arguably be called *query processing*. The last section of this chapter is called that, and the query processing algorithms presented there are based on the data structures presented earlier in the chapter.

Efficient query processing is a particularly important problem in web search, as it has reached a scale that would have been hard to imagine just 10 years ago. People all over the world type in over half a billion queries every day, searching indexes containing billions of web pages. Inverted indexes are at the core of all modern web search engines.

There are strong dependencies between the separate components of a search engine. The query processing algorithm depends on the retrieval model, and dictates the contents of the index. This works in reverse, too, since we are unlikely to choose a retrieval model that has no efficient query processing algorithm. Since we will not be discussing retrieval models in detail until Chapter 7, we start this chapter by describing an abstract model of ranking that motivates our choice of indexes. After that, there are four main parts to the chapter. In the first part, we discuss the different types of inverted index and what information about documents is captured in each index. The second part gives an overview of compression techniques, which are a critical part of the efficient implementation of inverted indexes for text retrieval. The third part of the chapter describes how indexes are constructed, including a discussion of the MapReduce framework that can be used for very large document collections. The final part of the chapter focuses on how the indexes are used to generate document rankings in response to queries.

5.2 Abstract Model of Ranking

Before we begin to look at how to build indexes for a search system, we will start by considering an abstract model of ranking. All of the techniques we will consider in this chapter can be seen as implementations of this model.

Figure 5.1 shows the basic components of our model. On the left side of the figure is a sample document. Documents are written in natural human languages, which are difficult for computers to analyze directly. So, as we saw in Chapter 4, the text is transformed into *index terms* or *document features*. For the purposes of this chapter, a document feature is some attribute of the document we can express numerically. In the figure, we show two kinds of features. On top, we have *topical* features, which estimate the degree to which the document is about a particular subject. On the bottom of the figure, we see two possible document *quality* features. One feature is the number of web pages that link to this document, and another is the number of days since this page was last updated. These features don't address whether the document is a good topical match for a query, but they do

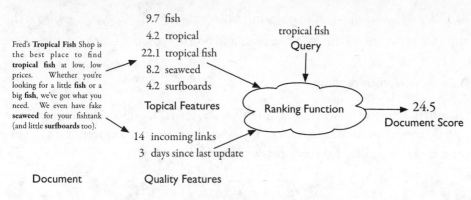

Fig. 5.1. The components of the abstract model of ranking: documents, features, queries, the retrieval function, and document scores

address its quality: a page with no incoming links that hasn't been edited in years is probably a poor match for any query. Each of these feature values is generated using a *feature function*, which is just a mathematical expression that generates numbers from document text. In Chapter 4 we discussed some of the important topical and quality features, and in Chapter 7 you will learn about the techniques for creating good feature functions. In this chapter, we assume that reasonable feature values have already been created.

On the right side of the figure, we see a cloud representing the *ranking function*. The ranking function takes data from document features combined with the query and produces a score. For now, the contents of that cloud are unimportant, except for the fact that most reasonable ranking functions ignore many of the document features, and focus only on the small subset that relate to the query. This fact makes the inverted index an appealing data structure for search.

The final output of the ranking function is a score, which we assume is some real number. If a document gets a high score, this means that the system thinks that document is a good match for the query, whereas lower numbers mean that the system thinks the document is a poor match for the query. To build a ranked list of results, the documents are sorted by score so that the highest-scoring documents come first.

Suppose that you are a human search engine, trying to sort documents in an appropriate order in response to a user query. Perhaps you would place the documents in piles, like "good," "not so good," and "bad." The computer is doing essentially the same thing with scoring. However, you might also break ties by looking carefully at each document to decide which one is more relevant. Unfortunately, finding deep meaning in documents is difficult for computers to do, so search engines focus on identifying good features and scoring based on those features.

A more concrete ranking model

Later in the chapter we will look at query evaluation techniques that assume something stronger about what happens in the ranking function. Specifically, we assume that the ranking function R takes the following form:

$$R(Q, D) = \sum_i g_i(Q)f_i(D)$$

Here, f_i is some feature function that extracts a number from the document text. g_i is a similar feature function that extracts a value from the query. These two functions form a pair of feature functions. Each pair of functions is multiplied together, and the results from all pairs are added to create a final document score.

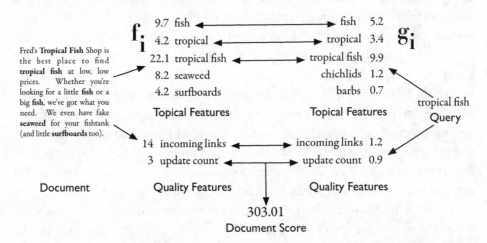

Fig. 5.2. A more concrete model of ranking. Notice how both the query and the document have feature functions in this model.

Figure 5.2 shows an example of this model. Just as in the abstract model of ranking, various features are extracted from the document. This picture shows only a few features, but in reality there will be many more. These correspond to the $f_i(D)$ functions in the equation just shown. We could easily name these $f_{\text{tropical}}(D)$ or $f_{\text{fish}}(D)$; these values will be larger for documents that contain the words "tropical" or "fish" more often or more prominently.

The document has some features that are not topical. For this example document, we see that the search engine notices that this document has been updated three times, and that it has 14 incoming links. Although these features don't tell us anything about whether this document would match the subject of a query, they do give us some hints about the quality of the document. We know that it wasn't just posted to the Web and then abandoned, since it gets updated occasionally. We also know that there are 14 other pages that have links pointing to it, which might mean that it has some useful information on it.

Notice that there are also feature functions that act on the query. The feature function $g_{\text{tropical}}(Q)$ evaluates to a large value because "tropical" is in the query. However, $g_{\text{barbs}}(Q)$ also has a small non-zero value because it is related to other terms in the query. These values from the query feature functions are multiplied by the document feature functions, then summed to create a document score.

The query also has some feature values that aren't topical, such as the update count feature. Of course, this doesn't mean that the query has been updated. The value of this feature indicates how important document updates are to relevance for this query. For instance, if the query was "today's weather in london", we would prefer documents that are updated frequently, since a document that isn't updated at least daily is unlikely to say anything interesting about today's weather. This query should have a high value for the update count feature. By contrast, a document that never changed could be very relevant for the query "full text of moby dick". This query could have a low feature value for update count.

If a retrieval system had to perform a sum over millions of features for every document, text search systems would not be practical. In practice, the query features ($g_i(Q)$) are mostly zero. This means that the sum for each document is only over the non-zero $g_i(Q)$ values.

5.3 Inverted Indexes

All modern search engine indexes are based on *inverted indexes*. Other index structures have been used in the past, most notably *signature files*,[1] but inverted indexes are considered the most efficient and flexible index structure.

---

[1] A signature is a concise representation of a block of text (or document) as a sequence of bits, similar to the fingerprints discussed in Chapter 3. A hash function is used for each word in the text block to set bits in specific positions in the signature to one.

An inverted index is the computational equivalent of the index found in the back of this textbook. You might want to look over the index in this book as an example. The book index is arranged in alphabetical order by *index term*. Each index term is followed by a list of pages about that word. If you want to know more about stemming, for example, you would look through the index until you found words starting with "s". Then, you would scan the entries until you came to the word "stemming." The list of page numbers there would lead you to Chapter 4.

Similarly, an inverted index is organized by index term. The index is *inverted* because usually we think of words being a part of documents, but if we invert this idea, documents are associated with words. Index terms are often alphabetized like a traditional book index, but they need not be, since they are often found directly using a hash table. Each index term has its own *inverted list* that holds the relevant data for that term. In an index for a book, the relevant data is a list of page numbers. In a search engine, the data might be a list of documents or a list of word occurrences. Each list entry is called a *posting*, and the part of the posting that refers to a specific document or location is often called a *pointer*. Each document in the collection is given a unique number to make it efficient for storing document pointers.

Indexes in books store more than just location information. For important words, often one of the page numbers is marked in boldface, indicating that this page contains a definition or extended discussion about the term. Inverted files can also have extended information, where postings can contain a range of information other than just locations. By storing the right information along with each posting, the feature functions we saw in the last section can be computed efficiently.

Finally, by convention, the page numbers in a book index are printed in ascending order, so that the smallest page numbers come first. Traditionally, inverted lists are stored the same way. These *document-ordered* lists are ordered by document number, which makes certain kinds of query processing more efficient and also improves list compression. However, some inverted files we will consider have other kinds of orderings.

Alternatives to inverted files generally have one or more disadvantages. The signature file, for example, represents each document in the collection as a small set of bits. To search a signature file, the query is converted to a signature and the bit patterns are compared. In general, all signatures must be scanned for every search. Even if the index is encoded compactly, this is a lot of processing. The inverted file's advantage is that only a small fraction of the index needs to be considered to process most queries. Also, matches in signature files are noisy, so a signature match is not guaranteed to be a match in the document text. Most importantly, it is difficult to generalize signature file techniques for ranked search (Zobel et al., 1998).

Another approach is to use spatial data structures, such as *k-d trees*. In this approach, each document is encoded as a point in some high-dimensional space, and the query is as well. The spatial data structure can then be used to find the closest documents to the query. Although many ranking approaches are fundamentally spatial, most spatial data structures are not designed for the number of dimensions associated with text applications.[2] As a result, it tends to be much faster to use an inverted list to rank documents than to use a typical spatial data structure.

In the next few sections, we will look at some different kinds of inverted files. In each case, the inverted file organization is dictated by the ranking function. More complex ranking functions require more information in the index. These more complicated indexes take additional space and computational power to process, but can be used to generate more effective document rankings. Index organization is by no means a solved problem, and research is ongoing into the best way to create indexes that can more efficiently produce effective document rankings.

5.3.1 Documents

The simplest form of an inverted list stores just the documents that contain each word, and no additional information. This kind of list is similar to the kind of index you would find at the back of this textbook.

Figure 5.3 shows an index of this type built from the four sentences in Table 5.1 (so in this case, the "documents" are sentences). The index contains every word found in all four sentences. Next to each word, there are a list of boxes, and each one contains the number of a sentence. Each one of these boxes is a posting. For example, look at the word "fish". You can quickly see that this word appears in all four sentences, because the numbers 1, 2, 3, and 4 appear by it. You can also quickly determine that "fish" is the only word that appears in all the sentences. Two words come close: "tropical" appears in every sentence but S_4, and "water" is not in S_3.

---

[2] Every term in a document corresponds to a dimension, so there are tens of thousands of dimensions in effect. This is in comparison to a typical database application with tens of dimensions at most.

S_1 Tropical fish include fish found in tropical environments around the world, including both freshwater and salt water species.

S_2 Fishkeepers often use the term tropical fish to refer only those requiring fresh water, with saltwater tropical fish referred to as marine fish.

S_3 Tropical fish are popular aquarium fish, due to their often bright coloration.

S_4 In freshwater fish, this coloration typically derives from iridescence, while salt water fish are generally pigmented.

Table 5.1. Four sentences from the Wikipedia entry for *tropical fish*

and	1				only	2		
aquarium	3				pigmented	4		
are	3	4			popular	3		
around	1				refer	2		
as	2				referred	2		
both	1				requiring	2		
bright	3				salt	1	4	
coloration	3	4			saltwater	2		
derives	4				species	1		
due	3				term	2		
environments	1				the	1	2	
fish	1	2	3	4	their	3		
fishkeepers	2				this	4		
found	1				those	2		
fresh	2				to	2	3	
freshwater	1	4			tropical	1	2	3
from	4				typically	4		
generally	4				use	2		
in	1	4			water	1	2	4
include	1				while	4		
including	1				with	2		
iridescence	4				world	1		
marine	2							
often	2	3						

Fig. 5.3. An inverted index for the documents (sentences) in Table 5.1

Notice that this index does not record the number of times each word appears; it only records the documents in which each word appears. For instance, S_2 contains the word "fish" twice, whereas S_1 contains "fish" only once. The inverted list for "fish" shows no distinction between sentences 1 and 2; both are listed in the same way. In the next few sections, we will look at indexes that include information about word frequencies.

Inverted lists become more interesting when we consider their intersection. Suppose we want to find the sentence that contains the words "coloration" and "freshwater". The inverted index tells us that "coloration" appears in S_3 and S_4, while "freshwater" appears in S_1 and S_4. We can quickly tell that only S_4 contains both "coloration" and "freshwater". Since each list is sorted by sentence number, finding the intersection of these lists takes $\mathcal{O}(\max(m, n))$ time, where m and n are the lengths of the two lists. The algorithm is the same as in merge sort. With list *skipping*, which we will see later in the chapter, this cost drops to $\mathcal{O}(\min(m, n))$.

5.3.2 Counts

Remember that our abstract model of ranking considers each document to be composed of features. With an inverted index, each word in the index corresponds to a document feature. This feature data can be processed by a ranking function into a document score. In an inverted index that contains only document information, the features are binary, meaning they are 1 if the document contains a term, 0 otherwise. This is important information, but it is too coarse to find the best few documents when there are a lot of possible matches.

For instance, consider the query "tropical fish". Three sentences match this query: S_1, S_2, and S_3. The data in the document-based index (Figure 5.3) gives us no reason to prefer any of these sentences over any other.

Now look at the index in Figure 5.4. This index looks similar to the previous one. We still have the same words and the same number of postings, and the first number in each posting is the same as in the previous index. However, each posting now has a second number. This second number is the number of times the word appears in the document. This small amount of additional data allows us to prefer S_2 over S_1 and S_3 for the query "tropical fish", since S_2 contains "tropical" twice and "fish" three times.

In this example, it may not be obvious that S_2 is much better than S_1 or S_3, but in general, word counts can be a powerful predictor of document relevance. In particular, word counts can help distinguish documents that are about a particular

and	1:1				only	2:1			
aquarium	3:1				pigmented	4:1			
are	3:1	4:1			popular	3:1			
around	1:1				refer	2:1			
as	2:1				referred	2:1			
both	1:1				requiring	2:1			
bright	3:1				salt	1:1	4:1		
coloration	3:1	4:1			saltwater	2:1			
derives	4:1				species	1:1			
due	3:1				term	2:1			
environments	1:1				the	1:1	2:1		
fish	1:2	2:3	3:2	4:2	their	3:1			
fishkeepers	2:1				this	4:1			
found	1:1				those	2:1			
fresh	2:1				to	2:2	3:1		
freshwater	1:1	4:1			tropical	1:2	2:2	3:1	
from	4:1				typically	4:1			
generally	4:1				use	2:1			
in	1:1	4:1			water	1:1	2:1	4:1	
include	1:1				while	4:1			
including	1:1				with	2:1			
iridescence	4:1				world	1:1			
marine	2:1								
often	2:1	3:1							

Fig. 5.4. An inverted index, with word counts, for the documents in Table 5.1

subject from those that discuss that subject in passing. Imagine two documents, one about tropical fish and another about tropical islands. The document about tropical islands would probably contain the word "fish", but only a few times. On the other hand, the document about tropical fish would contain the word "fish" many times. Using word occurrence counts helps us rank the most relevant document highest in this example.

5.3.3 Positions

When looking for matches for a query like "tropical fish", the location of the words in the document is an important predictor of relevance. Imagine a document about food that included a section on tropical fruits followed by a section on saltwater fish. So far, none of the indexes we have considered contain enough information to tell us that this document is not relevant. Although a document

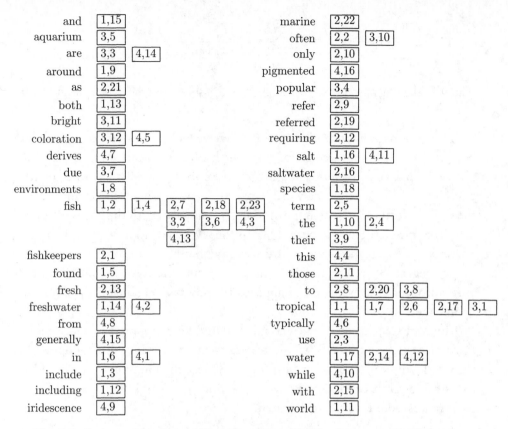

and	1,15					marine	2,22				
aquarium	3,5					often	2,2	3,10			
are	3,3	4,14				only	2,10				
around	1,9					pigmented	4,16				
as	2,21					popular	3,4				
both	1,13					refer	2,9				
bright	3,11					referred	2,19				
coloration	3,12	4,5				requiring	2,12				
derives	4,7					salt	1,16	4,11			
due	3,7					saltwater	2,16				
environments	1,8					species	1,18				
fish	1,2	1,4	2,7	2,18	2,23	term	2,5				
			3,2	3,6	4,3	the	1,10	2,4			
			4,13			their	3,9				
fishkeepers	2,1					this	4,4				
found	1,5					those	2,11				
fresh	2,13					to	2,8	2,20	3,8		
freshwater	1,14	4,2				tropical	1,1	1,7	2,6	2,17	3,1
from	4,8					typically	4,6				
generally	4,15					use	2,3				
in	1,6	4,1				water	1,17	2,14	4,12		
include	1,3					while	4,10				
including	1,12					with	2,15				
iridescence	4,9					world	1,11				

Fig. 5.5. An inverted index, with word positions, for the documents in Table 5.1

that contains the words "tropical" and "fish" is likely to be relevant, we really want to know if the document contains the exact phrase "tropical fish".

To determine this, we can add position information to our index, as in Figure 5.5. This index shares some structural characteristics with the previous indexes, in that it has the same index terms and each list contains some postings. These postings, however, are different. Each posting contains two numbers: a document number first, followed by a word position. In the previous indexes, there was just one posting per document. Now there is one posting per word occurrence.

Look at the long list for the word "fish". In the other indexes, this list contained just four postings. Now the list contains nine postings. The first two postings tell us that the word "fish" is the second word and fourth word in S_1. The next three postings tell us that "fish" is the seventh, eighteenth, and twenty-third word in S_2.

Fig. 5.6. Aligning posting lists for "tropical" and "fish" to find the phrase "tropical fish"

This information is most interesting when we look at intersections with other posting lists. Using an intersection with the list for "tropical", we find where the phrase "tropical fish" occurs. In Figure 5.6, the two inverted lists are lined up next to each other. We see that the word "tropical" is the first word in S_1, and "fish" is the second word in S_1, which means that S_1 must start with the phrase "tropical fish". The word "tropical" appears again as the seventh word in S_1, but "fish" does not appear as the eighth word, so this is not a phrase match. In all, there are four occurrences of the phrase "tropical fish" in the four sentences. The phrase matches are easy to see in the figure; they happen at the points where the postings are lined up in columns.

This same technique can be extended to find longer phrases or more general proximity expressions, such as "find **tropical** within 5 words of **fish**." Suppose that the word "tropical" appears at position p. We can then look in the inverted list for "fish" for any occurrences between position $p - 5$ and $p + 5$. Any of those occurrences would constitute a match.

5.3.4 Fields and Extents

Real documents are not just lists of words. They have sentences and paragraphs that separate concepts into logical units. Some documents have titles and headings that provide short summaries of the rest of the content. Special types of documents have their own sections; for example, every email contains sender information and a subject line. All of these are instances of what we will call *document fields*, which are sections of documents that carry some kind of semantic meaning.

It makes sense to include information about fields in the index. For example, suppose you have a professor named Dr. Brown. Dr. Brown sent you an email about when course projects are due, but you can't find it. You can type "brown" into your email program's search box, but the result you want will be mixed in with other uses of the word "brown", such as Brown University or brown socks. A search for "brown" in the From: line of the email will focus your search on exactly what you want.

Field information is useful even when it is not used explicitly in the query. Titles and headings tend to be good summaries of the rest of a document. Therefore, if a user searches for "tropical fish", it makes sense to prefer documents with the title "Tropical Fish," even if a document entitled "Mauritius" mentions the words "tropical" and "fish" more often. This kind of preference for certain document fields can be integrated into the ranking function.

In order to handle these kinds of searches, the search engine needs to be able to determine whether a word is in a particular field. One option is to make separate inverted lists for each kind of document field. Essentially, you could build one index for document titles, one for document headings, and one for body text. Searching for words in the title is as simple as searching the title index. However, finding a word in any section of the document is trickier, since you need to fetch inverted lists from many different indexes to make that determination.

Another option is to store information in each word posting about where the word occurred. For instance, we could specify that the number 0 indicates a title and 1 indicates body text. Each inverted list posting would then contain a 0 or a 1 at the end. This data could be used to quickly determine whether a posting was in a title, and it would require only one bit per posting. However, if you have more fields than just a title, the representation will grow.

Both of these suggestions have problems when faced with more complicated kinds of document structure. For instance, suppose we want to index books. Some books, like this one, have more than one author. Somewhere in the XML description of this book, you might find:

```
<author>W. Bruce Croft</author>,
<author>Donald Metzler</author>, and
<author>Trevor Strohman</author>
```

Suppose you would like to find books by an author named Croft Donald. If you type the phrase query "croft donald" into a search engine, should this book match? The words "croft" and "donald" appear in it, and in fact, they appear next to each other. However, they are in two distinct author fields. This probably is not a good match for the query "croft donald", but the previous two methods for dealing with fields (bits in the posting list, separate indexes) cannot make this kind of distinction.

This is where *extent lists* come in. An *extent* is a contiguous region of a document. We can represent these extents using word positions. For example, if the title of a book started on the fifth word and ended just before the ninth word, we could encode that as (5,9). For the author text shown earlier, we could write author: (1,4), (4,6), (7,9). The (1,4) means that the first three words ("W. Bruce Croft") constitute the first author, followed by the second author ("Donald Metzler"), which is two words. The word "and" is not in an author field, but the next two words are, so the last posting is (7,9).

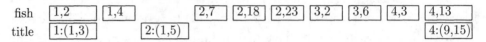

Fig. 5.7. Aligning posting lists for "fish" and title to find matches of the word "fish" in the title field of a document.

Figure 5.7 shows how this works in practice. Here we have the same positions posting list for "fish" that we used in the previous example. We also have an extent list for the title field. For clarity, there are gaps in the posting lists so that the appropriate postings line up next to each other. At the very beginning of both lists, we see that document 1 has a title that contains the first two words (1 and 2, ending just before the third word). We know that this title includes the word "fish", because the inverted list for "fish" tells us that "fish" is the second word in document 1. If the user wants to find documents with the word "fish" in the title, document 1 is a match. Document 2 does not match, because its title ends just before the fifth word, but "fish" doesn't appear until the seventh word. Document 3 apparently has no title at all, so no matches are possible. Document 4 has a title that starts at the ninth word (perhaps the document begins with a date or an author declaration), and it does contain the word "fish". In all, this example shows two matching documents: 1 and 4.

This concept can be extended to all kinds of fields, such as headings, paragraphs, or sentences. It can also be used to identify smaller pieces of text with specific meaning, such as addresses or names, or even just to record which words are verbs.

5.3.5 Scores

If the inverted lists are going to be used to generate feature function values, why not just store the value of the feature function? This is certainly possible, and some very efficient search engines do just this. This approach makes it possible to store feature function values that would be too computationally intensive to compute during the query processing phase. It also moves complexity out of the query processing engine and into the indexing code, where it may be more tolerable.

Let's make this more concrete. In the last section, there was an example about how a document with the title "Tropical Fish" should be preferred over a document "Mauritius" for the query "tropical fish", even if the Mauritius document contains the words "tropical" and "fish" many times. Computing the scores that reflect this preference requires some complexity at query evaluation time. The postings for "tropical fish" have to be segregated into groups, so we know which ones are in the title and which ones aren't. Then, we have to define some score for the title postings and the non-title postings and mix those numbers together, and this needs to be done for every document.

An alternate approach is to store the final value right in the inverted list. We could make a list for "fish" that has postings like [(1:3.6), (3:2.2)], meaning that the total feature value for "fish" in document 1 is 3.6, and in document 3 it is 2.2. Presumably the number 3.6 came from taking into account how many times "fish" appeared in the title, in the headings, in large fonts, in bold, and in links to the document. Maybe the document doesn't contain the word "fish" at all, but instead many names of fish, such as "carp" or "trout". The value 3.6 is then some indicator of how much this document is about fish.

Storing scores like this both increases and decreases the system's flexibility. It increases flexibility because computationally expensive scoring becomes possible, since much of the hard work of scoring documents is moved into the index. However, flexibility is lost, since we can no longer change the scoring mechanism once the index is built. More importantly, information about word proximity is gone in this model, meaning that we can't include phrase information in scoring unless we build inverted lists for phrases, too. These precomputed phrase lists require considerable additional space.

5.3.6 Ordering

So far, we have assumed that the postings of each inverted list would be ordered by document number. Although this is the most popular option, this is not the only way to order an inverted list. An inverted list can also be ordered by score, so that the highest-scoring documents come first. This makes sense only when the lists already store the score, or when only one kind of score is likely to be computed from the inverted list. By storing scores instead of documents, the query processing engine can focus only on the top part of each inverted list, where the highest-scoring documents are recorded. This is especially useful for queries consisting of a single word. In a traditional document-ordered inverted list, the query processing engine would need to scan the whole list to find the top k scoring documents, whereas it would only need to read the first k postings in a score-sorted list.

5.4 Compression

There are many different ways to store digital information. Usually we make a simple distinction between persistent and transient storage. We use persistent storage to store things in files and directories that we want to keep until we choose to delete them. Disks, CDs, DVDs, flash memory, and magnetic tape are commonly used for this purpose. Dynamic RAM (Random Access Memory), on the other hand, is used to store transient information, which is information we need only while the computer is running. We expect that when we turn off the computer, all of that information will vanish.

We can make finer distinctions between types of storage based on speed and capacity. Magnetic tape is slow, disks are faster, but dynamic RAM is much faster. Modern computers are so fast that even dynamic RAM isn't fast enough to keep up, so microprocessors contain at least two levels of cache memory. The very fastest kind of memory makes up the processor registers. In a perfect world, we could use registers or cache memory for all transient storage, but it is too expensive to be practical.

The reality, then, is that modern computers contain a *memory hierarchy*. At the top of the hierarchy we have memory that is tiny, but fast. The base consists of memory that is huge, but slow. The performance of a search engine strongly depends on how it makes use of the properties of each type of memory.

Compression techniques are the most powerful tool for managing the memory hierarchy. The inverted lists for a large collection are themselves very large. In fact, when it includes information about word position and document extents, the index can be comparable in size[3] to the document collection. Compression allows the same inverted list data to be stored in less space. The obvious benefit is that this could reduce disk or memory requirements, which would save

---

[3] As an example, indexes for TREC collections built using the Indri open source search engine range from 25–50% of the size of the collection. The lower figure is for a collection of web pages.

money. More importantly, compression allows data to move up the memory hierarchy. If index data is compressed by a factor of four, we can store four times more useful data in the processor cache, and we can feed data to the processor four times faster. On disk, compression also squeezes data closer together, which reduces seek times. In multicore and multiprocessor systems, where many processors share one memory system, compressing data allows the processors to share memory bandwidth more efficiently.

Unfortunately, nothing is free. The space savings of compression comes at a cost: the processor must decompress the data in order to use it. Therefore, it isn't enough to pick the compression technique that can store the most data in the smallest amount of space. In order to increase overall performance, we need to choose a compression technique that reduces space and is easy to decompress.

To see this mathematically, suppose some processor can process p inverted list postings per second. This processor is attached to a memory system that can supply the processor with m postings each second. The number of postings processed each second is then $\min(m, p)$. If $p > m$, then the processor will spend some of its time waiting for postings to arrive from memory. If $m > p$, the memory system will sometimes be idle.

Suppose we introduce compression into the system. Our compression system has a compression ratio of r, meaning that we can now store r postings in the same amount of space as one uncompressed posting. This lets the processor read mr postings each second. However, the processor first needs to decompress each posting before processing it. This slows processing by a decompression factor, d, and lets the processor process dp postings each second. Now we can process $\min(mr, dp)$ postings each second.

When we use no compression at all, $r = 1$ and $d = 1$. Any reasonable compression technique gives us $r > 1$, but $d < 1$. We can see that compression is a useful performance technique only when the $p > m$, that is, when the processor can process inverted list data faster than the memory system can supply it. A very simple compression scheme will raise r a little bit and reduce d a little bit. A complicated compression scheme will raise r a lot, while reducing d a lot. Ideally we would like to pick a compression scheme such that $\min(mr, dp)$ is maximized, which should happen when $mr = dp$.

In this section, we consider only *lossless* compression techniques. Lossless techniques store data in less space, but without losing information. There are also *lossy* data compression techniques, which are often used for video, images, and audio. These techniques achieve very high compression ratios (r in our previous discussion), but do this by throwing away the least important data. Inverted list pruning techniques, which we discuss later, could be considered a lossy compression technique, but typically when we talk about compression we mean only lossless methods.

In particular, our goal with these compression techniques is to reduce the size of the inverted lists we discussed previously. The compression techniques in this section are particularly well suited for document numbers, word counts, and document position information.

5.4.1 Entropy and Ambiguity

By this point in the book, you have already seen many examples of probability distributions. Compression techniques are based on probabilities, too. The fundamental idea behind compression is to represent common data elements with short codes while representing uncommon data elements with longer codes. The inverted lists that we have discussed are essentially lists of numbers, and without compression, each number takes up the same amount of space. Since some of those numbers are more frequent than others, if we encode the frequent numbers with short codes and the infrequent numbers with longer codes, we can end up with space savings.

For example, consider the numbers 0, 1, 2, and 3. We can encode these numbers using two binary bits. A sequence of numbers, like:

$$0, 1, 0, 3, 0, 2, 0$$

can be encoded in a sequence of binary digits:

$$00 \; 01 \; 00 \; 10 \; 00 \; 11 \; 00$$

Note that the spaces in the binary sequence are there to make it clear where each number starts and stops, and are not actually part of the encoding.

In our example sequence, the number 0 occurs four times, whereas each of the other numbers occurs just once. We may decide to save space by encoding 0 using just a single 0 bit. Our first attempt at an encoding might be:

$$0 \; 01 \; 0 \; 10 \; 0 \; 11 \; 0$$

This looks very successful because this encoding uses just 10 bits instead of the 14 bits used previously. This encoding is, however, *ambiguous*, meaning that it is not clear how to decode it. Remember that the spaces in the code are only there for our convenience and are not actually stored. If we add some different spaces, we arrive at a perfectly valid interpretation of this encoding:

$$0\ 01\ 01\ 0\ 0\ 11\ 0$$

which, when decoded, becomes:

$$0, 1, 1, 0, 0, 3, 0$$

Unfortunately, this isn't the data we encoded. The trouble is that when we see 010 in the encoded data, we can't be sure whether $(0, 2)$ or $(1, 0)$ was encoded.

The uncompressed encoding was not ambiguous. We knew exactly where to put the spaces because we knew that each number took exactly 2 bits. In our compressed code, encoded numbers consume either 1 or 2 bits, so it is not clear where to put the spaces. To solve this problem, we need to restrict ourselves to *unambiguous* codes, which are confusingly called both *prefix codes* and *prefix-free codes*. An unambiguous code is one where there is only one valid way to place spaces in encoded data.

Let's fix our code so that it is unambiguous:

Number	Code
0	0
1	101
2	110
3	111

This results in the following encoding:

$$0\ 101\ 0\ 111\ 0\ 110\ 0$$

This encoding requires 13 bits instead of the 14 bits required by the uncompressed version, so we are still saving some space. However, unlike the last code we considered, this one is unambiguous. Notice that if a code starts with 0, it consumes 1 bit; if a code starts with 1, it is 3 bits long. This gives us a deterministic algorithm for placing spaces in the encoded stream.

In the "Exercises" section, you will prove that there is no such thing as an unambiguous code that can compress every possible input; some inputs will get bigger. This is why it is so important to know something about what kind of data we want to encode. In our example, we notice that the number 0 appears frequently, and we can use that fact to reduce the amount of space that the encoded version requires. *Entropy* measures the predictability of the input. In our case, the input seems somewhat predictable, because the number 0 is more likely to appear than other numbers. We leverage this entropy to produce a usable code for our purposes.

5.4.2 Delta Encoding

All of the coding techniques we will consider in this chapter assume that small numbers are more likely to occur than large ones. This is an excellent assumption for word count data; many words appear just once in a document, and some appear two or three times. Only a small number of words appear more than 10 times. Therefore, it makes sense to encode small numbers with small codes and large numbers with large codes.

However, document numbers do not share this property. We expect that a typical inverted list will contain some small document numbers and some very large document numbers. It is true that some documents contain more words, and therefore will appear more times in the inverted lists, but otherwise there is not a lot of entropy in the distribution of document numbers in inverted lists.

The situation is different if we consider the differences between document numbers instead of the document numbers themselves. Remember that inverted list postings are typically ordered by document number. An inverted list without counts, for example, is just a list of document numbers, like these:

$$1, 5, 9, 18, 23, 24, 30, 44, 45, 48$$

Since these document numbers are ordered, we know that each document number in the sequence is more than the one before it and less than the one after it. This fact allows us to encode the list of numbers by the differences between adjacent document numbers:

$$1, 4, 4, 9, 5, 1, 6, 14, 1, 3$$

This encoded list starts with 1, indicating that 1 is the first document number. The next entry is 4, indicating that the second document number is 4 more than the first: $1 + 4 = 5$. The third number, 4, indicates that the third document number is 4 more than the second: $5 + 4 = 9$.

This process is called *delta encoding*, and the differences are often called *d-gaps*. Notice that delta encoding does not define the bit patterns that are used to store the data, and so it does not save any space on its own. However, delta encoding is particularly successful at changing an ordered list of numbers into a list of small numbers. Since we are about to discuss methods for compressing lists of small numbers, this is a useful property.

Before we move on, consider the inverted lists for the words "entropy" and "who." The word "who" is very common, so we expect that most documents will contain it. When we use delta encoding on the inverted list for "who," we would expect to see many small d-gaps, such as:

$$1, 1, 2, 1, 5, 1, 4, 1, 1, 3, \ldots$$

By contrast, the word "entropy" rarely appears in text, so only a few documents will contain it. Therefore, we would expect to see larger d-gaps, such as:

$$109, 3766, 453, 1867, 992, \ldots$$

However, since "entropy" is a rare word, this list of large numbers will not be very long. In general, we will find that inverted lists for frequent terms compress very well, whereas infrequent terms compress less well.

5.4.3 Bit-Aligned Codes

The code we invented in section 5.4.1 is a bit-aligned code, meaning that the breaks between the coded regions (the spaces) can happen after any bit position. In this section we will describe some popular bit-aligned codes. In the next section, we will discuss methods where code words are restricted to end on byte boundaries. In all of the techniques we'll discuss, we are looking at ways to store small numbers in inverted lists (such as word counts, word positions, and delta-encoded document numbers) in as little space as possible.

One of the simplest codes is the unary code. You are probably familiar with binary, which encodes numbers with two symbols, typically 0 and 1. A unary number system is a base-1 encoding, which means it uses a single symbol to encode numbers. Here are some examples:

Number	Code
0	0
1	10
2	110
3	1110
4	11110
5	111110

In general, to encode a number k in unary, we output k 1s, followed by a 0. We need the 0 at the end to make the code unambiguous.

This code is very efficient for small numbers such as 0 and 1, but quickly becomes very expensive. For instance, the number 1023 can be represented in 10 binary bits, but requires 1024 bits to represent in unary code.

Now we know about two kinds of numeric encodings. Unary is convenient because it is compact for small numbers and is inherently unambiguous. Binary is a better choice for large numbers, but it is not inherently unambiguous. A reasonable compression scheme needs to encode frequent numbers with fewer bits than infrequent numbers, which means binary encoding is not useful on its own for compression.

Elias-γ codes

The Elias-γ (Elias gamma) code combines the strengths of unary and binary codes. To encode a number k using this code, we compute two quantities:

- $k_d = \lfloor \log_2 k \rfloor$
- $k_r = k - 2^{\lfloor \log_2 k \rfloor}$

Suppose you wrote k in binary form. The first value, k_d, is the number of binary digits you would need to write. Assuming $k > 0$, the leftmost binary digit of k is 1. If you erase that digit, the remaining binary digits are k_r.

If we encode k_d in unary and k_r in binary (in k_d binary digits), we get the Elias-γ code. Some examples are shown in Table 5.2.

Number (k)	k_d	k_r	Code
1	0	0	0
2	1	0	10 0
3	1	1	10 1
6	2	2	110 10
15	3	7	1110 111
16	4	0	11110 0000
255	7	127	11111110 1111111
1023	9	511	1111111110 111111111

Table 5.2. Elias-γ code examples

The trick with this code is that the unary part of the code tells us how many bits to expect in the binary part. We end up with a code that uses no more bits than the unary code for any number, and for numbers larger than 2, it uses fewer bits. The savings for large numbers is substantial. We can, for example, now encode 1023 in 19 bits, instead of 1024 using just unary code.

For any number k, the Elias-γ code requires $\lfloor log_2 k \rfloor + 1$ bits for k_d in unary code and $\lfloor log_2 k \rfloor$ bits for k_r in binary. Therefore, $2\lfloor log_2 k \rfloor + 1$ bits are required in all.

Elias-δ codes

Although the Elias-γ code is a major improvement on the unary code, it is not ideal for inputs that might contain large numbers. We know that a number k can be expressed in $\log_2 k$ binary digits, but the Elias-γ code requires twice as many bits in order to make the encoding unambiguous.

The Elias-δ code attempts to solve this problem by changing the way that k_d is encoded. Instead of encoding k_d in unary, we can encode $k_d + 1$ in Elias-γ. In particular, we split k_d into:

- $k_{dd} = \lfloor \log_2(k_d + 1) \rfloor$
- $k_{dr} = k_d - 2^{\lfloor \log_2(k_d + 1) \rfloor}$

Notice that we use $k_d + 1$ here, since k_d may be zero, but $\log_2 0$ is undefined.

We then encode k_{dd} in unary, k_{dr} in binary, and k_r in binary. The value of k_{dd} is the length of k_{dr}, and k_{dr} is the length of k_r, which makes this code unambiguous. Table 5.3 gives some examples of Elias-δ encodings.

Number (k)	k_d	k_r	k_{dd}	k_{dr}	Code
1	0	0	0	0	0
2	1	0	1	0	10 0 0
3	1	1	1	0	10 0 1
6	2	2	1	1	10 1 10
15	3	7	2	0	110 00 111
16	4	0	2	1	110 01 0000
255	7	127	3	0	1110 000 1111111
1023	9	511	3	2	1110 010 111111111

Table 5.3. Elias-δ code examples

Elias-δ sacrifices some efficiency for small numbers in order to gain efficiency at encoding larger numbers. Notice that the code for the number 2 has increased to 4 bits instead of the 3 bits required by the Elias-γ code. However, for numbers larger than 16, the Elias-δ code requires no more space than the Elias-γ code, and for numbers larger than 32, the Elias-δ requires less space.

Specifically, the Elias-γ code requires $\lfloor \log_2(\lfloor \log_2 k \rfloor + 1) \rfloor + 1$ bits for k_{dd} in unary, followed by $\lfloor \log_2(\lfloor \log_2 k \rfloor + 1) \rfloor$ bits for k_{dr} in binary, and $\lfloor \log_2 k \rfloor$ bits for k_r in binary. The total cost is approximately $2 \log_2 \log_2 k + \log_2 k$.

5.4.4 Byte-Aligned Codes

Even though a few tricks can help us decode bit-aligned codes quickly, codes of variable bit length are cumbersome on processors that process bytes. The processor is built to handle bytes efficiently, not bits, so it stands to reason that byte-aligned codes would be faster in practice.

There are many examples of byte-aligned compression schemes, but we consider only one popular method here. This is the code commonly known as *v-byte*, which is an abbreviation for "variable byte length." The v-byte method is very similar to UTF-8 encoding, which is a popular way to represent text (see section 3.5.1).

Like the other codes we have studied so far, the v-byte method uses short codes for small numbers and longer codes for longer numbers. However, each code is a series of bytes, not bits. So, the shortest v-byte code for a single integer is one byte. In some circumstances, this could be very space-inefficient; encoding the number 1 takes eight times as much space in v-byte as in Elias-γ. Typically, the difference in space usage is not quite so dramatic.

The v-byte code is really quite simple. The low seven bits of each byte contain numeric data in binary. The high bit is a terminator bit. The last byte of each code has its high bit set to 1; otherwise, it is set to 0. Any number that can be represented in seven binary digits requires one byte to encode. More information about space usage is shown in Table 5.4.

Some example encodings are shown in Table 5.5. Numbers less than 128 are stored in a single byte in traditional binary form, except that the high bit is set. For larger numbers, the least significant seven bits are stored in the first byte. The next seven bits are stored in the next byte until all of the non-zero bits have been stored.

Storing compressed data with a byte-aligned code has many advantages over a bit-aligned code. Byte-aligned codes compress and decompress faster, since pro-

k	Number of bytes
$k < 2^7$	1
$2^7 \le k < 2^{14}$	2
$2^{14} \le k < 2^{21}$	3
$2^{21} \le k < 2^{28}$	4

Table 5.4. Space requirements for numbers encoded in v-byte

k	Binary Code	Hexadecimal
1	1 0000001	81
6	1 0000110	86
127	1 1111111	FF
128	0 0000001 1 0000000	01 80
130	0 0000001 1 0000010	01 82
20000	0 0000001 0 0011100 1 0100000	01 1C A0

Table 5.5. Sample encodings for v-byte

cessors (and programming languages) are designed to process bytes instead of bits. For these reasons, the Galago search engine associated with this book uses v-byte exclusively for compression.

5.4.5 Compression in Practice

The compression techniques we have covered are used to encode inverted lists in real retrieval systems. In this section, we'll look at how Galago uses compression to encode inverted lists in the PositionListWriter class.

Figure 5.5 illustrates how position information can be stored in inverted lists. Consider just the inverted list for tropical:

$$(1, 1)(1, 7)(2, 6)(2, 17)(3, 1)$$

In each pair, the first number represents the document and the second number represents the word position. For instance, the third entry in this list states that the word tropical is the sixth word in document 2. Because it helps the example, we'll add $(2, 197)$ to the list:

$$(1, 1)(1, 7)(2, 6)(2, 17)(2, 197)(3, 1)$$

We can group the positions for each document together so that each document has its own entry, (document, count, [positions]), where count is the number of occurrences in the document. Our example data now looks like this:

$$(1, 2, [1, 7])(2, 3, [6, 17, 197])(3, 1, [1])$$

The word count is important because it makes this list decipherable even without the parentheses and brackets. The count tells us how many positions lie within the brackets, and we can interpret these numbers unambiguously, even if they were printed as follows:

$$1, 2, 1, 7, 2, 3, 6, 17, 197, 3, 1, 1$$

However, we will leave the brackets in place for now for clarity.

These are small numbers, but with delta encoding we can make them smaller. Notice that the document numbers are sorted in ascending order, so we can safely use delta encoding to encode them:

$$(1, 2, [1, 7])(1, 3, [6, 17, 197])(1, 1, [1])$$

The second entry now starts with a 1 instead of a 2, but this 1 means "this document number is one more than the last document number." Since position information is also sorted in ascending order, we can delta-encode the positions as well:

$$(1, 2, [1, 6])(1, 3, [6, 11, 180])(1, 1, [1])$$

We can't delta-encode the word counts, because they're not in ascending order. If we did delta-encode them, some of the deltas might be negative, and the compression techniques we have discussed do not handle negative numbers without some extra work.

Now we can remove the brackets and consider this inverted list as just a list of numbers:

$$1, 2, 1, 6, 1, 2, 6, 11, 180, 1, 1, 1$$

Since most of these numbers are small, we can compress them with v-byte to save space:

81 82 81 86 81 82 86 8B 01 B4 81 81 81

The `01 B4` is 180, which is encoded in two bytes. The rest of the numbers were encoded as single bytes, giving a total of 13 bytes for the entire list.

5.4.6 Looking Ahead

This section described three compression schemes for inverted lists, and there are many others in common use. Even though compression is one of the older areas of computer science, new compression schemes are developed every year.

Why are these new schemes necessary? Remember at the beginning of this section we talked about how compression allows us to trade processor computation for data throughput. This means that the best choice for a compression algorithm is tightly coupled with the state of modern CPUs and memory systems. For a long time, CPU speed was increasing much faster than memory throughput, so compression schemes with higher compression ratios became more attractive. However, the dominant hardware trend now is toward many CPU cores with lower clock speeds. Depending on the memory throughput of these systems, lower compression ratios may be attractive.

More importantly, modern CPUs owe much of their speed to clever tricks such as branch prediction, which helps the processor guess about how code will execute. Code that is more predictable can run much faster than unpredictable code. Many of the newest compression schemes are designed to make the decode phase more predictable, and therefore faster.

5.4.7 Skipping and Skip Pointers

For many queries, we don't need all of the information stored in a particular inverted list. Instead, it would be more efficient to read just the small portion of the data that is relevant to the query. Skip pointers help us achieve that goal.

Consider the Boolean query "galago AND animal". The word "animal" occurs in about 300 million documents on the Web versus approximately 1 million for "galago." If we assume that the inverted lists for "galago" and "animal" are in document order, there is a very simple algorithm for processing this query:

- Let d_g be the first document number in the inverted list for "galago."
- Let d_a be the first document number in the inverted list for "animal."
- While there are still documents in the lists for "galago" and "animal," loop:
  - If $d_g < d_a$, set d_g to the next document number in the "galago" list.
  - If $d_a < d_g$, set d_a to the next document number in the "animal" list.

- If $d_a = d_g$, the document d_a contains both "galago" and "animal". Move both d_g and d_a to the next documents in the inverted lists for "galago" and "animal," respectively.

Unfortunately, this algorithm is very expensive. It processes almost all documents in both inverted lists, so we expect the computer to process this loop about 300 million times. Over 99% of the processing time will be spent processing the 299 million documents that contain "animal" but do not contain "galago."

We can change this algorithm slightly by skipping forward in the "animal" list. Every time we find that $d_a < d_g$, we skip ahead k documents in the "animal" list to a new document, s_a. If $s_a < d_g$, we skip ahead by another k documents. We do this until $s_a \geq d_g$. At this point, we have narrowed our search down to a range of k documents that might contain d_g, which we can search linearly.

How much time does the modified algorithm take? Since the word "galago" appears 1 million times, we know that the algorithm will perform 1 million linear searches of length k, giving an expected cost of $500,000 \times k$ steps. We also expect to skip forward $300,000,000/k$ times. This algorithm then takes about $500,000 \times k + 300,000,000/k$ steps in total.

k	Steps
5	62.5 million
10	35 million
20	25 million
25	24.5 million
40	27.5 million
50	31 million
100	53 million

Table 5.6. Skip lengths (k) and expected processing steps

Table 5.6 shows the number of processing steps required for some example values of k. We get the best expected performance when we skip 25 documents at a time. Notice that at this value of k, we expect to have to skip forward 12 times in the "animal" list for each occurrence of "galago." This is because of the cost of linear search: a larger value of k means more elements to check in the linear search. If we choose a binary search instead, the best value of k rises to about 208, with about 9.2 million expected steps.

If binary search combined with skipping is so much more efficient, why even consider linear search at all? The problem is compression. For binary search to work, we need to be able to jump directly to elements in the list, but after compression, every element could take a different amount of space. In addition, delta encoding may be used on the document numbers, meaning that even if we could jump to a particular location in the compressed sequence, we would need to decompress everything up to that point in order to decode the document numbers. This is discouraging because our goal is to reduce the amount of the list we need to process, and it seems that compression forces us to decompress the whole list.

We can solve the compression problem with a list of skip pointers. Skip pointer lists are small additional data structures built into the index to allow us to skip through the inverted lists efficiently.

A skip pointer (d, p) contains two parts, a document number d and a byte (or bit) position p. This means that there is an inverted list posting that starts at position p, and that the posting immediately before it is for document d. Notice that this definition of the skip pointer solves both of our compression problems: we can start decoding at position p, and since we know that d is the document immediately preceding p, we can use it for decoding.

As a simple example, consider the following list of document numbers, uncompressed:

$$5, 11, 17, 21, 26, 34, 36, 37, 45, 48, 51, 52, 57, 80, 89, 91, 94, 101, 104, 119$$

If we delta-encode this list, we end up with a list of d-gaps like this:

$$5, 6, 6, 4, 5, 9, 2, 1, 8, 3, 3, 1, 5, 23, 9, 2, 3, 7, 3, 15$$

We can then add some skip pointers for this list, using 0-based positions (that is, the number 5 is at position 0 in the list):

$$(17, 3), (34, 6), (45, 9), (52, 12), (89, 15), (101, 18)$$

Suppose we try decoding using the skip pointer $(34, 6)$. We move to position 6 in the d-gaps list, which is the number 2. We add 34 to 2, to decode document number 36.

More generally, if we want to find document number 80 in the list, we scan the list of skip pointers until we find $(52, 12)$ and $(89, 15)$. 80 is larger than 52 but less than 89, so we start decoding at position 12. We find:

- $52 + 5 = 57$
- $57 + 23 = 80$

At this point, we have successfully found 80 in the list. If instead we were searching for 85, we would again start at skip pointer (52, 12):

- $52 + 5 = 57$
- $57 + 23 = 80$
- $80 + 9 = 89$

At this point, since $85 < 89$, we would know that 85 is not in the list.

In the analysis of skip pointers for the "galago AND animal" example, the effectiveness of the skip pointers depended on the fact that "animal" was much more common than "galago." We found that 25 was a good value for k given this query, but we only get to choose one value for k for all queries. The best way to choose k is to find the best possible k for some realistic sample set of queries. For most collections and query loads, the optimal skip distance is around 100 bytes.

5.5 Auxiliary Structures

The inverted file is the primary data structure in a search engine, but usually other structures are necessary for a fully functional system.

Vocabulary and statistics

An inverted file, as described in this chapter, is just a collection of inverted lists. To search the index, some kind of data structure is necessary to find the inverted list for a particular term. The simplest way to solve this problem is to store each inverted list as a separate file, where each file is named after the corresponding search term. To find the inverted list for "dog," the system can simply open the file named dog and read the contents. However, as we saw in Chapter 4, document collections can have millions of unique words, and most of these words will occur only once or twice in the collection. This means that an index, if stored in files, would consist of millions of files, most of which are very small.

Unfortunately, modern file systems are not optimized for this kind of storage. A file system typically will reserve a few kilobytes of space for each file, even though most files will contain just a few bytes of data. The result is a huge amount of wasted space. As an example, in the AP89 collection, over 70,000 words occur just once (see Table 4.1). These inverted lists would require about 20 bytes each, for a total of about 2MB of space. However, if the file system requires 1KB for each file, the result is 70MB of space used to store 2MB of data. In addition, many file systems still store directory information in unsorted arrays, meaning that file lookups can be very slow for large file directories.

To fix these problems, inverted lists are usually stored together in a single file, which explains the name *inverted file*. An additional directory structure, called the *vocabulary* or *lexicon*, contains a lookup table from index terms to the byte offset of the inverted list in the inverted file.

In many cases, this vocabulary lookup table will be small enough to fit into memory. In this case, the vocabulary data can be stored in any reasonable way on disk and loaded into a hash table at search engine startup. If the search engine needs to handle larger vocabularies, some kind of tree-based data structure, such as a B-tree, should be used to minimize disk accesses during the search process.

Galago uses a hybrid strategy for its vocabulary structure. A small file in each index, called `vocabulary`, stores an abbreviated lookup table from vocabulary terms to offsets in the inverted file. This file contains just one vocabulary entry for each 32K of data in the inverted file. Therefore, a 32TB inverted file would require less than 1GB of vocabulary space, meaning that it can always be stored in memory for collections of a reasonable size. The lists in the inverted file are stored in alphabetical order. To find an inverted list, the search engine uses binary search to find the nearest entry in the vocabulary table, and reads the offset from that entry. The engine then reads 32KB of the inverted file, starting at the offset. This approach finds each inverted list with just one disk seek.

To compute some feature functions, the index needs to contain certain vocabulary statistics, such as the term frequency or document frequency (discussed in Chapter 4). When these statistics pertain to a specific term, they can be easily stored at the start of the inverted list. Some of these statistics pertain to the corpus, such as the total number of documents stored. When there are just a few of these kinds of statistics, efficient storage considerations can be safely ignored. Galago stores these collection-wide statistics in an XML file called `manifest`.

Documents, snippets, and external systems

The search engine, as described so far, returns a list of document numbers and scores. However, a real user-focused search engine needs to display textual information about each document, such as a document title, URL, or text summary

(Chapter 6 explains this in more detail). In order to get this kind of information, the text of the document needs to be retrieved.

In Chapter 3, we saw some ways that documents can be stored for fast access. There are many ways to approach this problem, but in the end, a separate system is necessary to convert search engine results from numbers into something readable by people.

5.6 Index Construction

Before an index can be used for query processing, it has to be created from the text collection. Building a small index is not particularly difficult, but as input sizes grow, some index construction tricks can be useful. In this section, we will look at simple in-memory index construction first, and then consider the case where the input data does not fit in memory. Finally, we will consider how to build indexes using more than one computer.

5.6.1 Simple Construction

Pseudocode for a simple indexer is shown in Figure 5.8. The process involves only a few steps. A list of documents is passed to the BuildIndex function, and the function parses each document into tokens, as discussed in Chapter 4. These tokens are words, perhaps with some additional processing, such as downcasing or stemming. The function removes duplicate tokens, using, for example, a hash table. Then, for each token, the function determines whether a new inverted list needs to be created in I, and creates one if necessary. Finally, the current document number, n, is added to the inverted list.

The result is a hash table of tokens and inverted lists. The inverted lists are just lists of integer document numbers and contain no special information. This is enough to do very simple kinds of retrieval, as we saw in section 5.3.1.

As described, this indexer can be used for many small tasks—for example, indexing less than a few thousand documents. However, it is limited in two ways. First, it requires that all of the inverted lists be stored in memory, which may not be practical for larger collections. Second, this algorithm is sequential, with no obvious way to parallelize it. The primary barrier to parallelizing this algorithm is the hash table, which is accessed constantly in the inner loop. Adding locks to the hash table would allow parallelism for parsing, but that improvement alone will

```
procedure BuildIndex(D)                    ▷ D is a set of text documents
    I ← HashTable()                              ▷ Inverted list storage
    n ← 0                                         ▷ Document numbering
    for all documents d ∈ D do
        n ← n + 1
        T ← Parse(d)                        ▷ Parse document into tokens
        Remove duplicates from T
        for all tokens t ∈ T do
            if I_t ∉ I then
                I_t ← Array()
            end if
            I_t.append(n)
        end for
    end for
    return I
end procedure
```

Fig. 5.8. Pseudocode for a simple indexer

not be enough to make use of more than a handful of CPU cores. Handling large collections will require less reliance on memory and improved parallelism.

5.6.2 Merging

The classic way to solve the memory problem in the previous example is by *merging*. We can build the inverted list structure I until memory runs out. When that happens, we write the partial index I to disk, then start making a new one. At the end of this process, the disk is filled with many partial indexes, $I_1, I_2, I_3, ..., I_n$. The system then merges these files into a single result.

By definition, it is not possible to hold even two of the partial index files in memory at one time, so the input files need to be carefully designed so that they can be merged in small pieces. One way to do this is to store the partial indexes in alphabetical order. It is then possible for a merge algorithm to merge the partial indexes using very little memory.

Figure 5.9 shows an example of this kind of merging procedure. Even though this figure shows only two indexes, it is possible to merge many at once. The algorithm is essentially the same as the standard merge sort algorithm. Since both I_1 and I_2 are sorted, at least one of them points to the next piece of data necessary to write to I. The data from the two files is interleaved to produce a sorted result.

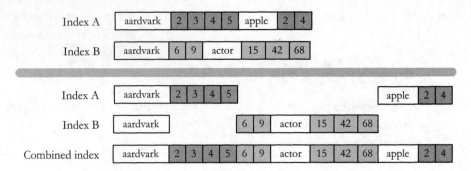

Fig. 5.9. An example of index merging. The first and second indexes are merged together to produce the combined index.

Since I_1 and I_2 may have used the same document numbers, the merge function renumbers documents in I_2.

This merging process can succeed even if there is only enough memory to store two words (w_1 and w_2), a single inverted list posting, and a few file pointers. In practice, a real merge function would read large chunks of I_1 and I_2, and then write large chunks to I in order to use the disk most efficiently.

This merging strategy also shows a possible parallel indexing strategy. If many machines build their own partial indexes, a single machine can combine all of those indexes together into a single, final index. However, in the next section, we will explore more recent distributed indexing frameworks that are becoming popular.

5.6.3 Parallelism and Distribution

The traditional model for search engines has been to use a single, fast machine to create the index and process queries. This is still the appropriate choice for a large number of applications, but it is no longer a good choice for the largest systems. Instead, for these large systems, it is increasingly popular to use many inexpensive servers together and use distributed processing software to coordinate their activities. MapReduce is a distributed processing tool that makes this possible.

Two factors have forced this shift. First, the amount of data to index in the largest systems is exploding. Modern web search engines already index tens of billions of pages, but even larger indexes are coming. Consider that if each person on earth wrote one blog post each day, the Web would increase in size by over two trillion pages every year. Optimistically, one typical modern computer can handle a few hundred million pages, although not with the kind of response times that most users expect. This leaves a huge gulf between the size of the Web and what we can handle with current single-computer technology. Note that this problem is not restricted to a few major web search companies; many more companies want to *analyze* the content of the Web instead of making it available for public search. These companies have the same scalability problem.

The second factor is simple economics. The incredible popularity of personal computers has made them very powerful and inexpensive. In contrast, large computers serve a very small market, and therefore have fewer opportunities to develop economies of scale. Over time, this difference in scale has made it difficult to make a computer that is much more powerful than a personal computer that is still sold for a reasonable amount of money. Many large information retrieval systems ran on mainframes in the past, but today's platform of choice consists of many inexpensive commodity servers.

Inexpensive servers have a few disadvantages when compared to mainframes. First, they are more likely to break, and the likelihood of at least one server failure goes up as you add more servers. Second, they are difficult to program. Most programmers are well trained for single-threaded programming, less well trained for threaded or multi-process programming, and not well trained at all for cooperative network programming. Many programming toolkits have been developed to help address this kind of problem. RPC, CORBA, Java RMI, and SOAP have been developed to allow function calls across machine boundaries. MPI provides a different abstraction, called *message passing*, which is popular for many scientific tasks. None of these techniques are particularly robust against system failures, and the programming models can be complex. In particular, these systems do not help distribute data evenly among machines; that is the programmer's job.

Data placement

Before diving into the mechanics of distributed processing, consider the problems of handling huge amounts of data on a single computer. Distributed processing and large-scale data processing have one major aspect in common, which is that not all of the input data is available at once. In distributed processing, the data might be scattered among many machines. In large-scale data processing, most of the data is on the disk. In both cases, the key to efficient data processing is placing the data correctly.

Let's take a simple example. Suppose you have a text file that contains data about credit card transactions. Each line of the file contains a credit card number and an amount of money. How might you determine the number of unique credit card numbers in the file?

If the file is not very big, you could read each line, parse the credit card number, and store the credit card number in a hash table. Once the entire file had been read, the hash table would contain one entry for each unique credit card number. Counting the number of entries in the hash table would give you the answer. Unfortunately, for a big file, the hash table would be too large to store in memory.

Now suppose you had the very same credit card data, but the transactions in the file were ordered by credit card number. Counting the number of unique credit card numbers in this case is very simple. Each line in the file is read and the credit card number on the line is parsed. If the credit card number found is different than the one on the line before it, a counter is incremented. When the end of the file is reached, the counter contains a count of the unique credit card numbers in the file. No hash table is necessary for this to work.

Now, back to distributed computation. Suppose you have more than one computer to use for this counting task. You can split the big file of transactions into small batches of transactions. Each computer can count its fraction, and then the results can be merged together to produce a final result.

Initially, we start with an unordered file of transactions. We split that file into small batches of transactions and count the unique credit card numbers in each batch. How do we combine the results? We could add the number of credit card numbers found in each batch, but this is incorrect, since the same credit card number might appear in more than one batch, and therefore would be counted more than once in the final total. Instead, we would need to keep a list of the unique credit card numbers found in each batch, and then merge those lists together to make a final result list. The size of this final list is the number of unique credit card numbers in the whole set.

In contrast, suppose the transactions are split into batches with more care, so that all transactions made with the same credit card end up in the same batch. With this extra restriction, each batch can be counted individually, and then the counts from each batch can be added to make a final result. No merge is necessary, because there is no possibility of double-counting. Each credit card number will appear in precisely one batch.

These examples might be a little bit tedious, but the point is that proper data grouping can radically change the performance characteristics of a task. Using a sorted input file made the counting task easy, reduced the amount of memory needed to nearly zero, and made it possible to distribute the computation easily.

MapReduce

MapReduce is a distributed programming framework that focuses on data placement and distribution. As we saw in the last few examples, proper data placement can make some problems very simple to compute. By focusing on data placement, MapReduce can unlock the parallelism in some common tasks and make it easier to process large amounts of data.

MapReduce gets its name from the two pieces of code that a user needs to write in order to use the framework: the *Mapper* and the *Reducer*. The MapReduce library automatically launches many Mapper and Reducer tasks on a cluster of machines. The interesting part about MapReduce, though, is the path the data takes between the Mapper and the Reducer.

Before we look at how the Mapper and Reducer work, let's look at the foundations of the MapReduce idea. The functions map and reduce are commonly found in functional languages. In very simple terms, the map function transforms a list of items into another list of items of the same length. The reduce function transforms a list of items into a single item. The MapReduce framework isn't quite so strict with its definitions: both Mappers and Reducers can return an arbitrary number of items. However, the general idea is the same.

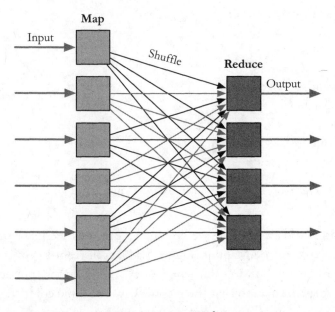

Fig. 5.10. MapReduce

We assume that the data comes in a set of records. The records are sent to the Mapper, which transforms these records into pairs, each with a key and a value. The next step is the shuffle, which the library performs by itself. This operation uses a hash function so that all pairs with the same key end up next to each other and on the same machine. The final step is the reduce stage, where the records are processed again, but this time in batches, meaning all pairs with the same key are processed at once. The MapReduce steps are summarized in Figure 5.10.

```
procedure MapCreditCards(input)
    while not input.done() do
        record ← input.next()
        card ← record.card
        amount ← record.amount
        Emit(card, amount)
    end while
end procedure
```

Fig. 5.11. Mapper for a credit card summing algorithm

```
procedure ReduceCreditCards(key, values)
    total ← 0
    card ← key
    while not values.done() do
        amount ← values.next()
        total ← total + amount
    end while
    Emit(card, total)
end procedure
```

Fig. 5.12. Reducer for a credit card summing algorithm

The credit card data example we saw in the previous section works well as a MapReduce task. In the Mapper (Figure 5.11), each record is split into a key (the credit card number) and a value (the money amount in the transaction). The shuffle stage sorts the data so that the records with the same credit card number end up next to each other. The reduce stage emits a record for each unique credit card number, so the total number of unique credit card numbers is the number of records emitted by the reducer (Figure 5.12).

Typically, we assume that both the Mapper and Reducer are *idempotent*. By idempotent, we mean that if the Mapper or Reducer is called multiple times on the same input, the output will always be the same. This idempotence allows the MapReduce library to be fault tolerant. If any part of the computation fails, perhaps because of a hardware machine failure, the MapReduce library can just process that part of the input again on a different machine. Even when machines don't fail, sometimes machines can be slow because of misconfiguration or slowly failing parts. In this case, a machine that appears to be normal could return results much more slowly than other machines in a cluster. To guard against this, as the computation nears completion, the MapReduce library issues *backup* Mappers and Reducers that duplicate the processing done on the slowest machines. This ensures that slow machines don't become the bottleneck of a computation. The idempotence of the Mapper and Reducer are what make this possible. If the Mapper or Reducer modified files directly, for example, multiple copies of them could not be run simultaneously.

Let's look at the problem of indexing a corpus with MapReduce. In our simple indexer, we will store inverted lists with word positions.

```
procedure MapDocumentsToPostings(input)
    while not input.done() do
        document ← input.next()
        number ← document.number
        position ← 0
        tokens ← Parse(document)
        for each word w in tokens do
            Emit(w, document:position)
            position = position + 1
        end for
    end while
end procedure
```

Fig. 5.13. Mapper for documents

MapDocumentsToPostings (Figure 5.13) parses each document in the input. At each word position, it emits a key/value pair: the key is the word itself, and the value is *document:position*, which is the document number and the position

```
procedure REDUCEPOSTINGSTOLISTS(key, values)
    word ← key
    WriteWord(word)
    while not input.done() do
        EncodePosting(values.next())
    end while
end procedure
```

Fig. 5.14. Reducer for word postings

concatenated together. When ReducePostingsToLists (Figure 5.14) is called, the emitted postings have been shuffled so that all postings for the same word are together. The Reducer calls WriteWord to start writing an inverted list and then uses EncodePosting to write each posting.

5.6.4 Update

So far, we have assumed that indexing is a batch process. This means that a set of documents is given to the indexer as input, the indexer builds the index, and then the system allows users to run queries. In practice, most interesting document collections are constantly changing. At the very least, collections tend to get bigger over time; every day there is more news and more email. In other cases, such as web search or file system search, the contents of documents can change over time as well. A useful search engine needs to be able to respond to dynamic collections.

We can solve the problem of update with two techniques: index merging and result merging. If the index is stored in memory, there are many options for quick index update. However, even if the search engine is evaluating queries in memory, typically the index is stored on a disk. Inserting data in the middle of a file is not supported by any common file system, so direct disk-based update is not straightforward. We do know how to merge indexes together, though, as we saw in section 5.6.2. This gives us a simple approach for adding data to the index: make a new, smaller index (I_2) and merge it with the old index (I_1) to make a new index containing all of the data (I). Postings in I_1 for any deleted documents can be ignored during the merge phase so they do not appear in I.

Index merging is a reasonable update strategy when index updates come in large batches, perhaps many thousands of documents at a time. For single document updates, it isn't a very good strategy, since it is time-consuming to write the entire index to disk. For these small updates, it is better to just build a small index for the new data, but not merge it into the larger index. Queries are evaluated separately against the small index and the big index, and the result lists are merged to find the top k results.

Result merging solves the problem of how to handle new documents: just put them in a new index. But how do we delete documents from the index? The common solution is to use a deleted document list. During query processing, the system checks the deleted document list to make sure that no deleted documents enter the list of results shown to the user. If the contents of a document change, we can delete the old version from the index by using a deleted document list and then add a new version to the recent documents index.

Results merging allows us to consider a small, in-memory index structure to hold new documents. This in-memory structure could be a hash table of arrays, as shown in Figure 5.8, and therefore would be simple and quick to update, even with only a single document.

To gain even more performance from the system, instead of using just two indexes (an in-memory index and a disk-based index), we can use many indexes. Using too many indexes is a bad idea, since each new index slows down query processing. However, using too few indexes results in slow index build throughput because of excessive disk traffic. A particularly elegant solution to this problem is *geometric partitioning*. In geometric partitioning, the smallest index, I_0, contains about as much data as would fit in memory. The next index, I_1, contains about r times as much data as I_1. If m is the amount of bytes of memory in the machine, index I_n then contains between mr^n and $(m + 1)r^n$ bytes of data. If index I_n ever contains more than $(m + 1)r^n$, it is merged into index I_{n+1}. If $r = 2$, the system can hold $1000m$ bytes of index data using just 10 indexes.

5.7 Query Processing

Once an index is built, we need to process the data in it to produce query results. Even with simple algorithms, processing queries using an index is much faster than it is without one. However, clever algorithms can boost query processing speed by ten to a hundred times over the simplest versions. We will explore the simplest two query processing techniques first, called document-at-a-time and term-at-a-time, and then move on to faster and more flexible variants.

5.7.1 Document-at-a-time Evaluation

Document-at-a-time retrieval is the simplest way, at least conceptually, to perform retrieval with an inverted file. Figure 5.15 is a picture of document-at-a-time retrieval for the query "salt water tropical". The inverted lists are shown horizontally, although the postings have been aligned so that each column represents a different document. The inverted lists in this example hold word counts, and the score, for this example, is just the sum of the word counts in each document. The vertical gray lines indicate the different steps of retrieval. In the first step, all the counts for the first document are added to produce the score for that document. Once the scoring for the first document has completed, the second document is scored, then the third, and then the fourth.

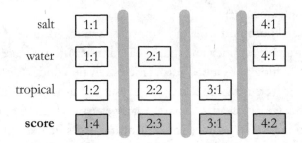

Fig. 5.15. Document-at-a-time query evaluation. The numbers $(x{:}y)$ represent a document number (x) and a word count (y).

Figure 5.16 shows a pseudocode implementation of this strategy. The parameters are Q, the query; I, the index; f and g, the sets of feature functions; and k, the number of documents to retrieve. This algorithm scores documents using the abstract model of ranking described in section 5.2. However, in this simplified example, we assume that the only non-zero feature values for $g(Q)$ correspond to the words in the query. This gives us a simple correspondence between inverted lists and features: there is one list for each query term, and one feature for each list. Later in this chapter we will explore structured queries, which are a standard way of moving beyond this simple model.

For each word w_i in the query, an inverted list is fetched from the index. These inverted lists are assumed to be sorted in order by document number. The InvertedList object starts by pointing at the first posting in each list. All of the fetched inverted lists are stored in an array, L.

procedure DOCUMENTATATIMERETRIEVAL(Q, I, f, g, k)
 $L \leftarrow$ Array()
 $R \leftarrow$ PriorityQueue(k)
 for all terms w_i in Q **do**
  $l_i \leftarrow$ InvertedList(w_i, I)
  L.add(l_i)
 end for
 for all documents $d \in I$ **do**
  for all inverted lists l_i in L **do**
   if l_i points to d **then**
    $s_D \leftarrow s_D + g_i(Q)f_i(l_i)$ ▷ Update the document score
    l_i.movePastDocument(d)
   end if
  end for
  R.add(s_D, D)
 end for
 return the top k results from R
end procedure

Fig. 5.16. A simple document-at-a-time retrieval algorithm

In the main loop, the function loops once for each document in the collection. At each document, all of the inverted lists are checked. If the document appears in one of the inverted lists, the feature function f_i is evaluated, and the document score s_D is computed by adding up the weighted function values. Then, the inverted list pointer is moved to point at the next posting. At the end of each document loop, a new document score has been computed and added to the priority queue R.

For clarity, this pseudocode is free of even simple performance-enhancing changes. Realistically, however, the priority queue R only needs to hold the top k results at any one time. If the priority queue ever contains more than k results, the lowest-scoring documents can be removed until only k remain, in order to save memory. Also, looping over all documents in the collection is unnecessary; we can change the algorithm to score only documents that appear in at least one of the inverted lists.

The primary benefit of this method is its frugal use of memory. The only major use of memory comes from the priority queue, which only needs to store k entries at a time. However, in a realistic implementation, large portions of the inverted lists would also be buffered in memory during evaluation.

5.7.2 Term-at-a-time Evaluation

Figure 5.17 shows term-at-a-time retrieval, using the same query, scoring function, and inverted list data as in the document-at-a-time example (Figure 5.15). Notice that the computed scores are exactly the same in both figures, although the structure of each figure is different.

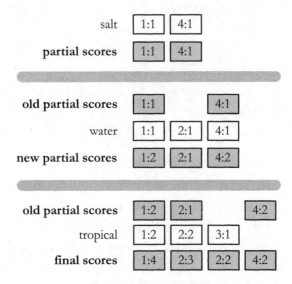

Fig. 5.17. Term-at-a-time query evaluation

As before, the gray lines indicate the boundaries between each step. In the first step, the inverted list for "salt" is decoded, and *partial scores* are stored in *accumulators*. These scores are called partial scores because they are only a part of the final document score. The accumulators, which get their name from their job, accumulate score information for each document. In the second step, partial scores from the accumulators are combined with data from the inverted list for "water" to produce a new set of partial scores. After the data from the list for "tropical" is added in the third step, the scoring process is complete.

The figure implies that a new set of accumulators is created for each list. Although this is one possible implementation technique, in practice accumulators are stored in a hash table. The information for each document is updated as the inverted list data is processed. The hash table contains the final document scores after all inverted lists have been processed.

procedure TERMATATIMERETRIEVAL$(Q, I, f, g \; k)$
    $A \leftarrow$ HashTable()
    $L \leftarrow$ Array()
    $R \leftarrow$ PriorityQueue(k)
    for all terms w_i in Q **do**
        $l_i \leftarrow$ InvertedList(w_i, I)
        L.add(l_i)
    end for
    for all lists $l_i \in L$ **do**
        while l_i is not finished **do**
            $d \leftarrow l_i$.getCurrentDocument()
            $A_d \leftarrow A_d + g_i(Q)f(l_i)$
            l_i.moveToNextDocument()
        end while
    end for
    for all accumulators A_d in A **do**
        $s_D \leftarrow A_d$ ▷ Accumulator contains the document score
        R.add(s_D, D)
    end for
    return the top k results from R
end procedure

Fig. 5.18. A simple term-at-a-time retrieval algorithm

The term-at-a-time retrieval algorithm for the abstract ranking model (Figure 5.18) is similar to the document-at-a-time version at the start. It creates a priority queue and fetches one inverted list for each term in the query, just like the document-at-a-time algorithm. However, the next step is different. Instead of a loop over each document in the index, the outer loop is over each list. The inner loop then reads each posting of the list, computing the feature functions f_i and g_i and adding its weighted contribution to the accumulator A_d. After the main loop completes, the accumulators are scanned and added to a priority queue, which determines the top k results to be returned.

The primary disadvantage of the term-at-a-time algorithm is the memory usage required by the accumulator table A. Remember that the document-at-a-time strategy requires only the small priority queue R, which holds a limited number of results. However, the term-at-a-time algorithm makes up for this because of its more efficient disk access. Since it reads each inverted list from start to finish, it requires minimal disk seeking, and it needs very little list buffering to achieve high speeds. In contrast, the document-at-a-time algorithm switches between lists and requires large list buffers to help reduce the cost of seeking.

In practice, neither the document-at-a-time nor term-at-a-time algorithms are used without additional optimizations. These optimizations dramatically improve the running speed of the algorithms, and can have a large effect on the memory footprint.

5.7.3 Optimization Techniques

There are two main classes of optimizations for query processing. The first is to read less data from the index, and the second is to process fewer documents. The two are related, since it would be hard to score the same number of documents while reading less data. When using feature functions that are particularly complex, focusing on scoring fewer documents should be the main concern. For simple feature functions, the best speed comes from ignoring as much of the inverted list data as possible.

List skipping

In section 5.4.7, we covered skip pointers in inverted lists. This kind of forward skipping is by far the most popular way to ignore portions of inverted lists (Figure 5.19). More complex approaches (for example, tree structures) are also possible but not frequently used.

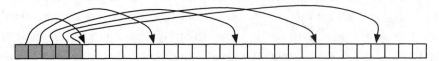

Fig. 5.19. Skip pointers in an inverted list. The gray boxes show skip pointers, which point into the white boxes, which are inverted list postings.

Skip pointers do not improve the asymptotic running time of reading an inverted list. Suppose we have an inverted list that is n bytes long, but we add skip pointers after each c bytes, and the pointers are k bytes long. Reading the entire list requires reading $\Theta(n)$ bytes, but jumping through the list using the skip pointers requires $\Theta(kn/c)$ time, which is equivalent to $\Theta(n)$. Even though there is no asymptotic gain in runtime, the factor of c can be huge. For typical values of $c = 100$ and $k = 4$, skipping through a list results in reading just 2.5% of the total data.

Notice that as c gets bigger, the amount of data you need to read to skip through the list drops. So, why not make c as big as possible? The problem is that if c gets too large, the average performance drops. Let's look at this problem in more detail.

Suppose you want to find p particular postings in an inverted list, and the list is n bytes long, with k-byte skip pointers located at c-byte intervals. Therefore, there are n/c total intervals in the list. To find those p postings, we need to read kn/c bytes in skip pointers, but we also need to read data in p intervals. On average, we assume that the postings we want are about halfway between two skip pointers, so we read an additional $pc/2$ bytes to find those postings. The total number of bytes read is then:

$$\frac{kn}{c} + \frac{pc}{2}$$

Notice that this analysis assumes that p is much smaller than n/c; that's what allows us to assume that each posting lies in its own interval. As p grows closer to n/c, it becomes likely that some of the postings we want will lie in the same intervals. However, notice that once p gets close to n/c, we need to read almost all of the inverted list, so the skip pointers aren't very helpful.

Coming back to the formula, you can see that while a larger value of c makes the first term smaller, it also makes the second term bigger. Therefore, picking the perfect value for c depends on the value of p, and we don't know what p is until a query is executed. However, it is possible to use previous queries to simulate skipping behavior and to get a good estimate for c. In the exercises, you will be asked to plot some of graphs of this formula and to solve for the equilibrium point.

Although it might seem that list skipping could save on disk accesses, in practice it rarely does. Modern disks are much better at reading sequential data than they are at skipping to random locations. Because of this, most disks require a skip of about 100,000 postings before any speedup is seen. Even so, skipping is still useful because it reduces the amount of time spent decoding compressed data that has been read from disk, and it dramatically reduces processing time for lists that are cached in memory.

Conjunctive processing

The simplest kind of query optimization is *conjunctive processing*. By conjunctive processing, we just mean that every document returned to the user needs to contain all of the query terms. Conjunctive processing is the default mode for many web search engines, in part because of speed and in part because users have come to expect it. With short queries, conjunctive processing can actually improve effectiveness and efficiency simultaneously. In contrast, search engines that use longer queries, such as entire paragraphs, will not be good candidates for conjunctive processing.

Conjunctive processing works best when one of the query terms is rare, as in the query "fish locomotion". The word "fish" occurs about 100 times as often as the word "locomotion". Since we are only interested in documents that contain both words, the system can skip over most of the inverted list for "fish" in order to find only the postings in documents that also contain the word "locomotion".

Conjunctive processing can be employed with both term-at-a-time and document-at-a-time systems. Figure 5.20 shows the updated term-at-a-time algorithm for conjunctive processing. When processing the first term, $(i = 0)$, processing proceeds normally. However, for the remaining terms, $(i > 0)$, the algorithm processes postings starting at line 14. It checks the accumulator table for the next document that contains all of the previous query terms, and instructs list l_i to skip forward to that document if there is a posting for it (line 17). If there is a posting, the accumulator is updated. If the posting does not exist, the accumulator is deleted (line 21).

The document-at-a-time version (Figure 5.21) is similar to the old document-at-a-time version, except in the inner loop. It begins by finding the largest document d currently pointed to by an inverted list (line 11). This document d is not guaranteed to contain all the query terms, but it is a reasonable candidate. The next loop tries to skip all lists forward to point at d (line 14). If this is not successful, the loop terminates and another document d is chosen. If it is successful, the document is scored and added to the priority queue.

In both algorithms, the system runs fastest when the first list (l_0) is the shortest and the last list (l_n) is the longest. This results in the biggest possible skip distances in the last list, which is where skipping will help most.

```
 1: procedure TERMATATIMERETRIEVAL(Q, I, f, g, k)
 2:     A ← HashTable()
 3:     L ← Array()
 4:     R ← PriorityQueue(k)
 5:     for all terms w_i in Q do
 6:         l_i ← InvertedList(w_i, I)
 7:         L.add( l_i )
 8:     end for
 9:     for all lists l_i ∈ L do
10:         while l_i is not finished do
11:             if i = 0 then
12:                 d ← l_i.getCurrentDocument()
13:                 A_d ← A_d + g_i(Q)f(l_i)
14:             else
15:                 d ← l_i.getCurrentDocument()
16:                 d ← A.getNextDocumentAfter(d)
17:                 l_i.skipForwardTo(d)
18:                 if l_i.getCurrentDocument() = d then
19:                     A_d ← A_d + g_i(Q)f(l_i)
20:                 else
21:                     A.remove(d)
22:                 end if
23:             end if
24:         end while
25:     end for
26:     for all accumulators A_d in A do
27:         s_D ← A_d                    ▷ Accumulator contains the document score
28:         R.add( s_D, D )
29:     end for
30:     return the top k results from R
31: end procedure
```

Fig. 5.20. A term-at-a-time retrieval algorithm with conjunctive processing

```
1:  procedure DocumentAtATimeRetrieval(Q, I, f, g, k)
2:      L ← Array()
3:      R ← PriorityQueue(k)
4:      for all terms wᵢ in Q do
5:          lᵢ ← InvertedList(wᵢ, I)
6:          L.add( lᵢ )
7:      end for
8:      while all lists in L are not finished do
9:          for all inverted lists lᵢ in L do
10:             if lᵢ.getCurrentDocument() > d then
11:                 d ← lᵢ.getCurrentDocument()
12:             end if
13:         end for
14:         for all inverted lists lᵢ in L do lᵢ.skipForwardToDocument(d)
15:             if lᵢ points to d then
16:                 s_d ← s_d + gᵢ(Q)fᵢ(lᵢ)            ▷ Update the document score
17:                 lᵢ.movePastDocument( d )
18:             else
19:                 break
20:             end if
21:         end for
22:         R.add( s_d, d )
23:     end while
24:     return the top k results from R
25: end procedure
```

Fig. 5.21. A document-at-a-time retrieval algorithm with conjunctive processing

Threshold methods

So far, the algorithms we have considered do not do much with the parameter k until the very last statement. Remember that k is the number of results requested by the user, and for many search applications this number is something small, such as 10 or 20. Because of this small value of k, most documents in the inverted lists will never be shown to the user. Threshold methods focus on this k parameter in order to score fewer documents.

In particular, notice that for every query, there is some minimum score that each document needs to reach before it can be shown to the user. This minimum score is the score of the kth-highest scoring document. Any document that does not score at least this highly will never be shown to the user. In this section, we will use the Greek letter tau (τ) to represent this value, which we call the *threshold*.

If we could know the appropriate value for τ before processing the query, many query optimizations would be possible. For instance, since a document needs a score of at least τ in order to be useful to the user, we could avoid adding documents to the priority queue (in the document-at-a-time case) that did not achieve a score of at least τ. In general, we could safely ignore any document with a score less than τ.

Unfortunately, we don't know how to compute the true value of τ without evaluating the query, but we can approximate it. These approximations will be called τ'. We want $\tau' \leq \tau$, so that we can safely ignore any document with a score less than τ'. Of course, the closer our estimate τ' gets to τ, the faster our algorithm will run, since it can ignore more documents.

Coming up with an estimate for τ' is easy with a document-at-a-time strategy. Remember that R maintains a list of the top k highest-scoring documents seen so far in the evaluation process. We can set τ' to the score of the lowest-scoring document currently in R, assuming R already has k documents in it. With term-at-a-time evaluation, we don't have full document scores until the query evaluation is almost finished. However, we can still set τ' to be the kth-largest score in the accumulator table.

MaxScore

With reasonable estimates for τ', it is possible to start ignoring some of the data in the inverted lists. This estimate, τ', represents a lower bound on the score a document needs in order to enter the final ranked list. Therefore, with a little bit of clever math, we can ignore parts of the inverted lists that will not generate document scores above τ'.

Let's look more closely at how this might happen with a simple example. Consider the query "eucalyptus tree". The word "tree" is about 100 times more common than the word "eucalyptus", so we expect that most of the time we spend evaluating this query will be spent scoring documents that contain the word "tree" and not "eucalyptus". This is a poor use of time, since we're almost certain to find a set of top k documents that contain both words.

Figure 5.22 shows this effect in action. We see the inverted lists for "eucalyptus" and "tree" extending across the page, with the postings lined up by document, as in previous figures in this chapter. This figure shows that there are many documents that contain the word "tree" and don't contain the word "eucalyptus".

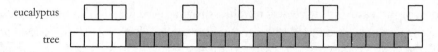

Fig. 5.22. MaxScore retrieval with the query "eucalyptus tree". The gray boxes indicate postings that can be safely ignored during scoring.

Suppose that the indexer computed the largest partial score in the "tree" list, and that value is called μ_{tree}. This is the maximum score (hence MaxScore) that any document that contains just this word could have.

Suppose that we are interested only in the top three documents in the ranked list (i.e., k is 3). The first scored document contains just the word "tree". The next three documents contain both "eucalyptus" and "tree". We will use τ' to represent the lowest score from these three documents. At this point, it is highly likely that $\tau' > \mu_{\text{tree}}$, because τ' is the score of a document that contains both query terms, whereas μ_{tree} is a query score for a document that contains just one of the query terms. This is where the gray boxes come into the story. Once $\tau' > \mu_{\text{tree}}$, we can safely skip over all of the gray postings, since we have proven that these documents will not enter the final ranked list.

The postings data in the figure is fabricated, but for real inverted lists for "eucalyptus" and "tree", 99% of the postings for "tree" would be gray boxes, and therefore would be safe to ignore. This kind of skipping can dramatically reduce query times without affecting the quality of the query results.

Early termination

The MaxScore approach guarantees that the result of query processing will be exactly the same in the optimized version as it is without optimization. In some cases, however, it may be interesting to take some risks with quality and process queries in a way that might lead to different results than the same queries in an unoptimized system.

Why might we choose to do this? One reason is that some queries are much, much more expensive than others. Consider the phrase query "to be or not to be". This query uses very common terms that would have very long inverted lists. Running this query to completion could severely reduce the amount of system resources available to serve other queries. Truncating query processing for this expensive query can help ensure fairness for others using the same system.

Another reason is that MaxScore is necessarily conservative. It will not skip over regions of the inverted list that might have a usable candidate document. Because of this, MaxScore can spend a lot of time looking for a document that might not exist. Taking a calculated risk to ignore these improbable documents can pay off in decreased system resource consumption.

How might early termination work? In term-at-a-time systems, we can terminate processing by simply ignoring some of the very frequent query terms. This is not so different from using a stopword list, except that in this case we would be ignoring words that usually would not be considered stopwords. Alternatively, we might decide that after some constant number of postings have been read, no other terms will be considered. The reasoning here is that, after processing a substantial number of postings, the ranking should be fairly well established. Reading more information will only change the rankings a little. This is especially true for queries with many (e.g., hundreds) of terms, which can happen when query expansion techniques are used.

In document-at-a-time systems, early termination means ignoring the documents at the very end of the inverted lists. This is a poor idea if the documents are sorted in random order, but this does not have to be the case. Instead, documents could be sorted in order by some quality metric, such as PageRank. Terminating early in that case would mean ignoring documents that are considered lower quality than the documents that have already been scored.

List ordering

So far, all the examples in this chapter assume that the inverted lists are stored in the same order, by document number. If the document numbers are assigned randomly, this means that the document sort order is random. The net effect is that the best documents for a query can easily be at the very end of the lists. With good documents scattered throughout the list, any reasonable query processing algorithm must read or skip through the whole list to make sure that no good documents are missed. Since these lists can be long, it makes sense to consider a more intelligent ordering.

One way to improve document ordering is to order documents based on document quality, as we discussed in the last section. There are plenty of quality metrics that could be used, such as PageRank or the total number of user clicks. If the smallest document numbers are assigned to the highest-quality documents, it becomes reasonable to consider stopping the search early if many good documents have been found. The threshold techniques from the MaxScore section can be used here. If we know that documents in the lists are decreasing in quality, we can compute an upper bound on the scores of the documents remaining in the lists at every point during retrieval. When τ' rises above the highest possible remaining document score, retrieval can be stopped safely without harming effectiveness.

Another option is to order each list by partial score. For instance, for the "food" list, we could store documents that contain many instances of the word "food" first. In a web application, this may correspond to putting restaurant pages early in the inverted list. For a "dog" list, we could store pages about dogs (i.e., containing many instances of "dog") first. Evaluating a query about food or dogs then becomes very easy. Other queries, however, can be more difficult. For example, how do we evaluate the query "dog food"? The best way to do it is to use an accumulator table, as in term-at-a-time retrieval. However, instead of reading a whole list at once, we read just small pieces of each list. Once the accumulator table shows that many good documents have been found, we can stop looking. As you can imagine, retrieval works fastest with terms that are likely to appear together, such as "tortilla guacamole". When the terms are not likely to appear together—for example, "dirt cheese"—it is likely to take much longer to find the top documents.

5.7.4 Structured Queries

In the query evaluation examples we have seen so far, our assumption is that each inverted list corresponds to a single feature, and that we add those features together to create a final document score. Although this works in simple cases, we might want a more interesting kind of scoring function. For instance, in Figure 5.2 the query had plenty of interesting features, including a phrase ("tropical fish"), a synonym ("chichlids"), and some non-topical features (e.g., incoming links).

One way to do this is to write specialized ranking code in the retrieval system that detects these extra features and uses inverted list data directly to compute scores, but in a way that is more complicated than just a linear combination of features. This approach greatly increases the kinds of scoring that you can use, and is very efficient. Unfortunately, it isn't very flexible.

Another option is to build a system that supports *structured queries*. Structured queries are queries written in a query language, which allows you to change the features used in a query and the way those features are combined. The query language is not used by normal users of the system. Instead, a *query translator* converts the user's input into a structured query representation. This translation process is where the intelligence of the system goes, including how to weight word features and what synonyms to use. Once this structured query has been created, it is passed to the retrieval system for execution.

You may already be familiar with this kind of model, since database systems work this way. Relational databases are controlled using Structured Query Language (SQL). Many important applications consist of a user interface and a structured query generator, with the rest of the logic controlled by a database. This separation of the application logic from the database logic allows the database to be both highly optimized and highly general.

Galago contains a structured query processing system that is described in detail in Chapter 7. This query language is also used in the exercises.

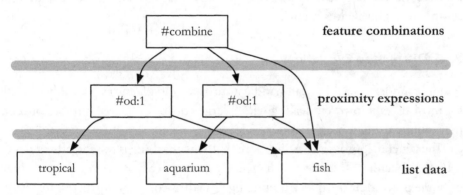

Fig. 5.23. Evaluation tree for the structured query #combine(#od:1(tropical fish) #od:1(aquarium fish) fish)

Figure 5.23 shows a tree representation of a structured query written in the Galago structured query language: #combine(#od:1(tropical fish) #od:1(aquarium fish) fish).

This query indicates that the document score should be a combination of the scores from three subqueries. The first query is #od:1(tropical fish). In the Galago query language, the #od:1 operator means that the terms inside it need to appear next to each other, in that order, in a matching document. The same is true of #od:1(aquarium fish). The final query term is fish. Each of these subqueries acts as a document feature that is combined using the #combine operator.

This query contains examples of the main types of structured query expressions. At the bottom of the tree, we have index terms. These are terms that correspond to inverted lists in the index. Above that level, we have proximity expressions. These expressions combine inverted lists to create more complex features, such as a feature for "fish" occurring in a document title, or "tropical fish" occurring as a phrase. At the top level, the feature data computed from the inverted lists is combined into a document score. At this level, the position information from the inverted lists is ignored.

Galago evaluates structured queries by making a tree of iterator objects that looks just like the tree shown in Figure 5.23. For instance, an iterator is created that returns the matching documents for #od:1(tropical fish). The iterator finds these matching documents by using data from inverted list iterators for "tropical" and "fish". The #combine operator is an iterator of document scores, which uses iterators for #od:1(tropical fish), #od:1(aquarium fish), and fish. Once a tree of iterators like this is made, scoring documents is just a matter of using the root iterator to step through the documents.

5.7.5 Distributed Evaluation

A single modern machine can handle a surprising load, and is probably enough for most tasks. However, dealing with a large corpus or a large number of users may require using more than one machine.

The general approach to using more than one machine is to send all queries to a *director* machine. The director then sends messages to many *index servers*, which do some portion of the query processing. The director then organizes the results of this process and returns them to the user.

The easiest distribution strategy is called *document distribution*. In this strategy, each index server acts as a search engine for a small fraction of the total document collection. The director sends a copy of the query to each of the index servers, each of which returns the top k results, including the document scores for these results. These results are merged into a single ranked list by the director, which then returns the results to the user.

Some ranking algorithms rely on collection statistics, such as the number of occurrences of a term in the collection or the number of documents containing a term. These statistics need to be shared among the index servers in order to produce comparable scores that can be merged effectively. In very large clusters of machines, the term statistics at the index server level can vary wildly. If each index server uses only its own term statistics, the same document could receive very different kinds of scores, depending on which index server is used.

Another distribution method is called *term distribution*. In term distribution, a single index is built for the whole cluster of machines. Each inverted list in that index is then assigned to one index server. For instance, the word "dog" might be handled by the third server, while "cat" is handled by the fifth server. For a system with n index servers and a k term query, the probability that all of the query terms would be on the same server is $1/n^{k-1}$. For a cluster of 10 machines, this probability is just 1% for a three-term query. Therefore, in most cases the data to process a query is not stored all on one machine.

One of the index servers, usually the one holding the longest inverted list, is chosen to process the query. If other index servers have relevant data, that data is sent over the network to the index server processing the query. When query processing is complete, the results are sent to a director machine.

The term distribution approach is more complex than document distribution because of the need to send inverted list data between machines. Given the size of inverted lists, the messages involved in shipping this data can saturate a network. In addition, each query is processed using just one processor instead of many, which increases overall query latency versus document distribution. The main advantage of term distribution is seek time. If we have a k-term query and n index servers, the total number of disk seeks necessary to process a query is $O(kn)$ for a document-distributed system, but just $O(k)$ in a term-distributed system. For a system that is disk-bound, and especially one that is seek-bound, term distribution might be attractive. However, recent research shows that term distribution is rarely worth the effort.

5.7.6 Caching

We saw in Chapter 4 how word frequencies in text follow a Zipfian distribution: a few words occur very often, but a huge number of words occur very infrequently. It turns out that query distributions are similar. Some queries, such as those about popular celebrities or current events, tend to be very popular with public search engines. However, about half of the queries that a search engine receives each day are unique.

This leads us into a discussion of *caching*. Broadly speaking, caching means storing something you might want to use later. With search engines, we usually want to cache ranked result lists for queries, but systems can also cache inverted lists from disk.

Caching is perfectly suited for search engines. Queries and ranked lists are small, meaning it doesn't take much space in a cache to store them. By contrast, processing a query against a large corpus can be very computationally intensive. This means that once a ranked list is computed, it usually makes sense to keep it around.

However, caching does not solve all of our performance problems, because about half of all queries received each day are unique. Therefore, the search engine itself must be built to handle query traffic very quickly. This leads to competition for resources between the search engine and the caching system. Recent research suggests that when memory space is tight, caching should focus on the most popular queries, leaving plenty of room to cache the index. Unique queries with multiple terms may still share a term and use the same inverted list. This explains why inverted list caching can have higher hit rates than query caching. Once the whole index is cached, all remaining resources can be directed toward caching query results.

When using caching systems, it is important to guard against stale data. Caching works because we assume that query results will not change over time, but eventually they do. Cache entries need acceptable timeouts that allow for fresh results. This is easier when dealing with partitioned indexes like the ones we discussed in section 5.6.4. Each cache can be associated with a particular index partition, and when that partition is deleted, the cache can also be deleted. Keep in mind that a system that is built to handle a certain peak throughput with caching enabled will handle a much smaller throughput with caching off. This means that if your system ever needs to destroy its cache, be prepared to have a slow system until the cache becomes suitably populated. If possible, cache flushes should happen at off-peak load times.

References and Further Reading

This chapter contains information about many topics: indexing, query processing, compression, index update, caching, and distribution just to name a few. All these topics are in one chapter to highlight how these components work together.

Because of how interconnected these components are, it is useful to look at studies of real, working systems. Brin and Page (1998) wrote a paper about the early Google system that is an instructive overview of what it takes to build a fully working system. Later papers show how the Google architecture has changed over time—for example Barroso et al. (2003). The MapReduce paper, by Dean and Ghemawat (2008), gives more detail than this chapter does about how MapReduce was developed and how it works in practice.

The inner workings of commercial search engines are often considered trade secrets, so the exact details of how they work is not often published. One important exception is the TodoBR engine, a popular Brazilian web search engine. Before TodoBR was acquired by Google, their engineers frequently published papers about its workings. One example is their paper on a two-level caching scheme (Saraiva et al., 2001), but there are many others.

The book *Managing Gigabytes* (Witten et al., 1999) is the standard reference for index construction, and is particularly detailed in its discussion of compression techniques. Work on compression for inverted lists continues to be an active area of research. One of the recent highlights of this research is the PFOR series of compressors from Zukowski et al. (2006), which exploit the performance characteristics of modern processors to make a scheme that is particularly fast for decompressing small integers. Büttcher and Clarke (2007) did a recent study on how compression schemes compare on the latest hardware.

Zobel and Moffat (2006) wrote a review article that outlines all of the important recent research in inverted indexes, both in index construction and in query processing. This article is the best place to look for an understanding of how this research fits together.

Turtle and Flood (1995) developed the MaxScore series of algorithms. Fagin et al. (2003) took a similar approach with score-sorted inputs, although they did not initially apply their ideas to information retrieval. Anh and Moffat (2006) refined these ideas to make a particularly efficient retrieval system.

Anh and Moffat (2005) and Metzler et al. (2008) cover methods for computing scores that can be stored in inverted lists. In particular, these papers describe how to compute scores that are both useful in retrieval and can be stored compactly in the list. Strohman (2007) explores the entire process of building scored indexes and processing queries efficiently with them.

Many of the algorithms from this chapter are based on merging two sorted inputs; index construction relies on this, as does any kind of document-at-a-time retrieval process. Knuth wrote an entire volume on just sorting and searching, which includes large amounts of material on merging, including disk-based merging (Knuth, 1998). If the Knuth book is too daunting, any standard algorithms textbook should be able to give you more detail about how merging works.

Lester et al. (2005) developed the geometric partitioning method for index update. Büttcher et al. (2006) added some extensions to this model, focusing on how very common terms should be handled during update. Strohman and Croft (2006) show how to update the index without halting query processing.

Exercises

5.1. Section 5.2 introduced an abstract model of ranking, where documents and queries are represented by features. What are some advantages of representing documents and queries by features? What are some disadvantages?

5.2. Our model of ranking contains a ranking function $R(Q, D)$, which compares each document with the query and computes a score. Those scores are then used to determine the final ranked list.

An alternate ranking model might contain a different kind of ranking function, $f(A, B, Q)$, where A and B are two different documents in the collection and Q is the query. When A should be ranked higher than B, $f(A, B, Q)$ evaluates to 1. When A should be ranked below B, $f(A, B, Q)$ evaluates to −1.

If you have a ranking function $R(Q, D)$, show how you can use it in a system that requires one of the form $f(A, B, Q)$. Why can you not go the other way (use $f(A, B, Q)$ in a system that requires $R(Q, D)$)?

5.3. Suppose you build a search engine that uses one hundred computers with a million documents stored on each one, so that you can search a collection of 100 million documents. Would you prefer a ranking function like $R(Q, D)$ or one like $f(A, B, Q)$ (from the previous problem). Why?

5.4. Documents can easily contain thousands of non-zero features. Why is it important that queries have only a few non-zero features?

5.5. Suppose your search engine has just retrieved the top 50 documents from your collection based on scores from a ranking function $R(Q, D)$. Your user interface can show only 10 results, but you can pick any of the top 50 documents to show. Why might you choose to show the user something other than the top 10 documents from the retrieved document set?

5.6. Indexes are not necessary to search documents. Your web browser, for instance, has a Find function in it that searches text without using an index. When should you use an inverted index to search text? What are some advantages to using an inverted index? What are some disadvantages?

5.7. Section 5.3 explains many different ways to store document information in inverted lists. What kind of inverted lists might you build if you needed a very small index? What kind would you build if you needed to find mentions of cities, such as Kansas City or São Paulo?

5.8. Write a program that can build a simple inverted index of a set of text documents. Each inverted list will contain the file names of the documents that contain that word.

Suppose the file A contains the text "the quick brown fox", and file B contains "the slow blue fox". The output of your program would be:

```
% ./your-program A B
blue B
brown A
fox A B
quick A
slow B
the A B
```

5.9. In section 5.4.1, we created an unambiguous compression scheme for 2-bit binary numbers. Find a sequence of numbers that takes up more space when it is "compressed" using our scheme than when it is "uncompressed."

5.10. Suppose a company develops a new unambiguous lossless compression scheme for 2-bit numbers called *SuperShrink*. Its developers claim that it will reduce the size of any sequence of 2-bit numbers by at least 1 bit. Prove that the developers are lying. More specifically, prove that either:

- *SuperShrink* never uses less space than an uncompressed encoding, or

- There is an input to *SuperShrink* such that the compressed version is larger than the uncompressed input

  You can assume that each 2-bit input number is encoded separately.

5.11. Develop an encoder for the Elias-γ code. Verify that your program produces the same codes as in Table 5.2.

5.12. Why do we need to know something about the kind of data we will compress before choosing a compression algorithm? Focus specifically on the result from Exercise 5.10.

5.13. Identify the optimal skip distance k when performing a two-term Boolean AND query where one term occurs 1 million times and the other term appears 100 million times. Assume that a linear search will be used once an appropriate region is found to search in.

5.14. In section 5.7.3, we saw that the optimal skip distance c can be determined by minimizing the quantity $kn/c + pc/2$, where k is the skip pointer length, n is the total inverted list size, c is the skip interval, and p is the number of postings to find.

Plot this function using $k = 4$, $n = 1,000,000$, and $p = 1,000$, but varying c. Then, plot the same function, but set $p = 10,000$. Notice how the optimal value for c changes.

Finally, take the derivative of the function $kn/c + pc/2$ in terms of c to find the optimum value for c for a given set of other parameters (k, n, and p).

5.15. In Chapter 4, you learned about Zipf's law, and how approximately 50% of words found in a collection of documents will occur only once. Your job is to design a program that will verify Zipf's law using MapReduce.

Your program will output a list of number pairs, like this:

```
195840,1
70944,2
34039,3
...
1,333807
```

This sample output indicates that 195,840 words appeared once in the collection, 70,944 appeared twice, and 34,039 appeared three times, but one word appeared 333,807 times. Your program will print this kind of list for a document collection.

Your program will use MapReduce twice (two Map phases and two Reduce phases) to produce this output.

5.16. Write the program described in Exercise 5.15 using the Galago search toolkit. Verify that it works by indexing the Wikipedia collection provided on the book website.

6

Queries and Interfaces

> "This is Information Retrieval, not Information Dispersal."
>
> Jack Lint, *Brazil*

6.1 Information Needs and Queries

Although the index structures and ranking algorithms are key components of a search engine, from the user's point of view the search engine is primarily an interface for specifying queries and examining results. People can't change the way the ranking algorithm works, but they can interact with the system during query formulation and reformulation, and while they are browsing the results. These interactions are a crucial part of the process of information retrieval, and can determine whether the search engine is viewed as providing an effective service. In this chapter, we discuss techniques for *query transformation and refinement*, and for assembling and displaying the *search results*. We also discuss *cross-language search engines* here because they rely heavily on the transformation of queries and results.

In Chapter 1, we described an information need as the motivation for a person using a search engine. There are many types of information needs, and researchers have categorized them using dimensions such as the number of relevant documents being sought, the type of information that is needed, and the tasks that led to the requirement for information. It has also been pointed out that in some cases it can be difficult for people to define exactly what their information need is, because that information is a gap in their knowledge.[1] From the point of view of the search engine designer, there are two important consequences of these observations about information needs:

- Queries can represent very different information needs and may require different search techniques and ranking algorithms to produce the best rankings.

---

[1] This is Belkin's well-known *Anomalous State of Knowledge* (ASK) hypothesis (Belkin et al., 1982/1997).

- A query can be a poor representation of the information need. This can happen because the user finds it difficult to express the information need. More often, however, it happens because the user is encouraged to enter short queries, both by the search engine interface and by the fact that long queries often fail.

The first point is discussed further in Chapter 7. The second point is a major theme in this chapter. We present techniques—such as *spelling correction*, *query expansion*, and *relevance feedback*—that are designed to refine the query, either automatically or through user interaction. The goal of this refinement process is to produce a query that is a better representation of the information need, and consequently to retrieve better documents. On the output side, the way that results are displayed is an important part of helping the user understand whether his information need has been met. We discuss techniques such as *snippet generation*, *result clustering*, and *document highlighting*, that are designed to help this process of understanding the results.

Short queries consisting of a small number of keywords (between two and three on average in most studies of web search) are by far the most popular form of query currently used in search engines. Given that such short queries can be ambiguous and imprecise,[2] why don't people use longer queries? There are a number of reasons for this. In the past, *query languages* for search engines were designed to be used by expert users, or *search intermediaries*. They were called intermediaries because they acted as the interface between the person looking for information and the search engine. These query languages were quite complex. For example, here is a query made up by an intermediary for a search engine that provides legal information:

> *User query:* Are there any cases that discuss negligent maintenance or failure to maintain aids to navigation such as lights, buoys, or channel markers?
>
> *Intermediary query:* NEGLECT! FAIL! NEGLIG! /5 MAINT! REPAIR! /P NAVIGAT! /5 AID EQUIP! LIGHT BUOY "CHANNEL MARKER"

This query language uses *wildcard* operators and various forms of *proximity* operators to specify the information need. A wildcard operator is used to define the minimum string match required for a word to match the query. For example, NEGLECT! will match "neglected", "neglects", or just "neglect". A proximity operator

---

[2] Would you go up to a person and say, "Tropical fish?", or even worse, "Fish?", if you wanted to ask what types of tropical fish were easiest to care for?

is used to define constraints on the distance between words that are required for them to match the query. One type of proximity constraint is adjacency. For example, the quotes around "CHANNEL MARKER" specify that the two words must occur next to each other. The more general window operator specifies a width (in words) of a text window that is allowed for the match. For example, /5 specifies that the words must occur within five words of each other. Other typical proximity operators are sentence and paragraph proximity. For example, /P specifies that the words must occur in the same paragraph. In this query language, if no constraint is specified, it is assumed to be a Boolean OR.

Some of these query language operators are still available in search engine interfaces, such as using quotes for a phrase or a "+" to indicate a mandatory term, but in general there is an emphasis on simple keyword queries (sometimes called "natural language" queries) in order to make it possible for most people to do their own searches.[3] But if we want to make querying as natural as possible, why not encourage people to type in better descriptions of what they are looking for instead of just a couple of keywords? Indeed, in applications where people expect other people to answer their questions, such as the community-based question answering systems described in section 10.3, the average query length goes up to around 30 words. The problem is that current search technology does not do a good job with long queries. Most web search engines, for example, only rank documents that contain all the query terms. If a person enters a query with 30 words in it, the most likely result is that nothing will be found. Even if documents containing all the words can be found, the subtle distinctions of language used in a long, grammatically correct query will often be lost in the results. Search engines use ranking algorithms based primarily on a statistical view of text as a collection of words, not on syntactic and semantic features.

Given what happens to long queries, people have quickly learned that they will get the most reliable results by thinking of a few keywords that are likely to be associated with the information they are looking for, and using these as the query. This places quite a burden on the user, and the query refinement techniques described here are designed to reduce this burden and compensate for poor queries.

---

[3] Note that the search engine may still be using a complex query language (such as that described in section 7.4.2) internally, but not in the interface.

6.2 Query Transformation and Refinement

6.2.1 Stopping and Stemming Revisited

As mentioned in the last section, the most common form of query used in current search engines consists of a small number of keywords. Some of these queries use quotes to indicate a phrase, or a "+" to indicate that a word must be present, but for the remainder of this chapter we will make the simplifying assumption that the query is simply text.[4] The initial stages of processing a text query should mirror the processing steps that are used for documents. Words in the query text must be transformed into the same terms that were produced by document texts, or there will be errors in the ranking. This sounds obvious, but it has been a source of problems in a number of search projects. Despite this restriction, there is scope for some useful differences between query and document transformation, particularly in stopping and stemming. Other steps, such as parsing the structure or tokenizing, will either not be needed (keyword queries have no structure) or will be essentially the same.

We mentioned in section 4.3.3 that stopword removal can be done at query time instead of during document indexing. Retaining the stopwords in the indexes increases the flexibility of the system to deal with queries that contain stopwords. Stopwords can be treated as normal words (by leaving them in the query), removed, or removed except under certain conditions (such as being used with quote or "+" operators).

Query-based stemming is another technique for increasing the flexibility of the search engine. If the words in documents are stemmed during indexing, the words in the queries must also be stemmed. There are circumstances, however, where stemming the query words will reduce the accuracy of the results. The query "fish village" will, for example, produce very different results from the query "fishing village", but many stemming algorithms would reduce "fishing" to "fish". By not stemming during document indexing, we are able to make the decision at query time whether or not to stem "fishing". This decision could be based on a number of factors, such as whether the word was part of a quoted phrase.

For query-based stemming to work, we must expand the query using the appropriate word variants, rather than reducing the query word to a word stem. This is because documents have not been stemmed. If the query word "fishing" was re-

---

[4] Based on a recent sample of web queries, about 1.5% of queries used quotes, and less than 0.5% used a "+" operator.

placed with the stem "fish", the query would no longer match documents that contained "fishing". Instead, the query should be expanded to include the word "fish". This expansion is done by the system (not the user) using some form of synonym operator, such as that described in section 7.4.2. Alternatively, we could index the documents using stems *as well as* words. This will make query execution more efficient, but increases the size of the indexes.

Every stemming algorithm implicitly generates *stem classes*. A stem class is the group of words that will be transformed into the same stem by the stemming algorithm. They are created by simply running the stemming algorithm on a large collection of text and recording which words map to a given stem. Stem classes can be quite large. For example, here are three stem classes created with the Porter Stemmer on TREC news collections (the first entry in each list is the stem):

```
/bank banked banking bankings banks
/ocean oceaneering oceanic oceanics oceanization oceans
/polic polical polically police policeable policed
-policement policer policers polices policial
-policically policier policiers policies policing
-policization policize policly policy policying policys
```

These classes are not only long (the "polic" class has 22 entries), but they also contain a number of errors. The words relating to "police" and "policy" should not be in the same class, and this will cause a loss in ranking accuracy. Other words are not errors, but may be used in different contexts. For example, "banked" is more often used in discussions of flying and pool, but this stem class will add words that are more common in financial discussions. The length of the lists is an issue if the stem classes are used to expand the query. Adding 22 words to a simple query will certainly negatively impact response time and, if not done properly using a synonym operator, could cause the search to fail.

Both of these issues can be addressed using an analysis of word co-occurrence in the collection of text. The assumption behind this analysis is that word variants that could be substitutes for each other should co-occur often in documents. More specifically, we do the following steps:

1. For all pairs of words in the stem classes, count how often they co-occur in text windows of W words. W is typically in the range 50–100.
2. Compute a co-occurrence or *association* metric for each pair. This measures how strong the association is between the words.

3. Construct a graph where the vertices represent words and the edges are between words whose co-occurrence metric is above a threshold T.

4. Find the *connected components* of this graph. These are the new stem classes.

The *term association measure* used in TREC experiments was based on *Dice's coefficient*. This measure has been used since the earliest studies of term similarity and automatic thesaurus construction in the 1960s and 1970s. If n_a is the number of windows (or documents) containing word a, n_b is the number of windows containing word b, n_{ab} is the number of windows containing both words a and b, and N is the number of text windows in the collection, then Dice's coefficient is defined as $2 \cdot n_{ab}/(n_a + n_b)$. This is simply the proportion of term occurrences that are co-occurrences. There are other possible association measures, which will be discussed later in section 6.2.3.

Two vertices are in the same connected component of a graph if there is a path between them. In the case of the graph representing word associations, the connected components will be *clusters* or groups of words, where each word has an association above the threshold T with at least one other member of the cluster. The parameter T is set empirically. We will discuss this and other clustering techniques in section 9.2.

Applying this technique to the three example stem classes, and using TREC data to do the co-occurrence analysis, results in the following connected components:

/policies policy
/police policed policing
/bank banking banks

The new stem classes are smaller, and the inappropriate groupings (e.g., policy/police) have been split up. In general, experiments show that this technique produces good ranking effectiveness with a moderate level of query expansion.

What about the "fishing village" query? The relevant stem class produced by the co-occurrence analysis is

/fish fished fishing

which means that we have not solved that problem. As mentioned before, the query context determines whether stemming is appropriate. It would be reasonable to expand the query "fishing in Alaska" with the words "fish" and "fished", but not the query "fishing village". The co-occurrence analysis described earlier uses context in a general way, but not at the level of co-occurrence with specific query words.

With the recent availability of large query logs in applications such as web search, the concept of validating or even generating stem classes through statistical analysis can be extended to these resources. In this case, the analysis would look for word variants that tended to co-occur with the same words in queries. This could be a solution to the fish/fishing problem, in that "fish" is unlikely to co-occur with "village" in queries.

Comparing this stemming technique to those described in section 4.3.4, it could be described as a dictionary-based approach, where the dictionary is generated automatically based on input from an algorithmic stemmer (i.e., the stem classes). This technique can also be used for stemming with languages that do not have algorithmic stemmers available. In that case, the stem classes are based on very simple criteria, such as grouping all words that have similar n-grams. A simple example would be to generate classes from words that have the same first three characters. These initial classes are much larger than those generated by an algorithmic stemmer, but the co-occurrence analysis reduces the final classes to similar sizes. Retrieval experiments confirm that typically there is little difference in ranking effectiveness between an algorithmic stemmer and a stemmer based on n-gram classes.

6.2.2 Spell Checking and Suggestions

Spell checking is an extremely important part of query processing. Approximately 10–15% of queries submitted to web search engines contain spelling errors, and people have come to rely on the "Did you mean: ..." feature to correct these errors. Query logs contain plenty of examples of simple errors such as the following (taken from a recent sample of web queries):

poiner sisters
brimingham news
catamarn sailing
hair extenssions
marshmellow world
miniture golf courses
psyhics
home doceration

These errors are similar to those that may be found in a word processing document. In addition, however, there will be *many* queries containing words related to websites, products, companies, and people that are unlikely to be found in any standard spelling dictionary. Some examples from the same query log are:

    realstateisting.bc.com
    akia 1080i manunal
    ultimatwarcade
    mainscourcebank
    dellottitouche

The wide variety in the type and severity of possible spelling errors in queries presents a significant challenge. In order to discuss which spelling correction techniques are the most effective for search engine queries, we first have to review how spelling correction is done for general text.

The basic approach used in many spelling checkers is to suggest corrections for words that are not found in the *spelling dictionary*. Suggestions are found by comparing the word that was not found in the dictionary to words that are in the dictionary using a similarity measure. The most common measure for comparing words (or more generally, strings) is the *edit distance*, which is the number of operations required to transform one of the words into the other. The *Damerau-Levenshtein distance* metric counts the minimum number of insertions, deletions, substitutions, or transpositions of single characters required to do the transformation.[5] Studies have shown that 80% or more of spelling errors are caused by an instance of one of these types of single-character errors.

As an example, the following transformations (shown with the type of error involved) all have Damerau-Levenshtein distance 1 since only a single operation or edit is required to produce the correct word:

    extenssions $\rightarrow$ extensions (insertion error)
    poiner $\rightarrow$ pointer (deletion error)
    marshmellow $\rightarrow$ marshmallow (substitution error)
    brimingham $\rightarrow$ birmingham (transposition error)

The transformation doceration $\rightarrow$ decoration, on the other hand, has edit distance 2 since it requires two edit operations:

---

[5] The *Levenshtein distance* is similar but does not include transposition as a basic operation.

doceration → deceration
deceration → decoration

A variety of techniques and data structures have been used to speed up the calculation of edit distances between the misspelled word and the words in the dictionary. These include restricting the comparison to words that start with the same letter (since spelling errors rarely change the first letter), words that are of the same or similar length (since spelling errors rarely change the length of the word), and words that sound the same.[6] In the latter case, phonetic rules are used to map words to codes. Words with the same codes are considered as possible corrections. The *Soundex* code is a simple type of phonetic encoding that was originally used for the problem of matching names in medical records. The rules for this encoding are:

1. Keep the first letter (in uppercase).
2. Replace these letters with hyphens: a, e, i, o, u, y, h, w.
3. Replace the other letters by numbers as follows:
   1: b, f, p, v
   2: c, g, j, k, q, s, x, z
   3: d, t
   4: l
   5: m, n
   6: r
4. Delete adjacent repeats of a number.
5. Delete the hyphens.
6. Keep the first three numbers or pad out with zeros.

Some examples of this code are:

extenssions → E235; extensions → E235
marshmellow → M625; marshmallow → M625
brimingham → B655; birmingham → B655
poiner → P560; pointer → P536

The last example shows that the correct word may not always have the same Soundex code. More elaborate phonetic encodings have been developed specifically for spelling correction (e.g., the GNU Aspell checker[7] uses a phonetic code).

---

[6] A word that is pronounced the same as another word but differs in meaning is called a *homophone*.

[7] http://aspell.net/

These encodings can be designed so that the edit distance for the *codes* can be used to narrow the search for corrections.

A given spelling error may have many possible corrections. For example, the spelling error "lawers" has the following possible corrections (among others) at edit distance 1: lawers → lowers, lawyers, layers, lasers, lagers. The spelling corrector has to decide whether to present all of these to the user, and in what order to present them. A typical policy would be to present them in decreasing order of their frequency in the language. Note that this process ignores the context of the spelling error. For example, if the error occurred in the query "trial lawers", this would have *no* impact on the presentation order of the suggested corrections. The lack of context in the spelling correction process also means that errors involving valid words will be missed. For example, the query "miniature golf curses" is clearly an example of a single-character deletion error, but this error has produced the valid word "curses" and so would not be detected.

The typical interface for the "Did you mean:..." feature requires the spell checker to produce the single best suggestion. This means that ranking the suggestions using context and frequency information is very important for query spell checking compared to spell checking in a word processor, where suggestions can be made available on a pull-down list. In addition, queries contain a large number of *run-on* errors, where word boundaries are skipped or mistyped. The two queries "ultimatwarcade" and "mainscourcebank" are examples of run-on errors that also contain single-character errors. With the appropriate framework, leaving out a separator such as a blank can be treated as just another class of single-character error.

The *noisy channel model* for spelling correction is a general framework that can address the issues of ranking, context, and run-on errors. The model is called a "noisy channel" because it is based on Shannon's theory of communication (Shannon & Weaver, 1963). The intuition is that a person chooses a word w to output (i.e., write), based on a probability distribution $P(w)$. The person then tries to write the word w, but the noisy channel (presumably the person's brain) causes the person to write the word e instead, with probability $P(e|w)$.

The probabilities $P(w)$, called the *language model*, capture information about the frequency of occurrence of a word in text (e.g., what is the probability of the word "lawyer" occurring in a document or query?), and contextual information such as the probability of observing a word given that another word has just been observed (e.g., what is the probability of "lawyer" following the word "trial"?). We will have more to say about language models in Chapter 7, but for now we can just assume it is a description of word occurrences in terms of probabilities.

The probabilities $P(e|w)$, called the *error model*, represent information about the frequency of different types of spelling errors. The probabilities for words (or strings) that are edit distance 1 away from the word w will be quite high, for example. Words with higher edit distances will generally have lower probabilities, although homophones will have high probabilities. Note that the error model will have probabilities for writing the correct word ($P(w|w)$) as well as probabilities for spelling errors. This enables the spelling corrector to suggest a correction for all words, even if the original word was correctly spelled. If the highest-probability correction is the same word, then no correction is suggested to the user. If, however, the context (i.e., the language model) suggests that another word may be more appropriate, then it can be suggested. This, in broad terms, is how a spelling corrector can suggest "course" instead of "curse" for the query "golf curse".

So how do we estimate the probability of a correction? What the person writes is the word e, so we need to calculate $P(w|e)$, which is the probability that the correct word is w given that we can see the person wrote e. If we are interested in finding the correction with the maximum value of this probability, or if we just want to rank the corrections, it turns out we can use $P(e|w)P(w)$, which is the product of the error model probability and the language model probability.[8]

To handle run-on errors and context, the language model needs to have information about pairs of words in addition to single words. The language model probability for a word is then calculated as a *mixture* of the probability that the word occurs in text and the probability that it occurs following the previous word, or

$$\lambda P(w) + (1 - \lambda)P(w|w_p)$$

where λ is a *parameter* that specifies the relative importance of the two probabilities, and $P(w|w_p)$ is the probability of a word w following the previous word w_p. As an example, consider the spelling error "fish tink". To rank the possible corrections for "tink", we multiply the error model probabilities for possible corrections by the language model probabilities for those corrections. The words "tank" and "think" will both have high error-model probabilities since they require only a single character correction. In addition, both words will have similar probabilities for $P(w)$ since both are quite common. The probability $P(tank|fish)$, however,

---

[8] *Bayes' Rule*, which is discussed in Chapter 7, is used to express $P(w|e)$ in terms of the component probabilities.

will be much higher than $P(think|fish)$, and this will result in "tank" being a more likely correction than "think".

Where does the information for the language model probabilities come from? In many applications, the best source for statistics about word occurrence in text will be the collection of documents that is being searched. In the case of web search (and some other applications), there will also be a query log containing millions of queries submitted to the search engine. Since our task is to correct the spelling of queries, the query log is likely to be the best source of information. It also reduces the number of pairs of words that need to be recorded in the language model, compared to analyzing all possible pairs in a large collection of documents. In addition to these sources, if a trusted dictionary is available for the application, it should be used.

The estimation of the $P(e|w)$ probabilities in the error model can be relatively simple or quite complex. The simple approach is to assume that all errors with the same edit distance have equal probability. Additionally, only strings within a certain edit distance (usually 1 or 2) are considered. More sophisticated approaches have been suggested that base the probability estimates on the likelihood of making certain types of errors, such as typing an "a" when the intention was to type an "e". These estimates are derived from large collections of text by finding many pairs of correctly and incorrectly spelled words.

Cucerzan and Brill (2004) describe an iterative process for spell checking queries using information from a query log and dictionary. The steps, in simplified form, are as follows:

1. Tokenize the query.
2. For each token, a set of alternative words and pairs of words is found using an edit distance modified by weighting certain types of errors, as described earlier. The data structure that is searched for the alternatives contains words and pairs from both the query log and the trusted dictionary.
3. The noisy channel model is then used to select the best correction.
4. The process of looking for alternatives and finding the best correction is repeated until no better correction is found.

By having multiple iterations, the spelling corrector can potentially make suggestions that are quite far (in terms of edit distance) from the original query. As an example, given the query "miniture golfcurses", the spelling corrector would go through the following iterations:

    miniture golfcurses
    miniature golfcourses
    miniature golf courses

Experiments with this spelling corrector show that the language model from the query log is the most important component in terms of correction accuracy. In addition, using context in the form of word pairs in the language model is critical. Having at least two iterations in the correction process also makes a significant difference. The error model was less important, however, and using a simple model where all errors have the same probability was nearly as effective as the more sophisticated model. Other studies of have shown that the error model is more important when the language model is based just on the collection of documents, rather than the query log.

The best approach to building a spelling corrector for queries in a search application obviously depends on the data available. If a large amount of query log information is available, then this should be incorporated. Otherwise, the sources available will be the collection of documents for the application and, in some cases, a trusted dictionary. One approach would be to use a general-purpose spelling corrector, such as Aspell, and create an application-specific dictionary. Building a spelling corrector based on the noisy channel model, however, is likely to be more effective and more adaptable, even if query log data is not available.

6.2.3 Query Expansion

In the early development of search engines, starting in the 1960s, an online *thesaurus* was considered an essential tool for the users of the system. The thesaurus described the indexing vocabulary that had been used for the document collection, and included information about synonyms and related words or phrases. This was particularly important because the collection had typically been manually indexed (tagged)[9] using the terms in the thesaurus. Because the terms in the thesaurus were carefully chosen and subject to quality control, the thesaurus was also referred to as a *controlled vocabulary*. Using the thesaurus, users could determine what words and phrases could be used in queries, and could *expand* an initial query using synonyms and related words. Table 6.1 shows part of an entry in

---

[9] In information retrieval, *indexing* is often used to refer to the process of representing a document using an index term, in addition to the process of creating the indexes to search the collection. More recently, the process of manual indexing has been called *tagging*, particularly in the context of social search applications (see Chapter 10).

the Medical Subject (MeSH) Headings thesaurus that is used in the National Library of Medicine search applications.[10] The "tree number" entries indicate, using a numbering scheme, where this term is found in the tree of broader and narrow terms. An "entry term" is a synonym or related phrase for the term.

MeSH Heading	Neck Pain
Tree Number	C10.597.617.576
Tree Number	C23.888.592.612.553
Tree Number	C23.888.646.501
Entry Term	Cervical Pain
Entry Term	Neckache
Entry Term	Anterior Cervical Pain
Entry Term	Anterior Neck Pain
Entry Term	Cervicalgia
Entry Term	Cervicodynia
Entry Term	Neck Ache
Entry Term	Posterior Cervical Pain
Entry Term	Posterior Neck Pain

Table 6.1. Partial entry for the Medical Subject (MeSH) Heading "Neck Pain"

Although the use of an explicit thesaurus is less common in current search applications, a number of techniques have been proposed for automatic and *semi-automatic* query expansion. A semi-automatic technique requires user interaction, such as selecting the expansion terms from a list suggested by the expansion technique. Web search engines, for example, provide query suggestions to the user in the form of the original query words expanded with one or more additional words, or replaced with alternative words.

Query expansion techniques are usually based on an analysis of word or term co-occurrence, in either the entire document collection, a large collection of queries, or the top-ranked documents in a result list. From this perspective, query-based stemming can also be regarded as a query expansion technique, with the expansion terms limited to word variants. Automatic expansion techniques that use a general thesaurus, such as Wordnet,[11] have not been shown to be effective.

---

[10] http://www.nlm.nih.gov/mesh/meshhome.html
[11] http://wordnet.princeton.edu/

The key to effective expansion is to choose words that are appropriate for the *context*, or topic, of the query. For example, "aquarium" may be a good expansion term for "tank" in the query "tropical fish tanks", but not appropriate for the query "armor for tanks". A general thesaurus lists related terms for many different contexts, which is why it is difficult to use automatically. The techniques we will describe use a variety of approaches to address this problem, such as using *all* the words in a query to find related words rather than expanding each word separately. One well-known expansion technique, called *pseudo-relevance feedback*, is discussed in the next section along with techniques that are based on user feedback about the relevance of documents in the results list.

Term association measures are an important part of many approaches to query expansion, and consequently a number of alternatives have been suggested. One of these, Dice's coefficient, was mentioned in section 6.2.1. The formula for this measure is

$$\frac{2 \cdot n_{ab}}{n_a + n_b} \overset{rank}{=} \frac{n_{ab}}{n_a + n_b}$$

where $\overset{rank}{=}$ means that the formula is *rank equivalent* (produces the same ranking of terms).[12]

Another measure, *mutual information*, has been used in a number of studies of word *collocation*. For two words (or terms) a and b, it is defined as

$$\log \frac{P(a,b)}{P(a)P(b)}$$

and measures the extent to which the words occur independently.[13] $P(a)$ is the probability that word a occurs in a text window of a given size, $P(b)$ is the probability that word b occurs in a text window, and $P(a,b)$ is the probability that a and b occur in the same text window. If the occurrences of the words are independent, $P(a,b) = P(a)P(b)$ and the mutual information will be 0. As an example, we might expect that the two words "fishing" and "automobile" would occur relatively independently of one another. If two words tend to co-occur, for

---

[12] More formally, two functions are defined to be rank equivalent if they produce the same ordering of items when sorted according to function value. Monotonic transforms (such as log), scaling (multiplying by a constant), and translation (adding a constant) are all examples of rank-preserving operations.

[13] This is actually the *pointwise* mutual information measure, just to be completely accurate.

example "fishing" and "boat", $P(a, b)$ will be greater than $P(a)P(b)$ and the mutual information will be higher.

To calculate mutual information, we use the following simple normalized frequency estimates for the probabilities: $P(a) = n_a/N$, $P(b) = n_b/N$, and $P(a, b) = n_{ab}/N$, where n_a is the number of windows (or documents) containing word a, n_b is the number of windows containing word b, n_{ab} is the number of windows containing both words a and b, and N is the number of text windows in the collection. This gives the formula:

$$\log \frac{P(a, b)}{P(a)P(b)} = \log N. \frac{n_{ab}}{n_a.n_b} \overset{rank}{=} \frac{n_{ab}}{n_a.n_b}$$

A problem that has been observed with this measure is that it tends to favor low-frequency terms. For example, consider two words with frequency 10 (i.e., $n_a = n_b = 10$) that co-occur half the time ($n_{ab} = 5$). The association measure for these two terms is 5×10^{-2}. For two terms with frequency 1,000 that co-occur half the time ($n_{ab} = 500$), the association measure is 5×10^{-4}. The *expected mutual information measure* addresses this problem by weighting the mutual information value using the probability $P(a, b)$. Although the expected mutual information in general is calculated over all combinations of the events of word occurrence and non-occurrence, we are primarily interested in the case where both terms occur, giving the formula:

$$P(a, b). \log \frac{P(a, b)}{P(a)P(b)} = \frac{n_{ab}}{N} \log(N. \frac{n_{ab}}{n_a.n_b}) \overset{rank}{=} n_{ab}. \log(N. \frac{n_{ab}}{n_a.n_b})$$

If we take the same example as before and assume $N = 10^6$, this gives an association measure of 23.5 for the low-frequency terms, and 1,350 for the high-frequency terms, clearly favoring the latter case. In fact, the bias toward high-frequency terms can be a problem for this measure.

Another popular association measure that has been used in a variety of applications is *Pearson's Chi-squared (χ^2) measure*. This measure compares the number of co-occurrences of two words with the expected number of co-occurrences if the two words were independent, and normalizes this comparison by the expected number. Using our estimates, this gives the formula:

$$\frac{(n_{ab} - N. \frac{n_a}{N}. \frac{n_b}{N})^2}{N. \frac{n_a}{N}. \frac{n_b}{N}} \overset{rank}{=} \frac{(n_{ab} - \frac{1}{N}.n_a.n_b)^2}{n_a.n_b}$$

The term $N.P(a).P(b) = N.\frac{n_a}{N}.\frac{n_b}{N}$ is the expected number of co-occurrences if the two terms occur independently. The χ^2 test is usually calculated over all combinations of the events of word occurrence and non-occurrence, similar to the expected mutual information measure, but our focus is on the case where both terms co-occur. In fact, when N is large, this restricted form of χ^2 produces the same term rankings as the full form. It should also be noted that χ^2 is very similar to the mutual information measure and may be expected to favor low-frequency terms.

Table 6.2 summarizes the association measures we have discussed. To see how they work in practice, we have calculated the top-ranked terms in a TREC news collection using each measure for the words in the sample query "tropical fish".

Measure	Formula
Mutual information (MIM)	$\frac{n_{ab}}{n_a.n_b}$
Expected Mutual Information $(EMIM)$	$n_{ab}.\log(N.\frac{n_{ab}}{n_a.n_b})$
Chi-square (χ^2)	$\frac{(n_{ab}-\frac{1}{N}.n_a.n_b)^2}{n_a.n_b}$
Dice's coefficient $(Dice)$	$\frac{n_{ab}}{n_a+n_b}$

Table 6.2. Term association measures

Table 6.3 shows the strongly associated words for "tropical" assuming an unlimited window size (in other words, co-occurrences are counted at the document level). There are two obvious features to note. The first is that the ranking for χ^2 is identical to the one for MIM. The second is that MIM and χ^2 favor low-frequency words, as expected. These words are not unreasonable ("itto", for example, is the International Tropical Timber Organization, and "xishuangbanna" is a Chinese tropical botanic garden), but they are so specialized that they are unlikely to be much use for many queries. The top terms for the $EMIM$ and $Dice$ measures are much more general and, in the case of $EMIM$, sometimes too general (e.g., "most").

Table 6.4 shows the top-ranked words for "fish". Note that because this is a higher-frequency term, the rankings for MIM and χ^2 are no longer identical, although both still favor low-frequency terms. The top-ranked words for $EMIM$

MIM	$EMIM$	χ^2	$Dice$
trmm	forest	trmm	forest
itto	tree	itto	exotic
ortuno	rain	ortuno	timber
kuroshio	island	kuroshio	rain
ivirgarzama	like	ivirgarzama	banana
biofunction	fish	biofunction	deforestation
kapiolani	most	kapiolani	plantation
bstilla	water	bstilla	coconut
almagreb	fruit	almagreb	jungle
jackfruit	area	jackfruit	tree
adeo	world	adeo	rainforest
xishuangbanna	america	xishuangbanna	palm
frangipani	some	frangipani	hardwood
yuca	live	yuca	greenhouse
anthurium	plant	anthurium	logging

Table 6.3. Most strongly associated words for "tropical" in a collection of TREC news stories. Co-occurrence counts are measured at the document level.

and *Dice* are quite similar, although in different ordering. To show the effect of changing the window size, Table 6.5 gives the top-ranked words found using a window of five words. The small window size has an effect on the results, although both *MIM* and χ^2 still find low-frequency terms. The words for *EMIM* are somewhat improved, being more specific. Overall, it appears that the simple Dice's coefficient is the most stable and reliable over a range of window sizes.

The most significant feature of these tables, however, is that even the best rankings contain virtually nothing that would be useful to expand the query "tropical fish"! Instead, the words are associated with other contexts, such as tropical forests and fruits, or fishing conservation. One way to address this problem would be to find words that are strongly associated with the phrase "tropical fish". Using Dice's coefficient with the same collection of TREC documents as the previous tables, this produces the following 10 words at the top of the ranking:

goldfish, reptile, aquarium, coral, frog, exotic, stripe, regent, pet, wet

Clearly, this is doing much better at finding words associated with the right context. To use this technique, however, we would have to find associations for every group of words that could be used in a query. This is obviously impractical, but

MIM	EMIM	χ^2	Dice
zoologico	water	arlsq	species
zapanta	species	happyman	wildlife
wrint	wildlife	outerlimit	fishery
wpfmc	fishery	sportk	water
weighout	sea	lingcod	fisherman
waterdog	fisherman	longfin	boat
longfin	boat	bontadelli	sea
veracruzana	area	sportfisher	habitat
ungutt	habitat	billfish	vessel
ulocentra	vessel	needlefish	marine
needlefish	marine	damaliscu	endanger
tunaboat	land	bontebok	conservation
tsolwana	river	taucher	river
olivacea	food	orangemouth	catch
motoroller	endanger	sheepshead	island

Table 6.4. Most strongly associated words for "fish" in a collection of TREC news stories. Co-occurrence counts are measured at the document level.

MIM	EMIM	χ^2	Dice
zapanta	wildlife	gefilte	wildlife
plar	vessel	mbmo	vessel
mbmo	boat	zapanta	boat
gefilte	fishery	plar	fishery
hapc	species	hapc	species
odfw	tuna	odfw	catch
southpoint	trout	southpoint	water
anadromous	fisherman	anadromous	sea
taiffe	salmon	taiffe	meat
mollie	catch	mollie	interior
frampton	nmf	frampton	fisherman
idfg	trawl	idfg	game
billingsgate	halibut	billingsgate	salmon
sealord	meat	sealord	tuna
longline	shellfish	longline	caught

Table 6.5. Most strongly associated words for "fish" in a collection of TREC news stories. Co-occurrence counts are measured in windows of five words.

there are other approaches that accomplish the same thing. One alternative would be to analyze the word occurrences in the retrieved documents for a query. This is the basis of pseudo-relevance feedback, which is discussed in the next section. Another approach that has been suggested is to index every word in the collection by the words that co-occur with it, creating a virtual document[14] representing that word. For example, the following list is the top 35 most strongly associated words for "aquarium" (using Dice's coefficient):

> zoology, cranmore, jouett, zoo, goldfish, fish, cannery, urchin, reptile, coral, animal, mollusk, marine, underwater, plankton, mussel, oceanography, mammal, species, exhibit, swim, biologist, cabrillo, saltwater, creature, reef, whale, oceanic, scuba, kelp, invertebrate, park, crustacean, wild, tropical

These words would form the index terms for the document representing "aquarium". To find expansion words for a query, these virtual documents are ranked in the same way as regular documents, giving a ranking for the corresponding words. In our example, the document for "aquarium" contains the words "tropical" and "fish" with high weights, so it is likely that it would be highly ranked for the query "tropical fish". This means that "aquarium" would be a highly ranked expansion term. The document for a word such as "jungle", on the other hand, would contain "tropical" with a high weight but is unlikely to contain "fish". This document, and the corresponding word, would be much further down the ranking than "aquarium".

All of the techniques that rely on analyzing the document collection face both computational and accuracy challenges due to the huge size and variability in quality of the collections in search applications. At the start of this section, it was mentioned that instead of analyzing the document collection, either the result list or a large collection of queries could be used. Recent studies and experience indicate that a large query log is probably the best resource for query expansion. Not only do these logs contain many short pieces of text that are are easier to analyze than full text documents, they also contain other data, such as information on which documents were clicked on during the search (i.e., *clickthrough* data).

As an example of how the query log can be used for expansion, the following list shows the 10 most frequent words associated with queries that contain "tropical fish" in a recent query log sample from a popular web search engine:

---

[14] Sometimes called a *context vector*.

stores, pictures, live, sale, types, clipart, blue, freshwater, aquarium, supplies

These words indicate the types of queries that people tend to submit about tropical fish (sales, supplies, pictures), and most would be good words to suggest for query expansion. In current systems, suggestions are usually made in the form of whole queries rather than expansion words, and here again the query log will be extremely useful in producing the best suggestions. For example, "tropical fish supplies" will be a much more common query than "supplies tropical fish" and would be a better suggestion for this expansion.

From this perspective, query expansion can be reformulated as a problem of finding similar queries, rather than expansion terms. Similar queries may not always contain the same words. For example, the query "pet fish sales" may be a reasonable suggestion as an alternative to "tropical fish", even though it doesn't contain the word "tropical". It has long been recognized that semantically similar queries can be found by grouping them based on the relevant documents they have in common, rather than just the words. Clickthrough data is very similar to relevance data, and recent studies have shown that queries can be successfully grouped or clustered based on the similarity of their clickthrough data. This means that every query is represented using the set of pages that are clicked on for that query, and the similarity between the queries is calculated using a measure such as Dice's coefficient, except that in this case n_{ab} will be the number of clicked-on pages the two queries have in common, and n_a, n_b are the number of pages clicked on for each query.

In summary, both automatic and semi-automatic query expansion methods have been proposed, although the default in many search applications is to suggest alternative queries to the user. Some term association measures are better than others, but term association based on single words does not produce good expansion terms, because it does not capture the context of the query. The best way to capture query context is to use a query log, both to analyze word associations and to find similar queries based on clickthrough data. If there is no query log available, the best alternative would be to use pseudo-relevance feedback, as described in the next section. Of the methods described for constructing an automatic thesaurus based on the document collection, the best alternative is to create virtual documents for each word and rank them for each query.

6.2.4 Relevance Feedback

Relevance feedback is a query expansion and refinement technique with a long history. First proposed in the 1960s, it relies on user interaction to identify relevant documents in a ranking based on the initial query. Other semi-automatic techniques were discussed in the last section, but instead of choosing from lists of terms or alternative queries, in relevance feedback the user indicates which documents are interesting (i.e., relevant) and possibly which documents are completely off-topic (i.e., non-relevant). Based on this information, the system automatically reformulates the query by adding terms and reweighting the original terms, and a new ranking is generated using this modified query.

This process is a simple example of using *machine learning* in information retrieval, where *training data* (the identified relevant and non-relevant documents) is used to improve the system's performance. Modifying the query is in fact equivalent to learning a classifier that distinguishes between relevant and non-relevant documents. We discuss classification and classification techniques further in Chapters 7 and 9. Relative to many other applications of machine learning, however, the amount of training data generated in relevance feedback is extremely limited since it is based on the user's input for this query session only, and not on historical data such as clickthrough.

The specific method for modifying the query depends on the underlying retrieval model. In the next chapter, we describe how relevance feedback works in the vector space model and the probabilistic model. In general, however, words that occur more frequently in the relevant documents than in the non-relevant documents, or in the collection as a whole, are added to the query or increased in weight. The same general idea is used in the technique of *pseudo-relevance feedback*, where instead of asking the user to identify relevant documents, the system simply *assumes* that the top-ranked documents are relevant. Words that occur frequently in these documents may then be used to expand the initial query. Once again, the specifics of how this is done depend on the underlying retrieval model. We describe pseudo-relevance feedback based on the language model approach to retrieval in the next chapter. The expansion terms generated by pseudo-relevance feedback will depend on the whole query, since they are extracted from documents ranked highly for that query, but the quality of the expansion will be determined by how many of the top-ranked documents in the initial ranking are in fact relevant.

As a simple example of how this process works, consider the ranking shown in Figure 6.1, which was generated using a popular search engine with the query

1. Badmans **Tropical Fish**

   A freshwater aquarium page covering all aspects of the **tropical fish** hobby. ... to Badman's **Tropical Fish**. ... world of aquariology with Badman's **Tropical Fish**. ...

2. **Tropical Fish**

   Notes on a few species and a gallery of photos of African cichlids.

3. The **Tropical** Tank Homepage - **Tropical Fish** and Aquariums

   Info on **tropical fish** and **tropical** aquariums, large **fish** species index with ... Here you will find lots of information on **Tropical Fish** and Aquariums. ...

4. **Tropical Fish** Centre

   Offers a range of aquarium products, advice on choosing species, feeding, and health care, and a discussion board.

5. **Tropical fish** - Wikipedia, the free encyclopedia

   Tropical fish are popular aquarium **fish** , due to their often bright coloration. ... Practical Fishkeeping • **Tropical Fish** Hobbyist • Koi. Aquarium related companies: ...

6. **Tropical Fish** Find

   Home page for **Tropical Fish** Internet Directory ... stores, forums, clubs, **fish** facts, **tropical fish** compatibility and aquarium ...

7. Breeding **tropical fish**

   ... intrested in keeping and/or breeding **Tropical**, Marine, Pond and Coldwater **fish**. ... Breeding **Tropical Fish** ... breeding **tropical**, marine, coldwater & pond **fish**. ...

8. FishLore

   Includes **tropical** freshwater aquarium how-to guides, FAQs, **fish** profiles, articles, and forums.

9. Cathy's **Tropical Fish** Keeping

   Information on setting up and maintaining a successful freshwater aquarium.

10. **Tropical Fish** Place

    Tropical Fish information for your freshwater **fish** tank ... great amount of information about a great hobby, a freshwater **tropical fish** tank. ...

Fig. 6.1. Top ten results for the query "tropical fish"

"tropical fish". To expand this query using pseudo-relevance feedback, we might assume that all these top 10 documents were relevant. By analyzing the full text of these documents, the most frequent terms, with their frequencies, can be identified as:

a (926), td (535), href (495), http (357), width (345), com (343), nbsp (316), www (260), tr (239), htm (233), class (225), jpg (221)

Clearly, these words are not appropriate to use as expansion terms, because they consist of stopwords and HTML expressions that will be common in the whole collection. In other words, they do not represent the topics covered in the top-ranked documents. A simple way to refine this process is to count words in the snippets of the documents and ignore stopwords. This analysis produces the following list of frequent words:

> tropical (26), fish (28), aquarium (8), freshwater (5), breeding (4), information (3), species (3), tank (2), Badman's (2), page (2), hobby (2), forums (2)

These words are much better candidates for query expansion, and do not have the problem of inadequate context that occurs when we try to expand "tropical" and "fish" separately. If the user was, however, specifically interested in breeding tropical fish, the expansion terms could be improved using true relevance feedback, where the document ranked seventh would be explicitly tagged as relevant. In this case, the most frequent terms are:

> breeding (4), fish (4), tropical (4), marine (2), pond (2), coldwater (2), keeping (1), interested (1)

The major effect of using this list would be to increase the weight of the expansion term "breeding". The specific weighting, as we have said, depends on the underlying retrieval model.

Both relevance feedback and pseudo-relevance feedback have been extensively investigated in the research literature, and have been shown to be effective techniques for improving ranking. They are, however, seldom incorporated into operational search applications. In the case of pseudo-relevance feedback, this appears to be primarily because the results of this automatic process can be unpredictable. If the initial ranking does not contain many relevant documents, the expansion terms found by pseudo-relevance feedback are unlikely to be helpful and, for some queries, can make the ranking significantly worse. To avoid this, the candidate expansion terms could be shown to the user, but studies have shown that this is not particularly effective. Suggesting alternative queries based on an analysis of query logs is a more reliable alternative for semi-automatic query expansion.

Relevance feedback, on the other hand, has been used in some applications, such as document filtering. Filtering involves tracking a person's interests over time, and some applications allow people to modify their profiles using relevance feedback. Another simple use of relevance feedback is the "more like this" feature in some early web search engines. This feature allowed users to click on a link associated with each document in a result list in order to generate a ranked list of other documents similar to the clicked-on document. The new ranked list of documents was based on a query formed by extracting and weighting important words from the clicked-on document. This is exactly the relevance feedback process, but limited to a single relevant document for training data.

Although these applications have had some success, the alternative approach of asking users to choose a different query from a list of suggested queries is currently more popular. There is no guarantee, of course, that the suggested queries will contain exactly what the user is looking for, and in that sense relevance feedback supports more precise query reformulation. There is an assumption, however, underlying the use of relevance feedback: that the user is looking for many relevant documents, not just the one or two that may be in the initial ranked list. For some queries, such as looking for background information on a topic, this may be true, but for many queries in the web environment, the user will be satisfied with the initial ranking and will not need relevance feedback. Lists of suggested queries will be helpful when the initial query fails, whereas relevance feedback is unlikely to help in that case.

6.2.5 Context and Personalization

One characteristic of most current search engines is that the results of a query will be the same regardless of who submitted the query, why the query was submitted, where the query was submitted, or what other queries were submitted in the same session. All that matters is what words were used to describe the query. The other factors, known collectively as the query *context*, will affect the relevance of retrieved documents and could potentially have a significant impact on the ranking algorithm. Most contextual information, however, has proved to be difficult to capture and represent in a way that provides consistent effectiveness improvements.

Much research has been done, in particular, on learning *user models* or profiles to represent a person's interests so that a search can be *personalized*. If the system knew that a person was interested in sports, for example, the documents retrieved for the query "vikings" may be different than those retrieved by the same query for a person interested in history. Although this idea is appealing, there are a number of problems with actually making it work. The first is the accuracy of the user models. The most common proposal is to create the profiles based on the documents that the person looks at, such as web pages visited, email messages, or word processing documents on the desktop. This type of profile represents a person using words weighted by their importance. Words that occur frequently in the documents associated with that person, but are not common words in general, will have the highest weights. Given that documents contain hundreds or even thousands of words, and the documents visited by the person represent only a snapshot of their interests, these models are not very specific. Experiments have shown that using such models does not improve the effectiveness of ranking on average.

An alternative approach would be to ask the user to describe herself using predefined categories. In addition to requiring additional (and optional) interactions that most people tend to avoid, there is still the fundamental problem that someone with a general interest in sports may still want to ask a question about history. This suggests that a category of interest could be specified for each query, such as specifying the "history" category for the query "vikings", but this is no different than simply entering a less ambiguous query. It is much more effective for a person to enter an extra word or two in her query to clarify it—such as "vikings quarterbacks" or "vikings exploration", for example—than to try to classify a query into a limited set of categories.

Another issue that is raised by any approach to personalization based on user models is *privacy*. People have understandable concerns about personal details being recorded in corporate and government databases. In response, techniques for maintaining anonymity while searching and browsing on the Web are becoming an increasingly popular area for research and development. Given this, a search engine that creates profiles based on web activity may be viewed negatively, especially since the benefit of doing this is currently not clear.

Problems with user modeling and privacy do not mean that contextual information is not useful, but rather that the benefits of any approach based on context need to be examined carefully. There are examples of applications where the use of contextual information is clearly effective. One of these is the use of query logs and clickthrough data to improve web search. The context in this case is the history of previous searches and search sessions that are the same or very similar. In general, this history is based on the entire user population. A particular person's search history may be useful for "caching" results for common search queries, but learning from a large number of queries across the population appears to be much more effective.

Another effective application of context is *local search*, which uses geographic information derived from the query, or from the location of the device that the query comes from, to modify the ranking of search results. For example, the query "fishing supplies" will generate a long list of web pages for suppliers from all over the country (or the world). The query "fishing supplies Cape Cod", however, should use the context provided by the location "Cape Cod" to rank suppliers in that region higher than any others. Similarly, if the query "fishing supplies" came from a mobile device in a town in Cape Cod, then this information could be used to rank suppliers by their proximity to that town.

Local search based on queries involves the following steps:

1. Identify the geographic region associated with web pages. This is done either by using location metadata that has been manually added to the document, or by automatically identifying locations, such as place names, city names, or country names, in the document text.
2. Identify the geographic region associated with the query using automatic techniques. Analysis of query logs has shown that 10–15% of queries contain some location reference.
3. Rank web pages using a comparison of the query and document location information in addition to the usual text- and link-based features.

Automatically identifying the location information in text is a specific example of the information extraction techniques mentioned in Chapter 4. Location names are mapped to specific regions and coordinates using a *geographic ontology*[15] and algorithms developed for spatial reasoning in *geographic information systems*. For example, the location "Cape Cod" in a document might be mapped to bounding rectangles based on latitude and longitude, as shown in Figure 6.2, whereas a town location would be mapped to more specific coordinates (or a smaller bounding rectangle). Although this sounds straightforward, there are many issues involved in identifying location names (for example, there are more than 35 places named Springfield in the United States), deciding which locations are significant (if a web page discusses the "problems with Washington lobbyists", should "Washington" be used as location metadata?), and combining multiple location references in a document.

---

[15] An ontology is essentially the same thing as a thesaurus. It is a representation of the concepts in a domain and the relationships between them, whereas a thesaurus describes words, phrases, and relationships between them. Ontologies usually have a richer set of relationships than a thesaurus. A *taxonomy* is another term used to describe categories of concepts.

The geographic comparison used in the ranking could involve inclusion (for example, the location metadata for a supplier's web page indicates that the supplier is located in the bounding box that represents Cape Cod), distance (for example, the supplier is within 10 miles of the town that the query mentioned), or other spatial relationships. From both an efficiency and effectiveness perspective, there will be implications for exactly how and when the geographic information is incorporated into the ranking process.

Fig. 6.2. Geographic representation of Cape Cod using bounding rectangles

To summarize, the most useful contextual information for improving search quality is based on past interactions with the search engine (i.e., the query log and session history). Local search based on geographic context can also produce substantial improvements for a subset of queries. In both cases, context is used to provide additional features to enhance the original query (query expansion provides additional words, and local search provides geographic distance). To understand the context for a specific query, however, there is no substitute for the user providing a more specific query. Indeed, local search in most cases relies on the location being specified in the query. Typically, more specific queries come from users examining the results and then reformulating the query. The results display, which we discuss next, must convey the context of the query term matches so that the user can decide which documents to look at in detail or how to reformulate the query.

6.3 Showing the Results

6.3.1 Result Pages and Snippets

Successful interactions with a search engine depend on the user understanding the results. Many different visualization techniques have been proposed for displaying search output (Hearst, 1999), but for most search engines the result pages consist of a ranked list of *document summaries* that are linked to the actual documents or web pages. A document summary for a web search typically contains the title and URL of the web page, links to live and cached versions of the page, and, most importantly, a short text summary, or *snippet*, that is used to convey the content of the page. In addition, most result pages contain advertisements consisting of short descriptions and links. Query words that occur in the title, URL, snippet, or advertisements are *highlighted* to make them easier to identify, usually by displaying them in a bold font.

Figure 6.3 gives an example of a document summary from a result page for a web search. In this case, the snippet consists of two partial sentences. Figure 6.1 gives more examples of snippets that are sometimes full sentences, but often text fragments, extracted from the web page. Some of the snippets do not even contain the query words. In this section, we describe some of the basic features of the algorithms used for snippet generation.

Tropical Fish

One of the U.K.s Leading suppliers of **Tropical**, Coldwater, Marine **Fish** and Invertebrates plus.. . next day **fish** delivery service ...

www.**tropicalfish**.org.uk/**tropical_fish**.htm   Cached page

Fig. 6.3. Typical document summary for a web search

Snippet generation is an example of text summarization. Summarization techniques have been developed for a number of applications, but primarily have been tested using news stories from the TREC collections. A basic distinction is made between techniques that produce *query-independent* summaries and those that produce *query-dependent* summaries. Snippets in web search engine result pages are clearly query-dependent summaries, since the snippet that is generated for a page will depend on the query that retrieved it, but some query-independent features, such as the position of the text in the page and whether the text is in a heading, are also used.

The development of text summarization techniques started with H. P. Luhn in the 1950s (Luhn, 1958). Luhn's approach was to rank each sentence in a document using a *significance factor* and to select the top sentences for the summary. The significance factor for a sentence is calculated based on the occurrence of significant words. Significant words are defined in his work as words of medium frequency in the document, where "medium" means that the frequency is between predefined high-frequency and low-frequency cutoff values. Given the significant words, portions of the sentence that are "bracketed" by these words are considered, with a limit set for the number of non-significant words that can be between two significant words (typically four). The significance factor for these bracketed text spans is computed by dividing the square of the number of significant words in the span by the total number of words. Figure 6.4 gives an example of a text span for which the significance factor is $4^2/7 = 2.3$. The significance factor for a sentence is the maximum calculated for any text span in the sentence.

```
W  W  W  W  W  W  W  W  W  W.
          (Initial sentence)

W  W  S  W  S  S  W  W  S  W  W.
        (Identify significant words)

W  W  [S  W  S  S  W  W  S]  W  W.
(Text span bracketed by significant words)
```

Fig. 6.4. An example of a text span of words (w) bracketed by significant words (s) using Luhn's algorithm

To be more specific about the definition of a significant word, the following is a frequency-based criterion that has been used successfully in more recent research. If $f_{d,w}$ is the frequency of word w in document d, then w is a significant word if it is not a stopword (which eliminates the high-frequency words), and

$$f_{d,w} \geq \begin{cases} 7 - 0.1 \times (25 - s_d), & \text{if } s_d < 25 \\ 7, & \text{if } 25 \leq s_d \leq 40 \\ 7 + 0.1 \times (s_d - 40), & \text{otherwise,} \end{cases}$$

where s_d is the number of sentences in document d. As an example, the second page of Chapter 1 of this book contains less than 25 sentences (roughly 20), and so the significant words will be non-stopwords with a frequency greater than or equal to 6.5. The only words that satisfy this criterion are "information" (frequency 9), "story" (frequency 8), and "text" (frequency 7).

Most work on summarization since Luhn has involved improvements to this basic approach, including better methods of selecting significant words and selecting sentences or sentence fragments. Snippet generation techniques can also be viewed as variations of Luhn's approach with query words being used as the significant words and different sentence selection criteria.

Typical features that would be used in selecting sentences for snippets to summarize a text document such as a news story would include whether the sentence is a heading, whether it is the first or second line of the document, the total number of query terms occurring in the sentence, the number of unique query terms in the sentence, the longest contiguous run of query words in the sentence, and a density measure of query words, such as Luhn's significance factor. In this approach, a weighted combination of features would be used to rank sentences. Web pages, however, often are much less structured than a news story, and can contain a lot of text that would not be appropriate for snippets. To address this, snippet sentences are often selected from the metadata associated with the web page, such as the "description" identified by the <meta name="description" content= ...> HTML tags, or from external sources, such as web directories.[16] Certain classes of web pages, such as Wikipedia entries, are more structured and have snippet sentences selected from the text.

Although many variations are possible for snippet generation and document summaries in result pages, some basic guidelines for effective summaries have been derived from an analysis of clickthrough data (Clarke et al., 2007). The most important is that whenever possible, all of the query terms should appear in the summary, showing their relationship to the retrieved page. When query terms are present in the title, however, they need not be repeated in the snippet. This allows for the possibility of using sentences from metadata or external descriptions that may not have query terms in them. Another guideline is that URLs should be selected and displayed in a manner that emphasizes their relationship to the query by, for example, highlighting the query terms present in the URL. Finally, search engine users appear to prefer readable prose in snippets (such as complete or near-complete sentences) rather than lists of keywords and phrases. A feature

---

[16] For example, the Open Directory Project, http://www.dmoz.org.

that measures readability should be included in the computation of the ranking for snippet selection.

The efficient implementation of snippet generation will be an important part of the search engine architecture since the obvious approach of finding, opening, and scanning document files would lead to unacceptable overheads in an environment requiring high query throughput. Instead, documents must be fetched from a local document store or cache at query time and decompressed. The documents that are processed for snippet generation should have all HTML tags and other "noise" (such as Javascript) removed, although metadata must still be distinguished from text content. In addition, sentence boundaries should be identified and marked at indexing time, to avoid this potentially time-consuming operation when selecting snippets.

6.3.2 Advertising and Search

Advertising is a key component of web search engines since that is how companies generate revenue. In the case of advertising presented with search results (*sponsored search*), the goal is to find advertisements that are appropriate for the query context. When browsing web pages, advertisements are selected for display based on the contents of pages. *Contextual advertising* is thought to lead to more user clicks on advertisements (clickthrough), which is how payments for advertising are determined. Search engine companies maintain a database of advertisements, which is searched to find the most relevant advertisements for a given query or web page. An advertisement in this database usually consists of a short text description and a link to a web page describing the product or service in more detail. Searching the advertisement database can therefore be considered a special case of general text search.

Nothing is ever that simple, however. Advertisements are not selected solely based on their ranking in a simple text search. Instead, advertisers bid for keywords that describe topics associated with their product. The amount bid for a keyword that matches a query is an important factor in determining which advertisement is selected. In addition, some advertisements generate more clickthrough because they are more appealing to the user population. The popularity of an advertisement, as measured by the clickthrough over time that is captured in the query log, is another significant factor in the selection process. The popularity of an advertisement can be measured over all queries or on a query-specific basis. Query-specific popularity can be used only for queries that occur on a regular basis. For the large number of queries that occur infrequently (so-called *long-tail* queries[17]), the general popularity of advertisements can be used. By taking all of these factors into account, namely relevance, bids, and popularity, the search engine company can devise strategies to maximize their expected profit.

As an example, a pet supplies company that specializes in tropical fish may place the highest bid for the keywords "aquarium" and "tropical fish". Given the query "tropical fish", this keyword is certainly relevant. The content of the advertisement for that company should also contain words that match the query. Given that, this company's advertisement will receive a high score for relevance and a high score based on the bid. Even though it has made the highest bid, however, there is still some chance that another advertisement will be chosen if it is very popular and has a moderately high bid for the same keywords.

Much ongoing research is directed at developing algorithms to maximize the advertiser's profit, drawing on fields such as economics and game theory. From the information retrieval perspective, the key issues are techniques for matching short pieces of text (the query and the advertisement) and selecting keywords to represent the content of web pages.

When searching the Web, there are usually many pages that contain all of the query terms. This is not the case, however, when queries are compared to advertisements. Advertisements contain a small number of words or keywords relative to a typical page, and the database of advertisements will be several orders of magnitude smaller than the Web. It is also important that variations of advertisement keywords that occur in queries are matched. For example, if a pet supply company has placed a high bid for "aquarium", they would expect to receive some traffic from queries about "fish tanks". This, of course, is the classic *vocabulary mismatch* problem, and many techniques have been proposed to address this, such as stemming and query expansion. Since advertisements are short, techniques for expanding the documents as well as the queries have been considered.

Two techniques that have performed well in experiments are query reformulation based on user sessions in query logs (Jones et al., 2006) and expansion of queries and documents using external sources, such as the Web (Metzler et al., 2007).

---

[17] The term "long-tail" comes from the long tail of the Zipf distribution described in Chapter 4. Assuming that a query refers to a specific combination of words, most queries occur infrequently, and a relatively small number account for the majority of the query instances that are processed by search engines.

Studies have shown that about 50% of the queries in a single session are reformulations, where the user modifies the original query through word replacements, insertions, and deletions. Given a large number of candidate associations between queries and phrases in those queries, statistical tests, such as those described in section 6.2.3, can be used to determine which associations are significant. For example, the association between the phrases "fish tank" and "aquarium" may occur often in search sessions as users reformulate their original query to find more web pages. If this happens often enough relative to the frequency of these phrases, it will be considered significant. The significant associations can be used as potential substitutions, so that, given an initial query, a ranked list of query reformulations can be generated, with the emphasis on generating queries that contain matches for advertising keywords.

The expansion technique consists of using the Web to expand either the query, the advertisement text, or both. A form of pseudo-relevance feedback is used where the advertisement text or keywords are used as a query for a web search, and expansion words are selected from the highest-ranking web pages. Experiments have shown that the most effective relevance ranking of advertisements is when exact matches of the whole query are ranked first, followed by exact matches of the whole query with words replaced by stems, followed by a probabilistic similarity match of the expanded query with the expanded advertisement. The type of similarity match used is described in section 7.3.

As an example, Figure 6.5 shows the list of advertisements generated by a search engine for the query "fish tanks". Two of the advertisements are obvious matches, in that "fish tanks" occurs in the titles. Two of the others (the second and fourth) have no words in common with the query, although they are clearly relevant. Using the simple pseudo-relevance feedback technique described in section 6.2.4 would produce both "aquarium" (frequency 10) and "acrylic" (frequency 7) as expansion terms based on the top 10 results. This would give advertisements containing "aquarium", such as the second one, a higher relevance score in the selection process. The fourth advertisement has presumably been selected because the pet supplier has bid on the keyword "aquarium", and potentially because many people have clicked on this advertisement. The third advertisement is similar and matches one of the query words.

In the case of contextual advertising for web pages, keywords typically are extracted from the contents of the page and then used to search the advertising database to select advertisements for display along with the contents of the page. Keyword selection techniques are similar to the summarization techniques de-

fish tanks at Target
Find **fish tanks** Online. Shop & Save at Target.com Today.
www.target.com

Aquariums
540+ Aquariums at Great Prices.
fishbowls.pronto.com

Freshwater **Fish** Species
Everything you need to know to keep your setup clean and beautiful
www.FishChannel.com

Pet Supplies at Shop.com
Shop millions of products and buy from our trusted merchants.
shop.com

Custom **Fish Tanks**
Choose From 6,500+ Pet Supplies. Save On Custom **Fish Tanks**!
shopzilla.com

Fig. 6.5. Advertisements displayed by a search engine for the query "fish tanks"

scribed in the last section, with the focus on keywords rather than sentences. A simple approach would be to select the top words ranked by a significance weight based on relative frequencies in the document and the collection of documents.

A more effective approach is to use a *classifier* based on machine learning techniques, as described in Chapter 9. A classifier uses a weighted combination of features to determine which words and phrases are significant. Typical features include the frequency in the document, the number of documents in which the word or phrase occurs, functions of those frequencies (such as taking the log or normalizing), frequency of occurrence in the query log, location of the word or phrase in the document (e.g., the title, body, anchor text, metadata, URL), and whether the word or phrase was capitalized or highlighted in some way. The most useful features are the document and query log frequency information (Yih et al., 2006).

6.3.3 Clustering the Results

The results returned by a search engine are often related to different aspects of the query topic. In the case of an ambiguous query, these groups of documents can represent very different interpretations of the query. For example, we have seen how the query "tropical fish" retrieves documents related to aquariums, pet supplies, images, and other *subtopics*. An even simpler query, such as "fish", is likely to retrieve a heterogeneous mix of documents about the sea, software products, a rock singer, and anything else that happens to use the name "fish". If a user is interested in a particular aspect of a query topic, scanning through many pages on different aspects could be frustrating. This is the motivation for the use of *clustering* techniques on search results. Clustering groups documents that are similar in content and labels the clusters so they can be quickly scanned for relevance.

Pictures (38)

Aquarium Fish (28)

Tropical Fish Aquarium (26)

Exporter (31)

Supplies (32)

Plants, Aquatic (18)

Fish Tank (15)

Breeding (16)

Marine Fish (16)

Aquaria (9)

Fig. 6.6. Clusters formed by a search engine from top-ranked documents for the query "tropical fish". Numbers in brackets are the number of documents in the cluster.

Figure 6.6 shows a list of clusters formed by a web search engine from the top-ranked documents for the query "tropical fish". This list, where each cluster is described or labeled using a single word or phrase and includes a number indicating the size of the cluster, is displayed to the side of the usual search results. Users that are interested in one of these clusters can click on the cluster label to see a list of those documents, rather than scanning the ranked list to find documents related to that aspect of the query. In this example, the clusters are clearly related to the subtopics we mentioned previously, such as supplies and pictures.

Clustering techniques are discussed in detail in Chapter 9. In this section, we focus on the specific requirements for the task of clustering search results. The first of these requirements is *efficiency*. The clusters that are generated must be specific to each query and are based on the top-ranked documents for that query. The clusters for popular queries could be cached, but clusters will still need to be generated online for most queries, and this process has to be efficient. One consequence of this is that cluster generation is usually based on the text of document snippets, rather than the full text. Snippets typically contain many fewer words than the full text, which will substantially speed up calculations that involve comparing word overlap. Snippet text is also designed to be focused on the query topic, whereas documents can contain many text passages that are only partially relevant.

The second important requirement for result clusters is that they are easy to understand. In the example in Figure 6.6, each cluster is labeled by a single word or phrase, and the user will assume that every document in that cluster will be described by that concept. In the cluster labeled "Pictures", for example, it is reasonable to expect that every document would contain some pictures of fish. This is an example of a *monothetic* classification, where every member of a class has the property that defines the class.[18] This may sound obvious, but in fact it is not the type of classification produced by most clustering algorithms. Membership of a class or cluster produced by an algorithm such as *K-means*[19] is based on word overlap. In other words, members of clusters share many properties, but there is no single defining property. This is known as a *polythetic* classification. For result clustering, techniques that produce monothetic classifications (or, at least, those that appear to be monothetic) are preferred because they are easier to understand.

As an example, consider documents in the search results D_1, D_2, D_3, and D_4 that contain the terms (i.e., words or phrases) $\{a, b, c, d, e, f, g\}$. The sets of terms representing each document are:

$$D_1 = \{a, b, c\}$$
$$D_2 = \{a, d, e\}$$
$$D_3 = \{d, e, f, g\}$$
$$D_4 = \{f, g\}$$

A monothetic algorithm may decide that a and e are significant terms and produce the two clusters $\{D_1, D_2\}$ (with cluster label a) and $\{D_2, D_3\}$ (labeled e). Note that these clusters are overlapping, in that a document may belong to more than one cluster. A polythetic algorithm may decide that, based on term overlap, the only significant cluster is $\{D_2, D_3, D_4\}$—D_2 has two terms in common with D_3, and D_3 has two terms in common with D_4. Note that these three documents have no single term in common, and it is not clear how this cluster would be labeled.

---

[18] This is also the definition of a class proposed by Aristotle over 2,400 years ago.

[19] *K*-means clustering is described in Chapter 9, but basically a document is compared to representatives of the existing clusters and added to the most similar cluster.

If we consider the list of snippets shown in Figure 6.1, a simple clustering based on the non-stopwords that occur in more than one document would give us:

aquarium (5)   (Documents 1, 3, 4, 5, 8)
freshwater (4)   (1, 8, 9, 10)
species (3)   (2, 3, 4)
hobby (3)   (1, 5, 10)
forums (2)   (6, 8)

In an actual implementation of this technique, both words and phrases would be considered and many more of the top-ranking snippets (say, 200) would be used. Additional features of the words and phrases, such as whether they occurred in titles or snippets, the length of the phrase, and the collection frequency of the phrase, as well as the overlap of the resulting clusters, would be considered in choosing the final set of clusters.

An alternative approach for organizing results into meaningful groups is to use *faceted classification* or, more simply, *facets*. A faceted classification consists of a set of categories, usually organized into a hierarchy, together with a set of facets that describe the important properties associated with the category. A product described by a faceted classification, for example, could be labeled by more than one category and will have values for every facet. Faceted classifications are primarily manually defined, although it is possible to support faceted browsing for data that has been structured using a database schema, and techniques for constructing faceted classifications automatically are being studied. The major advantage of manually defining facets is that the categories are in general easier for the user to understand than automatically generated cluster labels. The disadvantages are that a classification has to be defined for each new application and domain, and manual classifications tend to be static and not as responsive to new data as dynamically constructed clusters.

Facets are very common in e-commerce sites. Figure 6.7 shows the set of categories returned for the query "tropical fish" for a search on a popular retailer's site. The numbers refer to the number of products in each category that match the query. These categories are displayed to the side of the search results, similar to the clusters discussed earlier. If the "Home & Garden" category is selected, Figure 6.8 shows that what is displayed is a list of subcategories, such as "pet supplies", together with facets for this category, which include the brand name, supplier or vendor name, discount level, and price. A given product, such as an aquarium, can be found under "pet supplies" and in the appropriate price level, discount level, etc. This type of organization provides the user with both guidance and flexibility in browsing the search results.

Books (7,845)
Home & Garden (2,477)
Apparel (236)
Home Improvement (169)
Jewelry & Watches (76)
Sports & Outdoors (71)
Office Products (68)
Toys & Games (62)
Everything Else (44)
Electronics (26)
Baby (25)

DVD (12)
Music (11)
Software (10)
Gourmet Food (6)
Beauty (4)
Automotive (4)
Magazine Subscriptions (3)
Health & Personal Care (3)
Wireless Accessories (2)
Video Games (1)

Fig. 6.7. Categories returned for the query "tropical fish" in a popular online retailer

Home & Garden
Kitchen & Dining (149)
Furniture & Décor (1,776)
Pet Supplies (368)
Bedding & Bath (51)
Patio & Garden (22)
Art & Craft Supplies (12)
Home Appliances (2)
Vacuums, Cleaning & Storage (107)

Brand
   <brand names>
Seller
   <vendor names>

Discount
Up to 25% off (563)
25% - 50% off (472)
50% - 70% off (46)
70% off or more (46)

Price
$0-$24 (1,032)
$25-$49 (394)
$50-$99 (797)
$100-$199 (206)
$200-$499 (39)
$500-$999 (9)
$1000-$1999 (5)
$5000-$9999 (7)

Fig. 6.8. Subcategories and facets for the "Home & Garden" category

6.4 Cross-Language Search

By translating queries for one or more monolingual search engines covering different languages, it is possible to do *cross-language* search[20] (see Figure 6.9). A cross-language search engine receives a query in one language (e.g., English) and retrieves documents in a variety of other languages (e.g., French and Chinese). Users typically will not be familiar with a wide range of languages, so a cross-language search system must do the query translation automatically. Since the system also retrieves documents in multiple languages, some systems also translate these for the user.

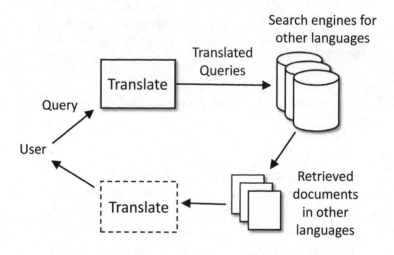

Fig. 6.9. Cross-language search

The most obvious approach to automatic translation would be to use a large bilingual dictionary that contained the translation of a word in the source language (e.g., English) to the target language (e.g., French). Sentences would then be translated by looking up each word in the dictionary. The main issue is how to deal with ambiguity, since many words have multiple translations. Simple dictionary-based translations are generally poor, but a number of techniques have been developed, such as query expansion (section 6.2.3), that reduce ambiguity and in-

---

[20] Also called cross-language information retrieval (CLIR), cross-lingual search, and multilingual search.

crease the ranking effectiveness of a cross-language system to be comparable to a monolingual system.

The most effective and general methods for automatic translation are based on *statistical machine translation models* (Manning & Schütze, 1999). When translating a document or a web page, in contrast to a query, not only is ambiguity a problem, but the translated sentences should also be grammatically correct. Words can change order, disappear, or become multiple words when a sentence is translated. Statistical translation models represent each of these changes with a probability. This means that the model describes the probability that a word is translated into another word, the probability that words change order, and the probability that words disappear or become multiple words. These probabilities are used to calculate the most likely translation for a sentence.[21]

Although a model that is based on word-to-word translation probabilities has some similarities to a dictionary-based approach, if the translation probabilities are accurate, they can make a large difference to the quality of the translation. Unusual translations for an ambiguous word can then be easily distinguished from more typical translations. More recent versions of these models, called *phrase-based translation models*, further improve the use of context in the translation by calculating the probabilities of translating sequences of words, rather than just individual words. A word such as "flight", for example, could be more accurately translated as the phrase "commercial flight", instead of being interpreted as "bird flight".

The probabilities in statistical machine translation models are estimated primarily by using *parallel corpora*. These are collections of documents in one language together with the translations into one or more other languages. The corpora are obtained primarily from government organizations (such as the United Nations), news organizations, and by mining the Web, since there are hundreds of thousands of translated pages. The sentences in the parallel corpora are *aligned* either manually or automatically, which means that sentences are paired with their translations. The aligned sentences are then used for training the translation model.

---

[21] The simplest form of a machine translation model is actually very similar to the query likelihood model described in section 7.3.1. The main difference is the incorporation of a translation probability $P(w_i|w_j)$, which is the probability that a word w_j can be translated into the word w_i, in the estimation of $P(Q|D)$. $P(Q|D)$ is the probability of generating a query from a document, which in the translation model becomes the probability that a query is a translation of the document.

Special attention has to be paid to the translation of unusual words, especially proper nouns such as people's names. For these words in particular, the Web is a rich resource. Automatic *transliteration* techniques are also used to address the problem of people's names. Proper names are not usually translated into another language, but instead are transliterated, meaning that the name is written in the characters of another language according to certain rules or based on similar sounds. This can lead to many alternative spellings for the same name. For example, the Libyan leader Muammar Qaddafi's name can found in many different transliterated variants on web pages, such as Qathafi, Kaddafi, Qadafi, Gadafi, Gaddafi, Kathafi, Kadhafi, Qadhafi, Qazzafi, Kazafi, Qaddafy, Qadafy, Quadhaffi, Gadhdhafi, al-Qaddafi, Al-Qaddafi, and Al Qaddafi. Similarly, there are a number of variants of "Bill Clinton" on Arabic web pages.

Although they are not generally regarded as cross-language search systems, web search engines can often retrieve pages in a variety of languages. For that reason, many search engines have made translation available on the result pages. Figure 6.10 shows an example of a page retrieved for the query "pecheur france", where the translation option is shown as a hyperlink. Clicking on this link produces a translation of the page (not the snippet), which makes it clear that the page contains links to archives of the sports magazine *Le pêcheur de France*, which is translated as "The fisherman of France". Although the translation provided is not perfect, it typically provides enough information for someone to understand the contents and relevance of the page. These translations are generated automatically using machine translation techniques, since any human intervention would be prohibitively expensive.

Le pêcheur de France archives @ peche poissons - [Translate this page]

Le **pêcheur** de **France** Les média Revues de pêche Revue de presse Archives de la revue Le **pêcheur** de **France** janvier 2003 n°234 Le **pêcheur** de **France** mars 2003 ...

Fig. 6.10. A French web page in the results list for the query "pecheur france"

References and Further Reading

This chapter has covered a wide range of topics that have been studied for a number of years. Consequently, there are many references that are relevant and provide more detail than we are able to cover here. The following papers and books represent some of the more significant contributions, but each contains pointers to other work for people interested in gaining a deeper understanding of a specific topic.

The advantages and disadvantages of Boolean queries relative to "natural language" or keyword queries has been discussed for more than 30 years. This debate has been particularly active in the legal retrieval field, which saw the introduction of the first search engines using ranking and simple queries on large collections in the early 1990s. Turtle (1994) describes one of the few quantitative comparisons of expert Boolean searching to ranking based on simple queries, and found that simple queries are surprisingly effective, even in this professional environment. The next chapter contains more discussion of the Boolean retrieval model.

A more detailed description of query-based stemming based on corpus analysis can be found in J. Xu and Croft (1998). A good source for the earlier history of association measures such as Dice's coefficient that have been used for information retrieval is van Rijsbergen (1979). Peng et al. (2007) describe a more recent version of corpus-based stemming for web search.

Kukich (1992) provides an overview of spelling correction techniques. For a more detailed introduction to minimum edit distance and the noisy channel model for spelling correction, see Jurafsky and Martin (2006). Guo et al. (2008) describe an approach that combines query refinement steps, such as spelling correction, stemming, and identification of phrases, into a single model. Their results indicate that the unified model can potentially improve effectiveness relative to carrying out these steps as separate processes.

Query expansion has been the subject of much research. Efthimiadis (1996) gives a general overview and history of query expansion techniques, including thesaurus-based expansion. As mentioned before, van Rijsbergen (1979) describes the development of association measures for information retrieval, including the mutual information measure. In computational linguistics, the paper by Church and Hanks (1989) is often referred to for the use of the mutual information measure in constructing lexicons (dictionaries). Manning and Schütze (1999) give a good overview of these and the other association measures mentioned in this chapter.

Jing and Croft (1994) describe a technique for constructing an "association thesaurus" from virtual documents consisting of the words that co-occur with other words. The use of query log data to support expansion is described in Beeferman and Berger (2000) and Cui et al. (2003).

Rocchio (1971) pioneered the work on relevance feedback, which was then followed up by a large amount of work that is reviewed in Salton and McGill (1983) and van Rijsbergen (1979). J. Xu and Croft (2000) is a frequently cited paper on pseudo-relevance feedback that compared "local" techniques based on top-ranked documents to "global" techniques based on the term associations in the collection. The book, based on 10 years of TREC experiments (Voorhees & Harman, 2005), contains many descriptions of both relevance feedback and pseudo-relevance feedback techniques.

Context and personalization is a popular topic. Many publications can be found in workshops and conferences, such as the Information Interaction in Context Symposium (IIiX).[22] Wei and Croft (2007) describe an experiment that raises questions about the potential benefit of user profiles. Chen et al. (2006) and Zhou et al. (2005) both discuss index structures for efficiently processing local search queries, but also provide general overviews of local search. V. Zhang et al. (2006) discusses local search with an emphasis on analyzing query logs.

The original work on text summarization was done by Luhn (1958). Goldstein et al. (1999) describe more recent work on summarization based on sentence selection. The work of Berger and Mittal (2000), in contrast, generates summaries based on statistical models of the document. Sun et al. (2005) describe a techniques based on clickthrough data. The papers of Clarke et al. (2007) and Turpin et al. (2007) focus specifically on snippet generation.

Feng et al. (2007) give a general overview of the issues in sponsored search. Metzler et al. (2007) and Jones et al. (2006) discuss specific techniques for matching queries to short advertisements. A discussion of the issues in contextual advertising (providing advertisements while browsing), as well as a specific technique for selecting keywords from a web page, can be found in Yih et al. (2006).

As mentioned earlier, many visualization techniques have been proposed over the years for search results, and we have ignored most of these in this book. Hearst (1999) provides a good overview of the range of techniques. Leouski and Croft (1996) presented one of the first evaluations of techniques for result clustering.

---

[22] This conference grew out of the Information Retrieval in Context (IRiX) workshops, whose proceedings can also be found on the Web.

Hearst and Pedersen (1996) show the potential benefits of this technique, and Zamir and Etzioni (1999) emphasize the importance of clusters that made sense to the user and were easy to label. Lawrie and Croft (2003) discuss a technique for building a hierarchical summary of the results, and Zeng et al. (2004) focus on the selection of phrases from the results as the basis of clusters. The relative advantages and disadvantages of clustering and facets are discussed in Hearst (2006).

More generally, there is a whole community of HCI[23] (Human-Computer Interaction) researchers concerned with the design and evaluation of interfaces for information systems. Shneiderman et al. (1998) is an example of this type of research, and Marchionini (2006) gives a good overview of the importance of the search interface for *interactive*, or *exploratory*, search.

Cross-language search has been studied at TREC (Voorhees & Harman, 2005) and at a European evaluation forum called CLEF[24] for a number of years. The first collection of papers in this area was in Grefenstette (1998). Issues that arise in specific CLIR systems, such as transliteration (AbdulJaleel & Larkey, 2003), are discussed in many papers in the literature. Manning and Schütze (1999) and Jurafsky and Martin (2006) give overviews of statistical machine translation models.

Finally, there has been a large body of work in the information science literature that has looked at how people actually search and interact with search engines. This research is complementary to the more systems-oriented approach taken in this chapter, and is a crucial part of understanding the process of looking for information and relevance. The *Journal of the American Society of Information Science and Technology* (JASIST) is the best source for these type of papers, and Ingwersen and Järvelin (2005) provide an interesting comparison of the computer science and information science perspectives on search.

Exercises

6.1. Using the Wikipedia collection provided at the book website, create a sample of stem clusters by the following process:

1. Index the collection without stemming.
2. Identify the first 1,000 words (in alphabetical order) in the index.

---

[23] Sometimes referred to as CHI.

[24] http://clef.isti.cnr.it/

3. Create stem classes by stemming these 1,000 words and recording which words become the same stem.
4. Compute association measures (Dice's coefficient) between all pairs of stems in each stem class. Compute co-occurrence at the document level.
5. Create stem clusters by thresholding the association measure. All terms that are still connected to each other form the clusters.

Compare the stem clusters to the stem classes in terms of size and the quality (in your opinion) of the groupings.

6.2. Create a simple spelling corrector based on the noisy channel model. Use a single-word language model, and an error model where all errors with the same edit distance have the same probability. Only consider edit distances of 1 or 2. Implement your own edit distance calculator (example code can easily be found on the Web).

6.3. Implement a simple pseudo-relevance feedback algorithm for the Galago search engine. Provide examples of the query expansions that your algorithm does, and summarize the problems and successes of your approach.

6.4. Assuming you had a gazetteer of place names available, sketch out an algorithm for detecting place names or locations in queries. Show examples of the types of queries where your algorithm would succeed and where it would fail.

6.5. Describe the snippet generation algorithm in Galago. Would this algorithm work well for pages with little text content? Describe in detail how you would modify the algorithm to improve it.

6.6. Pick a commercial web search engine and describe how you think the query is matched to the advertisements for sponsored search. Use examples as evidence for your ideas. Do the same thing for advertisements shown with web pages.

6.7. Implement a simple algorithm that selects phrases from the top-ranked pages as the basis for result clusters. Phrases should be considered as any two-word sequence. Your algorithm should take into account phrase frequency in the results, phrase frequency in the collection, and overlap in the clusters associated with the phrases.

6.8. Find four different types of websites that use facets, and describe them with examples.

6.9. Give five examples of web page translation that you think is poor. Why do you think the translation failed?

7

Retrieval Models

"There is no certainty, only opportunity."

V, *V for Vendetta*

7.1 Overview of Retrieval Models

During the last 45 years of information retrieval research, one of the primary goals has been to understand and formalize the processes that underlie a person making the decision that a piece of text is relevant to his information need. To develop a complete understanding would probably require understanding how language is represented and processed in the human brain, and we are a long way short of that. We can, however, propose theories about relevance in the form of mathematical retrieval models and test those theories by comparing them to human actions. Good models should produce outputs that correlate well with human decisions on relevance. To put it another way, ranking algorithms based on good retrieval models will retrieve relevant documents near the top of the ranking (and consequently will have high effectiveness).

How successful has modeling been? As an example, ranking algorithms for general search improved in effectiveness by over 100% in the 1990s, as measured using the TREC test collections. These changes in effectiveness corresponded to improvements in the associated retrieval models. Web search effectiveness has also improved substantially over the past 10 years. In experiments with TREC web collections, the most effective ranking algorithms come from well-defined retrieval models. In the case of commercial web search engines, it is less clear what the retrieval models are, but there is no doubt that the ranking algorithms rely on solid mathematical foundations.

It is possible to develop ranking algorithms without an explicit retrieval model through trial and error. Using a retrieval model, however, has generally proved to be the best approach. Retrieval models, like all mathematical models, provide a framework for defining new tasks and explaining assumptions. When problems are observed with a ranking algorithm, the retrieval model provides a structure for testing alternatives that will be much more efficient than a *brute force* (try everything) approach.

In this discussion, we must not overlook the fact that relevance is a complex concept. It is quite difficult for a person to explain why one document is more relevant than another, and when people are asked to judge the relevance of documents for a given query, they can often disagree. Information scientists have written volumes about the nature of relevance, but we will not dive into that material here. Instead, we discuss two key aspects of relevance that are important for both retrieval models and evaluation measures.

The first aspect is the difference between *topical* and *user* relevance, which was mentioned in section 1.1. A document is topically relevant to a query if it is judged to be on the same topic. In other words, the query and the document are about the same thing. A web page containing a biography of Abraham Lincoln would certainly be topically relevant to the query "Abraham Lincoln", and would also be topically relevant to the queries "U.S. presidents" and "Civil War". User relevance takes into account all the other factors that go into a user's judgment of relevance. This may include the age of the document, the language of the document, the intended target audience, the novelty of the document, and so on. A document containing just a list of all the U.S. presidents, for example, would be topically relevant to the query "Abraham Lincoln" but may not be considered relevant to the person who submitted the query because they were looking for more detail on Lincoln's life. Retrieval models cannot incorporate all the additional factors involved in user relevance, but some do take these factors into consideration.

The second aspect of relevance that we consider is whether it is *binary* or *multivalued*. Binary relevance simply means that a document is either relevant or not relevant. It seems obvious that some documents are less relevant than others, but still more relevant than documents that are completely off-topic. For example, we may consider the document containing a list of U.S. presidents to be less topically relevant than the Lincoln biography, but certainly more relevant than an advertisement for a Lincoln automobile. Based on this observation, some retrieval models and evaluation measures explicitly introduce relevance as a multivalued variable. Multiple levels of relevance are certainly important in evaluation, when people are asked to judge relevance. Having just three levels (relevant, nonrelevant, unsure) has been shown to make the judges' task much easier. In the case of retrieval models, however, the advantages of multiple levels are less clear. This is because most ranking algorithms calculate a *probability* of relevance and can represent the uncertainty involved.

Many retrieval models have been proposed over the years. Two of the oldest are the *Boolean* and *vector space* models. Although these models have been largely superseded by probabilistic approaches, they are often mentioned in discussions about information retrieval, and so we describe them briefly before going into the details of other models.

7.1.1 Boolean Retrieval

The Boolean retrieval model was used by the earliest search engines and is still in use today. It is also known as *exact-match retrieval* since documents are retrieved if they exactly match the query specification, and otherwise are not retrieved. Although this defines a very simple form of ranking, Boolean retrieval is not generally described as a ranking algorithm. This is because the Boolean retrieval model assumes that all documents in the retrieved set are equivalent in terms of relevance, in addition to the assumption that relevance is binary. The name Boolean comes from the fact that there only two possible outcomes for query evaluation (**TRUE** and **FALSE**) and because the query is usually specified using operators from Boolean logic (**AND, OR, NOT**). As mentioned in Chapter 6, proximity operators and wildcard characters are also commonly used in Boolean queries. Searching with a regular expression utility such as grep is another example of exact-match retrieval.

There are some advantages to Boolean retrieval. The results of the model are very predictable and easy to explain to users. The operands of a Boolean query can be any document feature, not just words, so it is straightforward to incorporate metadata such as a document date or document type in the query specification. From an implementation point of view, Boolean retrieval is usually more efficient than ranked retrieval because documents can be rapidly eliminated from consideration in the scoring process.

Despite these positive aspects, the major drawback of this approach to search is that the effectiveness depends entirely on the user. Because of the lack of a sophisticated ranking algorithm, simple queries will not work well. All documents containing the specified query words will be retrieved, and this retrieved set will be presented to the user in some order, such as by publication date, that has little to do with relevance. It is possible to construct complex Boolean queries that narrow the retrieved set to mostly relevant documents, but this is a difficult task that requires considerable experience. In response to the difficulty of formulating queries, a class of users known as search intermediaries (mentioned in the last chapter) became associated with Boolean search systems. The task of an intermediary is to translate a user's information need into a complex Boolean query for a particular search engine. Intermediaries are still used in some specialized areas, such as in legal offices. The simplicity and effectiveness of modern search engines, however, has enabled most people to do their own searches.

As an example of Boolean query formulation, consider the following queries for a search engine that has indexed a collection of news stories. The simple query:

> lincoln

would retrieve a large number of documents that mention Lincoln cars and places named Lincoln in addition to stories about President Lincoln. All of these documents would be equivalent in terms of ranking in the Boolean retrieval model, regardless of how many times the word "lincoln" occurs or in what context it occurs. Given this, the user may attempt to narrow the scope of the search with the following query:

> president AND lincoln

This query will retrieve a set of documents that contain both words, occurring anywhere in the document. If there are a number of stories involving the management of the Ford Motor Company and Lincoln cars, these will be retrieved in the same set as stories about President Lincoln, for example:

> Ford Motor Company today announced that Darryl Hazel will succeed
> Brian Kelley as **president** of **Lincoln** Mercury.

If enough of these types of documents were retrieved, the user may try to eliminate documents about cars by using the NOT operator, as follows:

> president AND lincoln AND NOT (automobile OR car)

This would remove any document that contains even a single mention of the words "automobile" or "car" anywhere in the document. The use of the NOT operator, in general, removes too many relevant documents along with non-relevant documents and is not recommended. For example, one of the top-ranked documents in a web search for "President Lincoln" was a biography containing the sentence:

> **Lincoln**'s body departs Washington in a nine-**car** funeral train.

Using NOT (automobile OR car) in the query would have removed this document. If the retrieved set is still too large, the user may try to further narrow the query by adding in additional words that should occur in biographies:

> president AND lincoln AND biography AND life AND birthplace AND gettysburg AND NOT (automobile OR car)

Unfortunately, in a Boolean search engine, putting too many search terms into the query with the AND operator often results in nothing being retrieved. To avoid this, the user may try using an OR instead:

> president AND lincoln AND (biography OR life OR birthplace OR gettysburg) AND NOT (automobile OR car)

This will retrieve any document containing the words "president" and "lincoln", along with any one of the words "biography", "life", "birthplace", or "gettysburg" (and does not mention "automobile" or "car").

After all this, we have a query that may do a reasonable job at retrieving a set containing some relevant documents, but we still can't specify which words are more important or that having more of the associated words is better than any one of them. For example, a document containing the following text was retrieved at rank 500 by a web search (which does use measures of word importance):

> **President**'s Day - Holiday activities - crafts, mazes, word searches, ... "The **Life** of Washington" Read the entire book online! Abraham **Lincoln** Research Site ...

A Boolean retrieval system would make no distinction between this document and the other 499 that are ranked higher by the web search engine. It could, for example, be the first document in the result list.

The process of developing queries with a focus on the size of the retrieved set has been called *searching by numbers*, and is a consequence of the limitations of the Boolean retrieval model. To address these limitations, researchers developed models, such as the vector space model, that incorporate ranking.

7.1.2 The Vector Space Model

The vector space model was the basis for most of the research in information retrieval in the 1960s and 1970s, and papers using this model continue to appear at conferences. It has the advantage of being a simple and intuitively appealing framework for implementing term weighting, ranking, and relevance feedback.

Historically, it was very important in introducing these concepts, and effective techniques have been developed through years of experimentation. As a retrieval model, however, it has major flaws. Although it provides a convenient computational framework, it provides little guidance on the details of how weighting and ranking algorithms are related to relevance.

In this model, documents and queries are assumed to be part of a t-dimensional vector space, where t is the number of index terms (words, stems, phrases, etc.). A document D_i is represented by a vector of index terms:

$$D_i = (d_{i1}, d_{i2}, \ldots, d_{it}),$$

where d_{ij} represents the weight of the jth term. A document collection containing n documents can be represented as a matrix of term weights, where each row represents a document and each column describes weights that were assigned to a term for a particular document:

$$
\begin{array}{ccccc}
 & Term_1 & Term_2 & \ldots & Term_t \\
Doc_1 & d_{11} & d_{12} & \ldots & d_{1t} \\
Doc_2 & d_{21} & d_{22} & \ldots & d_{2t} \\
\vdots & \vdots & & & \\
Doc_n & d_{n1} & d_{n2} & \ldots & d_{nt}
\end{array}
$$

Figure 7.1 gives a simple example of the vector representation for four documents. The term-document matrix has been rotated so that now the terms are the rows and the documents are the columns. The term weights are simply the count of the terms in the document. Stopwords are not indexed in this example, and the words have been stemmed. Document D_3, for example, is represented by the vector $(1, 1, 0, 2, 0, 1, 0, 1, 0, 0, 1)$.

Queries are represented the same way as documents. That is, a query Q is represented by a vector of t weights:

$$Q = (q_1, q_2, \ldots, q_t),$$

where q_j is the weight of the jth term in the query. If, for example the query was "tropical fish", then using the vector representation in Figure 7.1, the query would be $(0, 0, 0, 1, 0, 0, 0, 0, 0, 0, 1)$. One of the appealing aspects of the vector space model is the use of simple diagrams to visualize the documents and queries. Typically, they are shown as points or vectors in a three-dimensional picture, as in

D$_1$ Tropical Freshwater Aquarium Fish.
D$_2$ Tropical Fish, Aquarium Care, Tank Setup.
D$_3$ Keeping Tropical Fish and Goldfish in Aquariums,
      and Fish Bowls.
D$_4$ The Tropical Tank Homepage - Tropical Fish and
      Aquariums.

Terms	Documents			
	D$_1$	D$_2$	D$_3$	D$_4$
aquarium	1	1	1	1
bowl	0	0	1	0
care	0	1	0	0
fish	1	1	2	1
freshwater	1	0	0	0
goldfish	0	0	1	0
homepage	0	0	0	1
keep	0	0	1	0
setup	0	1	0	0
tank	0	1	0	1
tropical	1	1	1	2

Fig. 7.1. Term-document matrix for a collection of four documents

Figure 7.2. Although this can be helpful for teaching, it is misleading to think that an intuition developed using three dimensions can be applied to the actual high-dimensional document space. Remember that the t terms represent all the document features that are indexed. In enterprise and web applications, this corresponds to hundreds of thousands or even *millions* of dimensions.

Given this representation, documents could be ranked by computing the distance between the points representing the documents and the query. More commonly, a *similarity measure* is used (rather than a distance or *dissimilarity* measure), so that the documents with the highest scores are the most similar to the query. A number of similarity measures have been proposed and tested for this purpose. The most successful of these is the *cosine correlation* similarity measure. The cosine correlation measures the cosine of the angle between the query and the document vectors. When the vectors are *normalized* so that all documents and queries are represented by vectors of equal length, the cosine of the angle between two identical vectors will be 1 (the angle is zero), and for two vectors that do not share any non-zero terms, the cosine will be 0. The cosine measure is defined as:

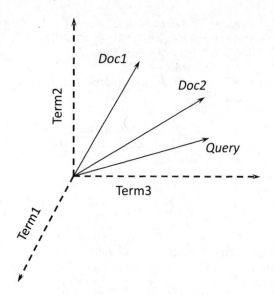

Fig. 7.2. Vector representation of documents and queries

$$Cosine(D_i, Q) = \frac{\sum\limits_{j=1}^{t} d_{ij} \cdot q_j}{\sqrt{\sum\limits_{j=1}^{t} d_{ij}{}^2 \cdot \sum\limits_{j=1}^{t} q_j{}^2}}$$

The numerator of this measure is the sum of the products of the term weights for the matching query and document terms (known as the *dot product* or inner product). The denominator normalizes this score by dividing by the product of the lengths of the two vectors. There is no theoretical reason why the cosine correlation should be preferred to other similarity measures, but it does perform somewhat better in evaluations of search quality.

As an example, consider two documents $D_1 = (0.5, 0.8, 0.3)$ and $D_2 = (0.9, 0.4, 0.2)$ indexed by three terms, where the numbers represent term weights. Given the query $Q = (1.5, 1.0, 0)$ indexed by the same terms, the cosine measures for the two documents are:

$$Cosine(D_1, Q) = \frac{(0.5 \times 1.5) + (0.8 \times 1.0)}{\sqrt{(0.5^2 + 0.8^2 + 0.3^2)(1.5^2 + 1.0^2)}}$$

$$= \frac{1.55}{\sqrt{(0.98 \times 3.25)}} = 0.87$$

$$Cosine(D_2, Q) = \frac{(0.9 \times 1.5) + (0.4 \times 1.0)}{\sqrt{(0.9^2 + 0.4^2 + 0.2^2)(1.5^2 + 1.0^2)}}$$

$$= \frac{1.75}{\sqrt{(1.01 \times 3.25)}} = 0.97$$

The second document has a higher score because it has a high weight for the first term, which also has a high weight in the query. Even this simple example shows that ranking based on the vector space model is able to reflect term importance and the number of matching terms, which is not possible in Boolean retrieval.

In this discussion, we have yet to say anything about the form of the term weighting used in the vector space model. In fact, many different weighting schemes have been tried over the years. Most of these are variations on *tf.idf* weighting, which was described briefly in Chapter 2. The term frequency component, *tf*, reflects the importance of a term in a document D_i (or query). This is usually computed as a normalized count of the term occurrences in a document, for example by

$$tf_{ik} = \frac{f_{ik}}{\sum\limits_{j=1}^{t} f_{ij}}$$

where tf_{ik} is the term frequency weight of term k in document D_i, and f_{ik} is the number of occurrences of term k in the document. In the vector space model, normalization is part of the cosine measure. A document collection can contain documents of many different lengths. Although normalization accounts for this to some degree, long documents can have many terms occurring once and others occurring hundreds of times. Retrieval experiments have shown that to reduce the impact of these frequent terms, it is effective to use the logarithm of the number of term occurrences in *tf* weights rather than the raw count.

The inverse document frequency component (idf) reflects the importance of the term in the collection of documents. The more documents that a term occurs in, the less *discriminating* the term is between documents and, consequently, the less useful it will be in retrieval. The typical form of this weight is

$$idf_k = \log \frac{N}{n_k}$$

where idf_k is the inverse document frequency weight for term k, N is the number of documents in the collection, and n_k is the number of documents in which term k occurs. The form of this weight was developed by intuition and experiment, although an argument can be made that idf measures the amount of information carried by the term, as defined in *information theory* (Robertson, 2004).

The effects of these two weights are combined by multiplying them (hence the name *tf.idf*). The reason for combining them this way is, once again, mostly empirical. Given this, the typical form of document term weighting in the vector space model is:

$$d_{ik} = \frac{(\log(f_{ik}) + 1) \cdot \log(N/n_k)}{\sqrt{\sum_{k=1}^{t} [(\log(f_{ik}) + 1.0) \cdot \log(N/n_k)]^2}}$$

The form of query term weighting is essentially the same. Adding 1 to the term frequency component ensures that terms with frequency 1 have a non-zero weight. Note that, in this model, term weights are computed only for terms that occur in the document (or query). Given that the cosine measure normalization is incorporated into the weights, the score for a document is computed using simply the dot product of the document and query vectors.

Although there is no explicit definition of relevance in the vector space model, there is an implicit assumption that relevance is related to the similarity of query and document vectors. In other words, documents "closer" to the query are more likely to be relevant. This is primarily a model of topical relevance, although features related to user relevance could be incorporated into the vector representation. No assumption is made about whether relevance is binary or multivalued.

In the last chapter we described relevance feedback, a technique for query modification based on user-identified relevant documents. This technique was first introduced using the vector space model. The well-known *Rocchio algorithm* (Rocchio, 1971) was based on the concept of an *optimal query*, which maximizes the difference between the average vector representing the relevant documents and the average vector representing the non-relevant documents. Given that only limited relevance information is typically available, the most common (and effective) form of the Rocchio algorithm modifies the initial weights in query vector Q to produce a new query Q' according to

$$q'_j = \alpha.q_j + \beta.\frac{1}{|Rel|} \sum_{D_i \in Rel} d_{ij} - \gamma.\frac{1}{|Nonrel|} \sum_{D_i \in Nonrel} d_{ij}$$

where q_j is the initial weight of query term j, Rel is the set of identified relevant documents, $Nonrel$ is the set of non-relevant documents, $|.|$ gives the size of a set, d_{ij} is the weight of the jth term in document i, and α, β, and γ are parameters that control the effect of each component. Previous studies have shown that the set of non-relevant documents is best approximated by all unseen documents (i.e., all documents not identified as relevant), and that reasonable values for the parameters are 8, 16, and 4 for α, β, and γ, respectively.

This formula modifies the query term weights by adding a component based on the average weight in the relevant documents and subtracting a component based on the average weight in the non-relevant documents. Query terms with weights that are negative are dropped. This results in a longer or expanded query because terms that occur frequently in the relevant documents but not in the original query will be added (i.e., they will have non-zero positive weights in the modified query). To restrict the amount of expansion, typically only a certain number (say, 50) of the terms with the highest average weights in the relevant documents will be added to the query.

7.2 Probabilistic Models

One of the features that a retrieval model should provide is a clear statement about the assumptions upon which it is based. The Boolean and vector space approaches make implicit assumptions about relevance and text representation that impact the design and effectiveness of ranking algorithms. The ideal situation would be to show that, given the assumptions, a ranking algorithm based on the retrieval model will achieve better effectiveness than any other approach. Such proofs are actually very hard to come by in information retrieval, since we are trying to formalize a complex human activity. The validity of a retrieval model generally has to be validated empirically, rather than theoretically.

One early theoretical statement about effectiveness, known as the *Probability Ranking Principle* (Robertson, 1977/1997), encouraged the development of probabilistic retrieval models, which are the dominant paradigm today. These models have achieved this status because *probability theory* is a strong foundation for representing and manipulating the uncertainty that is an inherent part of the information retrieval process. The Probability Ranking Principle, as origi-nally stated, is as follows:

> If a reference retrieval system's[1] response to each request is a ranking of the documents in the collection in order of decreasing probability of rel-evance to the user who submitted the request, where the probabilities are estimated as accurately as possible on the basis of whatever data have been made available to the system for this purpose, the overall effectiveness of the system to its user will be the best that is obtainable on the basis of those data.

Given some assumptions, such as that the relevance of a document to a query is independent of other documents, it is possible to show that this statement is true, in the sense that ranking by probability of relevance will maximize preci-sion, which is the proportion of relevant documents, at any given rank (for exam-ple, in the top 10 documents). Unfortunately, the Probability Ranking Principle doesn't tell us *how* to calculate or estimate the probability of relevance. There are many probabilistic retrieval models, and each one proposes a different method for estimating this probability. Most of the rest of this chapter discusses some of the most important probabilistic models.

In this section, we start with a simple probabilistic model based on treating information retrieval as a classification problem. We then describe a popular and effective ranking algorithm that is based on this model.

7.2.1 Information Retrieval as Classification

In any retrieval model that assumes relevance is binary, there will be two sets of documents, the relevant documents and the non-relevant documents, for each query. Given a new document, the task of a search engine could be described as deciding whether the document belongs in the relevant set or the non-relevant[2] set. That is, the system should *classify* the document as relevant or non-relevant, and retrieve it if it is relevant.

Given some way of calculating the *probability* that the document is relevant and the probability that it is non-relevant, then it would seem reasonable to clas-sify the document into the set that has the highest probability. In other words,

---

[1] A "reference retrieval system" would now be called a search engine.

[2] Note that we never talk about "irrelevant" documents in information retrieval; instead they are "non-relevant."

we would decide that a document D is relevant if $P(R|D) > P(NR|D)$, where $P(R|D)$ is a *conditional* probability representing the probability of relevance given the representation of that document, and $P(NR|D)$ is the conditional probability of non-relevance (Figure 7.3). This is known as the *Bayes Decision Rule*, and a system that classifies documents this way is called a *Bayes classifier*.

In Chapter 9, we discuss other applications of classification (such as spam filtering) and other classification techniques, but here we focus on the ranking algorithm that results from this probabilistic retrieval model based on classification.

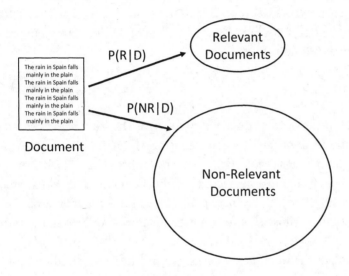

Fig. 7.3. Classifying a document as relevant or non-relevant

The question that faces us now is how to compute these probabilities. To start with, let's focus on $P(R|D)$. It's not clear how we would go about calculating this, but given information about the relevant set, we should be able to calculate $P(D|R)$. For example, if we had information about how often specific words occurred in the relevant set, then, given a new document, it would be relatively straightforward to calculate how likely it would be to see the combination of words in the document occurring in the relevant set. Let's assume that the probability of the word "president" in the relevant set is 0.02, and the probability of "lincoln" is 0.03. If a new document contains the words "president" and "lincoln", we could say that the probability of observing that combination of words in the relevant set is $0.02 \times 0.03 = 0.0006$, assuming that the two words occur independently.[3]

So how does calculating $P(D|R)$ get us to the probability of relevance? It turns out there is a relationship between $P(R|D)$ and $P(D|R)$ that is expressed by *Bayes' Rule*:[4]

$$P(R|D) = \frac{P(D|R)P(R)}{P(D)}$$

where $P(R)$ is the *a priori* probability of relevance (in other words, how likely any document is to be relevant), and $P(D)$ acts as a normalizing constant. Given this, we can express our decision rule in the following way: classify a document as relevant if $P(D|R)P(R) > P(D|NR)P(NR)$. This is the same as classifying a document as relevant if:

$$\frac{P(D|R)}{P(D|NR)} > \frac{P(NR)}{P(R)}$$

The left-hand side of this equation is known as the *likelihood ratio*. In most classification applications, such as spam filtering, the system must decide which class the document belongs to in order to take the appropriate action. For information retrieval, a search engine only needs to rank documents, rather than make that decision (which is hard). If we use the likelihood ratio as a score, the highly ranked documents will be those that have a high likelihood of belonging to the relevant set.

To calculate the document scores, we still need to decide how to come up with values for $P(D|R)$ and $P(D|NR)$. The simplest approach is to make the same assumptions that we made in our earlier example; that is, we represent documents as a combination of words and the relevant and non-relevant sets using word probabilities. In this model, documents are represented as a vector of binary features, $D = (d_1, d_2, \ldots, d_t)$, where $d_i = 1$ if term i is present in the document, and 0 otherwise. The other major assumption we make is *term independence* (also known as the *Naïve Bayes* assumption). This means we can estimate $P(D|R)$ by the product of the individual term probabilities $\prod_{i=1}^{t} P(d_i|R)$ (and similarly for $P(D|NR)$). Because this model makes the assumptions of term independence and binary features in documents, it is known as the *binary independence model*.

---

[3] Given two events A and B, the joint probability $P(A \cap B)$ is the probability of both events occurring together. In general, $P(A \cap B) = P(A|B)P(B)$. If A and B are independent, this means that $P(A \cap B) = P(A)P(B)$.

[4] Named after Thomas Bayes, a British mathematician.

Words obviously do not occur independently in text. If the word "Microsoft" occurs in a document, it is very likely that the word "Windows" will also occur. The assumption of term independence, however, is a common one since it usually simplifies the mathematics involved in the model. Models that allow some form of dependence between terms will be discussed later in this chapter.

Recall that a document in this model is a vector of 1s and 0s representing the presence and absence of terms. For example, if there were five terms indexed, one of the document representations might be $(1, 0, 0, 1, 1)$, meaning that the document contains terms 1, 4, and 5. To calculate the probability of this document occurring in the relevant set, we need the probabilities that the terms are 1 or 0 in the relevant set. If p_i is the probability that term i occurs (has the value 1) in a document from the relevant set, then the probability of our example document occurring in the relevant set is $p_1 \times (1 - p_2) \times (1 - p_3) \times p_4 \times p_5$. The probability $(1 - p_2)$ is the probability of term 2 *not* occurring in the relevant set. For the non-relevant set, we use s_i to represent the probability of term i occurring.[5]

Going back to the likelihood ratio, using p_i and s_i gives us a score of

$$\frac{P(D|R)}{P(D|NR)} = \prod_{i:d_i=1} \frac{p_i}{s_i} \cdot \prod_{i:d_i=0} \frac{1 - p_i}{1 - s_i}$$

where $\prod_{i:d_i=1}$ means that it is a product over the terms that have the value 1 in the document. We can now do a bit of mathematical manipulation to get:

$$\prod_{i:d_i=1} \frac{p_i}{s_i} \cdot \left(\prod_{i:d_i=1} \frac{1 - s_i}{1 - p_i} \cdot \prod_{i:d_i=1} \frac{1 - p_i}{1 - s_i} \right) \cdot \prod_{i:d_i=0} \frac{1 - p_i}{1 - s_i}$$

$$= \prod_{i:d_i=1} \frac{p_i(1 - s_i)}{s_i(1 - p_i)} \cdot \prod_{i} \frac{1 - p_i}{1 - s_i}$$

The second product is over all terms and is therefore the same for all documents, so we can ignore it for ranking. Since multiplying lots of small numbers can lead to problems with the accuracy of the result, we can equivalently use the logarithm of the product, which means that the scoring function is:

$$\sum_{i:d_i=1} \log \frac{p_i(1 - s_i)}{s_i(1 - p_i)}$$

---

[5] In many descriptions of this model, p_i and q_i are used for these probabilities. We use s_i to avoid confusion with the q_i used to represent query terms.

You might be wondering where the query has gone, given that this is a document ranking algorithm for a specific query. In many cases, the query provides us with the only information we have about the relevant set. We can assume that, in the absence of other information, terms that are not in the query will have the same probability of occurrence in the relevant and non-relevant documents (i.e., $p_i = s_i$). In that case, the summation will only be over terms that are both in the query and in the document. This means that, given a query, the score for a document is simply the sum of the term weights for all matching terms.

If we have no other information about the relevant set, we could make the additional assumptions that p_i is a constant and that s_i could be estimated by using the term occurrences in the whole collection as an approximation. We make the second assumption based on the fact that the number of relevant documents is much smaller than the total number of documents in the collection. With a value of 0.5 for p_i in the scoring function described earlier, this gives a term weight for term i of

$$\log \frac{0.5(1 - \frac{n_i}{N})}{\frac{n_i}{N}(1 - 0.5)} = \log \frac{N - n_i}{n_i}$$

where n_i is the number of documents that contain term i, and N is the number of documents in the collection. This shows that, in the absence of information about the relevant documents, the term weight derived from the binary independence model is very similar to an idf weight. There is no tf component, because the documents were assumed to have binary features.

If we do have information about term occurrences in the relevant and non-relevant sets, it can be summarized in a *contingency table*, shown in Table 7.1. This information could be obtained through relevance feedback, where users identify relevant documents in initial rankings. In this table, r_i is the number of relevant documents containing term i, n_i is the number of documents containing term i, N is the total number of documents in the collection, and R is the number of relevant documents for this query.

	Relevant	Non-relevant	Total
$d_i = 1$	r_i	$n_i - r_i$	n_i
$d_i = 0$	$R - r_i$	$N - n_i - R + r_i$	$N - r_i$
Total	R	$N - R$	N

Table 7.1. Contingency table of term occurrences for a particular query

Given this table, the obvious *estimates*[6] for p_i and s_i would be $p_i = r_i/R$ (the number of relevant documents that contain a term divided by the total number of relevant documents) and $s_i = (n_i - r_i)/(N - R)$ (the number of non-relevant documents that contain a term divided by the total number of non-relevant documents). Using these estimates could cause a problem, however, if some of the entries in the contingency table were zeros. If r_i was zero, for example, the term weight would be $\log 0$. To avoid this, a standard solution is to add 0.5 to each count (and 1 to the totals), which gives us estimates of $p_i = (r_i + 0.5)/(R + 1)$ and $s_i = (n_i - r_i + 0.5)/(N - R + 1.0)$. Putting these estimates into the scoring function gives us:

$$\sum_{i:d_i=q_i=1} \log \frac{(r_i + 0.5)/(R - r_i + 0.5)}{(n_i - r_i + 0.5)/(N - n_i - R + r_i + 0.5)}$$

Although this document score sums term weights for just the matching query terms, with relevance feedback the query can be *expanded* to include other important terms from the relevant set. Note that if we have no relevance information, we can set r and R to 0, which would give a p_i value of 0.5, and would produce the *idf*-like term weight discussed before.

So how good is this document score when used for ranking? Not very good, it turns out. Although it does provide a method of incorporating relevance information, in most cases we don't have this information and instead would be using term weights that are similar to *idf* weights. The absence of a tf component makes a significant difference to the effectiveness of the ranking, and most effectiveness measures will drop by about 50% if the ranking ignores this information. This means, for example, that we might see 50% fewer relevant documents in the top ranks if we used the binary independence model ranking instead of the best $tf.idf$ ranking.

It turns out, however, that the binary independence model is the basis for one of the most effective and popular ranking algorithms, known as BM25.[7]

---

[6] We use the term *estimate* for a probability value calculated using data such as a contingency table because this value is only an estimate for the true value of the probability and would change if more data were available.

[7] BM stands for Best Match, and 25 is just a numbering scheme used by Robertson and his co-workers to keep track of weighting variants (Robertson & Walker, 1994).

7.2.2 The BM25 Ranking Algorithm

BM25 extends the scoring function for the binary independence model to include document and query term weights. The extension is based on probabilistic arguments and experimental validation, but it is not a formal model.

BM25 has performed very well in TREC retrieval experiments and has influenced the ranking algorithms of commercial search engines, including web search engines. There are some variations of the scoring function for BM25, but the most common form is:

$$\sum_{i \in Q} \log \frac{(r_i + 0.5)/(R - r_i + 0.5)}{(n_i - r_i + 0.5)/(N - n_i - R + r_i + 0.5)} \cdot \frac{(k_1 + 1)f_i}{K + f_i} \cdot \frac{(k_2 + 1)qf_i}{k_2 + qf_i}$$

where the summation is now over all terms in the query; and N, R, n_i, and r_i are the same as described in the last section, with the additional condition that r and R are set to zero if there is no relevance information; f_i is the frequency of term i in the document; qf_i is the frequency of term i in the query; and k_1, k_2, and K are parameters whose values are set empirically.

The constant k_1 determines how the tf component of the term weight changes as f_i increases. If $k_1 = 0$, the term frequency component would be ignored and only term presence or absence would matter. If k_1 is large, the term weight component would increase nearly linearly with f_i. In TREC experiments, a typical value for k_1 is 1.2, which causes the effect of f_i to be very non-linear, similar to the use of $\log f$ in the term weights discussed in section 7.1.2. This means that after three or four occurrences of a term, additional occurrences will have little impact. The constant k_2 has a similar role in the query term weight. Typical values for this parameter are in the range 0 to 1,000, meaning that performance is less sensitive to k_2 than it is to k_1. This is because query term frequencies are much lower and less variable than document term frequencies.

K is a more complicated parameter that normalizes the tf component by document length. Specifically

$$K = k_1((1 - b) + b \cdot \frac{dl}{avdl})$$

where b is a parameter, dl is the length of the document, and $avdl$ is the average length of a document in the collection. The constant b regulates the impact of the length normalization, where $b = 0$ corresponds to no length normalization, and

$b = 1$ is full normalization. In TREC experiments, a value of $b = 0.75$ was found to be effective.

As an example calculation, let's consider a query with two terms, "president" and "lincoln", each of which occurs only once in the query ($qf = 1$). We will consider the typical case where we have no relevance information (r and R are zero). Let's assume that we are searching a collection of 500,000 documents (N), and that in this collection, "president" occurs in 40,000 documents ($n_1 = 40,000$) and "lincoln" occurs in 300 documents ($n_2 = 300$). In the document we are scoring (which is about President Lincoln), "president" occurs 15 times ($f_1 = 15$) and "lincoln" occurs 25 times ($f_2 = 25$). The document length is 90% of the average length ($dl/avdl = 0.9$). The parameter values we use are $k_1 = 1.2, b = 0.75$, and $k_2 = 100$. With these values, $K = 1.2 \cdot (0.25 + 0.75 \cdot 0.9) = 1.11$, and the document score is:

$$BM25(Q, D) =$$

$$\log \frac{(0 + 0.5)/(0 - 0 + 0.5)}{(40000 - 0 + 0.5)/(500000 - 40000 - 0 + 0 + 0.5)}$$

$$\times \frac{(1.2 + 1)15}{1.11 + 15} \times \frac{(100 + 1)1}{100 + 1}$$

$$+ \log \frac{(0 + 0.5)/(0 - 0 + 0.5)}{(300 - 0 + 0.5)/(500000 - 300 - 0 + 0 + 0.5)}$$

$$\times \frac{(1.2 + 1)25}{1.11 + 25} \times \frac{(100 + 1)1}{100 + 1}$$

$$= \log 460000.5/40000.5 \cdot 33/16.11 \cdot 101/101$$
$$+ \log 499700.5/300.5 \cdot 55/26.11 \cdot 101/101$$
$$= 2.44 \cdot 2.05 \cdot 1 + 7.42 \cdot 2.11 \cdot 1$$
$$= 5.00 + 15.66 = 20.66$$

Notice the impact from the first part of the weight that, without relevance information, is nearly the same as an *idf* weight (as we discussed in section 7.2.1). Because the term "lincoln" is much less frequent in the collection, it has a much higher *idf* component (7.42 versus 2.44). Table 7.2 gives scores for different numbers of term occurrences. This shows the importance of the "lincoln" term and that even one occurrence of a term can make a large difference in the score. Reducing the number of term occurrences from 25 or 15 to 1 makes a significant but not dramatic difference. This example also demonstrates that it is possible for a document containing a large number of occurrences of a single important term to score higher than a document containing both query terms (15.66 versus 12.74).

Frequency of "president"	Frequency of "lincoln"	BM25 score
15	25	20.66
15	1	12.74
15	0	5.00
1	25	18.2
0	25	15.66

Table 7.2. BM25 scores for an example document

The score calculation may seem complicated, but remember that some of the calculation of term weights can occur at indexing time, before processing any query. If there is no relevance information, scoring a document simply involves adding the weights for matching query terms, with a small additional calculation if query terms occur more than once (i.e., if $qf > 1$). Another important point is that the parameter values for the BM25 ranking algorithm can be tuned (i.e., adjusted to obtain the best effectiveness) for each application. The process of tuning is described further in section 7.7 and Chapter 8.

To summarize, BM25 is an effective ranking algorithm derived from a model of information retrieval viewed as classification. This model focuses on topical relevance and makes an explicit assumption that relevance is binary. In the next section, we discuss another probabilistic model that incorporates term frequency directly in the model, rather than being added in as an extension to improve performance.

7.3 Ranking Based on Language Models

Language models are used to represent text in a variety of *language technologies*, such as speech recognition, machine translation, and handwriting recognition. The simplest form of language model, known as a *unigram* language model, is a *probability distribution* over the words in the language. This means that the language model associates a probability of occurrence with every word in the index vocabulary for a collection. For example, if the documents in a collection contained just five different words, a possible language model for that collection might be $(0.2, 0.1, 0.35, 0.25, 0.1)$, where each number is the probability of a word occurring. If we treat each document as a *sequence* of words, then the probabilities in the language model predict what the next word in the sequence will be. For example, if the five words in our language were "girl", "cat", "the", "boy", and "touched", then the probabilities predict which of these words will be next. These words cover all the possibilities, so the probabilities must add to 1. Because this is a unigram model, the previous words have no impact on the prediction. With this model, for example, it is just as likely to get the sequence "girl cat" (probability 0.2×0.1) as "girl touched" (probability 0.2×0.1).

In applications such as speech recognition, n-gram language models that predict words based on longer sequences are used. An n-gram model predicts a word based on the previous $n - 1$ words. The most common n-gram models are *bigram* (predicting based on the previous word) and *trigram* (predicting based on the previous two words) models. Although bigram models have been used in information retrieval to represent two-word phrases (see section 4.3.5), we focus our discussion on unigram models because they are simpler and have proven to be very effective as the basis for ranking algorithms.

For search applications, we use language models to represent the topical content of a document. A *topic* is something that is talked about often but rarely defined in information retrieval discussions. In this approach, we define a topic as a probability distribution over words (in other words, a language model). For example, if a document is about fishing in Alaska, we would expect to see words associated with fishing and locations in Alaska with high probabilities in the language model. If it is about fishing in Florida, some of the high-probability words will be the same, but there will be more high probability words associated with locations in Florida. If instead the document is about fishing games for computers, most of the high-probability words will be associated with game manufacturers and computer use, although there will still be some important words about fishing. Note that a topic language model, or *topic model* for short, contains probabilities for all words, not just the most important. Most of the words will have "default" probabilities that will be the same for any text, but the words that are important for the topic will have unusually high probabilities.

A language model representation of a document can be used to "generate" new text by sampling words according to the probability distribution. If we imagine the language model as a big bucket of words, where the probabilities determine how many instances of a word are in the bucket, then we can generate text by reaching in (without looking), drawing out a word, writing it down, putting the word back in the bucket, and drawing again. Note that we are not saying that we can generate the original document by this process. In fact, because we are only using a unigram model, the generated text is going to look pretty bad, with no syntactic structure. Important words for the topic of the document will, however, appear often. Intuitively, we are using the language model as a very approximate model for the topic the author of the document was thinking about when he was writing it.

When text is modeled as a finite sequence of words, where at each point in the sequence there are t different possible words, this corresponds to assuming a *multinomial* distribution over words. Although there are alternatives, multinomial language models are the most common in information retrieval.[8] One of the limitations of multinomial models that has been pointed out is that they do not describe text *burstiness* well, which is the observation that once a word is "pulled out of the bucket," it tends to be pulled out repeatedly.

In addition to representing documents as language models, we can also represent the topic of the query as a language model. In this case, the intuition is that the language model is a representation of the topic that the information seeker had in mind when she was writing the query. This leads to three obvious possibilities for retrieval models based on language models: one based on the probability of generating the query text from a document language model, one based on generating the document text from a query language model, and one based on comparing the language models representing the query and document topics. In the next two sections, we describe these retrieval models in more detail.

7.3.1 Query Likelihood Ranking

In the *query likelihood* retrieval model, we rank documents by the probability that the query text could be generated by the document language model. In other words, we calculate the probability that we could pull the query words out of the "bucket" of words representing the document. This is a model of topical relevance, in the sense that the probability of query generation is the measure of how likely it is that a document is about the same topic as the query.

Since we start with a query, we would in general like to calculate $P(D|Q)$ to rank the documents. Using Bayes' Rule, we can calculate this by

---

[8] We discuss the multinomial model in the context of classification in Chapter 9.

$$p(D|Q) \stackrel{rank}{=} P(Q|D)P(D)$$

where the symbol $\stackrel{rank}{=}$, as we mentioned previously, means that the right-hand side is rank equivalent to the left-hand side (i.e., we can ignore the normalizing constant $P(Q)$), $P(D)$ is the prior probability of a document, and $P(Q|D)$ is the query likelihood given the document. In most cases, $P(D)$ is assumed to be *uniform* (the same for all documents), and so will not affect the ranking. Models that assign non-uniform prior probabilities based on, for example, document date or document length can be useful in some applications, but we will make the simpler uniform assumption here. Given that assumption, the retrieval model specifies ranking documents by $P(Q|D)$, which we calculate using the unigram language model for the document

$$P(Q|D) = \prod_{i=1}^{n} P(q_i|D)$$

where q_i is a query word, and there are n words in the query.

To calculate this score, we need to have estimates for the language model probabilities $P(q_i|D)$. The obvious estimate would be

$$P(q_i|D) = \frac{f_{q_i,D}}{|D|}$$

where $f_{q_i,D}$ is the number of times word qi occurs in document D, and $|D|$ is the number of words in D. For a multinomial distribution, this is the *maximum likelihood* estimate, which means this this is the estimate that makes the observed value of $f_{q_i,D}$ most likely. The major problem with this estimate is that if any of the query words are missing from the document, the score given by the query likelihood model for $P(Q|D)$ will be zero. This is clearly not appropriate for longer queries. For example, missing one word out of six should not produce a score of zero. We will also not be able to distinguish between documents that have different numbers of query words missing. Additionally, because we are building a topic model for a document, words associated with that topic should have some probability of occurring, even if they were not mentioned in the document. For example, a language model representing a document about computer games should have some non-zero probability for the word "RPG" even if that word was not mentioned in the document. A small probability for that word will enable the document to receive a non-zero score for the query "RPG computer games", although it will be lower than the score for a document that contains all three words.

Smoothing is a technique for avoiding this estimation problem and overcoming *data sparsity*, which means that we typically do not have large amounts of text to use for the language model probability estimates. The general approach to smoothing is to lower (or *discount*) the probability estimates for words that are seen in the document text, and assign that "leftover" probability to the estimates for the words that are not seen in the text. The estimates for unseen words are usually based on the frequency of occurrence of words in the whole document collection. If $P(q_i|C)$ is the probability for query word i in the *collection language model* for document collection C, then the estimate we use for an unseen word in a document is $\alpha_D P(q_i|C)$, where α_D is a coefficient controlling the probability assigned to unseen words.[9] In general, α_D can depend on the document. In order that the probabilities sum to one, the probability estimate for a word that is seen in a document is $(1 - \alpha_D)P(q_i|D) + \alpha_D P(q_i|C)$.

To make this clear, consider a simple example where there are only three words, w_1, w_2, and w_3, in our index vocabulary. If the collection probabilities for these three words, based on maximum likelihood estimates, are 0.3, 0.5, and 0.2, and the document probabilities based on maximum likelihood estimates are 0.5, 0.5, and 0.0, then the *smoothed* probability estimates for the document language model are:

$$
\begin{aligned}
P(w_1|D) &= (1 - \alpha_D)P(w_1|D) + \alpha_D P(w_1|C) \\
&= (1 - \alpha_D) \cdot 0.5 + \alpha_D \cdot 0.3 \\
P(w_2|D) &= (1 - \alpha_D) \cdot 0.5 + \alpha_D \cdot 0.5 \\
P(w_3|D) &= (1 - \alpha_D) \cdot 0.0 + \alpha_D \cdot 0.2 = \alpha_D \cdot 0.2
\end{aligned}
$$

Note that term w_3 has a non-zero probability estimate, even though it did not occur in the document text. If we add these three probabilities, we get

$$
\begin{aligned}
P(w_1|D) + P(w_2|D) + P(w_3|D) &= (1 - \alpha_D) \cdot (0.5 + 0.5) \\
&\quad + \alpha_D \cdot (0.3 + 0.5 + 0.2) \\
&= 1 - \alpha_D + \alpha_D \\
&= 1
\end{aligned}
$$

which confirms that the probabilities are consistent.

---

[9] The collection language model probability is also known as the *background* language model probability, or just the background probability.

Different forms of estimation result from specifying the value of α_D. The simplest choice would be to set it to a constant, i.e., $\alpha_D = \lambda$. The collection language model probability estimate we use for word q_i is $c_{q_i}/|C|$, where c_{q_i} is the number of times a query word occurs in the collection of documents, and $|C|$ is the total number of word occurrences in the collection. This gives us an estimate for $P(q_i|D)$ of:

$$p(q_i|D) = (1 - \lambda)\frac{f_{q_i,D}}{|D|} + \lambda\frac{c_{q_i}}{|C|}$$

This form of smoothing is known as the *Jelinek-Mercer* method. Substituting this estimate in the document score for the query-likelihood model gives:

$$P(Q|D) = \prod_{i=1}^{n}((1 - \lambda)\frac{f_{q_i,D}}{|D|} + \lambda\frac{c_{q_i}}{|C|})$$

As we have said before, since multiplying many small numbers together can lead to accuracy problems, we can use logarithms to turn this score into a rank-equivalent sum as follows:

$$\log P(Q|D) = \sum_{i=1}^{n}\log((1 - \lambda)\frac{f_{q_i,D}}{|D|} + \lambda\frac{c_{q_i}}{|C|})$$

Small values of λ produce less smoothing, and consequently the query tends to act more like a Boolean **AND** since the absence of any query word will penalize the score substantially. In addition, the relative weighting of words, as measured by the maximum likelihood estimates, will be important in determining the score. As λ approaches 1, the relative weighting will be less important, and the query acts more like a Boolean **OR** or a *coordination level match*.[10] In TREC evaluations, it has been shown that values of λ around 0.1 work well for short queries, whereas values around 0.7 are better for much longer queries. Short queries tend to contain only significant words, and a low λ value will favor documents that contain all the query words. With much longer queries, missing a word is much less important, and a high λ places more emphasis on documents that contain a number of the high-probability words.

At this point, it may occur to you that the query likelihood retrieval model doesn't have anything that looks like a *tf.idf* weight, and yet experiments show

---

[10] A coordination level match simply ranks documents by the number of matching query terms.

that it is as least as effective as the BM25 ranking algorithm. We can, however, demonstrate a relationship to *tf.idf* weights by manipulating the query likelihood score in the following way:

$$\log P(Q|D) = \sum_{i=1}^{n} \log((1-\lambda)\frac{f_{q_i,D}}{|D|} + \lambda\frac{c_{q_i}}{|C|})$$

$$= \sum_{i:f_{q_i,D}>0} \log((1-\lambda)\frac{f_{q_i,D}}{|D|} + \lambda\frac{c_{q_i}}{|C|}) + \sum_{i:f_{q_i,D}=0} \log(\lambda\frac{c_{q_i}}{|C|})$$

$$= \sum_{i:f_{q_i,D}>0} \log\frac{((1-\lambda)\frac{f_{q_i,D}}{|D|} + \lambda\frac{c_{q_i}}{|C|})}{\lambda\frac{c_{q_i}}{|C|}} + \sum_{i=1}^{n} \log(\lambda\frac{c_{q_i}}{|C|})$$

$$\stackrel{rank}{=} \sum_{i:f_{q_i,D}>0} \log\left(\frac{((1-\lambda)\frac{f_{q_i,D}}{|D|}}{\lambda\frac{c_{q_i}}{|C|}} + 1\right)$$

In the second line, we split the score into the words that occur in the document and those that don't occur ($f_{q_i,D} = 0$). In the third line, we add

$$\sum_{i:f_{q_i,D}>0} \log(\lambda\frac{c_{q_i}}{|C|})$$

to the last term and subtract it from the first (where it ends up in the denominator), so there is no net effect. The last term is now the same for all documents and can be ignored for ranking. The final expression gives the document score in terms of a "weight" for matching query terms. Although this weight is not identical to a *tf.idf* weight, there are clear similarities in that it is directly proportional to the document term frequency and inversely proportional to the collection frequency.

A different form of estimation, and one that is generally more effective, comes from using a value of α_D that is dependent on document length. This approach is known as *Dirichlet* smoothing, for reasons we will discuss later, and uses

$$\alpha_D = \frac{\mu}{|D| + \mu}$$

where μ is a parameter whose value is set empirically. Substituting this expression for α_D in $(1 - \alpha_D)P(q_i|D) + \alpha_D P(q_i|C)$ results in the probability estimation formula

$$p(q_i|D) = \frac{f_{q_i,D} + \mu\frac{c_{q_i}}{|C|}}{|D| + \mu}$$

which in turn leads to the following document score:

$$\log P(Q|D) = \sum_{i=1}^{n} \log \frac{f_{q_i,D} + \mu\frac{c_{q_i}}{|C|}}{|D| + \mu}$$

Similar to the Jelinek-Mercer smoothing, small values of the parameter (μ in this case) give more importance to the relative weighting of words, and large values favor the number of matching terms. Typical values of μ that achieve the best results in TREC experiments are in the range 1,000 to 2,000 (remember that collection probabilities are very small), and Dirichlet smoothing is generally more effective than Jelinek-Mercer, especially for the short queries that are common in most search applications.

So where does Dirichlet smoothing come from? It turns out that a Dirichlet distribution[11] is the natural way to specify prior knowledge when estimating the probabilities in a multinomial distribution. The process of *Bayesian estimation* determines probability estimates based on this prior knowledge and the observed text. The resulting probability estimate can be viewed as combining actual word counts from the text with *pseudo-counts* from the Dirichlet distribution. If we had no text, the probability estimate for term q_i would be $\mu(c_{q_i}/|C|)/\mu$, which is a reasonable guess based on the collection. The more text we have (i.e., for longer documents), the less influence the prior knowledge will have.

We can demonstrate the calculation of query likelihood document scores using the example given in section 7.2.2. The two query terms are "president" and "lincoln". For the term "president", $f_{q_i,D} = 15$, and let's assume that $c_{q_i} = 160,000$. For the term "lincoln", $f_{q_i,D} = 25$, and we will assume that $c_{q_i} = 2,400$. The number of word occurrences in the document $|d|$ is assumed to be 1,800, and the number of word occurrences in the collection is 10^9 (500,000 documents times an average of 2,000 words). The value of μ used is 2,000. Given these numbers, the score for the document is:

---

[11] Named after the German mathematician Johann Peter Gustav Lejeune Dirichlet (the first name used seems to vary).

$$QL(Q, D) = \log \frac{15 + 2000 \times (1.6 \times 10^5/10^9)}{1800 + 2000}$$
$$+ \log \frac{25 + 2000 \times (2400/10^9)}{1800 + 2000}$$
$$= \log(15.32/3800) + \log(25.005/3800)$$
$$= -5.51 + -5.02 = -10.53$$

A negative number? Remember that we are taking logarithms of probabilities in this scoring function, and the probabilities of word occurrence are small. The important issue is the effectiveness of the rankings produced using these scores. Table 7.3 shows the query likelihood scores for the same variations of term occurrences that were used in Table 7.2. Although the scores look very different for BM25 and QL, the rankings are similar, with the exception that the document containing 15 occurrences of "president" and 1 of "lincoln" is ranked higher than the document containing 0 occurrences of "president" and 25 occurrences of "lincoln" in the QL scores, whereas the reverse is true for BM25.

Frequency of "president"	Frequency of "lincoln"	QL score
15	25	−10.53
15	1	−13.75
15	0	−19.05
1	25	−12.99
0	25	−14.40

Table 7.3. Query likelihood scores for an example document

To summarize, query likelihood is a simple probabilistic retrieval model that directly incorporates term frequency. The problem of coming up with effective term weights is replaced by probability estimation, which is better understood and has a formal basis. The basic query likelihood score with Dirichlet smoothing has similar effectiveness to BM25, although it does do better on most TREC collections. If more sophisticated smoothing based on topic models is used (described further in section 7.6), query likelihood consistently outperforms BM25. This means that instead of smoothing using the collection probabilities for words, we instead use word probabilities from similar documents.

The simplicity of the language model framework, combined with the ability to describe a variety of retrieval applications and the effectiveness of the associated ranking algorithms, make this approach a good choice for a retrieval model based on topical relevance.

7.3.2 Relevance Models and Pseudo-Relevance Feedback

Although the basic query likelihood model has a number of advantages, it is limited in terms of how it models information needs and queries. It is difficult, for example, to incorporate information about relevant documents into the ranking algorithm, or to represent the fact that a query is just one of many possible queries that could be used to describe a particular information need. In this section, we show how this can be done by extending the basic model.

In the introduction to section 7.3, we mentioned that it is possible to represent the topic of a query as a language model. Instead of calling this the query language model, we use the name *relevance model* since it represents the topic covered by relevant documents. The query can be viewed as a very small sample of text generated from the relevance model, and relevant documents are much larger samples of text from the same model. Given some examples of relevant documents for a query, we could estimate the probabilities in the relevance model and then use this model to predict the relevance of new documents. In fact, this is a version of the classification model presented in section 7.2.1, where we interpret $P(D|R)$ as the probability of generating the text in a document given a relevance model. This is also called the *document likelihood* model. Although this model, unlike the binary independence model, directly incorporates term frequency, it turns out that $P(D|R)$ is difficult to calculate and compare across documents. This is because documents contain a large and extremely variable number of words compared to a query. Consider two documents D_a and D_b, for example, containing 5 and 500 words respectively. Because of the large difference in the number of words involved, the comparison of $P(D_a|R)$ and $P(D_b|R)$ for ranking will be more difficult than comparing $P(Q|D_a)$ and $P(Q|D_b)$, which use the same query and smoothed representations for the documents. In addition, we still have the problem of obtaining examples of relevant documents.

There is, however, another alternative. If we can estimate a relevance model from a query, we can compare this language model directly with the model for a document. Documents would then be ranked by the similarity of the document model to the relevance model. A document with a model that is very similar to the relevance model is likely to be on the same topic. The obvious next question is how to compare two language models. A well-known measure from probability theory and information theory, the *Kullback-Leibler divergence* (referred to as

KL-divergence in this book),[12] measures the difference between two probability distributions. Given the *true* probability distribution P and another distribution Q that is an approximation to P, the KL divergence is defined as:

$$KL(P||Q) = \sum_x P(x) \log \frac{P(x)}{Q(x)}$$

Since KL-divergence is always positive and is larger for distributions that are further apart, we use the *negative* KL-divergence as the basis for the ranking function (i.e., smaller differences mean higher scores). In addition, KL-divergence is not symmetric, and it matters which distribution we pick as the true distribution. If we assume the true distribution to be the relevance model for the query (R) and the approximation to be the document language model (D), then the negative KL-divergence can be expressed as

$$\sum_{w \in V} P(w|R) \log P(w|D) - \sum_{w \in V} P(w|R) \log P(w|R)$$

where the summation is over all words w in the vocabulary V. The second term on the right-hand side of this equation does not depend on the document, and can be ignored for ranking. Given a simple maximum likelihood estimate for $P(w|R)$, based on the frequency in the query text ($f_{w,Q}$) and the number of words in the query ($|Q|$), the score for a document will be:

$$\sum_{w \in V} \frac{f_{w,Q}}{|Q|} \log P(w|D)$$

Although this summation is over all words in the vocabulary, words that do not occur in the query have a zero maximum likelihood estimate and will not contribute to the score. Also, query words with frequency k will contribute $k \times \log P(w|D)$ to the score. This means that this score is rank equivalent to the query likelihood score described in the previous section. In other words, query likelihood is a special case of a retrieval model that ranks by comparing a relevance model based on a query to a document language model.

The advantage of the more general model is that it is not restricted to the simple method of estimating the relevance model using query term frequencies. If we

---

[12] KL-divergence is also called information divergence, information gain, or relative entropy.

regard the query words as a sample from the relevance model, then it seems reasonable to base the probability of a new sample word on the query words we have seen. In other words, the probability of pulling a word w out of the "bucket" representing the relevance model should depend on the n query words we have just pulled out. More formally, we can relate the probability of w to the conditional probability of observing w given that we just observed the query words $q_1 \ldots q_n$ by the approximation:

$$P(w|R) \approx P(w|q_1 \ldots q_n)$$

By definition, we can express the conditional probability in terms of the joint probability of observing w with the query words:

$$P(w|R) \approx \frac{P(w, q_1 \ldots q_n)}{P(q_1 \ldots q_n)}$$

$P(q_1 \ldots q_n)$ is a normalizing constant and is calculated as:

$$P(q_1 \ldots q_n) = \sum_{w \in V} P(w, q_1 \ldots q_n)$$

Now the question is how to estimate the joint probability $P(w, q_1 \ldots q_n)$. Given a set of documents $\mathcal{C}$ represented by language models, we can calculate the joint probability as follows:

$$P(w, q_1 \ldots q_n) = \sum_{D \in \mathcal{C}} p(D) P(w, q_1 \ldots q_n | D)$$

We can also make the assumption that:

$$P(w, q_1 \ldots q_n | D) = P(w|D) \prod_{i=1}^{n} P(q_i|D)$$

When we substitute this expression for $P(w, q_1 \ldots q_n | D)$ into the previous equation, we get the following estimate for the joint probability:

$$P(w, q_1 \ldots q_n) = \sum_{D \in \mathcal{C}} P(D) P(w|D) \prod_{i=1}^{n} P(q_i|D)$$

How do we interpret this formula? The prior probability $P(D)$ is usually assumed to be uniform and can be ignored. The expression $\prod_{i=1}^{n} P(q_i|D)$ is, in fact, the query likelihood score for the document D. This means that the estimate for $P(w, q_1 \ldots q_n)$ is simply a weighted average of the language model probabilities for w in a set of documents, where the weights are the query likelihood scores for those documents.

Ranking based on relevance models actually requires two passes. The first pass ranks documents using query likelihood to obtain the weights that are needed for relevance model estimation. In the second pass, we use KL-divergence to rank documents by comparing the relevance model and the document model. Note also that we are in effect adding words to the query by smoothing the relevance model using documents that are similar to the query. Many words that had zero probabilities in the relevance model based on query frequency estimates will now have non-zero values. What we are describing here is *exactly* the pseudo-relevance feedback process described in section 6.2.4. In other words, relevance models provide a formal retrieval model for pseudo-relevance feedback and query expansion. The following is a summary of the steps involved in ranking using relevance models:

1. Rank documents using the query likelihood score for query Q.
2. Select some number of the top-ranked documents to be the set C.
3. Calculate the relevance model probabilities $P(w|R)$ using the estimate for $P(w, q_1 \ldots q_n)$.
4. Rank documents again using the KL-divergence score:[13]

$$\sum_w P(w|R) \log P(w|D)$$

Some of these steps require further explanation. In steps 1 and 4, the document language model probabilities ($P(w|D)$) should be estimated using Dirichlet smoothing. In step 2, the model allows the set C to be the whole collection, but because low-ranked documents have little effect on the estimation of $P(w|R)$, usually only 10–50 of the top-ranked documents are used. This also makes the computation of $P(w|R)$ substantially faster.

For similar reasons, the summation in step 4 is not done over all words in the vocabulary. Typically only a small number (10–25) of the highest-probability words are used. In addition, the importance of the original query words is emphasized by combining the original query frequency estimates with the relevance

---

[13] More accurately, this score is the negative *cross entropy* because we removed the term $\sum_{w \in V} P(w|R) \log P(w|R)$.

model estimates using a similar approach to Jelinek-Mercer, i.e., $\lambda P(w|Q) + (1 - \lambda)P(w|R)$, where λ is a mixture parameter whose value is determined empirically (0.5 is a typical value for TREC experiments). This combination makes it clear that estimating relevance models is basically a process for query expansion and smoothing.

The next important question, as for all retrieval models, is how well it works. Based on TREC experiments, ranking using relevance models is one of the best pseudo-relevance feedback techniques. In addition, relevance models produce a significant improvement in effectiveness compared to query likelihood ranking averaged over a number of queries. Like all current pseudo-relevance feedback techniques, however, the improvements are not consistent, and some queries can produce worse rankings or strange results.

Tables 7.4 and 7.5 show the 16 highest-probability words from relevance models estimated using this technique with some example queries and a large collection of TREC news stories from the 1990s.[14] Table 7.4 uses the top 10 documents from the query likelihood ranking to construct the relevance model, whereas Table 7.5 uses the top 50 documents.

The first thing to notice is that, although the words are reasonable, they are very dependent on the collection of documents that is used. In the TREC news collection, for example, many of the stories that mention Abraham Lincoln are on the topic of the Lincoln Bedroom in the White House, which President Clinton used for guests and President Lincoln used as an office during the Civil War. These types of stories are reflected in the top probability words for the queries "president lincoln" and "abraham lincoln". Expanding the query using these words would clearly favor the retrieval of this type of story rather than more general biographies of Lincoln. The second observation is that there is not much difference between the words based on 10 documents and the words based on 50 documents. The words based on 50 documents are, however, somewhat more general because the larger set of documents contains a greater variety of topics. In the case of the query "tropical fish", the relevance model words based on 10 documents are clearly more related to the topic.

In summary, ranking by comparing a model of the query to a model of the document using KL-divergence is a generalization of query likelihood scoring.

---

[14] This is a considerably larger collection than was used to generate the term association tables in Chapter 6. Those tables were based on the ROBUST track data, which consists of just over half a million documents. These tables were generated using all the TREC news collections, which total more than six million documents.

president lincoln	abraham lincoln	fishing	tropical fish
lincoln	lincoln	fish	fish
president	america	farm	tropic
room	president	salmon	japan
bedroom	faith	new	aquarium
house	guest	wild	water
white	abraham	water	species
america	new	caught	aquatic
guest	room	catch	fair
serve	christian	tag	china
bed	history	time	coral
washington	public	eat	source
old	bedroom	raise	tank
office	war	city	reef
war	politics	people	animal
long	old	fishermen	tarpon
abraham	national	boat	fishery

Table 7.4. Highest-probability terms from relevance model for four example queries (estimated using top 10 documents)

This generalization allows for more accurate queries that reflect the relative importance of the words in the topic that the information seeker had in mind when he was writing the query. Relevance model estimation is an effective pseudo-relevance feedback technique based on the formal framework of language models, but as with all these techniques, caution must be used in applying relevance model–based query expansion to a specific retrieval application.

Language models provide a formal but straightforward method of describing retrieval models based on topical relevance. Even more sophisticated models can be developed by incorporating term dependence and phrases, for example. Topical relevance is, however, only part of what is needed for effective search. In the next section, we focus on a retrieval model for combining all the pieces of evidence that contribute to user relevance, which is what people who use a search engine really care about.

president lincoln	abraham lincoln	fishing	tropical fish
lincoln	lincoln	fish	fish
president	president	water	tropic
america	america	catch	water
new	abraham	reef	storm
national	war	fishermen	species
great	man	river	boat
white	civil	new	sea
war	new	year	river
washington	history	time	country
clinton	two	bass	tuna
house	room	boat	world
history	booth	world	million
time	time	farm	state
center	politics	angle	time
kennedy	public	fly	japan
room	guest	trout	mile

Table 7.5. Highest-probability terms from relevance model for four example queries (estimated using top 50 documents)

7.4 Complex Queries and Combining Evidence

Effective retrieval requires the combination of many pieces of evidence about a document's potential relevance. In the case of the retrieval models described in previous sections, the evidence consists of word occurrences that reflect topical content. In general, however, there can be many other types of evidence that should be considered. Even considering words, we may want to take into account whether certain words occur near each other, whether words occur in particular document structures, such as section headings or titles, or whether words are related to each other. In addition, evidence such as the date of publication, the document type, or, in the case of web search, the PageRank number will also be important. Although a retrieval algorithm such as query likelihood or BM25 could be extended to include some of these types of evidence, it is difficult not to resort to heuristic "fixes" that make the retrieval algorithm difficult to tune and adapt to new retrieval applications. Instead, what we really need is a framework where we can describe the different types of evidence, their relative importance, and how they should be combined. The *inference network* retrieval model, which has been used in both commercial and open source search engines (and is incorporated in Galago), is one approach to doing this.

The inference network model is based on the formalism of *Bayesian networks* and is a probabilistic model. The model provides a mechanism for defining and evaluating operators in a query language. Some of these operators are used to specify types of evidence, and others describe how it should be combined. The version of the inference network we will describe uses language models to estimate the probabilities that are needed to evaluate the queries.

In this section, we first give an overview of the inference network model, and then show how that model is used as the basis of a powerful query language for search applications. In the next section, we describe web search and explain how the inference network model would be used to combine the many sources of evidence required for effective ranking.

Queries described using the inference network query language appear to be much more complicated than a simple text query with two or three words. Most users will not understand this language, just as most relational database users do not understand Structured Query Language (SQL). Instead, applications translate simple user queries into more complex inference network versions. The more complex query incorporates additional features and weights that reflect the best combination of evidence for effective ranking. This point will become clearer as we discuss examples in the next two sections.

7.4.1 The Inference Network Model

A Bayesian network is a probabilistic model that is used to specify a set of events and the dependencies between them. The networks are directed, acyclic graphs (DAGs), where the nodes in the graph represent events with a set of possible outcomes and arcs represent probabilistic dependencies between the events. The probability, or belief,[15] of a particular event outcome can be determined given the probabilities of the parent events (or a prior probability in the case of a root node). When used as a retrieval model, the nodes represent events such as observing a particular document, or a particular piece of evidence, or some combination of pieces of evidence. These events are all binary, meaning that TRUE and FALSE are the only possible outcomes.

---

[15] *Belief network* is the name for a range of techniques used to model uncertainty. A Bayesian network is a probabilistic belief network.

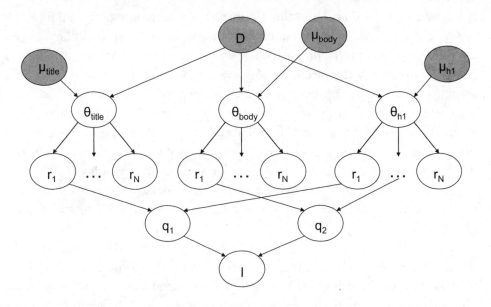

Fig. 7.4. Example inference network model

Figure 7.4 shows an inference net where the evidence being combined are words in a web page's title, body, and <h1> headings. In this figure, D is a document node. This node corresponds to the event that a document (the web page) is observed. There is one document node for every document in the collection, and we assume that only one document is observed at any time. The r_i or representation nodes are document features (evidence), and the probabilities associated with those features are based on language models θ estimated using the parameters μ. There is one language model for each significant document structure (title, body, or headings). In addition to features based on word occurrence, r_i nodes also represent proximity features. Proximity features take a number of different forms, such as requiring words to co-occur within a certain "window" (length) of text, and will be described in detail in the next section. Features that are not based on language models, such as document date, are allowed but not shown in this example.

The query nodes q_i are used to combine evidence from representation nodes and other query nodes. These nodes represent the occurrence of more complex evidence and document features. A number of forms of combination are available, with Boolean **AND** and **OR** being two of the simplest. The network as a whole computes $P(I|D,\mu)$, which is the probability that an information need is met given the document and the parameters μ. The information need node I is a special query node that combines all of the evidence from the other query nodes into a single probability or belief score. This score is used to rank documents. Conceptually, this means we must evaluate an inference network for every document in the collection, but as with every other ranking algorithm, indexes are used to speed up the computation. In general, representation nodes are indexed, whereas query nodes are specified for each query by the user or search application. This means that indexes for a variety of proximity features, in addition to words, will be created (as described in Chapter 5), significantly expanding the size of the indexes. In some applications, the probabilities associated with proximity features are computed at query time in order to provide more flexibility in specifying queries.

The connections in the inference network graph are defined by the query and the representation nodes connected to every document in the collection. The probabilities for the representation nodes are estimated using language models for each document. Note that these nodes do not represent the occurrence of a particular feature in a document, but instead capture the probability that the feature is *characteristic* of the document, in the sense that the language model could generate it. For example, a node for the word "lincoln" represents the binary event that a document is about that topic (or not), and the language model for the document is used to calculate the probability of that event being TRUE.

Since all the events in the inference network are binary, we cannot really use a multinomial model of a document as a sequence of words. Instead, we use a *multiple-Bernoulli*[16] model, which is the basis for the binary independence model in section 7.2.1. In that case, a document is represented as a binary feature vector, which simply records whether a feature is present or not. In order to capture term frequency information, a different multiple-Bernoulli model is used where the document is represented by a multiset[17] of vectors, with one vector for each term occurrence (Metzler, Lavrenko, & Croft, 2004). It turns out that with the appropriate choice of parameters, the probability estimate based on the multiple-Bernoulli distribution is the *same* as the estimate for the multinomial distribution with Dirichlet smoothing, which is

---

[16] Named after the Swiss mathematician Jakob Bernoulli (also known as James or Jacques, and one of eight famous mathematicians in the same family). The multiple-Bernoulli model is discussed further in Chapter 9.

[17] A multiset (also called a *bag*) is a set where each member has an associated number recording the number of times it occurs.

$$P(r_i|D,\mu) = \frac{f_{r_i,D} + \mu P(r_i|C)}{|D| + \mu}$$

where $f_{i,D}$ is the number of times feature r_i occurs in document D, $P(r_i|C)$ is the collection probability for feature r_i, and μ is the Dirichlet smoothing parameter. To be more precise, for the model shown in Figure 7.4 we would use $f_{i,D}$ counts, collection probabilities, and a value for μ that are specific to the document structure of interest. For example, if $f_{i,D}$ was the number of times feature r_i occurs in a document title, the collection probabilities would be estimated from the collection of all title texts, and the μ parameter would be specific to titles. Also note that the same estimation formula is used for proximity-based features as for words. For example, for a feature such as "New York" where the words must occur next to each other, $f_{i,D}$ is the number of times "New York" occurs in the text.

The query nodes, which specify how to combine evidence, are the basis of the operators in the query language. Although Bayesian networks permit arbitrary combinations (constrained by the laws of probability), the inference network retrieval model is based on operators that can be computed efficiently. At each node in the network, we need to specify the probability of each outcome given all possible states of the parent nodes. When the number of parent nodes is large, this could clearly get expensive. Fortunately, many of the interesting combinations can be expressed as simple formulas.

As an example of the combination process and how it can be done efficiently, consider Boolean **AND**. Given a simple network for a query node q with two parent nodes a and b, as shown in Figure 7.5, we can describe the conditional probabilities as shown in Table 7.6.

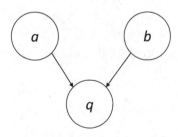

Fig. 7.5. Inference network with three nodes

We can refer to the values in the first column of Table 7.6 using p_{ij}, where i and j refer to the states of the parents. For example, p_{10} refers to the probability

$P(q = \text{TRUE}|a, b)$	a	b
0	FALSE	FALSE
0	FALSE	TRUE
0	TRUE	FALSE
1	TRUE	TRUE

Table 7.6. Conditional probabilities for example network

that q is **TRUE** given that a is **TRUE** and b is **FALSE**. To compute the probability of q, we use this table and the probabilities of the parent nodes (which come from the representation nodes) as follows:

$$
\begin{aligned}
bel_{and}(q) &= p_{00}P(a = \text{FALSE})P(b = \text{FALSE}) \\
&\quad +p_{01}P(a = \text{FALSE})P(b = \text{TRUE}) \\
&\quad +p_{10}P(a = \text{TRUE})P(b = \text{FALSE}) \\
&\quad +p_{11}P(a = \text{TRUE})P(b = \text{TRUE}) \\
&= 0 \cdot (1 - p_a)(1 - p_b) + 0 \cdot (1 - p_a)p_b + 0 \cdot p_a(1 - p_b) + 1 \cdot p_a p_b \\
&= p_a p_b
\end{aligned}
$$

where p_a is the probability that a is true, and p_b is the probability that b is true. We use the name $bel_{and}(q)$ to indicate that this is the belief value (probability) that results from an **AND** combination.

This means that the **AND** combination of evidence is computed by simply multiplying the probabilities of the parent nodes. If one of the parent probabilities is low (or zero if smoothing is not used), then the combination will have a low probability. This seems reasonable for this type of combination. We can define a number of other combination operators in the same way. If a q node has n parents with probability of being true p_i, then the following list defines the common operators:

$$
bel_{not}(q) = 1 - p_1
$$

$$
bel_{or}(q) = 1 - \prod_{i}^{n}(1 - p_i)
$$

$$
bel_{and}(q) = \prod_{i}^{n} p_i
$$

$$bel_{wand}(q) = \prod_{i}^{n} p_i^{wt_i}$$

$$bel_{max}(q) = max\{p_1, p_2, \ldots, p_n\}$$

$$bel_{sum}(q) = \frac{\sum_{i}^{n} p_i}{n}$$

$$bel_{wsum}(q) = \frac{\sum_{i}^{n} wt_i p_i}{\sum_{i}^{n} wt_i}$$

where wt_i is a weight associated with the ith parent, which indicates the relative importance of that evidence. Note that **NOT** is a unary operator (i.e., has only one parent).

The weighted **AND** operator is very important and one of the most commonly used in the query language described in the next section. Using this form of combination and restricting the evidence (representation nodes) to individual words gives the same ranking as query likelihood.

Given this description of the underlying model and combination operators, we can now define a query language that can be used in a search engine to produce rankings based on complex combinations of evidence.

7.4.2 The Galago Query Language

The Galago query language presented here is similar to query languages used in open source search engines that are based on the inference network retrieval model.[18] This version focuses on the most useful aspects of those languages for a variety of search applications, and adds the ability to use arbitrary features. Note that the Galago search engine is not based on a specific retrieval model, but instead provides an efficient framework for implementing retrieval models.

Although the query language can easily handle simple unstructured text documents, many of the more interesting features make use of evidence based on document structure. We assume that structure is specified using tag pairs, as in HTML or XML. Consider the following document:

```
<html>
<head>
<title>Department Descriptions</title>
</head>
```

---

[18] Such as Inquery and Indri.

```
<body>
The following list describes ...
<h1>Agriculture</h1> ...
<h1>Chemistry</h1> ...
<h1>Computer Science</h1> ...
<h1>Electrical Engineering</h1> ...
</body>
</html>
```

In the Galago query language, a document is viewed as a sequence of text that may contain arbitrary tags. In the example just shown, the document consists of text marked up with HTML tags.

For each tag type T within a document (e.g., title, body, h1, etc.), we define the *context*[19] of T to be all of the text and tags that appear within tags of type T. In the example, all of the text and tags appearing between <body> and </body> tags define the body context. A single context is generated for each unique tag name. Therefore, a context defines a subdocument. Note that because of nested tags, certain word occurrences may appear in many contexts. It is also the case that there may be nested contexts. For example, within the <body> context there is a nested <h1> context made up of all of the text and tags that appear within the body context and within <h1> and </h1> tags. Here are the tags for the title, h1, and body contexts in this example document:

title context:

```
<title>Department Descriptions</title>
```

h1 context:

```
<h1>Agriculture</h1>
<h1>Chemistry</h1> ...
<h1>Computer Science</h1> ...
<h1>Electrical Engineering</h1> ...
```

body context:

```
<body> The following list describes ...
<h1>Agriculture</h1> ...
<h1>Chemistry</h1> ...
```

---

[19] Contexts are sometimes referred to as *fields*.

```
<h1>Computer Science</h1> ...
<h1>Electrical Engineering</h1> ...
</body>
```

Each context is made up of one or more *extents*. An extent is a sequence of text that appears within a single begin/end tag pair of the same type as the context. For this example, in the `<h1>` context, there are extents `<h1>Agriculture</h1>`, `<h1>Chemistry<h1>`, etc. Both the title and body contexts contain only a single extent because there is only a single pair of `<title>` and `<body>` tags, respectively. The number of extents for a given tag type is determined by the number of tag pairs of that type that occur within the document.

In addition to the structure defined when a document is created, contexts are also used to represent structure added by feature extraction tools. For example, dates, people's names, and addresses can be identified in text and tagged by a feature extraction tool. As long as this information is represented using tag pairs, it can be referred to in the query language in the same way as other document structures.

Terms are the basic building blocks of the query language, and correspond to representation nodes in the inference network model. A variety of types of terms can be defined, such as simple terms, ordered and unordered phrases, synonyms, and others. In addition, there are a number of options that can be used to specify that a term should appear within a certain context, or that it should be scored using a language model that is estimated using a given context.

Simple terms:

term – term that will be normalized and stemmed.
"term" – term is not normalized or stemmed.
Examples:
presidents
"NASA"

Proximity terms:

#od:N(...) – ordered window – terms must appear ordered, with at most N-1 terms between each.
#od(...) – unlimited ordered window – all terms must appear ordered anywhere within current context.
#uw:N(...) – unordered window – all terms must appear within a window of length N in any order.

#uw(...) – unlimited unordered window – all terms must appear within current context in any order.
Examples:
#od:1(white house) – matches "white house" as an exact phrase.
#od:2(white house) – matches "white * house" (where * is any word or null).
#uw:2(white house) – matches "white house" and "house white".

Synonyms:

#syn(...)
#wsyn(...)
The first two expressions are equivalent. They each treat all of the terms listed as synonyms. The #wsyn operator treats the terms as synonyms, and allows weights to be assigned to each term. The arguments given to these operators can only be simple terms or proximity terms.
Examples:
#syn(dog canine) – simple synonym based on two terms.
#syn(#od:1(united states) #od:1(united states of america)) – creates a synonym from two proximity terms.
#wsyn(1.0 donald 0.8 don 0.5 donnie) – weighted synonym indicating relative importance of terms.

Anonymous terms:

#any:.() – used to match extent types
Examples:
#any:person() – matches any occurrence of a person extent.
#od:1(lincoln died in #any:date()) – matches exact phrases of the form: "lincoln died in <date>...</date>".

Context restriction and evaluation:

expression.C1,,...,CN – matches when the expression appears in all contexts C1 through CN.
expression.(C1,...,CN) – evaluates the expression using the language model defined by the concatenation of contexts C1...CN within the document.
Examples:
dog.title – matches the term "dog" appearing in a title extent.
#uw(smith jones).author – matches when the two names "smith" and "jones" appear in an author extent.

dog.(title) – evaluates the term based on the title language model for the document. This means that the estimate of the probability of occurrence for **dog** for a given document will be based on the number of times that the word occurs in the title field for that document and will be normalized using the number of words in the title rather than the document. Similarly, smoothing is done using the probabilities of occurrence in the title field over the whole collection.

#od:1(abraham lincoln).person.(header) – builds a language model from all of the "header" text in the document and evaluates **#od:1(abraham lincoln).person** in that context (i.e., matches only the exact phrase appearing within a person extent within the header context).

Belief operators are used to combine evidence about terms, phrases, etc. There are both unweighted and weighted belief operators. With the weighted operator, the relative importance of the evidence can be specified. This allows control over how much each expression within the query impacts the final score. The filter operator is used to screen out documents that do not contain required evidence. All belief operators can be nested.

Belief operators:

#combine(...) – this operator is a normalized version of the $bel_{and}(q)$ operator in the inference network model. See the discussion later for more details.

#weight(...) – this is a normalized version of the $bel_{wand}(q)$ operator.

#filter(...) – this operator is similar to **#combine**, but with the difference that the document must contain at least one instance of all terms (simple, proximity, synonym, etc.). The evaluation of nested belief operators is not changed.

Examples:

#combine(#syn(dog canine) training) – rank by two terms, one of which is a synonym.

#combine(biography #syn(#od:1(president lincoln) #od:1(abraham lincoln))) – rank using two terms, one of which is a synonym of "president lincoln" and "abraham lincoln".

#weight(1.0 #od:1(civil war) 3.0 lincoln 2.0 speech) – rank using three terms, and weight the term "lincoln" as most important, followed by "speech", then "civil war".

#filter(aquarium #combine(tropical fish)) – consider only those documents

containing the word "aquarium" and "tropical" or "fish", and rank them according to the query #combine(aquarium #combine(tropical fish)).
#filter(#od:1(john smith).author) #weight(2.0 europe 1.0 travel) – rank documents about "europe" or "travel" that have "John Smith" in the author context.

As we just described, the #combine and #weight operators are normalized versions of the bel_{and} and bel_{wand} operators, respectively. The beliefs of these operators are computed as follows:

$$bel_{combine} = \prod_{i}^{n} p_i^{1/n}$$

$$bel_{weight} = \prod_{i}^{n} p_i^{wt_i / \sum_{i'}^{n} wt_{i'}}$$

This normalization is done in order to make the operators behave more like the original bel_{sum} and bel_{wsum} operators, which are both normalized. One advantage of the normalization is that it allows us to describe the belief computation of these operators in terms of various types of means (averages). For example, bel_{sum} computes the arithmetic mean over the beliefs of the parent nodes, whereas bel_{wsum} computes a weighted arithmetic mean. Similarly, $bel_{combine}$ and bel_{wand} compute a geometric mean and weighted geometric mean, respectively.

The filter operator also could be used with numeric and date field operators so that non-textual evidence can be combined into the score. For example, the query

#filter(news.doctype #dateafter(12/31/1999).docdate
#uw:20(brown.person #any:company() #syn(money cash payment))

ranks documents that are news stories, that appeared after 1999, and that contained at least one text segment of length 20 that mentioned a person named "brown", a company name, and at least one of the three words dealing with money. The inference network model can easily deal with the combination of this type of evidence, but for simplicity, we have not implemented these operators in Galago.

Another part of the inference network model that we do support in the Galago query language is document priors. Document priors allow the specification of a prior probability over the documents in a collection. These prior probabilities influence the rankings by preferring documents with certain characteristics, such as those that were written recently or are short.

Prior:

#prior:name() – uses the document prior specified by the name given. Priors are files or functions that provide prior probabilities for each document.

Example:

#combine(#prior:recent() global warming) – uses a prior named recent to give greater weight to documents that were published more recently.

As a more detailed example of the use of this query language, in the next section we discuss web search and the types of evidence that have to be combined for effective ranking. The use of the #feature operator to define arbitrary features (new evidence) is discussed in Chapter 11.

7.5 Web Search

Measured in terms of popularity, web search is clearly the most important search application. Millions of people use web search engines every day to carry out an enormous variety of tasks, from shopping to research. Given its importance, web search is the obvious example to use for explaining how the retrieval models we have discussed are applied in practice.

There are some major differences between web search and an application that provides search for a collection of news stories, for example. The primary ones are the size of the collection (billions of documents), the connections between documents (i.e., links), the range of document types, the volume of queries (tens of millions per day), and the types of queries. Some of these issues we have discussed in previous chapters, and others, such as the impact of spam, will be discussed later. In this section, we will focus on the features of the queries and documents that are most important for the ranking algorithm.

There are a number of different types of search in a web environment. One popular way of describing searches was suggested by Broder (2002). In this taxonomy, searches are either *informational*, *navigational*, or *transactional*. An informational search has the goal of finding information about some topic that may be on one or more web pages. Since every search is looking for some type of information, we call these *topical searches* in this book. A navigational search has the goal of finding a particular web page that the user has either seen before or assumes must exist.[20] A transactional search has the goal of finding a site where a task such as shopping or downloading music can be performed. Each type of search has an information need associated with it, but a different type of information need. Retrieval models based on topical relevance have focused primarily on the first type of information need (and search). To produce effective rankings for the other types of searches, a retrieval model that can combine evidence related to user relevance is required.

Commercial web search engines incorporate *hundreds* of features (types of evidence) in their ranking algorithms, many derived from the huge collection of user interaction data in the query logs. These can be broadly categorized into features relating to page content, page metadata, anchor text, links (e.g., PageRank), and user behavior. Although anchor text is derived from the links in a page, it is used in a different way than features that come from an analysis of the link structure of pages, and so is put into a separate category. Page metadata refers to information about a page that is not part of the content of the page, such as its "age," how often it is updated, the URL of the page, the domain name of its site, and the amount of text content in the page relative to other material, such as images and advertisements.

It is interesting to note that understanding the relative importance of these features and how they can be manipulated to obtain better search rankings for a web page is the basis of *search engine optimization* (SEO). A search engine optimizer may, for example, improve the text used in the title tag of the web page, improve the text in heading tags, make sure that the domain name and URL contain important keywords, and try to improve the anchor text and link structure related to the page. Some of these techniques are not viewed as appropriate by the web search engine companies, and will be discussed further in section 9.1.5.

In the TREC environment, retrieval models have been compared using test collections of web pages and a mixture of query types. The features related to user behavior and some of the page metadata features, such as frequency of update, are not available in the TREC data. Of the other features, the most important for navigational searches are the text in the title, body, and heading (h1, h2, h3, and h4) parts of the document; the anchor text of all links pointing to the document; the PageRank number; and the inlink count (number of links pointing to the page).

---

[20] In the TREC world, navigational searches are called *home-page* and *named-page* searches. Topical searches are called *ad hoc* searches. Navigational searches are similar to *known-item* searches, which have been discussed in the information retrieval literature for many years.

Note that we are not saying that other features do not affect the ranking in web search engines, just that these were the ones that had the most significant impact in TREC experiments.

Given the size of the Web, many pages will contain all the query terms. Some ranking algorithms rank only those pages which, in effect, filters the results using a Boolean **AND**. This can cause problems if only a subset of the Web is used (such as in a site search application) and is particularly risky with topical searches. For example, only about 50% of the pages judged relevant in the TREC topical web searches contain all the query terms. Instead of filtering, the ranking algorithm should strongly favor pages that contain all query terms. In addition, *term proximity* will be important. The additional evidence of terms occurring near each other will significantly improve the effectiveness of the ranking. A number of retrieval models incorporating term proximity have been developed. The following approach is designed to work in the inference network model, and produces good results.[21]

The *dependence model* is based on the assumption that query terms are likely to appear in close proximity to each other within relevant documents. For example, given the query "Green party political views", relevant documents will likely contain the phrases "green party" and "political views" within relatively close proximity to one another. If the query is treated as a set of terms Q, we can define S_Q as the set of all non-empty subsets of Q. A Galago query attempts to capture dependencies between query terms as follows:

1. Every $s \in S_Q$ that consists of contiguous query terms is likely to appear as an exact phrase in a relevant document (i.e., represented using the #od:1 operator).
2. Every $s \in S_Q$ such that $|s| > 1$ is likely to appear (ordered or unordered) within a reasonably sized window of text in a relevant document (i.e., in a window represented as #uw:8 for $|s| = 2$ and #uw:12 for $|s| = 3$).

As an example, this model produces the Galago query language representation shown in Figure 7.6 for the TREC query "embryonic stem cells", where the weights were determined empirically to produce the best results.

Given the important pieces of evidence for web search ranking, we can now give an example of a Galago query that combines this evidence into an effective ranking. For the TREC query "pet therapy", we would produce the Galago query shown in Figure 7.7. The first thing to note about this query is that it clearly shows

---

[21] The formal model is described in Metzler and Croft (2005b).

```
#weight(
        0.8 #combine(embryonic stem cells)
        0.1 #combine( #od:1(stem cells) #od:1(embryonic stem)
                #od:1(embryonic stem cells))
        0.1 #combine( #uw:8(stem cells) #uw:8(embryonic cells)
                #uw:8(embryonic stem) #uw:12(embryonic stem cells)))
```

Fig. 7.6. Galago query for the dependence model

how a complex query expression can be generated from a simple user query. A number of proximity terms have been added, and all terms are evaluated using contexts based on anchor text, title text, body text, and heading text. From an efficiency perspective, the proximity terms may be indexed, even though this will increase the index size substantially. The benefit is that these relatively large query expressions will be able to be evaluated very efficiently at query time.

```
#weight(
        0.1 #weight( 0.6 #prior(pagerank) 0.4 #prior(inlinks))
        1.0 #weight(
            0.9 #combine(
                #weight( 1.0 pet.(anchor) 1.0 pet.(title)
                        3.0 pet.(body) 1.0 pet.(heading))
                #weight( 1.0 therapy.(anchor) 1.0 therapy.(title)
                        3.0 therapy.(body) 1.0 therapy.(heading)))
            0.1 #weight(
                1.0 #od:1(pet therapy).(anchor) 1.0 #od:1(pet therapy).(title)
                3.0 #od:1(pet therapy).(body) 1.0 #od:1(pet therapy).(heading))
            0.1 #weight(
                1.0 #uw:8(pet therapy).(anchor) 1.0 #uw:8(pet therapy).(title)
                3.0 #uw:8(pet therapy).(body) 1.0 #uw:8(pet therapy).(heading)))
        )
```

Fig. 7.7. Galago query for web data

The PageRank and inlink evidence is incorporated into this query as prior probabilities. In other words, this evidence is independent of specific queries and can be calculated at indexing time. The weights in the query were determined by experiments with TREC Web page collections, which are based on a crawl of the .gov domain. The relative importance of the evidence could be different for the full Web or for other collections. The text in the main body of the page was found to be more important than the other parts of the document and anchor text, and this is reflected in the weights.

Experiments with the TREC data have also shown that much of the evidence that is crucial for effective navigational search is not important for topical searches. In fact, the only features needed for topical search are the simple terms and proximity terms for the body part of the document. The other features do not improve effectiveness, but they also do not reduce it. Another difference between topical and navigational searches is that query expansion using pseudo-relevance feedback was found to help topical searches, but made navigational searches worse. Navigational searches are looking for a specific page, so it is not surprising that smoothing the query by adding a number of extra terms may increase the "noise" in the results. If a search was known to be in the topical category, query expansion could be used, but this is difficult to determine reliably, and since the potential effectiveness benefits of expansion are variable and somewhat unpredictable, this technique is generally not used. Given that the evidence needed to identify good sites for transaction searches seems to be similar to that needed for navigational searches, this means that the same ranking algorithm can be used for the different categories of web search.

Other research has shown that user behavior information, such as clickthrough data (e.g., which documents have been clicked on in the past, which rank positions were clicked) and browsing data (e.g., dwell time on page, links followed), can have a significant impact on the effectiveness of the ranking. This type of evidence can be added into the inference network framework using additional operators, but as the number of pieces of evidence grows, the issue of how to determine the most effective way of combining and weighting the evidence becomes more important. In the next section, we discuss techniques for learning both the weights and the ranking algorithm using explicit and implicit feedback data from the users.

7.6 Machine Learning and Information Retrieval

There has been considerable overlap between the fields of information retrieval and machine learning. In the 1960s, relevance feedback was introduced as a technique to improve ranking based on user feedback about the relevance of documents in an initial ranking. This was an example of a simple machine-learning algorithm that built a classifier to separate relevant from non-relevant documents based on training data. In the 1980s and 1990s, information retrieval researchers used machine learning approaches to learn ranking algorithms based on user feedback. In the last 10 years, there has been a lot of research on machine-learning approaches to text categorization. Many of the applications of machine learning to information retrieval, however, have been limited by the amount of training data available. If the system is trying to build a separate classifier for every query, there is very little data about relevant documents available, whereas other machine-learning applications may have hundreds or even thousands of training examples. Even the approaches that tried to learn ranking algorithms by using training data from all the queries were limited by the small number of queries and relevance judgments in typical information retrieval test collections.

With the advent of web search engines and the huge query logs that are collected from user interactions, the amount of potential training data is enormous. This has led to the development of new techniques that are having a significant impact in the field of information retrieval and on the design of search engines. In the next section, we describe techniques for learning ranking algorithms that can combine and weight the many pieces of evidence that are important for web search.

Another very active area of machine learning has been the development of sophisticated statistical models of text. In section 7.6.2, we describe how these models can be used to improve ranking based on language models.

7.6.1 Learning to Rank

All of the probabilistic retrieval models presented so far fall into the category of *generative* models. A generative model for text classification assumes that documents were generated from some underlying model (in this case, usually a multinomial distribution) and uses training data to estimate the parameters of the model. The probability of belonging to a class (i.e., the relevant documents for a query) is then estimated using Bayes' Rule and the document model. A *discriminative* model, in contrast, estimates the probability of belonging to a class directly from the observed features of the document based on the training data.[22] In general classification problems, a generative model performs better with low numbers of training examples, but the discriminative model usually has the advantage

---

[22] We revisit the discussion of generative versus discriminative classifiers in Chapter 9.

given enough data. Given the amount of potential training data available to web search engines, discriminative models may be expected to have some advantages in this application. It is also easier to incorporate new features into a discriminative model and, as we have mentioned, there can be hundreds of features that are considered for web ranking.

Early applications of learning a discriminative model (*discriminative learning*) in information retrieval used logistic regression to predict whether a document belonged to the relevant class. The problem was that the amount of training data and, consequently, the effectiveness of the technique depended on explicit relevance judgments obtained from people. Even given the resources of a commercial web search company, explicit relevance judgments are costly to obtain. On the other hand, query logs contain a large amount of implicit relevance information in the form of clickthroughs and other user interactions. In response to this, discriminative learning techniques based on this form of training data have been developed.

The best-known of the approaches used to learn a ranking function for search is based on the *Support Vector Machine (SVM)* classifier. This technique will be discussed in more detail in Chapter 9, so in this section we will just give a brief description of how a *Ranking SVM* can learn to rank.[23]

The input to the Ranking SVM is a training set consisting of partial rank information for a set of queries

$$(q_1, r_1), (q_2, r_2), \ldots, (q_n, r_n)$$

where q_i is a query and r_i is partial information about the *desired* ranking, or relevance level, of documents for that query. This means that if document d_a should be ranked higher than d_b, then $(d_a, d_b) \in r_i$; otherwise, $(d_a, d_b) \notin r_i$. Where do these rankings come from? If relevance judgments are available, the desired ranking would put all documents judged to be at a higher relevance level above those at a lower level. Note that this accommodates multiple levels of relevance, which are often used in evaluations of web search engines.

If relevance judgments are not available, however, the ranking can be based on clickthrough and other user data. For example, if a person clicks on the third document in a ranking for a query and not on the first two, we can assume that it should be ranked higher in r. If d_1, d_2, and d_3 are the documents in the first,

---

[23] This description is based on Joachims' paper on learning to rank using clickthrough data (Joachims, 2002b).

second, and third rank of the search output, the clickthrough data will result in pairs (d_3, d_1) and (d_3, d_2) being in the desired ranking for this query. This ranking data will be noisy (because clicks are not relevance judgments) and incomplete, but there will be a lot of it, and experiments have shown that this type of training data can be used effectively.

Let's assume that we are learning a linear ranking function $\vec{w}.\vec{d_a}$, where $\vec{w}$ is a weight vector that is adjusted by learning, and $\vec{d_a}$ is the vector representation of the features of document d_a. These features are, as we described in the last section, based on page content, page metadata, anchor text, links, and user behavior. Instead of language model probabilities, however, the features used in this model that depend on the match between the query and the document content are usually simpler and less formal. For example, there may be a feature for the number of words in common between the query and the document body, and similar features for the title, header, and anchor text. The weights in the $\vec{w}$ vector determine the relative importance of these features, similar to the weights in the inference network operators. If a document is represented by three features with integer values $\vec{d} = (2, 4, 1)$ and the weights $\vec{w} = (2, 1, 2)$, then the score computed by the ranking function is just:

$$\vec{w}.\vec{d} = (2, 1, 2).(2, 4, 1) = 2.2 + 1.4 + 2.1 = 10$$

Given the training set of queries and rank information, we would like to find a weight vector $\vec{w}$ that would satisfy as many of the following conditions as possible:

$$\forall(d_i, d_j) \in r_1 : \vec{w}.\vec{d_i} > \vec{w}.\vec{d_j}$$

$$\cdots$$

$$\forall(d_i, d_j) \in r_n : \vec{w}.\vec{d_i} > \vec{w}.\vec{d_j}$$

This simply means that for all document pairs in the rank data, we would like the score for the document with the higher relevance rating (or rank) to be greater than the score for the document with the lower relevance rating. Unfortunately, there is no efficient algorithm to find the exact solution for $\vec{w}$. We can, however, reformulate this problem as a standard SVM optimization as follows:

$$minimize: \quad \frac{1}{2}\vec{w}.\vec{w} + C\sum \xi_{i,j,k}$$

$$subject\ to:$$

$$\forall(d_i, d_j) \in r_1 : \vec{w}.\vec{d_i} > \vec{w}.\vec{d_j} + 1 - \xi_{i,j,1}$$

$$\cdots$$

$$\forall(d_i, d_j) \in r_n : \vec{w}.\vec{d_i} > \vec{w}.\vec{d_j} + 1 - \xi_{i,j,n}$$

$$\forall i \forall j \forall k : \xi_i, j, k \geq 0$$

where ξ, known as a *slack variable*, allows for misclassification of difficult or noisy training examples, and C is a parameter that is used to prevent *overfitting*. Overfitting happens when the learning algorithm produces a ranking function that does very well at ranking the training data, but does not do well at ranking documents for a new query. Software packages are available[24] that do this optimization and produce a classifier.

Where did this optimization come from? The impatient reader will have to jump ahead to the explanation for a general SVM classifier in Chapter 9. For the time being, we can say that the SVM algorithm will find a classifier (i.e., the vector $\vec{w}$) that has the following property. Each pair of documents in our training data can be represented by the vector $(\vec{d_i} - \vec{d_j})$. If we compute the score for this pair as $\vec{w}.(\vec{d_i} - \vec{d_j})$, the SVM classifier will find a $\vec{w}$ that makes the smallest score as large as possible. The same thing is true for negative examples (pairs of documents that are not in the rank data). This means that the classifier will make the differences in scores as large as possible for the pairs of documents that are hardest to rank.

Note that this model does not specify the features that should be used. It could even be used to learn the weights for features corresponding to scores from completely different retrieval models, such as BM25 and language models. Combining multiple searches for a given query has been shown to be effective in a number of experiments, and is discussed further in section 10.5.1. It should also be noted that the weights learned by Ranking SVM (or some other discriminative technique) can be used directly in the inference network query language.

Although linear discriminative classifiers such as Ranking SVM may have an advantage for web search, there are other search applications where there will be less training data and less features available. For these applications, the generative models of topical relevance may be more effective, especially as the models continue to improve through better estimation techniques. The next section discusses

---

[24] Such as SVM^{light}; see http://svmlight.joachims.org.

how estimation can be improved by modeling a document as a mixture of topic models.

7.6.2 Topic Models and Vocabulary Mismatch

One of the important issues in general information retrieval is vocabulary mismatch. This refers to a situation where relevant documents do not match a query, because they are using different words to describe the same topic. In the web environment, many documents will contain all the query words, so this may not appear to be an issue. In search applications with smaller collections, however, it will be important, and even in web search, TREC experiments have shown that topical queries produce better results using query expansion. Query expansion (using, for example, pseudo-relevance feedback) is the standard technique for reducing vocabulary mismatch, although stemming also addresses this issue to some extent. A different approach would be to expand the *documents* by adding related terms. For documents represented as language models, this is equivalent to smoothing the probabilities in the language model so that words that did not occur in the text have non-zero probabilities. Note that this is different from smoothing using the collection probabilities, which are the same for all documents. Instead, we need some way of increasing the probabilities of words that are associated with the topic of the document.

A number of techniques have been proposed to do this. If a document is known to belong to a category or cluster of documents, then the probabilities of words in that cluster can be used to smooth the document language model. We describe the details of this in Chapter 9. A technique known as *Latent Semantic Indexing*, or *LSI*,[25] maps documents and terms into a reduced dimensionality space, so that documents that were previously indexed using a vocabulary of hundreds of thousands of words are now represented using just a few hundred features. Each feature in this new space is a mixture or cluster of many words, and it is this mixing that in effect smooths the document representation.

The *Latent Dirichlet Allocation* (*LDA*) model, which comes from the machine learning community, models documents as a mixture of topics. A topic is a language model, just as we defined previously. In a retrieval model such as query likelihood, each document is assumed to be associated with a single topic. There are,

---

[25] This technique is also called Latent Semantic Analysis or LSA (Deerwester et al., 1990). Note that "latent" is being used in the sense of "hidden."

in effect, as many topics as there are documents in the collection. In the LDA approach, in contrast, the assumption is that there is a fixed number of underlying (or latent) topics that can be used to describe the contents of documents. Each document is represented as a mixture of these topics, which achieves a smoothing effect that is similar to LSI. In the LDA model, a document is generated by first picking a distribution over topics, and then, for the next word in the document, we choose a topic and generate a word from that topic.

Using our "bucket" analogy for language models, we would need multiple buckets to describe this process. For each document, we would have one bucket of topics, with the number of instances of each topic depending on the distribution of topics we had picked. For each topic, there would be another bucket containing words, with the number of instances of the words depending on the probabilities in the topic language model. Then, to generate a document, we first select a topic from the topic bucket (still without looking), then go to the bucket of words for the topic that had been selected and pick out a word. The process is then repeated for the next word.

More formally, the LDA process for generating a document is:

1. For each document D, pick a multinomial distribution θ_D from a Dirichlet distribution with parameter α.
2. For each word position in document D:
   a) Pick a topic z from the multinomial distribution θ_D.
   b) Choose a word w from $P(w|z, \beta)$, a multinomial probability conditioned on the topic z with parameter β.

A variety of techniques are available for learning the topic models and the θ distributions using the collection of documents as the training data, but all of these methods tend to be quite slow. Once we have these distributions, we can produce language model probabilities for the words in documents:

$$P_{lda}(w|D) = P(w|\theta_D, \beta) = \sum_z P(w|z, \beta)P(z|\theta_D)$$

These probabilities can then be used to smooth the document representation by mixing them with the query likelihood probability as follows:

$$P(w|D) = \lambda \left(\frac{f_{w,D} + \mu \frac{c_w}{|C|}}{|D| + \mu} \right) + (1 - \lambda)P_{lda}(w|D)$$

So the final language model probabilities are, in effect, a mixture of the maximum likelihood probabilities, collection probabilities, and the LDA probabilities.

If the LDA probabilities are used directly as the document representation, the effectiveness of the ranking will be significantly reduced because the features are *too* smoothed. In TREC experiments, K (the number of topics) has a value of around 400. This means that all documents in the collection are represented as mixtures of just 400 topics. Given that there can be millions of words in a collection vocabulary, matching on topics alone will lose some of the precision of matching individual words. When used to smooth the document language model, however, the LDA probabilities can significantly improve the effectiveness of query likelihood ranking. Table 7.7 shows the high-probability words from four LDA topics (out of 100) generated from a sample of TREC news stories.[26] Note that the names of the topics were not automatically generated.

Arts	Budgets	Children	Education
new	million	children	school
film	tax	women	students
show	program	people	schools
music	budget	child	education
movie	billion	years	teachers
play	federal	families	high
musical	year	work	public
best	spending	parents	teacher
actor	new	says	bennett
first	state	family	manigat
york	plan	welfare	namphy
opera	money	men	state
theater	programs	percent	president
actress	government	care	elementary
love	congress	life	haiti

Table 7.7. Highest-probability terms from four topics in LDA model

The main problem with using LDA for search applications is that estimating the probabilities in the model is expensive. Until faster methods are developed,

---

[26] This table is from Blei et al. (2003).

this technique will be limited to smaller collections (hundreds of thousands of documents, but not millions).

7.7 Application-Based Models

In this chapter we have described a wide variety of retrieval models and ranking algorithms. From the point of view of someone involved in designing and implementing a search application, the question is which of these techniques should be used and when? The answer depends on the application and the tools available. Most search applications involve much smaller collections than the Web and a lot less connectivity in terms of links and anchor text. Ranking algorithms that work well in web search engines often do not produce the best rankings in other applications. Customizing a ranking algorithm for the application will nearly always produce the best results.

The first step in doing this is to construct a test collection of queries, documents, and relevance judgments so that different versions of the ranking algorithm can be compared quantitatively. Evaluation is discussed in detail in Chapter 8, and it is the key to an effective search engine.

The next step is to identify what evidence or features might be used to represent documents. Simple terms and proximity terms are almost always useful. Significant document structure—such as titles, authors, and date fields—are also nearly always important for search. In some applications, numeric fields may be important. Text processing techniques such as stemming and stopwords also must be considered.

Another important source of information that can be used for query expansion is an application-specific thesaurus. These are surprisingly common since often an attempt will have been made to build them either manually or automatically for a previous information system. Although they are often very incomplete, the synonyms and related words they contain can make a significant difference to ranking effectiveness.

Having identified the various document features and other evidence, the next task is to decide how to combine it to calculate a document score. An open source search engine such as Galago makes this relatively easy since the combination and weighting of evidence can be expressed in the query language and many variations can be tested quickly. Other search engines do not have this degree of flexibility. If a search engine based on a simple retrieval model is being used for the search application, the descriptions of how scores are calculated in the BM25 or query likelihood models and how they are combined in the inference network model can be used as a guide to achieve similar effects by appropriate query transformations and additional code for scoring. For example, the synonym and related word information in a thesaurus should not be used to simply add words to a query. Unless some version of the #syn operator is used, the effectiveness of the ranking will be reduced. The implementation of #syn in Galago can be used as an example of how to add this operator to a search engine.

Much of the time spent in developing a search application will be spent on tuning the retrieval effectiveness of the ranking algorithm. Doing this without some concept of the underlying retrieval model can be very unrewarding. The retrieval models described in this chapter (namely BM25, query likelihood, relevance models, inference network, and Ranking SVM) provide the best possible blueprints for a successful ranking algorithm. For these models, good parameter values and weights are already known from extensive published experiments. These values can be used as a starting point for the process of determining whether modifications are needed for an application. If enough training data is available, a discriminative technique such as Ranking SVM will learn the best weights directly.

References and Further Reading

Since retrieval models are one of the most important topics in information retrieval, there are many papers describing research in this area, starting in the 1950s. One of the most valuable aspects of van Rijsbergen's book (van Rijsbergen, 1979) is the coverage of the older research in this area. In this book, we will focus on some of the major papers, rather than attempting to be comprehensive. These references will be discussed in the order of the topics presented in this chapter.

The discussion of the nature of relevance has, understandably, been going on in information retrieval for a long time. One of the earlier papers that is often cited is Saracevic (1975). A more recent article gives a review of work in this area (Mizzaro, 1997).

On the topic of Boolean versus ranked search, Turtle (1994) carried out an experiment comparing the performance of professional searchers using the best Boolean queries they could generate against keyword searches using ranked output and found no advantage for the Boolean search. When simple Boolean queries are compared against ranking, as in Turtle and Croft (1991), the effectiveness of ranking is much higher.

The vector space model was first mentioned in Salton et al. (1975), and is described in detail in Salton and McGill (1983). The most comprehensive paper in weighting experiments with this model is Salton and Buckley (1988), although the term-weighting techniques described in section 7.1.2 are a later improvement on those described in the paper.

The description of information retrieval as a classification problem appears in van Rijsbergen (1979). The best paper on the application of the binary independence model and its development into the BM25 ranking function is Sparck Jones et al. (2000).

The use of language models in information retrieval started with Ponte and Croft (1998), who described a retrieval model based on multiple-Bernoulli language models. This was quickly followed by a number of papers that developed the multinomial version of the retrieval model (Hiemstra, 1998; F. Song & Croft, 1999). Miller et al. (1999) described the same approach using a Hidden Markov Model. Berger and Lafferty (1999) showed how translation probabilities for words could be incorporated into the language model approach. We will refer to this translation model again in section 10.3. The use of non-uniform prior probabilities was studied by Kraaij et al. (2002). A collection of papers relating to language models and information retrieval appears in Croft and Lafferty (2003).

Zhai and Lafferty (2004) give an excellent description of smoothing techniques for language modeling in information retrieval. Smoothing using clusters and nearest neighbors is described in Liu and Croft (2004) and Kurland and Lee (2004).

An early term-dependency model was described in van Rijsbergen (1979). A bigram language model for information retrieval was described in F. Song and Croft (1999), but the more general models in Gao et al. (2004) and Metzler and Croft (2005b) produced significantly better retrieval results, especially with larger collections.

The relevance model approach to query expansion appeared in Lavrenko and Croft (2001). Lafferty and Zhai (2001) proposed a related approach that built a query model and compared it to document models.

There have been many experiments reported in the information retrieval literature showing that the combination of evidence significantly improves the ranking effectiveness. Croft (2000) reviews these results and shows that this is not surprising, given that information retrieval can be viewed as a classification problem with a huge choice of features. Turtle and Croft (1991) describe the inference network model. This model was used as the basis for the Inquery search engine (Callan et al., 1992) and the WIN version of the commercial search engine WESTLAW (Pritchard-Schoch, 1993). The extension of this model to include language model probabilities is described in Metzler and Croft (2004). This extension was implemented as the Indri search engine (Strohman et al., 2005; Metzler, Strohman, et al., 2004). The Galago query language is based on the query language for Indri.

The approach to web search described in section 7.5, which scores documents based on a combination or mixture of language models representing different parts of the document structure, is based on Ogilvie and Callan (2003). The BM25F ranking function (Robertson et al., 2004) is an extension of BM25 that is also designed to effectively combine information from different document fields.

Spam is of such importance in web search that an entire subfield, called *adversarial information retrieval*, has developed to deal with search techniques for document collections that are being manipulated by parties with different interests (such as spammers and search engine optimizers). We discuss the topic of spam in Chapter 9.

The early work on learning ranking functions includes the use of logistic regression (Cooper et al., 1992). Fuhr and Buckley (1991) were the first to describe clearly how using features that are independent of the actual query words (e.g., using a feature like the number of matching terms rather than which terms matched) enable the learning of ranking functions across queries. The use of Ranking SVM for information retrieval was described by Joachims (2002b). Cao et al. (2006) describe modifications of this approach that improve ranking effectiveness. *RankNet* (C. Burges et al., 2005) is a neural network approach to learning a ranking function that is used in the Microsoft web search engine. Agichtein, Brill, and Dumais (2006) describe how user behavior features can be incorporated effectively into ranking based on RankNet. Both Ranking SVMs and RankNet learn using partial rank information (i.e., pairwise preferences). Another class of learning models, called listwise models, use the entire ranked list for learning. Examples of these models include the linear discriminative model proposed by Gao et al. (2005), which learns weights for features that are based on language models. This approach has some similarities to the inference network model being used to combine language model and other features. Another listwise approach is the term dependence model proposed by Metzler and Croft (2005b), which is also based on a linear combination of features. Both the Gao and Metzler models provide a learning technique that maximizes average precision (an important information retrieval metric) directly. More information about listwise learning models can be found in Xia et al. (2008).

Hofmann (1999) described a probabilistic version of LSI (pLSI) that introduced the modeling of documents as a mixture of topics. The LDA model was described by Blei et al. (2003). A number of extensions of this model have been proposed since then, but they have not been applied to information retrieval. The application of LDA to information retrieval was described in Wei and Croft (2006).

Exercises

7.1. Use the "advanced search" feature of a web search engine to come up with three examples of searches using the Boolean operators **AND**, **OR**, and **NOT** that work better than using the same query in the regular search box. Do you think the search engine is using a strict Boolean model of retrieval for the advanced search?

7.2. If each term represents a dimension in a t-dimensional space, the vector space model is making an assumption that the terms are *orthogonal*. Explain this assumption and discuss whether you think it is reasonable.

7.3. Can you think of another measure of similarity that could be used in the vector space model? Compare your measure with the cosine correlation using some example documents and queries with made-up weights. Browse the IR literature on the Web and see whether your measure has been studied (start with van Rijsbergen's book).

7.4. Derive Bayes' Rule from the definition of a conditional probability:

$$P(A|B) = \frac{P(A \cap B)}{P(B)}$$

Give an example of a conditional and a joint probability using the occurrence of words in documents as the events.

7.5. Implement a BM25 module for Galago. Show that it works and document it.

7.6. Show the effect of changing parameter values in your BM25 implementation.

7.7. What is the "bucket" analogy for a bigram language model? Give examples.

7.8. Using the Galago implementation of query likelihood, study the impact of short queries and long queries on effectiveness. Do the parameter settings make a difference?

7.9. Implement the relevance model approach to pseudo-relevance feedback in Galago. Show it works by generating some expansion terms for queries and document it.

7.10. Implement a #not operator for the inference network query language in Galago. Show some examples of how it works.

7.11. Show that the bel_{wand} operator computes the query likelihood score with simple terms. What does the bel_{wsum} operator compute?

7.12. Do a detailed design for numeric operators for the inference network query language in Galago.

7.13. Write an interface program that will take a user's query as text and transform it into an inference network query. Make sure you use proximity operators. Compare the performance of the simple queries and the transformed queries.

8

Evaluating Search Engines

"Evaluation, Mr. Spock."

Captain Kirk, *Star Trek: The Motion Picture*

8.1 Why Evaluate?

Evaluation is the key to making progress in building better search engines. It is also essential to understanding whether a search engine is being used effectively in a specific application. Engineers don't make decisions about a new design for a commercial aircraft based on whether it *feels* better than another design. Instead, they test the performance of the design with simulations and experiments, evaluate everything again when a prototype is built, and then continue to monitor and tune the performance of the aircraft after it goes into service. Experience has shown us that ideas that we intuitively feel must improve search quality, or models that have appealing formal properties often have little or no impact when tested using quantitative experiments.

One of the primary distinctions made in the evaluation of search engines is between *effectiveness* and *efficiency*. Effectiveness, loosely speaking, measures the ability of the search engine to find the right information, and efficiency measures how quickly this is done. For a given query, and a specific definition of relevance, we can more precisely define effectiveness as a measure of how well the ranking produced by the search engine corresponds to a ranking based on user relevance judgments. Efficiency is defined in terms of the time and space requirements for the algorithm that produces the ranking. Viewed more generally, however, search is an interactive process involving different types of users with different information problems. In this environment, effectiveness and efficiency will be affected by many factors, such as the interface used to display search results and query refinement techniques, such as query suggestion and relevance feedback. Carrying out this type of holistic evaluation of effectiveness and efficiency, while important, is very difficult because of the many factors that must be controlled. For this reason, evaluation is more typically done in tightly defined experimental settings, and this is the type of evaluation we focus on here.

Effectiveness and efficiency are related in that techniques that give a small boost to effectiveness may not be included in a search engine implementation if they have a significant adverse effect on an efficiency measure such as query throughput. Generally speaking, however, information retrieval research focuses on improving the effectiveness of search, and when a technique has been established as being potentially useful, the focus shifts to finding efficient implementations. This is not to say that research on system architecture and efficiency is not important. The techniques described in Chapter 5 are a critical part of building a scalable and usable search engine and were primarily developed by research groups. The focus on effectiveness is based on the underlying goal of a search engine, which is to find the relevant information. A search engine that is extremely fast is of no use unless it produces good results.

So is there a trade-off between efficiency and effectiveness? Some search engine designers discuss having "knobs," or parameters, on their system that can be turned to favor either high-quality results or improved efficiency. The current situation, however, is that there is no reliable technique that significantly improves effectiveness that cannot be incorporated into a search engine due to efficiency considerations. This may change in the future.

In addition to efficiency and effectiveness, the other significant consideration in search engine design is cost. We may know how to implement a particular search technique efficiently, but to do so may require a huge investment in processors, memory, disk space, and networking. In general, if we pick targets for any two of these three factors, the third will be determined. For example, if we want a particular level of effectiveness and efficiency, this will determine the cost of the system configuration. Alternatively, if we decide on efficiency and cost targets, it may have an impact on effectiveness. Two extreme cases of choices for these factors are searching using a pattern-matching utility such as grep, or searching using an organization such as the Library of Congress. Searching a large text collection using grep will have poor effectiveness and poor efficiency, but will be very cheap. Searching using the staff analysts at the Library of Congress will produce excellent results (high effectiveness) due to the manual effort involved, will be efficient in terms of the user's time (although it will involve a delay waiting for a response from the analysts), and will be very expensive. Searching directly using an effective search engine is designed to be a reasonable compromise between these extremes.

An important point about terminology is the meaning of "optimization" as it is discussed in the context of evaluation. The retrieval and indexing techniques in a search engine have many parameters that can be adjusted to optimize performance, both in terms of effectiveness and efficiency. Typically the best values for these parameters are determined using training data and a cost function. Training data is a sample of the real data, and the cost function is the quantity based on the data that is being maximized (or minimized). For example, the training data could be samples of queries with relevance judgments, and the cost function for a ranking algorithm would be a particular effectiveness measure. The optimization process would use the training data to learn parameter settings for the ranking algorithm that maximized the effectiveness measure. This use of optimization is very different from "search engine optimization", which is the process of tailoring web pages to ensure high rankings from search engines.

In the remainder of this chapter, we will discuss the most important evaluation measures, both for effectiveness and efficiency. We will also describe how experiments are carried out in controlled environments to ensure that the results are meaningful.

8.2 The Evaluation Corpus

One of the basic requirements for evaluation is that the results from different techniques can be compared. To do this comparison fairly and to ensure that experiments are repeatable, the experimental settings and data used must be fixed. Starting with the earliest large-scale evaluations of search performance in the 1960s, generally referred to as the Cranfield[1] experiments (Cleverdon, 1970), researchers assembled *test collections* consisting of documents, queries, and relevance judgments to address this requirement. In other language-related research fields, such as linguistics, machine translation, or speech recognition, a *text corpus* is a large amount of text, usually in the form of many documents, that is used for statistical analysis of various kinds. The test collection, or *evaluation corpus*, in information retrieval is unique in that the queries and relevance judgments for a particular search task are gathered in addition to the documents.

Test collections have changed over the years to reflect the changes in data and user communities for typical search applications. As an example of these changes,

---

[1] Named after the place in the United Kingdom where the experiments were done.

the following three test collections were created at intervals of about 10 years, starting in the 1980s:

- CACM: Titles and abstracts from the Communications of the ACM from 1958–1979. Queries and relevance judgments generated by computer scientists.

- AP: Associated Press newswire documents from 1988–1990 (from TREC disks 1–3). Queries are the title fields from TREC topics 51–150. Topics and relevance judgments generated by government information analysts.

- GOV2: Web pages crawled from websites in the .gov domain during early 2004. Queries are the title fields from TREC topics 701–850. Topics and relevance judgments generated by government analysts.

The CACM collection was created when most search applications focused on *bibliographic records* containing titles and abstracts, rather than the full text of documents. Table 8.1 shows that the number of documents in the collection (3,204) and the average number of words per document (64) are both quite small. The total size of the document collection is only 2.2 megabytes, which is considerably less than the size of a single typical music file for an MP3 player. The queries for this collection of abstracts of computer science papers were generated by students and faculty of a computer science department, and are supposed to represent actual information needs. An example of a CACM query is:

> Security considerations in local networks, network operating systems, and distributed systems.

Relevance judgments for each query were done by the same people, and were relatively *exhaustive* in the sense that most relevant documents were identified. This was possible since the collection is small and the people who generated the questions were very familiar with the documents. Table 8.2 shows that the CACM queries are quite long (13 words on average) and that there are an average of 16 relevant documents per query.

The AP and GOV2 collections were created as part of the TREC conference series sponsored by the National Institute of Standards and Technology (NIST). The AP collection is typical of the full-text collections that were first used in the early 1990s. The availability of cheap magnetic disk technology and online text entry led to a number of search applications for full-text documents such as news

Collection	Number of documents	Size	Average number of words/doc.
CACM	3,204	2.2 MB	64
AP	242,918	0.7 GB	474
GOV2	25,205,179	426 GB	1073

Table 8.1. Statistics for three example text collections. The average number of words per document is calculated without stemming.

stories, legal documents, and encyclopedia articles. The AP collection is much bigger (by two orders of magnitude) than the CACM collection, both in terms of the number of documents and the total size. The average document is also considerably longer (474 versus 64 words) since they contain the full text of a news story. The GOV2 collection, which is another two orders of magnitude larger, was designed to be a testbed for web search applications and was created by a crawl of the .gov domain. Many of these government web pages contain lengthy policy descriptions or tables, and consequently the average document length is the largest of the three collections.

Collection	Number of queries	Average number of words/query	Average number of relevant docs/query
CACM	64	13.0	16
AP	100	4.3	220
GOV2	150	3.1	180

Table 8.2. Statistics for queries from example text collections

The queries for the AP and GOV2 collections are based on TREC topics. The topics were created by government information analysts employed by NIST. The early TREC topics were designed to reflect the needs of professional analysts in government and industry and were quite complex. Later TREC topics were supposed to represent more general information needs, but they retained the TREC topic format. An example is shown in Figure 8.1. TREC topics contain three fields indicated by the tags. The title field is supposed to be a short query, more typical of a web application. The description field is a longer version of the query, which as this example shows, can sometimes be more precise than the short query. The narrative field describes the criteria for relevance, which is used by the people doing relevance judgments to increase consistency, and should not be considered as a query. Most recent TREC evaluations have focused on using the title field of the topic as the query, and our statistics in Table 8.2 are based on that field.

```
<top>
<num> Number: 794

<title> pet therapy

<desc> Description:
How are pets or animals used in therapy for humans and what are the
benefits?

<narr> Narrative:
Relevant documents must include details of how pet- or animal-assisted
therapy is or has been used.  Relevant details include information
about pet therapy programs, descriptions of the circumstances in which
pet therapy is used, the benefits of this type of therapy, the degree
of success of this therapy, and any laws or regulations governing it.

</top>
```

Fig. 8.1. Example of a TREC topic

The relevance judgments in TREC depend on the task that is being evaluated. For the queries in these tables, the task emphasized high recall, where it is important not to miss information. Given the context of that task, TREC analysts judged a document as relevant if it contained information that could be used to help write a report on the query topic. In Chapter 7, we discussed the difference between *user relevance* and *topical relevance*. Although the TREC relevance definition does refer to the usefulness of the information found, analysts are instructed to judge all documents containing the same useful information as relevant. This is not something a real user is likely to do, and shows that TREC is primarily focused on topical relevance. Relevance judgments for the CACM collections are binary, meaning that a document is either relevant or it is not. This is also true of most of the TREC collections. For some tasks, multiple levels of relevance may be appropriate. Some TREC collections, including GOV2, were judged using three levels of relevance (not relevant, relevant, and highly relevant). We discuss effectiveness measures for both binary and graded relevance in section 8.4. Different retrieval tasks can affect the number of relevance judgments required, as well as the type of judgments and the effectiveness measure. For example, in Chapter 7 we described *navigational* searches, where the user is looking for a particular page. In this case, there is only one relevant document for the query.

Creating a new test collection can be a time-consuming task. Relevance judgments in particular require a considerable investment of manual effort for the high-recall search task. When collections were very small, most of the documents in a collection could be evaluated for relevance. In a collection such as GOV2, however, this would clearly be impossible. Instead, a technique called *pooling* is used. In this technique, the top k results (for TREC, k varied between 50 and 200) from the rankings obtained by different search engines (or retrieval algorithms) are merged into a pool, duplicates are removed, and the documents are presented in some random order to the people doing the relevance judgments. Pooling produces a large number of relevance judgments for each query, as shown in Table 8.2. However, this list is incomplete and, for a new retrieval algorithm that had not contributed documents to the original pool, this could potentially be a problem. Specifically, if a new algorithm found many relevant documents that were not part of the pool, they would be treated as being not relevant, and consequently the effectiveness of that algorithm could be significantly underestimated. Studies with the TREC data, however, have shown that the relevance judgments are complete enough to produce accurate comparisons for new search techniques.

TREC corpora have been extremely useful for evaluating new search techniques, but they have limitations. A high-recall search task and collections of news articles are clearly not appropriate for evaluating product search on an e-commerce site, for example. New TREC "tracks" can be created to address important new applications, but this process can take months or years. On the other hand, new search applications and new data types such as blogs, forums, and annotated videos are constantly being developed. Fortunately, it is not that difficult to develop an evaluation corpus for any given application using the following basic guidelines:

- Use a document collection that is representative for the application in terms of the number, size, and type of documents. In some cases, this may be the actual collection for the application; in others it will be a sample of the actual collection, or even a similar collection. If the target application is very general, then more than one collection should be used to ensure that results are not corpus-specific. For example, in the case of the high-recall TREC task, a number of different news and government collections were used for evaluation.

- The queries that are used for the test collection should also be representative of the queries submitted by users of the target application. These may be acquired either from a query log from a similar application or by asking potential users for examples of queries. Although it may be possible to gather tens of thousands of queries in some applications, the need for relevance judgments is a major constraint. The number of queries must be sufficient to establish that a new technique makes a significant difference. An analysis of TREC experiments has shown that with 25 queries, a difference in the effectiveness measure MAP (section 8.4.2) of 0.05 will result in the wrong conclusion about which system is better in about 13% of the comparisons. With 50 queries, this error rate falls below 4%. A difference of 0.05 in MAP is quite large. If a *significance test*, such as those discussed in section 8.6.1, is used in the evaluation, a *relative* difference of 10% in MAP is sufficient to guarantee a low error rate with 50 queries. If resources or the application make more relevance judgments possible, in terms of generating reliable results it will be more productive to judge more queries rather than to judge more documents from existing queries (i.e., increasing k). Strategies such as judging a small number (e.g., 10) of the top-ranked documents from many queries or selecting documents to judge that will make the most difference in the comparison (Carterette et al., 2006) have been shown to be effective. If a small number of queries are used, the results should be considered indicative, not conclusive. In that case, it is important that the queries should be at least representative and have good coverage in terms of the goals of the application. For example, if algorithms for local search were being tested, the queries in the test collection should include many different types of location information.

- Relevance judgments should be done either by the people who asked the questions or by independent judges who have been instructed in how to determine relevance for the application being evaluated. Relevance may seem to be a very subjective concept, and it is known that relevance judgments can vary depending on the person making the judgments, or even vary for the same person at different times. Despite this variation, analysis of TREC experiments has shown that conclusions about the relative performance of systems are very stable. In other words, differences in relevance judgments do not have a significant effect on the error rate for comparisons. The number of documents that are evaluated for each query and the type of relevance judgments will depend on the effectiveness measures that are chosen. For most applications, it is generally easier for people to decide between at least three levels of relevance: *definitely relevant*, *definitely not relevant*, and *possibly relevant*. These can be converted into binary judgments by assigning the "possibly relevant" level to either one of the other levels, if that is required for an effectiveness measure. Some applications and effectiveness measures, however, may support more than three levels of relevance.

As a final point, it is worth emphasizing that many user actions can be considered *implicit* relevance judgments, and that if these can be exploited, this can substantially reduce the effort of constructing a test collection. For example, actions such as clicking on a document in a result list, moving it to a folder, or sending it to a printer may indicate that it is relevant. In previous chapters, we have described how query logs and clickthrough can be used to support operations such as query expansion and spelling correction. In the next section, we discuss the role of query logs in search engine evaluation.

8.3 Logging

Query logs that capture user interactions with a search engine have become an extremely important resource for web search engine development. From an evaluation perspective, these logs provide large amounts of data showing how users browse the results that a search engine provides for a query. In a general web search application, the number of users and queries represented can number in the tens of millions. Compared to the hundreds of queries used in typical TREC collections, query log data can potentially support a much more extensive and realistic evaluation. The main drawback with this data is that it is not as precise as explicit relevance judgments.

An additional concern is maintaining the *privacy* of the users. This is particularly an issue when query logs are shared, distributed for research, or used to construct user profiles (see section 6.2.5). Various techniques can be used to *anonymize* the logged data, such as removing identifying information or queries that may contain personal data, although this can reduce the utility of the log for some purposes.

A typical query log will contain the following data for each query:

- User identifier or user session identifier. This can be obtained in a number of ways. If a user logs onto a service, uses a search toolbar, or even allows cookies, this information allows the search engine to identify the user. A session is a series of queries submitted to a search engine over a limited amount of time. In some circumstances, it may be possible to identify a user only in the context of a session.

- Query terms. The query is stored exactly as the user entered it.
- List of URLs of results, their ranks on the result list, and whether they were clicked on.[2]
- Timestamp(s). The timestamp records the time that the query was submitted. Additional timestamps may also record the times that specific results were clicked on.

The clickthrough data in the log (the third item) has been shown to be highly correlated with explicit judgments of relevance when interpreted appropriately, and has been used for both training and evaluating search engines. More detailed information about user interaction can be obtained through a client-side application, such as a search toolbar in a web browser. Although this information is not always available, some user actions other than clickthroughs have been shown to be good predictors of relevance. Two of the best predictors are page *dwell time* and search exit action. The page dwell time is the amount of time the user spends on a clicked result, measured from the initial click to the time when the user comes back to the results page or exits the search application. The search exit action is the way the user exits the search application, such as entering another URL, closing the browser window, or timing out. Other actions, such as printing a page, are very predictive but much less frequent.

Although clicks on result pages are highly correlated with relevance, they cannot be used directly in place of explicit relevance judgments, because they are very biased toward pages that are highly ranked or have other features such as being popular or having a good snippet on the result page. This means, for example, that pages at the top rank are clicked on much more frequently than lower-ranked pages, even when the relevant pages are at the lower ranks. One approach to removing this bias is to use clickthrough data to predict user *preferences* between pairs of documents rather than relevance judgments. User preferences were first mentioned in section 7.6, where they were used to train a ranking function. A preference for document d_1 compared to document d_2 means that d_1 is more rel-

---

[2] In some logs, only the clicked-on URLs are recorded. Logging all the results enables the generation of preferences and provides a source of "negative" examples for various tasks.

evant or, equivalently, that it should be ranked higher. Preferences are most appropriate for search tasks where documents can have multiple levels of relevance, and are focused more on user relevance than purely topical relevance. Relevance judgments (either multi-level or binary) can be used to generate preferences, but preferences do not imply specific relevance levels.

The bias in clickthrough data is addressed by "strategies," or policies that generate preferences. These strategies are based on observations of user behavior and verified by experiments. One strategy that is similar to that described in section 7.6 is known as *Skip Above and Skip Next* (Agichtein, Brill, Dumais, & Ragno, 2006). This strategy assumes that given a set of results for a query and a clicked result at rank position p, all unclicked results ranked above p are predicted to be less relevant than the result at p. In addition, unclicked results immediately following a clicked result are less relevant than the clicked result. For example, given a result list of ranked documents together with click data as follows:

d_1
d_2
d_3 (clicked)
d_4,

this strategy will generate the following preferences:

$d_3 > d_2$
$d_3 > d_1$
$d_3 > d_4$

Since preferences are generated only when higher-ranked documents are ignored, a major source of bias is removed.

The "Skip" strategy uses the clickthrough patterns of individual users to generate preferences. This data can be noisy and inconsistent because of the variability in users' behavior. Since query logs typically contain many instances of the same query submitted by different users, clickthrough data can be aggregated to remove potential noise from individual differences. Specifically, *click distribution* information can be used to identify clicks that have a higher frequency than would be expected based on typical click patterns. These clicks have been shown to correlate well with relevance judgments. For a given query, we can use all the instances of that query in the log to compute the observed click frequency $O(d, p)$ for the result d in rank position p. We can also compute the expected click frequency $E(p)$ at rank p by averaging across all queries. The *click deviation* $CD(d, p)$ for a result d in position p is computed as:

$$CD(d, p) = O(d, p) - E(p).$$

We can then use the value of $CD(d, p)$ to "filter" clicks and provide more reliable click information to the Skip strategy.

A typical evaluation scenario involves the comparison of the result lists for two or more systems for a given set of queries. Preferences are an alternate method of specifying which documents should be retrieved for a given query (relevance judgments being the typical method). The quality of the result lists for each system is then summarized using an effectiveness measure that is based on either preferences or relevance judgments. The following section describes the measures that are most commonly used in research and system development.

8.4 Effectiveness Metrics

8.4.1 Recall and Precision

The two most common effectiveness measures, *recall* and *precision*, were introduced in the Cranfield studies to summarize and compare search results. Intuitively, recall measures how well the search engine is doing at finding all the relevant documents for a query, and precision measures how well it is doing at rejecting non-relevant documents.

The definition of these measures assumes that, for a given query, there is a set of documents that is *retrieved* and a set that is *not retrieved* (the rest of the documents). This obviously applies to the results of a Boolean search, but the same definition can also be used with a ranked search, as we will see later. If, in addition, relevance is assumed to be binary, then the results for a query can be summarized as shown in Table 8.3. In this table, A is the relevant set of documents for the query, $\overline{A}$ is the non-relevant set, B is the set of retrieved documents, and $\overline{B}$ is the set of documents that are not retrieved. The operator $\cap$ gives the intersection of two sets. For example, $A \cap B$ is the set of documents that are both relevant *and* retrieved.

A number of effectiveness measures can be defined using this table. The two we are particularly interested in are:

$$Recall = \frac{|A \cap B|}{|A|}$$

$$Precision = \frac{|A \cap B|}{|B|}$$

	Relevant	Non-Relevant
Retrieved	$A \cap B$	$\overline{A} \cap B$
Not Retrieved	$A \cap \overline{B}$	$\overline{A} \cap \overline{B}$

Table 8.3. Sets of documents defined by a simple search with binary relevance

where $|.|$ gives the size of the set. In other words, recall is the proportion of relevant documents that are retrieved, and precision is the proportion of retrieved documents that are relevant. There is an implicit assumption in using these measures that the task involves retrieving as many of the relevant documents as possible and minimizing the number of non-relevant documents retrieved. In other words, even if there are 500 relevant documents for a query, the user is interested in finding them all.

We can also view the search results summarized in Table 8.3 as the output of a binary classifier, as was mentioned in section 7.2.1. When a document is retrieved, it is the same as making a prediction that the document is relevant. From this perspective, there are two types of errors that can be made in prediction (or retrieval). These errors are called *false positives* (a non-relevant document is retrieved) and *false negatives* (a relevant document is not retrieved). Recall is related to one type of error (the false negatives), but precision is not related directly to the other type of error. Instead, another measure known as *fallout*,[3] which is the proportion of non-relevant documents that are retrieved, is related to the false positive errors:

$$Fallout = \frac{|\overline{A} \cap B|}{|\overline{A}|}$$

---

[3] In the classification and signal detection literature, the errors are known as Type I and Type II errors. Recall is often called the true positive rate, or sensitivity. Fallout is called the false positive rate, or the false alarm rate. Another measure, specificity, is 1 − fallout. Precision is known as the positive predictive value, and is often used in medical diagnostic tests where the probability that a positive test is correct is particularly important. The true positive rate and the false positive rate are used to draw ROC (receiver operating characteristic) curves that show the trade-off between these two quantities as the discrimination threshold varies. This threshold is the value at which the classifier makes a positive prediction. In the case of search, the threshold would correspond to a position in the document ranking. In information retrieval, recall-precision graphs are generally used instead of ROC curves.

Given that fallout and recall together characterize the effectiveness of a search as a classifier, why do we use precision instead? The answer is simply that precision is more meaningful to the user of a search engine. If 20 documents were retrieved for a query, a precision value of 0.7 means that 14 out of the 20 retrieved documents would be relevant. Fallout, on the other hand, will always be very small because there are so many non-relevant documents. If there were 1,000,000 non-relevant documents for the query used in the precision example, fallout would be $6/1000000 = 0.000006$. If precision fell to 0.5, which would be noticeable to the user, fallout would be 0.00001. The skewed nature of the search task, where most of the corpus is not relevant to any given query, also means that evaluating a search engine as a classifier can lead to counterintuitive results. A search engine trained to minimize classification errors would tend to retrieve nothing, since classifying a document as non-relevant is always a good decision!

The *F measure* is an effectiveness measure based on recall and precision that is used for evaluating classification performance and also in some search applications. It has the advantage of summarizing effectiveness in a single number. It is defined as the *harmonic mean* of recall and precision, which is:

$$F = \frac{1}{\frac{1}{2}(\frac{1}{R} + \frac{1}{P})} = \frac{2RP}{(R + P)}$$

Why use the harmonic mean instead of the usual arithmetic mean or average? The harmonic mean emphasizes the importance of small values, whereas the arithmetic mean is affected more by values that are unusually large (outliers). A search result that returned nearly the entire document collection, for example, would have a recall of 1.0 and a precision near 0. The arithmetic mean of these values is 0.5, but the harmonic mean will be close to 0. The harmonic mean is clearly a better summary of the effectiveness of this retrieved set.[4]

Most of the retrieval models we have discussed produce ranked output. To use recall and precision measures, retrieved sets of documents must be defined based on the ranking. One possibility is to calculate recall and precision values at every

---

[4] The more general form of the F measure is the *weighted harmonic mean*, which allows weights reflecting the relative importance of recall and precision to be used. This measure is $F = RP/(\alpha R + (1 - \alpha)P)$, where α is a weight. This is often transformed using $\alpha = 1/(\beta^2 + 1)$, which gives $F_\beta = (\beta^2 + 1)RP/(R + \beta^2 P)$. The common F measure is in fact F_1, where recall and precision have equal importance. In some evaluations, precision or recall is emphasized by varying the value of β. Values of $\beta > 1$ emphasize recall.

rank position. Figure 8.2 shows the top ten documents of two possible rankings, together with the recall and precision values calculated at every rank position for a query that has six relevant documents. These rankings might correspond to, for example, the output of different retrieval algorithms or search engines.

At rank position 10 (i.e., when ten documents are retrieved), the two rankings have the same effectiveness as measured by recall and precision. Recall is 1.0 because all the relevant documents have been retrieved, and precision is 0.6 because both rankings contain six relevant documents in the retrieved set of ten documents. At higher rank positions, however, the first ranking is clearly better. For example, at rank position 4 (four documents retrieved), the first ranking has a recall of 0.5 (three out of six relevant documents retrieved) and a precision of 0.75 (three out of four retrieved documents are relevant). The second ranking has a recall of 0.17 (1/6) and a precision of 0.25 (1/4).

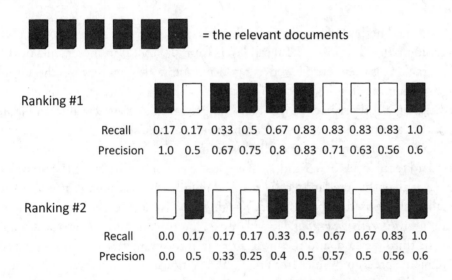

Fig. 8.2. Recall and precision values for two rankings of six relevant documents

If there are a large number of relevant documents for a query, or if the relevant documents are widely distributed in the ranking, a list of recall-precision values for every rank position will be long and unwieldy. Instead, a number of techniques have been developed to summarize the effectiveness of a ranking. The first of these is simply to calculate recall-precision values at a small number of predefined rank positions. In fact, to compare two or more rankings for a given query, only the precision at the predefined rank positions needs to be calculated. If the precision for a ranking at rank position p is higher than the precision for another ranking, the recall will be higher as well. This can be seen by comparing the corresponding recall-precision values in Figure 8.2. This effectiveness measure is known as *precision at rank p*. There are many possible values for the rank position p, but this measure is typically used to compare search output at the top of the ranking, since that is what many users care about. Consequently, the most common versions are precision at 10 and precision at 20. Note that if these measures are used, the implicit search task has changed to finding the most relevant documents at a given rank, rather than finding as many relevant documents as possible. Differences in search output further down the ranking than position 20 will not be considered. This measure also does not distinguish between differences in the rankings at positions 1 to p, which may be considered important for some tasks. For example, the two rankings in Figure 8.2 will be the same when measured using precision at 10.

Another method of summarizing the effectiveness of a ranking is to calculate precision at fixed or *standard* recall levels from 0.0 to 1.0 in increments of 0.1. Each ranking is then represented using 11 numbers. This method has the advantage of summarizing the effectiveness of the ranking of *all* relevant documents, rather than just those in the top ranks. Using the recall-precision values in Figure 8.2 as an example, however, it is clear that values of precision at these standard recall levels are often not available. In this example, only the precision values at the standard recall levels of 0.5 and 1.0 have been calculated. To obtain the precision values at all of the standard recall levels will require *interpolation*.[5] Since standard recall levels are used as the basis for averaging effectiveness across queries and generating *recall-precision graphs*, we will discuss interpolation in the next section.

The third method, and the most popular, is to summarize the ranking by averaging the precision values from the rank positions where a relevant document was retrieved (i.e., when recall increases). If a relevant document is not retrieved for some reason,[6] the contribution of this document to the average is 0.0. For the first ranking in Figure 8.2, the *average precision* is calculated as:

$$(1.0 + 0.67 + 0.75 + 0.8 + 0.83 + 0.6)/6 = 0.78$$

---

[5] Interpolation refers to any technique for calculating a new point between two existing data points.

[6] One common reason is that only a limited number of the top-ranked documents (e.g., 1,000) are considered.

For the second ranking, it is:

$$(0.5 + 0.4 + 0.5 + 0.57 + 0.56 + 0.6)/6 = 0.52$$

Average precision has a number of advantages. It is a single number that is based on the ranking of all the relevant documents, but the value depends heavily on the highly ranked relevant documents. This means it is an appropriate measure for evaluating the task of finding as many relevant documents as possible while still reflecting the intuition that the top-ranked documents are the most important.

All three of these methods summarize the effectiveness of a ranking for a single query. To provide a realistic assessment of the effectiveness of a retrieval algorithm, it must be tested on a number of queries. Given the potentially large set of results from these queries, we will need a method of summarizing the performance of the retrieval algorithm by calculating the average effectiveness for the entire set of queries. In the next section, we discuss the averaging techniques that are used in most evaluations.

8.4.2 Averaging and Interpolation

In the following discussion of averaging techniques, the two rankings shown in Figure 8.3 are used as a running example. These rankings come from using the same ranking algorithm on two *different* queries. The aim of an averaging technique is to summarize the effectiveness of a specific ranking algorithm across a collection of queries. Different queries will often have different numbers of relevant documents, as is the case in this example. Figure 8.3 also gives the recall-precision values calculated for the top 10 rank positions.

Given that the average precision provides a number for each ranking, the simplest way to summarize the effectiveness of rankings from multiple queries would be to average these numbers. This effectiveness measure, *mean average precision*,[7] or *MAP*, is used in most research papers and some system evaluations.[8] Since

---

[7] This sounds a lot better than average average precision!

[8] In some evaluations the *geometric mean* of the average precision (*GMAP*) is used instead of the arithmetic mean. This measure, because it multiplies average precision values, emphasizes the impact of queries with low performance. It is defined as

$$GMAP = \exp \frac{1}{n} \sum_{i=1}^{n} \log AP_i$$

where n is the number of queries, and AP_i is the average precision for query i.

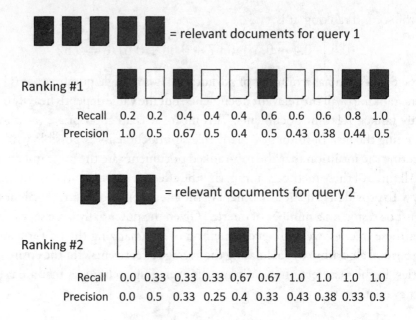

Ranking #1
Recall   0.2 0.2 0.4 0.4 0.4 0.6 0.6 0.6 0.8 1.0
Precision 1.0 0.5 0.67 0.5 0.4 0.5 0.43 0.38 0.44 0.5

Ranking #2
Recall   0.0 0.33 0.33 0.33 0.67 0.67 1.0 1.0 1.0 1.0
Precision 0.0 0.5 0.33 0.25 0.4 0.33 0.43 0.38 0.33 0.3

Fig. 8.3. Recall and precision values for rankings from two different queries

it is based on average precision, it assumes that the user is interested in finding many relevant documents for each query. Consequently, using this measure for comparison of retrieval algorithms or systems can require a considerable effort to acquire the relevance judgments, although methods for reducing the number of judgments required have been suggested (e.g., Carterette et al., 2006).

For the example in Figure 8.3, the mean average precision is calculated as follows:

average precision query 1 $= (1.0 + 0.67 + 0.5 + 0.44 + 0.5)/5 = 0.62$
average precision query 2 $= (0.5 + 0.4 + 0.43)/3 = 0.44$
mean average precision $= (0.62 + 0.44)/2 = 0.53$

The MAP measure provides a very succinct summary of the effectiveness of a ranking algorithm over many queries. Although this is often useful, sometimes too much information is lost in this process. *Recall-precision graphs*, and the tables of recall-precision values they are based on, give more detail on the effectiveness of the ranking algorithm at different recall levels. Figure 8.4 shows the recall-precision graph for the two queries in the example from Figure 8.3. Graphs for individual queries have very different shapes and are difficult to compare. To gen-

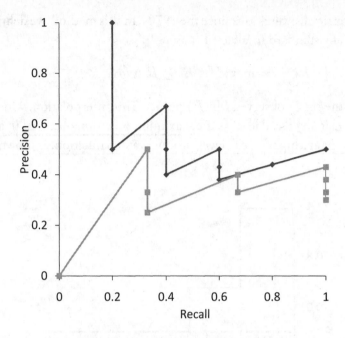

Fig. 8.4. Recall-precision graphs for two queries

erate a recall-precision graph that summarizes effectiveness over all the queries, the recall-precision values in Figure 8.3 should be averaged. To simplify the averaging process, the recall-precision values for each query are converted to precision values at standard recall levels, as mentioned in the last section. The precision values for all queries at each standard recall level can then be averaged.[9]

The standard recall levels are 0.0 to 1.0 in increments of 0.1. To obtain precision values for each query at these recall levels, the recall-precision data points, such as those in Figure 8.3, must be interpolated. That is, we have to define a function based on those data points that has a value at each standard recall level. There are many ways of doing interpolation, but only one method has been used in in-

---

[9] This is called a *macroaverage* in the literature. A macroaverage computes the measure of interest for each query and then averages these measures. A *microaverage* combines all the applicable data points from every query and computes the measure from the combined data. For example, a microaverage precision at rank 5 would be calculated as $\sum_{i=1}^{n} r_i / 5n$, where r_i is the number of relevant documents retrieved in the top five documents by query i, and n is the number of queries. Macroaveraging is used in most retrieval evaluations.

formation retrieval evaluations since the 1970s. In this method, we define the precision P at any standard recall level R as

$$P(R) = \max\{P' : R' \geq R \wedge (R', P') \in S\}$$

where S is the set of observed (R, P) points. This interpolation, which defines the precision at any recall level as the <u>maximum precision observed in any recall-precision point at a higher recall level, produces a step function, as shown in Figure 8.5.</u>

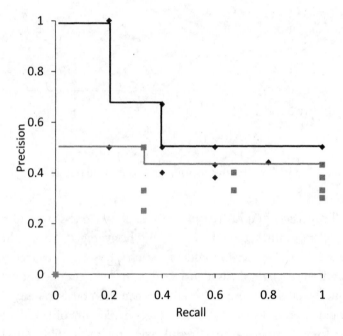

Fig. 8.5. Interpolated recall-precision graphs for two queries

Because search engines are imperfect and nearly always retrieve some non-relevant documents, precision tends to decrease with increasing recall (although this is not always true, as is shown in Figure 8.4). This interpolation method is consistent with this observation in that it produces a function that is monotonically decreasing. This means that precision values always go down (or stay the same) with increasing recall. The interpolation also defines a precision value for the recall level of 0.0, which would not be obvious otherwise! The general intuition behind this interpolation is that the recall-precision values are defined by the sets of documents in the ranking with the best possible precision values. In query 1, for example, there are three sets of documents that would be the best possible for the user to look at in terms of finding the highest proportion of relevant documents.

The average precision values at the standard recall levels are calculated by simply averaging the precision values for each query. Table 8.4 shows the interpolated precision values for the two example queries, along with the average precision values. The resulting average recall-precision graph is shown in Figure 8.6.

Recall	0.0	0.1	0.2	0.3	0.4	0.5	0.6	0.7	0.8	0.9	1.0
Ranking 1	1.0	1.0	1.0	0.67	0.67	0.5	0.5	0.5	0.5	0.5	0.5
Ranking 2	0.5	0.5	0.5	0.5	0.43	0.43	0.43	0.43	0.43	0.43	0.43
Average	0.75	0.75	0.75	0.59	0.47	0.47	0.47	0.47	0.47	0.47	0.47

Table 8.4. Precision values at standard recall levels calculated using interpolation

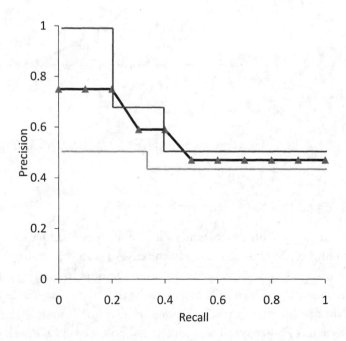

Fig. 8.6. Average recall-precision graph using standard recall levels

The average recall-precision graph is plotted by simply joining the average precision points at the standard recall levels, rather than using another step function. Although this is somewhat inconsistent with the interpolation method, the intermediate recall levels are never used in evaluation. When graphs are averaged over many queries, they tend to become smoother. Figure 8.7 shows a typical recall-precision graph from a TREC evaluation using 50 queries.

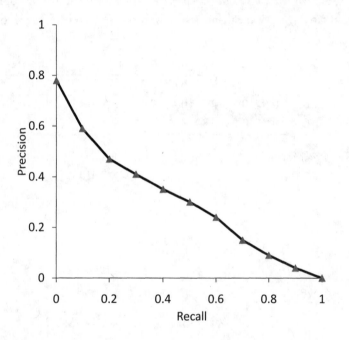

Fig. 8.7. Typical recall-precision graph for 50 queries from TREC

8.4.3 Focusing on the Top Documents

In many search applications, users tend to look at only the top part of the ranked result list to find relevant documents. In the case of web search, this means that many users look at just the first page or two of results. In addition, tasks such as *navigational* search (Chapter 7) or *question answering* (Chapter 1) have just a single relevant document. In these situations, recall is not an appropriate measure. Instead, the focus of an effectiveness measure should be on how well the search engine does at retrieving relevant documents at very high ranks (i.e., close to the top of the ranking).

One measure with this property that has already been mentioned is *precision at rank* p, where p in this case will typically be 10. This measure is easy to compute, can be averaged over queries to produce a single summary number, and is readily understandable. The major disadvantage is that it does not distinguish between different rankings of a given number of relevant documents. For example, if only one relevant document was retrieved in the top 10, according to the precision measure a ranking where that document is in the top position would be the same as one where it was at rank 10. Other measures have been proposed that are more sensitive to the rank position.

The *reciprocal rank* measure has been used for applications where there is typically a single relevant document. It is defined as the reciprocal of the rank at which the first relevant document is retrieved. The *mean reciprocal rank (MRR)* is the average of the reciprocal ranks over a set of queries. For example, if the top five documents retrieved for a query were d_n, d_r, d_n, d_n, d_n, where d_n is a non-relevant document and d_r is a relevant document, the reciprocal rank would be $1/2 = 0.5$. Even if more relevant documents had been retrieved, as in the ranking d_n, d_r, d_n, d_r, d_n, the reciprocal rank would still be 0.5. The reciprocal rank is very sensitive to the rank position. It falls from 1.0 to 0.5 from rank 1 to 2, and the ranking d_n, d_n, d_n, d_n, d_r would have a reciprocal rank of $1/5 = 0.2$. The MRR for these two rankings would be $(0.5 + 0.2)/2 = 0.35$.

The *discounted cumulative gain (DCG)* has become a popular measure for evaluating web search and related applications (Järvelin & Kekäläinen, 2002). It is based on two assumptions:

- Highly relevant documents are more useful than marginally relevant documents.
- The lower the ranked position of a relevant document (i.e., further down the ranked list), the less useful it is for the user, since it is less likely to be examined.

These two assumptions lead to an evaluation that uses graded relevance as a measure of the usefulness, or *gain*, from examining a document. The gain is accumulated starting at the top of the ranking and may be reduced, or *discounted*, at lower ranks. The DCG is the total gain accumulated at a particular rank p. Specifically, it is defined as:

$$DCG_p = rel_1 + \sum_{i=2}^{p} \frac{rel_i}{\log_2 i}$$

where rel_i is the graded relevance level of the document retrieved at rank i. For example, web search evaluations have been reported that used manual relevance judgments on a six-point scale ranging from "Bad" to "Perfect" (i.e., $0 \leq rel_i \leq 5$). Binary relevance judgments can also be used, in which case rel_i would be either 0 or 1.

The denominator $\log_2 i$ is the discount or reduction factor that is applied to the gain. There is no theoretical justification for using this particular discount factor, although it does provide a relatively smooth (gradual) reduction.[10] By varying the base of the logarithm, the discount can be made sharper or smoother. With base 2, the discount at rank 4 is 1/2, and at rank 8 it is 1/3. As an example, consider the following ranking where each number is a relevance level on the scale 0–3 (not relevant–highly relevant):

$$3, 2, 3, 0, 0, 1, 2, 2, 3, 0$$

These numbers represent the gain at each rank. The discounted gain would be:

$$3, 2/1, 3/1.59, 0, 0, 1/2.59, 2/2.81, 2/3, 3/3.17, 0 =$$
$$3, 2, 1.89, 0, 0, 0.39, 0.71, 0.67, 0.95, 0$$

The DCG at each rank is formed by accumulating these numbers, giving:

$$3, 5, 6.89, 6.89, 6.89, 7.28, 7.99, 8.66, 9.61, 9.61$$

Similar to precision at rank p, specific values of p are chosen for the evaluation, and the DCG numbers are averaged across a set of queries. Since the focus of this measure is on the top ranks, these values are typically small, such as 5 and 10. For this example, DCG at rank 5 is 6.89 and at rank 10 is 9.61. To facilitate averaging across queries with different numbers of relevant documents, these numbers can be normalized by comparing the DCG at each rank with the DCG value for the *perfect* ranking for that query. For example, if the previous ranking contained all

---

[10] In some publications, DCG is defined as:

$$DCG_p = \sum_{i=1}^{p} (2^{rel_i} - 1)/log(1 + i)$$

For binary relevance judgments, the two definitions are the same, but for graded relevance this definition puts a strong emphasis on retrieving highly relevant documents. This version of the measure is used by some search engine companies and, because of this, may become the standard.

the relevant documents for that query, the perfect ranking would have gain values at each rank of:

3, 3, 3, 2, 2, 2, 1, 0, 0, 0

which would give *ideal* DCG values of:

3, 6, 7.89, 8.89, 9.75, 10.52, 10.88, 10.88, 10.88, 10.88

Normalizing the actual DCG values by dividing by the ideal values gives us the *normalized discounted cumulative gain (NDCG)* values:

1, 0.83, 0.87, 0.76, 0.71, 0.69, 0.73, 0.8, 0.88, 0.88

Note that the NDCG measure is ≤ 1 at any rank position. To summarize, the NDCG for a given query can be defined as:

$$NDCG_p = \frac{DCG_p}{IDCG_p}$$

where IDCG is the ideal DCG value for that query.

8.4.4 Using Preferences

In section 8.3, we discussed how user preferences can be inferred from query logs. Preferences have been used for training ranking algorithms, and have been suggested as an alternative to relevance judgments for evaluation. Currently, however, there is no standard effectiveness measure based on preferences.

In general, two rankings described using preferences can be compared using the *Kendall tau coefficient* (τ). If P is the number of preferences that agree and Q is the number that disagree, Kendall's τ is defined as:

$$\tau = \frac{P - Q}{P + Q}$$

This measure varies between 1 (when all preferences agree) and –1 (when they all disagree). If preferences are derived from clickthrough data, however, only a partial ranking is available. Experimental evidence shows that this partial information can be used to learn effective ranking algorithms, which suggests that effectiveness can be measured this way. Instead of using the complete set of preferences to calculate P and Q, a new ranking would be evaluated by comparing it to the *known* set of preferences. For example, if there were 15 preferences learned from clickthrough data, and a ranking agreed with 10 of these, the τ measure would be $(10 - 5)/15 = 0.33$. Although this seems reasonable, no studies are available that show that this effectiveness measure is useful for comparing systems.

For preferences derived from binary relevance judgments, the BPREF[11] measure has been shown to be robust with partial information and to give similar results (in terms of system comparisons) to recall-precision measures such as MAP. In this measure, the number of relevant and non-relevant documents is balanced to facilitate averaging across queries. For a query with R relevant documents, only the first R non-relevant documents are considered. This is equivalent to using $R \times R$ preferences (all relevant documents are preferred to all non-relevant documents). Given this, the measure is defined as:

$$BPREF = \frac{1}{R} \sum_{d_r} (1 - \frac{N_{d_r}}{R})$$

where d_r is a relevant document and N_{d_r} gives the number of non-relevant documents (from the set of R non-relevant documents that are considered) that are ranked higher than d_r. If this is expressed in terms of preferences, N_{d_r} is actually a method for counting the number of preferences that disagree (for binary relevance judgments). Since $R \times R$ is the number of preferences being considered, an alternative definition of BPREF is:

$$BPREF = \frac{P}{P + Q}$$

which means it is very similar to Kendall's τ. The main difference is that BPREF varies between 0 and 1. Given that BPREF is a useful effectiveness measure, this suggests that the same measure or τ could be used with preferences associated with graded relevance.

8.5 Efficiency Metrics

Compared to effectiveness, the efficiency of a search system seems like it should be easier to quantify. Most of what we care about can be measured automatically with a timer instead of with costly relevance judgments. However, like effectiveness, it is important to determine exactly what aspects of efficiency we want to measure. Table 8.5 shows some of the measures that are used.

---

[11] Binary Preference

Metric name	Description
Elapsed indexing time	Measures the amount of time necessary to build a document index on a particular system.
Indexing processor time	Measures the CPU seconds used in building a document index. This is similar to elapsed time, but does not count time waiting for I/O or speed gains from parallelism.
Query throughput	Number of queries processed per second.
Query latency	The amount of time a user must wait after issuing a query before receiving a response, measured in milliseconds. This can be measured using the mean, but is often more instructive when used with the median or a percentile bound.
Indexing temporary space	Amount of temporary disk space used while creating an index.
Index size	Amount of storage necessary to store the index files.

Table 8.5. Definitions of some important efficiency metrics

The most commonly quoted efficiency metric is query throughput, measured in queries processed per second. Throughput numbers are comparable only for the same collection and queries processed on the same hardware, although rough comparisons can be made between runs on similar hardware. As a single-number metric of efficiency, throughput is good because it is intuitive and mirrors the common problems we want to solve with efficiency numbers. A real system user will want to use throughput numbers for capacity planning, to help determine whether more hardware is necessary to handle a particular query load. Since it is simple to measure the number of queries per second currently being issued to a service, it is easy to determine whether a system's query throughput is adequate to handle the needs of an existing service.

The trouble with using throughput alone is that it does not capture latency. Latency measures the elapsed time the system takes between when the user issues a query and when the system delivers its response. Psychology research suggests that users consider any operation that takes less than about 150 milliseconds to be instantaneous. Above that level, users react very negatively to the delay they perceive.

This brings us back to throughput, because latency and throughput are not orthogonal: generally we can improve throughput by increasing latency, and reducing latency leads to poorer throughput. To see why this is so, think of the difference between having a personal chef and ordering food at a restaurant. The personal chef prepares your food with the lowest possible latency, since she has no other demands on her time and focuses completely on preparing your food. Unfortunately, the personal chef has low throughput, since her focus on you leads to idle time when she is not completely occupied. The restaurant is a high throughput operation with lots of chefs working on many different orders simultaneously. Having many orders and many chefs leads to certain economies of scale—for instance, when a single chef prepares many identical orders at the same time. Note that the chef is able to process these orders simultaneously precisely because some latency has been added to some orders: instead of starting to cook immediately upon receiving an order, the chef may decide to wait a few minutes to see if anyone else orders the same thing. The result is that the chefs are able to cook food with high throughput but at some cost in latency.

Query processing works the same way. It is possible to build a system that handles just one query at a time, devoting all resources to the current query, just like the personal chef devotes all her time to a single customer. This kind of system is low throughput, because only one query is processed at a time, which leads to idle resources. The radical opposite approach is to process queries in large batches. The system can then reorder the incoming queries so that queries that use common subexpressions are evaluated at the same time, saving valuable execution time. However, interactive users will hate waiting for their query batch to complete.

Like recall and precision in effectiveness, low latency and high throughput are both desirable properties of a retrieval system, but they are in conflict with each other and cannot be maximized at the same time. In a real system, query throughput is not a variable but a requirement: the system needs to handle every query the users submit. The two remaining variables are latency (how long the users will have to wait for a response) and hardware cost (how many processors will be applied to the search problem). A common way to talk about latency is with percentile bounds, such as "99% of all queries will complete in under 100 milliseconds." System designers can then add hardware until this requirement is met.

Query throughput and latency are the most visible system efficiency metrics, but we should also consider the costs of indexing. For instance, given enough time and space, it is possible to cache every possible query of a particular length. A system that did this would have excellent query throughput and query latency, but at the cost of enormous storage and indexing costs. Therefore, we also need to measure the size of the index structures and the time necessary to create them. Because indexing is often a distributed process, we need to know both the total amount of processor time used during indexing and the elapsed time. Since the process of inversion often requires temporary storage, it is interesting to measure the amount of temporary storage used.

8.6 Training, Testing, and Statistics

8.6.1 Significance Tests

Retrieval experiments generate data, such as average precision values or NDCG values. In order to decide whether this data shows that there is a meaningful difference between two retrieval algorithms or search engines, *significance tests* are needed. Every significance test is based on a *null hypothesis*. In the case of a typical retrieval experiment, we are comparing the value of an effectiveness measure for rankings produced by two retrieval algorithms. The null hypothesis is that there is no difference in effectiveness between the two retrieval algorithms. The *alternative hypothesis* is that there is a difference. In fact, given two retrieval algorithms A and B, where A is a *baseline* algorithm and B is a new algorithm, we are usually trying to show that the effectiveness of B is better than A, rather than simply finding a difference. Since the rankings that are compared are based on the same set of queries for both retrieval algorithms, this is known as a *matched pair* experiment.

We obviously cannot conclude that B is better than A on the basis of the results of a single query, since A may be better than B on all other queries. So how many queries do we have to look at to make a decision about which is better? If, for example, B is better than A for 90% of 200 queries in a test collection, we should be more confident that B is better for that effectiveness measure, but how confident? Significance tests allow us to quantify the confidence we have in any judgment about effectiveness.

More formally, a significance test enables us to reject the null hypothesis in favor of the alternative hypothesis (i.e., show that B is better than A) on the basis of the data from the retrieval experiments. Otherwise, we say that the null hypothesis cannot be rejected (i.e., B might not be better than A). As with any binary decision process, a significance test can make two types of error. A Type I error is when the null hypothesis is rejected when it is in fact true. A Type II error is when the null hypothesis is accepted when it is in fact false.[12] Significance tests

---

[12] Compare to the discussion of errors in section 8.4.1.

are often described by their *power*, which is the probability that the test will reject the null hypothesis correctly (i.e., decide that B is better than A). In other words, a test with high power will reduce the chance of a Type II error. The power of a test can also be increased by increasing the sample size, which in this case is the number of queries in the experiment. Increasing the number of queries will also reduce the chance of a Type I error.

The procedure for comparing two retrieval algorithms using a particular set of queries and a significance test is as follows:

1. Compute the effectiveness measure for every query for both rankings.
2. Compute a *test statistic* based on a comparison of the effectiveness measures for each query. The test statistic depends on the significance test, and is simply a quantity calculated from the sample data that is used to decide whether or not the null hypothesis should be rejected.
3. The test statistic is used to compute a *P-value*, which is the probability that a test statistic value at least that extreme could be observed if the null hypothesis were true. Small P-values suggest that the null hypothesis may be false.
4. The null hypothesis (no difference) is rejected in favor of the alternate hypothesis (i.e., B is more effective than A) if the P-value is $\leq \alpha$, the *significance level*. Values for α are small, typically 0.05 and 0.1, to reduce the chance of a Type I error.

In other words, if the probability of getting a specific test statistic value is very small assuming the null hypothesis is true, we reject that hypothesis and conclude that ranking algorithm B is more effective than the baseline algorithm A.

The computation of the test statistic and the corresponding P-value is usually done using tables or standard statistical software. The significance tests discussed here are also provided in Galago.

The procedure just described is known as a *one-sided* or *one-tailed* test since we want to establish that B is better than A. If we were just trying to establish that there is a difference between B and A, it would be a *two-sided* or *two-tailed* test, and the P-value would be doubled. The "side" or "tail" referred to is the tail of a probability distribution. For example, Figure 8.8 shows a distribution for the possible values of a test statistic assuming the null hypothesis. The shaded part of the distribution is the *region of rejection* for a one-sided test. If a test yielded the test statistic value x, the null hypothesis would be rejected since the probability of getting that value or higher (the P-value) is less than the significance level of 0.05.

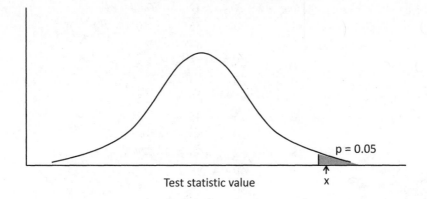

Fig. 8.8. Probability distribution for test statistic values assuming the null hypothesis. The shaded area is the region of rejection for a one-sided test.

The significance tests most commonly used in the evaluation of search engines are the *t-test*,[13] the *Wilcoxon signed-rank test*, and the *sign test*. To explain these tests, we will use the data shown in Table 8.6, which shows the effectiveness values of the rankings produced by two retrieval algorithms for 10 queries. The values in the table are artificial and could be average precision or NDCG, for example, on a scale of 0–100 (instead of 0–1). The table also shows the difference in the effectiveness measure between algorithm B and the baseline algorithm A. The small number of queries in this example data is not typical of a retrieval experiment.

In general, the t-test assumes that data values are sampled from normal distributions. In the case of a matched pair experiment, the assumption is that the difference between the effectiveness values is a sample from a normal distribution. The null hypothesis in this case is that the mean of the distribution of differences is zero. The test statistic for the paired t-test is:

$$ t = \frac{\overline{B - A}}{\sigma_{B-A}} \cdot \sqrt{N} $$

where $\overline{B - A}$ is the mean of the differences, σ_{B-A} is the standard deviation[14] of the differences, and N is the size of the sample (the number of queries). For

---

[13] Also known as Student's t-test, where "student" was the pen name of the inventor, William Gosset, not the type of person who should use it.

[14] For a set of data values x_i, the standard deviation can be calculated by $\sigma = \sqrt{\sum_{i=1}^{N}(x_i - \overline{x})^2/N}$, where $\overline{x}$ is the mean.

Query	A	B	B – A
1	25	35	10
2	43	84	41
3	39	15	-24
4	75	75	0
5	43	68	25
6	15	85	70
7	20	80	60
8	52	50	-2
9	49	58	9
10	50	75	25

Table 8.6. Artificial effectiveness data for two retrieval algorithms (A and B) over 10 queries. The column B – A gives the difference in effectiveness.

the data in Table 8.6, $\overline{B-A} = 21.4$, $\sigma_{B-A} = 29.1$, and $t = 2.33$. For a one-tailed test, this gives a P-value of 0.02, which would be significant at a level of $\alpha = 0.05$. Therefore, for this data, the t-test enables us to reject the null hypothesis and conclude that ranking algorithm B is more effective than A.

There are two objections that could be made to using the t-test in search evaluations. The first is that the assumption that the data is sampled from normal distributions is generally not appropriate for effectiveness measures, although the distribution of differences can resemble a normal distribution for large N. Recent experimental results have supported the validity of the t-test by showing that it produces very similar results to the *randomization test* on TREC data (Smucker et al., 2007). The randomization test does not assume the data comes from normal distributions, and is the most powerful of the *nonparametric* tests.[15] The randomization test, however, is much more expensive to compute than the t-test.

The second objection that could be made is concerned with the level of *measurement* associated with effectiveness measures. The t-test (and the randomization test) assume the the evaluation data is measured on an *interval scale*. This means that the values can be ordered (e.g., an effectiveness of 54 is greater than an effectiveness of 53), and that differences between values are meaningful (e.g., the difference between 80 and 70 is the same as the difference between 20 and 10). Some people have argued that effectiveness measures are an *ordinal scale*, which

---

[15] A nonparametric test makes less assumptions about the data and the underlying distribution than parametric tests.

means that the magnitude of the differences are not significant. The Wilcoxon signed-rank test and the sign test, which are both nonparametric, make less assumptions about the effectiveness measure. As a consequence, they do not use all the information in the data, and it can be more difficult to show a significant difference. In other words, if the effectiveness measure did satisfy the conditions for using the t-test, the Wilcoxon and sign tests have less power.

The Wilcoxon signed-rank test assumes that the differences between the effectiveness values for algorithms A and B can be ranked, but the magnitude is not important. This means, for example, that the difference for query 8 in Table 8.6 will be ranked first because it is the smallest non-zero absolute value, but the magnitude of 2 is not used directly in the test. The test statistic is:

$$w = \sum_{i=1}^{N} R_i$$

where R_i is a signed-rank, and N is the number of differences $\neq 0$. To compute the signed-ranks, the differences are ordered by their absolute values (increasing), and then assigned rank values (ties are assigned the average rank). The rank values are then given the sign of the original difference. The null hypothesis for this test is that the sum of the positive ranks will be the same as the sum of the negative ranks.

For example, the nine non-zero differences from Table 8.6, in rank order of absolute value, are:

   2, 9, 10, 24, 25, 25, 41, 60, 70

The corresponding signed-ranks are:

   −1, +2, +3, −4, +5.5, +5.5, +7, +8, +9

Summing these signed-ranks gives a value of $w = 35$. For a one-tailed test, this gives a P-value of approximately 0.025, which means the null hypothesis can be rejected at a significance level of $\alpha = 0.05$.

The sign test goes further than the Wilcoxon signed-ranks test, and completely ignores the magnitude of the differences. The null hypothesis for this test is that $P(B > A) = P(A > B) = \frac{1}{2}$. In other words, over a large sample we would expect that the number of pairs where B is "better" than A would be the same as the number of pairs where A is "better" than B. The test statistic is simply the number of pairs where $B > A$. The issue for a search evaluation is deciding what difference in the effectiveness measure is "better." We could assume that even small differences in average precision or NDCG—such as 0.51 compared to 0.5—are significant. This has the risk of leading to a decision that algorithm B is more effective than A when the difference is, in fact, not noticeable to the users. Instead, an appropriate threshold for the effectiveness measure should be chosen. For example, an old rule of thumb in information retrieval is that there has to be at least 5% difference in average precision to be noticeable (10% for a more conservative threshold). This would mean that a difference of $0.51 - 0.5 = 0.01$ would be considered a tie for the sign test. If the effectiveness measure was precision at rank 10, on the other hand, any difference might be considered significant since it would correspond directly to additional relevant documents in the top 10.

For the data in Table 8.6, we will consider any difference to be significant. This means there are seven pairs out of ten where B is better than A. The corresponding P-value is 0.17, which is the chance of observing seven "successes" in ten trials where the probability of success is 0.5 (just like flipping a coin). Using the sign test, we cannot reject the null hypothesis. Because so much information from the effectiveness measure is discarded in the sign test, it is more difficult to show a difference, and more queries are needed to increase the power of the test. On the other hand, it can be used in addition to the t-test to provide a more user-focused perspective. An algorithm that is significantly more effective according to both the t-test and the sign test, perhaps using different effectiveness measures, is more likely to be noticeably better.

8.6.2 Setting Parameter Values

Nearly every ranking algorithm has *parameters* that can be tuned to improve the effectiveness of the results. For example, BM25 has the parameters k_1, k_2, and b used in term weighting, and query likelihood with Dirichlet smoothing has the parameter μ. Ranking algorithms for web search can have hundreds of parameters that give the weights for the associated features. The values of these parameters can have a major impact on retrieval effectiveness, and values that give the best effectiveness for one application may not be appropriate for another application, or even for a different document collection. Not only is choosing the right parameter values important for the performance of a search engine when it is deployed, it is an important part of comparing the effectiveness of two retrieval algorithms. An algorithm that has had its parameters tuned for optimal performance for the test collection may appear to be much more effective than it really is when compared to a baseline algorithm with poor parameter values.

The appropriate method of setting parameters for both maximizing effectiveness and making fair comparisons of algorithms is to use a *training set* and a *test set* of data. The training set is used to learn the best parameter values, and the test set is used for validating these parameter values and comparing ranking algorithms. The training and test sets are two separate test collections of documents, queries, and relevance judgments, although they may be created by splitting a single collection. In TREC experiments, for example, the training set is usually documents, queries, and relevance judgments from previous years. When there is not a large amount of data available, *cross-validation* can be done by partitioning the data into K subsets. One subset is used for testing, and $K - 1$ are used for training. This is repeated using each of the subsets as a test set, and the best parameter values are averaged across the K runs.

Using training and test sets helps to avoid the problem of *overfitting* (mentioned in Chapter 7), which occurs when the parameter values are tuned to fit a particular set of data too well. If this was the only data that needed to be searched in an application, that would be appropriate, but a much more common situation is that the training data is only a sample of the data that will be encountered when the search engine is deployed. Overfitting will result in a choice of parameter values that do not generalize well to this other data. A symptom of overfitting is that effectiveness on the training set improves but effectiveness on the test set gets worse.

A fair comparison of two retrieval algorithms would involve getting the best parameter values for both algorithms using the training set, and then using those values with the test set. The effectiveness measures are used to tune the parameter values in multiple retrieval runs on the training data, and for the final comparison, which is a single retrieval run, on the test data. The "cardinal sin" of retrieval experiments, which should be avoided in nearly all situations, is testing on the training data. This typically will artificially boost the measured effectiveness of a retrieval algorithm. It is particularly problematic when one algorithm has been trained in some way using the testing data and the other has not. Although it sounds like an easy problem to avoid, it can sometimes occur in subtle ways in more complex experiments.

Given a training set of data, there a number of techniques for finding the best parameter settings for a particular effectiveness measure. The most common method is simply to explore the space of possible parameter values by *brute force*. This requires a large number of retrieval runs with small variations in parameter values (a *parameter sweep*). Although this could be computationally infeasible for large numbers of parameters, it is guaranteed to find the parameter settings that give the best effectiveness for any given effectiveness measure. The Ranking SVM method described in section 7.6 is an example of a more sophisticated procedure for learning good parameter values efficiently with large numbers of parameters. This method, as well as similar optimization techniques, will find the best possible parameter values if the function being optimized meets certain conditions.[16] Because many of the effectiveness measures we have described do not meet these conditions, different functions are used for the optimization, and the parameter values are not guaranteed to be optimal. This is, however, a very active area of research, and new methods for learning parameters are constantly becoming available.

8.6.3 Online Testing

All of the evaluation strategies described thus far have assumed that training and testing are done offline. That is, we have assumed that all of the training and test data are fixed ahead of time. However, with real search engines, it may be possible to test (or even train) using live traffic. This is often called *online testing*. For example, suppose that you just developed a new sponsored-search advertising algorithm. Rather than evaluating your system using human relevance judgments, it is possible to deploy the new ranking algorithm and observe the amount of revenue generated using the new algorithm versus some baseline algorithm. This makes it possible to test various search engine components, such as ranking algorithms, query suggestion algorithms, and snippet generation algorithms, using live traffic and real users. Notice that this is similar to logging, which was discussed earlier in this chapter. With logging, evaluations are typically done retrospectively on "stale" data, whereas online testing uses live data.

There are several benefits to online testing. First, it allows real users to interact with the system. These interactions provide information, such as click data, that can be used for various kinds of evaluation. Second, online testing is less biased, since the evaluation is being done over a real sample of users and traffic. This

---

[16] Specifically, the function should be *convex* (or *concave*; a function $f(x)$ is concave if and only if $-f(x)$ is convex). A convex function is a continuous function that satisfies the following constraint for all λ in [0,1]:

$$f(\lambda x_1 + (1 - \lambda)x_2) \leq \lambda f(x_1) + (1 - \lambda)f(x_2)$$

is valuable because it is often difficult to build test collections that accurately reflect real search engine users and traffic. Finally, online testing can produce a large amount of data very cheaply, since it does not require paying any humans to do relevance judgments.

Unfortunately, online testing also has its fair share of drawbacks. The primary drawback is that the data collected is typically very noisy. There are many different reasons why users behave the way they do in an online environment. For example, if a user does not click on a search result, it does not necessarily mean the result is bad. The user may have clicked on an advertisement instead, lost interest, or simply gone to eat dinner. Therefore, typically a very large amount of online testing data is required to eliminate noise and produce meaningful conclusions. Another drawback to online testing is that it requires live traffic to be altered in potentially harmful ways. If the algorithm being tested is highly experimental, then it may significantly degrade retrieval effectiveness and drive users away. For this reason, online testing must be done very carefully, so as not to negatively affect the user experience. One way of minimizing the effect of an online test on the general user population is to use the experimental algorithm only for a small percentage, such as 1% to 5%, of the live traffic. Finally, online tests typically provide only a very specific type of data—click data. As we described earlier in this section, click data is not always ideal for evaluating search engines, since the data is noisy and highly biased. However, for certain search engine evaluation metrics, such as clickthrough rate[17] and revenue, online testing can be very useful.

Therefore, online testing can be a useful, inexpensive way of training or testing new algorithms, especially those that can be evaluated using click data. Special care must be taken to ensure that the data collected is analyzed properly and that the overall user experience is not degraded.

8.7 The Bottom Line

In this chapter, we have presented a number of effectiveness and efficiency measures. At this point, it would be reasonable to ask which of them is the right measure to use. The answer, especially with regard to effectiveness, is that no single measure is the correct one for any search application. Instead, a search engine should be evaluated through a combination of measures that show different as-

---

[17] The percentage of times that some item is clicked on.

pects of the system's performance. In many settings, *all* of the following measures and tests could be carried out with little additional effort:

- Mean average precision - single number summary, popular measure, pooled relevance judgments.
- Average NDCG - single number summary for each rank level, emphasizes top ranked documents, relevance judgments needed only to a specific rank depth (typically to 10).
- Recall-precision graph - conveys more information than a single number measure, pooled relevance judgments.
- Average precision at rank 10 - emphasizes top ranked documents, easy to understand, relevance judgments limited to top 10.

Using MAP and a recall-precision graph could require more effort in relevance judgments, but this analysis could also be limited to the relevant documents found in the top 10 for the NDCG and precision at 10 measures.

All these evaluations should be done relative to one or more baseline searches. It generally does not make sense to do an effectiveness evaluation without a good baseline, since the effectiveness numbers depend strongly on the particular mix of queries and documents in the test collection. The t-test can be used as the significance test for the average precision, NDCG, and precision at 10 measures.

All of the standard evaluation measures and significance tests are available using the evaluation program provided as part of Galago.

In addition to these evaluations, it is also very useful to present a summary of the number of queries that were improved and the number that were degraded, relative to a baseline. Figure 8.9 gives an example of this summary for a TREC run, where the query numbers are shown as a distribution over various percentage levels of improvement for a specific evaluation measure (usually MAP). Each bar represents the number of queries that were better (or worse) than the baseline by the given percentage. This provides a simple visual summary showing that many more queries were improved than were degraded, and that the improvements were sometimes quite substantial. By setting a threshold on the level of improvement that constitutes "noticeable," the sign test can be used with this data to establish significance.

Given this range of measures, both developers and users will get a better picture of where the search engine is performing well and where it may need improvement. It is often necessary to look at individual queries to get a better understand-

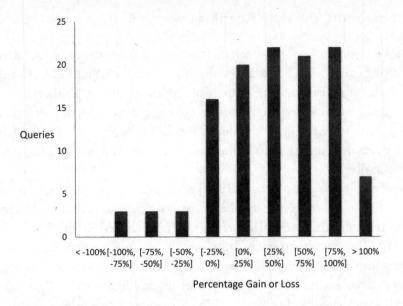

Fig. 8.9. Example distribution of query effectiveness improvements

ing of what is causing the ranking behavior of a particular algorithm. Query data such as Figure 8.9 can be helpful in identifying interesting queries.

References and Further Reading

Despite being discussed for more than 40 years, the measurement of effectiveness in search engines is still a hot topic, with many papers being published in the major conferences every year. The chapter on evaluation in van Rijsbergen (1979) gives a good historical perspective on effectiveness measurement in information retrieval. Another useful general source is the TREC book (Voorhees & Harman, 2005), which describes the test collections and evaluation procedures used and how they evolved.

Saracevic (1975) and Mizzaro (1997) are the best papers for general reviews of the critical topic of relevance. The process of obtaining relevance judgments and the reliability of retrieval experiments are discussed in the TREC book. Zobel (1998) shows that some incompleteness of relevance judgments does not affect experiments, although Buckley and Voorhees (2004) suggest that substantial incompleteness can be a problem. Voorhees and Buckley (2002) discuss the error rates associated with different numbers of queries. Sanderson and Zobel (2005) show how using a significance test can affect the reliability of comparisons and also compare shallow versus in-depth relevance judgments. Carterette et al. (2006) describe a technique for reducing the number of relevance judgments required for reliable comparisons of search engines. Kelly and Teevan (2003) review approaches to acquiring and using implicit relevance information. Fox et al. (2005) studied implicit measures of relevance in the context of web search, and Joachims et al. (2005) introduced strategies for deriving preferences based on clickthrough data. Agichtein, Brill, Dumais, and Ragno (2006) extended this approach and carried out more experiments introducing click distributions and deviation, and showing that a number of features related to user behavior are useful for predicting relevance.

The F measure was originally proposed by van Rijsbergen (1979) in the form of $E = 1 - F$. He also provided a justification for the E measure in terms of measurement theory, raised the issue of whether effectiveness measures were interval or ordinal measures, and suggested that the sign and Wilcoxon tests would be appropriate for significance. Cooper (1968) wrote an important early paper that introduced the expected search length (ESL) measure, which was the expected number of documents that a user would have to look at to find a specified number of relevant documents. Although this measure has not been widely used, it was the ancestor of measures such as NDCG (Järvelin & Kekäläinen, 2002) that focus on the top-ranked documents. Another measure of this type that has recently been introduced is rank-biased precision (Moffat et al., 2007).

Yao (1995) provides one of the first discussions of preferences and how they could be used to evaluate a search engine. The paper by Joachims (2002b) that showed how to train a linear feature-based retrieval model using preferences also used Kendall's τ as the effectiveness measure for defining the best ranking. The recent paper by Carterette and Jones (2007) shows how search engines can be evaluated using relevance information directly derived from clickthrough data, rather than converting clickthrough to preferences.

A number of recent studies have focused on *interactive* information retrieval. These studies involve a different style of evaluation than the methods described in this chapter, but are more formal than online testing. Belkin (2008) describes the challenges of evaluating interactive experiments and points to some interesting papers on this topic.

Another area related to effectiveness evaluation is the *prediction* of query effectiveness. Cronen-Townsend et al. (2006) describe the Clarity measure, which is used to predict whether a ranked list for a query has good or bad precision. Other measures have been suggested that have even better correlations with average precision.

There are very few papers that discuss guidelines for efficiency evaluations of search engines. Zobel et al. (1996) is an example from the database literature.

Exercises

8.1. Find three other examples of test collections in the information retrieval literature. Describe them and compare their statistics in a table.

8.2. Imagine that you were going to study the effectiveness of a search engine for blogs. Specify the retrieval task(s) for this application, and then describe the test collection you would construct and how you would evaluate your ranking algorithms.

8.3. For one query in the CACM collection (provided at the book website), generate a ranking using Galago, and then calculate average precision, NDCG at 5 and 10, precision at 10, and the reciprocal rank by hand.

8.4. For two queries in the CACM collection, generate two uninterpolated recall-precision graphs, a table of interpolated precision values at standard recall levels, and the average interpolated recall-precision graph.

8.5. Generate the mean average precision, recall-precision graph, average NDCG at 5 and 10, and precision at 10 for the entire CACM query set.

8.6. Compare the MAP value calculated in the previous problem to the GMAP value. Which queries have the most impact on this value?

8.7. Another measure that has been used in a number of evaluations is *R-precision*. This is defined as the precision at R documents, where R is the number of relevant documents for a query. It is used in situations where there is a large variation in the number of relevant documents per query. Calculate the average R-precision for the CACM query set and compare it to the other measures.

8.8. Generate another set of rankings for 10 CACM queries by adding structure to the queries manually. Compare the effectiveness of these queries to the simple queries using MAP, NDCG, and precision at 10. Check for significance using the t-test, Wilcoxon test, and the sign test.

8.9. For one query in the CACM collection, generate a ranking and calculate BPREF. Show that the two formulations of BPREF give the same value.

8.10. Consider a test collection that contains judgments for a large number of time-sensitive queries, such as "olympics" and "miss universe". Suppose that the judgments for these queries were made in 2002. Why is this a problem? How can online testing be used to alleviate the problem?

9

Classification and Clustering

"What kind of thing? I need a clear definition."

Ripley, *Alien*

We now take a slight detour from search to look at classification and clustering. Classification and clustering have many things in common with document retrieval. In fact, many of the techniques that proved to be useful for ranking documents can also be used for these tasks. Classification and clustering algorithms are heavily used in most modern search engines, and thus it is important to have a basic understanding of how these techniques work and how they can be applied to real-world problems. We focus here on providing general background knowledge and a broad overview of these tasks. In addition, we provide examples of how they can be applied in practice. It is not our goal to dive too deeply into the details or the theory, since there are many other excellent references devoted entirely to these subjects, some of which are described in the "References and Future Reading" section at the end of this chapter. Instead, at the end of this chapter, you should know what classification and clustering are, the most commonly used algorithms, examples of how they are applied in practice, and how they are evaluated. On that note, we begin with a brief description of classification and clustering.

Classification, also referred to as categorization, is the task of automatically applying labels to data, such as emails, web pages, or images. People classify items throughout their daily lives. It would be infeasible, however, to manually label every page on the Web according to some criteria, such as "spam" or "not spam." Therefore, there is a need for automatic classification and categorization techniques. In this chapter, we describe several classification algorithms that are applicable to a wide range of tasks, including spam detection, sentiment analysis, and applying semantic labels to web advertisements.

Clustering, the other topic covered in this chapter, can be broadly defined as the task of grouping related items together. In classification, each item is assigned a label, such as "spam" or "not spam." In clustering, however, each item is assigned to one or more clusters, where the cluster does not necessarily correspond to a meaningful concept, such as "spam" or "not spam." Instead, as we will describe later in this chapter, items are grouped together according to their similarity. Therefore, rather than mapping items onto a predefined set of labels, clustering allows the data to "speak for itself" by uncovering the implicit structure that relates the items.

Both classification and clustering have been studied for many years by information retrieval researchers, with the aim of improving the effectiveness, or in some cases the efficiency, of search applications. From another perspective, these two tasks are classic machine learning problems. In machine learning, the learning algorithms are typically characterized as supervised or unsupervised. In *supervised learning*, a model is learned using a set of fully labeled items, which is often called the *training set*. Once a model is learned, it can be applied to a set of unlabeled items, called the *test set*, in order to automatically apply labels. Classification is often cast as a supervised learning problem. For example, given a set of emails that have been labeled as "spam" or "not spam" (the training set), a classification model can be learned. The model then can be applied to incoming emails in order to classify them as "spam" or "not spam".

Unsupervised learning algorithms, on the other hand, learn entirely based on unlabeled data. Unsupervised learning tasks are often posed differently than supervised learning tasks, since the input data is not mapped to a predefined set of labels. Clustering is the most common example of unsupervised learning. As we will show, clustering algorithms take a set of unlabeled data as input and then group the items using some notion of similarity.

There are many other types of learning paradigms beyond supervised and unsupervised, such as *semi-supervised learning*, *active learning*, and *online learning*. However, these subjects are well beyond the scope of this book. Instead, in this chapter, we provide an overview of basic yet effective classification and clustering algorithms and methods for evaluating them.

9.1 Classification and Categorization

Applying labels to observations is a very natural task, and something that most of us do, often without much thought, in our everyday lives. For example, consider a trip to the local grocery store. We often implicitly assign labels such as "ripe" or "not ripe," "healthy" or "not healthy," and "cheap" or "expensive" to the groceries that we see. These are examples of binary labels, since there are only two options for each. It is also possible to apply multivalued labels to foods, such as "starch," "meat," "vegetable," or "fruit." Another possible labeling scheme would arrange categories into a hierarchy, in which the "vegetable" category would be split by color into subcategories, such as "green," "red," and "yellow." Under this scheme, foods would be labeled according to their position within the hierarchy. These different labeling or categorization schemes, which include binary, multivalued, and hierarchical, are called *ontologies* (see Chapter 6).

It is important to choose an ontology that is appropriate for the underlying task. For example, for detecting whether or not an email is spam, it is perfectly reasonable to choose a label set that consists of "spam" and "not spam". However, if one were to design a classifier to automatically detect what language a web page is written in, then the set of all possible languages would be a more reasonable ontology. Typically, the correct choice of ontology is dictated by the problem, but in cases when it is not, it is important to choose a set of labels that is expressive enough to be useful for the underlying task. However, since classification is a supervised learning task, it is important not to construct an overly complex ontology, since most learning algorithms will fail (i.e., not generalize well to unseen data) when there is little or no data associated with one or more of the labels. In the web page language classifier example, if we had only one example page for each of the Asian languages, then, rather than having separate labels for each of the languages, such as "Chinese", "Korean", etc., it would be better to combine all of the languages into a single label called "Asian languages". The classifier will then be more likely to classify things as "Asian languages" correctly, since it has more training examples.

In order to understand how machine learning algorithms work, we must first take a look at how people classify items. Returning to the grocery store example, consider how we would classify a food as "healthy" or "not healthy." In order to make this classification, we would probably look at the amount of saturated fat, cholesterol, sugar, and sodium in the food. If these values, either separately or in combination, are above some threshold, then we would label the food "healthy" or "unhealthy." To summarize, as humans we classify items by first identifying a number of important *features* that will help us distinguish between the possible labels. We then *extract* these features from each item. We then *combine evidence* from the extracted features in some way. Finally, we *classify* the item using some decision mechanism based on the combined evidence.

In our example, the features are things such as the amount of saturated fat and the amount of cholesterol. The features are extracted by reading the nutritional information printed on the packaging or by performing laboratory tests. There are various ways to combine the evidence in order to quantify the "healthiness" (denoted H) of the food, but one simple way is to weight the importance of each feature and then add the weighted feature values together, such as:

$$H(food) \approx w_{fat}fat(food) + w_{chol}chol(food) + $$
$$w_{sugar}sugar(food) + w_{sodium}sodium(food)$$

where w_{fat}, w_{chol}, etc., are the weights associated with each feature. Of course, in this case, it is likely that each of the weights would be negative.

Once we have a healthiness score, H, for a given food, we must apply some decision mechanism in order to apply a "healthy" or "not healthy" label to the food. Again, there are various ways of doing this, but one of the most simple is to apply a simple threshold rule that says "a food is healthy if $H(food) \geq t$" for some threshold value t.

Although this is an idealized model of how people classify items, it provides valuable insights into how a computer can be used to automatically classify items. Indeed, the two classification algorithms that we will now describe follow the same steps as we outlined earlier. The only difference between the two algorithms is in the details of how each step is actually implemented.

9.1.1 Naïve Bayes

We are now ready to describe how items can be automatically classified. One of the most straightforward yet effective classification techniques is called *Naïve Bayes*. We introduced the Bayes classifier in Chapter 7 as a framework for a probabilistic retrieval model. In that case, there were just two classes of interest, the *relevant* class and the *non-relevant* class. In general, classification tasks can involve more than two labels or classes. In that situation, *Bayes' Rule*, which is the basis of a Bayes classifier, states that:

$$P(C|D) = \frac{P(D|C)P(C)}{P(D)}$$
$$= \frac{P(D|C)P(C)}{\sum_{c \in \mathcal{C}} P(D|C = c)P(C = c)}$$

where C and D are *random variables*. Random variables are commonly used when modeling uncertainty. Such variables do not have a fixed (deterministic) value. Instead, the value of the variable is random. Every random variable has a set of possible outcomes associated with it, as well as a probability distribution over the outcomes. As an example, the outcome of a coin toss can be modeled as a random variable X. The possible outcomes of the random variable are "heads" (h) and "tails" (t). Given a fair coin, the probability associated with both the heads outcome and the tails outcome is 0.5. Therefore, $P(X = h) = P(X = t) = 0.5$.

Consider another example, where you have the algebraic expression $Y = 10 + 2X$. If X was a deterministic variable, then Y would be deterministic as well. That is, for a fixed X, Y would always evaluate to the same value. However, if X is a random variable, then Y is also a random variable. Suppose that X had possible outcomes -1 (with probability 0.1), 0 (with probability 0.25), and 1 (with probability 0.65). The possible outcomes for Y would then be 8, 10, and 12, with $P(Y = 8) = 0.1$, $P(Y = 10) = 0.25$, and $P(Y = 12) = 0.65$.

In this chapter, we denote random variables with capital letters (e.g., C, D) and outcomes of random variables as lowercase letters (e.g., c, d). Furthermore, we denote the entire set of outcomes with caligraphic letters (e.g., $\mathcal{C}, \mathcal{D}$). Finally, for notational convenience, instead of writing $P(X = x)$, we write $P(x)$. Similarly for conditional probabilities, rather than writing $P(X = x | Y = y)$, we write $P(x|y)$.

Bayes' Rule is important because it allows us to write a conditional probability (such as $P(C|D)$) in terms of the "reverse" conditional ($P(D|C)$). This is a very powerful theorem, because it is often easy to estimate or compute the conditional probability in one direction but not the other. For example, consider spam classification, where D represents a document's text and C represents the class label (e.g., "spam" or "not spam"). It is not immediately clear how to write a program that detects whether a document is spam; that program is represented by $P(C|D)$. However, it is easy to find examples of documents that are and are not spam. It is possible to come up with estimates for $P(D|C)$ given examples or training data. The magic of Bayes' Rule is that it tells us how to get what we want ($P(C|D)$), but may not immediately know how to estimate, from something we do know how to estimate ($P(D|C)$).

It is straightforward to use this rule to classify items if we let C be the random variable associated with observing a class label and let D be the random variable associated with observing a document, as in our spam example. Given a document[1] d (an outcome of random variable D) and a set of classes $\mathcal{C} = c_1, \ldots, c_N$ (outcomes of the random variable C), we can use Bayes' Rule to compute $P(c_1|d), \ldots, P(c_N|d)$, which computes the likelihood of observing class label c_i given that document d was observed. Document d can then be labeled with the class with the highest probability of being observed given the document. That is, Naïve Bayes classifies a document d as follows:

$$\text{Class}(d) = \arg\max_{c \in \mathcal{C}} P(c|d)$$

$$= \arg\max_{c \in \mathcal{C}} \frac{P(d|c)P(c)}{\sum_{c \in C} P(d|c)P(c)}$$

where $\arg\max_{c \in \mathcal{C}} P(c|d)$ means "return the class c, out of the set of all possible classes $\mathcal{C}$, that maximizes $P(c|d)$." This is a mathematical way of saying that we are trying to find the most likely class c given the document d.

Instead of computing $P(c|d)$ directly, we can compute $P(d|c)$ and $P(c)$ instead and then apply Bayes' Rule to obtain $P(c|d)$. As we explained before, one reason for using Bayes' Rule is when it is easier to estimate the probabilities of one conditional, but not the other. We now explain how these values are typically estimated in practice.

We first describe how to estimate the class prior, $P(c)$. The estimation is straightforward. It is estimated according to:

$$P(c) = \frac{N_c}{N}$$

where N_c is the number of training instances that have label c, and N is the total number of training instances. Therefore, $P(c)$ is simply the proportion of training instances that have label c.

Estimating $P(d|c)$ is a little more complicated because the same "counting" estimate that we were able to use for estimating $P(c)$ would not work. (Why? See exercise 9.3.) In order to make the estimation feasible, we must impose the simplifying assumption that d can be represented as $d = w_1, \ldots, w_n$ and that w_i is independent of w_j for every $i \neq j$. Simply stated, this says that document d

---

[1] Throughout most of this chapter, we assume that the items being classified are textual documents. However, it is important to note that the techniques described here can be used in a more general setting and applied to non-textual items such as images and videos.

can be factored into a set of elements (terms) and that the elements (terms) are independent of each other.[2] This assumption is the reason for calling the classifier *naïve*, because it requires documents to be represented in an overly simplified way. In reality, terms are not independent of each other. However, as we will show in Chapter 11, properly modeling term dependencies is possible, but typically more difficult. Despite the independence assumption, the Naïve Bayes classifier has been shown to be robust and highly effective for various classification tasks.

This naïve independence assumption allows us to invoke a classic result from probability that states that the joint probability of a set of (conditionally) independent random variables can be written as the product of the individual conditional probabilities. That means that $P(d|c)$ can be written as:

$$P(d|c) = \prod_{i=1}^{n} P(w_i|c)$$

Therefore, we must estimate $P(w|c)$ for every possible term w in the vocabulary $\mathcal{V}$ and class c in the ontology $\mathcal{C}$. It turns out that this is a much easier task than estimating $P(d|c)$ since there is a finite number of terms in the vocabulary and a finite number of classes, but an infinite number of possible documents. The independence assumption allows us to write the probability $P(c|d)$ as:

$$P(c|d) = \frac{P(d|c)P(c)}{\sum_{c \in \mathcal{C}} P(d|c)P(c)}$$

$$= \frac{\prod_{i=1}^{\mathcal{V}} P(w_i|c)P(c)}{\sum_{c \in \mathcal{C}} \prod_{i=1}^{\mathcal{V}} P(w_i|c)P(c)}$$

The only thing left to describe is how to estimate $P(w|c)$. Before we can estimate the probability, we must first decide on what the probability actually means. For example, $P(w|c)$ could be interpreted as "the probability that term w is related to class c," "the probability that w has nothing to do with class c," or any number of other things. In order to make the meaning concrete, we must explicitly define the event space that the probability is defined over. An *event space* is the

---

[2] This is the same assumption that lies at the heart of most of the retrieval models described in Chapter 7. It is also equivalent to the *bag of words* assumption discussed in Chapter 11.

set of possible events (or outcomes) from some process. A probability is assigned to each event in the event space, and the sum of the probabilities over all of the events in the event space must equal one.

The probability estimates and the resulting classification will vary depending on the choice of event space. We will now briefly describe two of the more popular event spaces and show how $P(w|c)$ is estimated in each.

Multiple-Bernoulli model

The first event space that we describe is very simple. Given a class c, we define a *binary* random variable w_i for every term in the vocabulary. The outcome for the binary event is either 0 or 1. The probability $P(w_i = 1|c)$ can then be interpreted as "the probability that term w_i is generated by class c." Conversely, $P(w_i = 0|c)$ can be interpreted as "the probability that term w_i is not generated by class c." This is exactly the event space used by the binary independence model (see Chapter 7), and is known as the *multiple-Bernoulli* event space.

Under this event space, for each term in some class c, we estimate the probability that the term is generated by the class. For example, in a spam classifier, $P(cheap = 1|spam)$ is likely to have a high probability, whereas $P(dinner = 1|spam)$ is going to have a much lower probability.

document id	cheap	buy	banking	dinner	the	*class*
1	0	0	0	0	1	not spam
2	1	0	1	0	1	spam
3	0	0	0	0	1	not spam
4	1	0	1	0	1	spam
5	1	1	0	0	1	spam
6	0	0	1	0	1	not spam
7	0	1	1	0	1	not spam
8	0	0	0	0	1	not spam
9	0	0	0	0	1	not spam
10	1	1	0	1	1	not spam

Fig. 9.1. Illustration of how documents are represented in the multiple-Bernoulli event space. In this example, there are 10 documents (each with a unique id), two classes (spam and not spam), and a vocabulary that consists of the terms "cheap", "buy", "banking", "dinner", and "the".

Figure 9.1 shows how a set of training documents can be represented in this event space. In the example, there are 10 documents, two classes (spam and not spam), and a vocabulary that consists of the terms "cheap", "buy", "banking", "dinner", and "the". In this example, $P(\text{spam}) = \frac{3}{10}$ and $P(\text{not spam}) = \frac{7}{10}$. Next, we must estimate $P(w|c)$ for every pair of terms and classes. The most straightforward way is to estimate the probabilities using what is called the maximum likelihood estimate, which is:

$$P(w|c) = \frac{df_{w,c}}{N_c}$$

where $df_{w,c}$ is the number of training documents with class label c in which term w occurs, and N_c is the total number of training documents with class label c. As we see, the maximum likelihood estimate is nothing more than the proportion of documents in class c that contain term w. Using the maximum likelihood estimate, we can easily compute $P(the|\text{spam}) = 1$, $P(the|\text{not spam}) = 1$, $P(dinner|\text{spam}) = 0$, $P(dinner|\text{not spam}) = \frac{1}{7}$, and so on.

Using the multiple-Bernoulli model, the document likelihood, $P(d|c)$, can be written as:

$$P(d|c) = \prod_{w \in V} P(w|c)^{\delta(w,d)} \left(1 - P(w|c)\right)^{1-\delta(w,d)}$$

where $\delta(w, D)$ is 1 if and only if term w occurs in document d.

In practice, it is not possible to use the maximum likelihood estimate because of the *zero probability problem*. In order to illustrate the zero probability problem, let us return to the spam classification example from Figure 9.1. Suppose that we receive a spam email that happens to contain the term "dinner". No matter what other terms the email does or does not contain, the probability $P(d|c)$ will always be zero because $P(dinner|\text{spam}) = 0$ and the term occurs in the document (i.e., $\delta_{dinner,d} = 1$). Therefore, any document that contains the term "dinner" will automatically have zero probability of being spam. This problem is more general, since a zero probability will result whenever a document contains a term that never occurs in one or more classes. The problem here is that the maximum likelihood estimate is based on counting occurrences in the training set. However, the training set is finite, so not every possible event is observed. This is known as data sparseness. Sparseness is often a problem with small training sets, but it can also happen with relatively large data sets. Therefore, we must alter the estimates in such a way that all terms, including those that have not been observed for a given class, are given some probability mass. That is, we must ensure that $P(w|c)$ is non-zero for all terms in $\mathcal{V}$. By doing so, we will avoid all of the problems associated with the zero probability problem.

As was described in Chapter 7, smoothing is a useful technique for overcoming the zero probability problem. One popular smoothing technique is often called *Bayesian smoothing*, which assumes some prior probability over models and uses a *maximum a posteriori* estimate. The resulting smoothed estimate for the multiple-Bernoulli model has the form:

$$P(w|c) = \frac{df_{w,c} + \alpha_w}{N_c + \alpha_w + \beta_w}$$

where α_w and β_w are parameters that depend on w. Different settings of these parameters result in different estimates. One popular choice is to set $\alpha_w = 1$ and $\beta_w = 0$ for all w, which results in the following estimate:

$$P(w|c) = \frac{df_{w,c} + 1}{N_c + 1}$$

Another choice is to set $\alpha_w = \mu \frac{N_w}{N}$ and $\beta_w = \mu(1 - \frac{N_w}{N})$ for all w, where N_w is the total number of training documents in which term w occurs, and μ is a single tunable parameter. This results in the following estimate:

$$P(w|c) = \frac{df_{w,c} + \mu \frac{N_w}{N}}{N_c + \mu}$$

This event space only captures whether or not the term is generated; it fails to capture *how many* times the term occurs, which can be an important piece of information. We will now describe an event space that takes term frequency into account.

Multinomial model

The binary event space of the multiple-Bernoulli model is overly simplistic, as it does not model the number of times that a term occurs in a document. Term frequency has been shown to be an important feature for retrieval and classification, especially when used on long documents. When documents are very short, it is unlikely that many terms will occur more than one time, and therefore the multiple-Bernoulli model will be an accurate model. However, more often than not, real collections contain documents that are both short and long, and therefore it is important to take term frequency and, subsequently, document length into account.

The *multinomial* event space is very similar to the multiple-Bernoulli event space, except rather than assuming that term occurrences are binary ("term occurs" or "term does not occur"), it assumes that terms occur zero or more times ("term occurs zero times", "term occurs one time", etc.).

document *id*	cheap	buy	banking	dinner	the	*class*
1	0	0	0	0	2	not spam
2	3	0	1	0	1	spam
3	0	0	0	0	1	not spam
4	2	0	3	0	2	spam
5	5	2	0	0	1	spam
6	0	0	1	0	1	not spam
7	0	1	1	0	1	not spam
8	0	0	0	0	1	not spam
9	0	0	0	0	1	not spam
10	1	1	0	1	2	not spam

Fig. 9.2. Illustration of how documents are represented in the multinomial event space. In this example, there are 10 documents (each with a unique *id*), two classes (spam and not spam), and a vocabulary that consists of the terms "cheap", "buy", "banking", "dinner", and "the".

Figure 9.2 shows how the documents from our spam classification example are represented in the multinomial event space. The only difference between this representation and the multiple-Bernoulli representation is that the events are no longer binary. The maximum likelihood estimate for the multinomial model is very similar to the multiple-Bernoulli model. It is computed as:

$$P(w|c) = \frac{tf_{w,c}}{|c|}$$

where $tf_{w,c}$ is the number of times that term w occurs in class c in the training set, and $|c|$ is the total number of terms that occur in training documents with class label c. In the spam classification example, $P(the|\text{spam}) = \frac{4}{20}$, $P(the|\text{not spam}) = \frac{9}{15}$, $P(dinner|\text{spam}) = 0$, and $P(dinner|\text{not spam}) = \frac{1}{15}$.

Since terms are now distributed according to a multinomial distribution, the likelihood of a document d given a class c is computed according to:

$$P(d|c) = P(|d|) \left(tf_{w_1,d}, tf_{w_2,d}, \ldots, tf_{w_V,d}\right)! \prod_{w \in \mathcal{V}} P(w|c)^{tf_{w,d}}$$

$$\propto \prod_{w \in \mathcal{V}} P(w|c)^{tf_{w,d}}$$

where $tf_{w,d}$ is the number of times that term w occurs in document d, $|d|$ is the total number of terms that occur in d, $P(|d|)$ is the probability of generating a document of length $|d|$, and $\left(tf_{w_1,d}, tf_{w_2,d}, \ldots, tf_{w_V,d}\right)!$ is the multinomial coefficient.[3] Notice that $P(|d|)$ and the multinomial coefficient are document-dependent and, for the purposes of classification, can be ignored.

The Bayesian smoothed estimates of the term likelihoods are computed according to:

$$P(w|c) = \frac{tf_{w,c} + \alpha_w}{|c| + \sum_{w \in \mathcal{V}} \alpha_w}$$

where α_w is a parameter that depends on w. As with the multiple-Bernoulli model, different settings of the smoothing parameters result in different types of estimates. Setting $\alpha_w = 1$ for all w is one possible option. This results in the following estimate:

$$P(w|c) = \frac{tf_{w,c} + 1}{|c| + |\mathcal{V}|}$$

Another popular choice is to set $\alpha_w = \mu \frac{cf_w}{|C|}$, where cf_w is the total number of times that term w occurs in any training document, $|C|$ is the total number of terms in all training documents, and μ, as before, is a tunable parameter. Under this setting, we obtain the following estimate:

$$P(w|c) = \frac{tf_{w,c} + \mu \frac{cf_w}{|C|}}{|c| + \mu}$$

This estimate may look familiar, as it is exactly the Dirichlet smoothed language modeling estimate that was described in Chapter 7.

---

[3] The multinomial coefficient is a generalization of the binomial coefficient. It is computed as $(N_1, N_2, \ldots, N_k)! = \frac{N!}{N_1! N_2! \cdots N_k!}$. It counts the total number of unique ways that $\sum_i N_i$ items (terms) can be arranged given that item i occurs N_i times.

In practice, the multinomial model has been shown to consistently outperform the multiple-Bernoulli model. Implementing a classifier based on either of these models is straightforward. Training consists of computing simple term occurrence statistics. In most cases, these statistics can be stored in memory, which means that classification can be done efficiently. The simplicity of the model, combined with good accuracy, makes the Naïve Bayes classifier a popular and attractive choice as a general-purpose classification algorithm.

9.1.2 Support Vector Machines

Unlike the Naïve Bayes classifier, which is based purely on probabilistic principles, the next classifier we describe is based on geometric principles. *Support Vector Machines*, often called *SVMs*, treat inputs such as documents as points in some geometric space. For simplicity, we first describe how SVMs are applied to classification problems with binary class labels, which we will refer to as the "positive" and "negative" classes. In this setting, the goal of SVMs is to find a *hyperplane*[4] that separates the positive examples from the negative examples.

In the Naïve Bayes model, documents were treated as binary vectors in the multiple-Bernoulli model and as term frequency vectors in the multinomial case. SVMs provide more flexibility in terms of how documents can be represented. With SVMs, rather than defining some underlying event space, we must instead define a set of *feature functions* $f_1(\cdot), \ldots, f_N(\cdot)$ that take a document as input and produce what is known as a *feature value*. Given a document d, the document is represented in an N-dimensional space by the vector $x_d = [f_1(d), \ldots, f_N(d)]$. Given a set of training data, we can use the feature functions to embed the training documents in this N-dimensional space. Notice that different feature functions will result in different embeddings. Since SVMs find a hyperplane that separates the data according to classes, it is important to choose feature functions that will help discriminate between the different classes.

Two common feature functions are $f_w(d) = \delta(w, d)$ and $f_w(d) = tf_{w,d}$. The first feature function is 1 if term w occurs in d, which is analogous to the multiple-Bernoulli model. The second feature function counts the number of times that w occurs in d, which is analogous to the multinomial model. Notice that these feature functions are indexed by w, which means that there is a total of $|\mathcal{V}|$ such functions. This results in documents being embedded in a $|\mathcal{V}|$-dimensional space. It is also possible to define similar feature functions over bigrams or trigrams, which

---

[4] A hyperplane generalizes the notion of a plane to N-dimensional space.

would cause the dimensionality of the feature space to explode. Furthermore, other information can be encoded in the feature functions, such as the document length, the number of sentences in the document, the last time the document was updated, and so on.

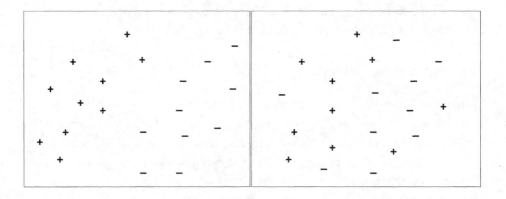

Fig. 9.3. Data set that consists of two classes (pluses and minuses). The data set on the left is linearly separable, whereas the one on the right is not.

Now that we have a mechanism for representing documents in an N-dimensional space, we describe how SVMs actually classify the points in this space. As described before, the goal of SVMs is to find a hyperplane that separates the negative and positive examples. The hyperplane is learned from the training data. An unseen test point is classified according to which side of the hyperplane the point falls on. For example, if the point falls on the negative side, then we classify it as negative. Similarly, if it falls on the positive side, then it is classified as positive. It is not always possible to draw a hyperplane that perfectly separates the negative training data from the positive training data, however, since no such hyperplane may exist for some embedding of the training data. For example, in Figure 9.3, it is possible to draw a line (hyperplane) that separates the positive class (denoted by "+") from the negative class (denoted by "-") in the left panel. However, it is impossible to do so in the right panel. The points in the left panel are said to be *linearly separable*, since we can draw a linear hyperplane that separates the points.

It is much easier to define and find a good hyperplane when the data is linearly separable. Therefore, we begin our explanation of how SVMs work by focusing on this special case. We will then extend our discussion to the more general and common case where the data points are not linearly separable.

Case 1: Linearly separable data

Suppose that you were given a linearly separable training set, such as the one in Figure 9.3, and were asked to find the optimal hyperplane that separates the data points. How would you proceed? You would very likely first ask what exactly is meant by optimal. One might first postulate that optimal means *any* hyperplane that separates the positive training data from the negative training data. However, we must also consider the ultimate goal of any classification algorithm, which is to *generalize* well to unseen data. If a classifier can perfectly classify the training data but completely fails at classifying the test set data, then it is of little value. This scenario is known as *overfitting*.

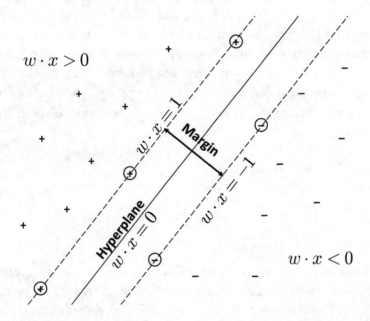

Fig. 9.4. Graphical illustration of Support Vector Machines for the linearly separable case. Here, the hyperplane defined by w is shown, as well as the margin, the decision regions, and the support vectors, which are indicated by circles.

In order to avoid overfitting, SVMs choose the hyperplane that maximizes the separation between the positive and negative data points. This selection criteria makes sense intuitively, and is backed up by strong theoretical results as well. Assuming that our hyperplane is defined by the vector w, we want to find the w that separates the positive and negative training data *and* maximizes the separation between the data points. The maximal separation is defined as follows. Suppose that x^- is the closest negative training point to the hyperplane and that x^+ is the closest positive training point to the hyperplane.[5] Then, we define the *margin* as the distance from x^- to the hyperplane plus the distance from x^+ to the hyperplane. Figure 9.4 shows a graphical illustration of the margin, with respect to the hyperplane and the support vectors (i.e., x^+ and x^-). The margin can be computed using simple vector mathematics as follows:

$$\text{Margin}(w) = \frac{|w \cdot x^-| + |w \cdot x^+|}{||w||}$$

where $\cdot$ is the dot product (inner product) between two vectors, and $||w|| = (w \cdot w)^{1/2}$ is the length of the vector w. The SVM algorithm's notion of an optimal hyperplane, therefore, is the hyperplane w that maximizes the margin while still separating the data. In order to simplify things, it is typically assumed that $w \cdot x^- = -1$ and $w \cdot x^+ = 1$. These assumptions, which do not change the solution to the problem, result in the margin being equal to $\frac{2}{||w||}$. An alternative yet equivalent formulation is to find the hyperplane w that solves the following optimization problem:

$$\text{minimize:} \quad \tfrac{1}{2}||w||^2$$
$$\text{subject to:}$$
$$w \cdot x_i \geq 1 \quad \forall i \text{ s.t. } \text{Class}(i) = +$$
$$w \cdot x_i \leq -1 \quad \forall i \text{ s.t. } \text{Class}(i) = -$$

This formulation is often used because it is easier to solve. In fact, this optimization problem can be solved using a technique called *quadratic programming*, the details of which are beyond the scope of this book. However, there many excellent open source SVM packages available. In the "References and Further Reading" section at the end of this chapter we provide pointers to several such software packages.

Once the best w has been found, an unseen document d can be classified using the following rule:

$$\text{Class}(d) = \begin{cases} + & \text{if } w \cdot x_d > 0 \\ - & \text{otherwise} \end{cases}$$

---

[5] The vectors x^- and x^+ are known as *support vectors*. The optimal hyperplane w is a linear combination of these vectors. Therefore, they provide the *support* for the decision boundary. This is the origin of the name "Support Vector Machine."

Therefore, the rule classifies documents based on which side of the hyperplane the document's feature vector is on. Referring back to Figure 9.4, we see that in this example, those points to the left of the hyperplane are classified as positive examples and those to the right of the hyperplane are classified as negative examples.

Case 2: Non-linearly separable data

Very few real-world data sets are actually linearly separable. Therefore, the SVM formulation just described must be modified in order to account for this. This can be achieved by adding a penalty factor to the problem that accounts for training instances that do not satisfy the constraints of the linearly separable formulation.

Suppose that, for some training point x in the positive class, $w \cdot x = -0.5$. This violates the constraint $w \cdot x \geq 1$. In fact, x falls on the entirely wrong side of the hyperplane. Since the target for $w \cdot x$ is (at least) 1, we can apply a linear penalty based on the difference between the target and actual value. That is, the penalty given to x is $1 - (-0.5) = 1.5$. If $w \cdot x = 1.25$, then no penalty would be assigned, since the constraint would not be violated. This type of penalty is known as the *hinge loss function*. It is formally defined as:

$$L(x) = \begin{cases} \max(1 - w \cdot x, 0) \text{ if Class}(i) = + \\ \max(1 + w \cdot x, 0) \text{ if Class}(i) = - \end{cases}$$

This loss function is incorporated into the SVM optimization as follows:

$$\textit{minimize: } \tfrac{1}{2}||w||^2 + C\sum_{i=1}^{N} \xi_i$$
$$\textit{subject to:}$$
$$w \cdot x_i \geq 1 - \xi_i \quad \forall i \text{ s.t. Class}(i) = +$$
$$w \cdot x_i \leq -1 + \xi_i \quad \forall i \text{ s.t. Class}(i) = -$$
$$\xi_i \geq 0 \quad \forall i$$

where ξ_i is known as a *slack variable* that allows the target values to be violated. The slack variables enforce the hinge loss function. Notice that if all of the constraints are satisfied, all of the slack variables would be equal to 0, and therefore the loss function would reduce to the linearly separable case. In addition, if any constraint is violated, then the amount by which it is violated is added into the objective function and multiplied by C, which is a free parameter that controls how much to penalize constraint violations. It is standard to set C equal to 1. This optimization problem finds a hyperplane that maximizes the margin while allowing for some slack. As in the linearly separable case, this optimization problem can be solved using quadratic programming. In addition, classification is performed in the same way as the linearly separable case.

The kernel trick

The example in Figure 9.3 illustrates the fact that certain embeddings of the training data are not linearly separable. It may be possible, however, that a *transformation* or *mapping* of the data into a higher dimensional space results in a set of linearly separable points. This may result in improved classification effectiveness, although it is not guaranteed.

There are many ways to map an N-dimensional vector into a higher dimensional space. For example, given the vector $[f_1(d), \ldots, f_N(d)]$, one could augment the vector by including squared feature values. That is, the data items would now be represented by the $2N$-dimensional vector:

$$\left[f_1(d), \ldots, f_N(d), f_1(d)^2, \ldots, f_N(d)^2\right]$$

The higher the dimensionality of the feature vectors, however, the less efficient the algorithm becomes, both in terms of space requirements and computation time.

One important thing to notice is that the key mathematical operation involved in training and testing SVMs is the dot product. If there was an efficient way to compute the dot product between two very high-dimensional vectors without having to store them, then it would be feasible to perform such a mapping. In fact, this is possible for certain classes of high-dimensional mappings. This can be achieved by using a *kernel function*. A kernel function takes two N-dimensional vectors and computes a dot product between them in a higher dimensional space. This higher dimensional space is *implicit*, in that the higher dimensional vectors are never actually constructed.

Let us now consider an example. Suppose that we have two 2-dimensional vectors $w = [w_1 w_2]$ and $x = [x_1 x_2]$. Furthermore, we define $\Phi(\cdot)$ as follows:

$$\Phi(x) = \begin{pmatrix} x_1^2 \\ \sqrt{2}x_1x_2 \\ x_2^2 \end{pmatrix}$$

Here, $\Phi(\cdot)$ maps 2-dimensional vectors into 3-dimensional vectors. As we described before, this may be useful because the original inputs may actually be linearly separable in the 3-dimensional space to which $\Phi(\cdot)$ maps the points. One can imagine many, many ways of mapping the original inputs into higher dimensional spaces. However, as we will now show, certain mappings have very nice properties that allow us to efficiently compute dot products in the higher dimensional space.

Given this mapping, the naïve way to compute $\Phi(w) \cdot \Phi(x)$ would be to first explicitly construct $\Phi(w)$ and $\Phi(x)$ and then perform the dot product in the 3-dimensional space. However, surprisingly, it turns out that this is not necessary, since:

$$\Phi(w) \cdot \Phi(x) = w_1^2 x_1^2 + 2 w_1 w_2 x_1 x_2 + w_2^2 x_2^2$$
$$= (w \cdot x)^2$$

where $w \cdot x$ is computed in the original, 2-dimensional space. Therefore, rather than explicitly computing the dot product in the higher 3-dimensional space, we only need to compute the dot product in the original 2-dimensional space and then square the value. This "trick," which is often referred to as the *kernel trick*, allows us to efficiently compute dot products in some higher dimensional space.

Of course, the example given here is rather trivial. The true power of the kernel trick becomes more apparent when dealing with mappings that project into much higher dimensional spaces. In fact, some kernels perform a dot product in an infinite dimensional space!

Kernel Type	Value	Implicit Dimension
Linear	$K(x_1, x_2) = x_1 \cdot x_2$	N
Polynomial	$K(x_1, x_2) = (x_1 \cdot x_2)^p$	$\binom{N + p - 1}{N}$
Gaussian	$K(x_1, x_2) = \exp{-\|x_1 - x_2\|^2 / 2\sigma^2}$	Infinite

Table 9.1. A list of kernels that are typically used with SVMs. For each kernel, the name, value, and implicit dimensionality are given.

A list of the most widely used kernels is given in Table 9.1. Note that the Gaussian kernel is also often called a radial basis function (RBF) kernel. The best choice of kernel depends on the geometry of the embedded data. Each of these kernels has been shown to be effective on textual features, although the Gaussian kernel tends to work well across a wide range of data sets, as long as the variance (σ^2) is properly set. Most standard SVM software packages have these kernels built in, so using them is typically as easy as specifying a command-line argument. Therefore, given their potential power and their ease of use, it is often valuable to experiment with each of the kernels to determine the best one to use for a specific data set and task.

The availability of these software packages, together with the SVM's flexibility in representation and, most importantly, their demonstrated effectiveness in many applications, has resulted in SVMs being very widely used in classification applications.

Non-binary classification

Up until this point, our discussion has focused solely on how support vector machines can be used for binary classification tasks. We will now describe two of the most popular ways to turn a binary classifier, such as a support vector machine, into a multi-class classifier. These approaches are relatively simple to implement and have been shown to be work effectively.

The first technique is called the *one versus all* (OVA) approach. Suppose that we have a $K \geq 2$ class classification problem. The OVA approach works by training K classifiers. When training the kth classifier, the kth class is treated as the positive class and *all* of the other classes are treated as the negative class. That is, each classifier treats the instances of a single class as the positive class, and the remaining instances are the negative class. Given a test instance x, it is classified using all K classifiers. The class for x is the (positive) class associated with the classifier that yields the largest value of $w \cdot x$. That is, if w_c is the "class c versus not class c" classifier, then items are classified according to:

$$\text{Class}(x) = \arg \max_c w_c \cdot x$$

The other technique is called the *one versus one* (OVO) approach. In the OVO approach, a binary classifier is trained for every unique pair of classes. For example, for a ternary classification problem with the labels "excellent", "fair", and "bad", it would be necessary to train the following classifiers: "excellent versus fair", "excellent versus bad", and "fair versus bad". In general, the OVO approach requires $\frac{K(K-1)}{2}$ classifiers to be trained, which can be computationally expensive for large data sets and large values of K. To classify a test instance x, it is run through each of the classifiers. Each time x is classified as c, a vote for c is recorded. The class that has the most votes at the end is then assigned to x.

Both the OVA and OVO approaches work well in practice. There is no concrete evidence that suggests that either should be preferred over the other. Instead, the effectiveness of the approaches largely depends on the underlying characteristics of the data set.

9.1.3 Evaluation

Most classification tasks are evaluated using standard information retrieval metrics, such as *accuracy*,[6] *precision*, *recall*, the F measure, and *ROC* curve analysis. Each of these metrics were described in detail in Chapter 8. Of these metrics, the most commonly used are accuracy and the F measure.

There are two major differences between evaluating classification tasks and other retrieval tasks. The first difference is that the notion of "relevant" is replaced with "is classified correctly." The other major difference is that microaveraging, which is not commonly used to evaluate retrieval tasks, is widely used in classification evaluations. Macroaveraging for classification tasks involves computing some metric for each *class* and then computing the average of the per-class metrics. On the other hand, microaveraging computes a metric for every test instance (document) and then averages over all such instances. It is often valuable to compute and analyze both the microaverage and the macroaverage, especially when the class distribution $P(c)$ is highly skewed.

9.1.4 Classifier and Feature Selection

Up until this point we have covered the basics of two popular classifiers. We have described the principles the classifiers are built upon, their underlying assumptions, the pros and cons, and how they can be used in practice. As classification is a deeply complex and rich subject, we cover advanced classification topics in this section that may be of interest to those who would like a deeper or more complete understanding of the topic.

Generative, discriminative, and non-parametric models

The Naïve Bayes classifier was based on probabilistic modeling. The model requires us to assume that documents are generated from class labels according to a probabilistic model that corresponds to some underlying event space. The Naïve Bayes classifier is an example of a wider class of probabilistic models called *generative models*. These models assume that some underlying probability distribution

---

[6] Accuracy is another name for precision at rank 1.

generates both documents and classes. In the Naïve Bayes case, the classes and documents are generated as follows. First, a class is generated according to $P(c)$. Then, a document is generated according to $P(d|c)$. This process is summarized in Figure 9.5. Generative models tend to appeal to intuition by mimicking how people may actually generate (write) documents.

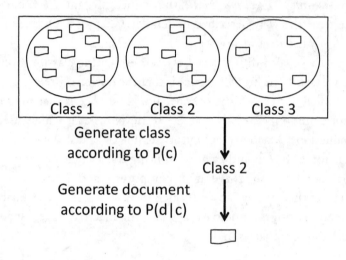

Fig. 9.5. Generative process used by the Naïve Bayes model. First, a class is chosen according to $P(c)$, and then a document is chosen according to $P(d|c)$.

Of course, the accuracy of generative models largely depends on how accurately the probabilistic model captures this generation process. If the model is a reasonable reflection of the actual generation process, then generative models can be very powerful, especially when there are very few training examples.

As the number of training examples grows, however, the power of the generative model can be limited by simplifying distributional assumptions, such as the independence assumption in the Naïve Bayes classifier. In such cases, *discriminative models* often outperform generative models. Discriminative models are those that do not model the generative process of documents and classes. Instead, they directly model the class assignment problem given a document as input. In this way, they discriminate between class labels. Since these models do not need to model the generation of documents, they often have fewer distributional assumptions, which is one reason why they are often preferred to generative models when there are many training examples. Support vector machines are an example of a discriminative model. Notice that no assumptions about the document generation process are made anywhere in the SVM formulation. Instead, SVMs directly learn a hyperplane that effectively discriminates between the classes.

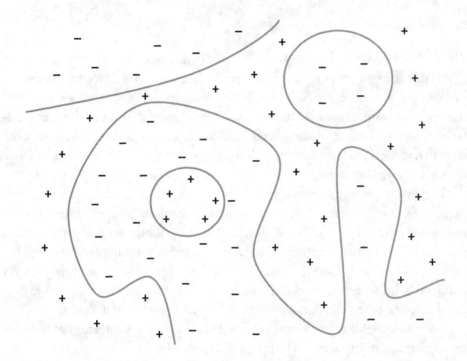

Fig. 9.6. Example data set where non-parametric learning algorithms, such as a nearest neighbor classifier, may outperform parametric algorithms. The pluses and minuses indicate positive and negative training examples, respectively. The solid gray line shows the actual decision boundary, which is highly non-linear.

Non-parametric classifiers are another option when there is a large number of training examples. Non-parametric classifiers let the data "speak for itself" by eliminating all distributional assumptions. One simple example of a non-parametric classifier is the *nearest neighbor classifier*. Given an unseen example, the nearest neighbor classifier finds the training example that is nearest (according to some distance metric) to it. The unseen example is then assigned the label of this nearest neighbor. Figure 9.6 shows an example output of a nearest neighbor classifier. Notice the irregular, highly non-linear decision boundary induced by the classifier. Generative and discriminative models, even SVMs with a non-linear kernel, would have a difficult time fitting a model to this data. For this reason, the nearest neighbor classifier is optimal as the number of training examples approaches infinity. However, the classifier tends to have a very high variance for smaller data sets, which often limits its applicability.

Feature selection

The SVM classifier embeds inputs, such as documents, into some feature space that is defined by a set of feature functions. As we described, it is common to define one (or more) feature functions for every word in the vocabulary. This $|\mathcal{V}|$-dimensional feature space can be extremely large, especially for very large vocabularies. Since the feature set size affects both the efficiency and effectiveness of the classifier, researchers have devised techniques for pruning the feature space. These are known as *feature selection* techniques.

The goal of feature selection is to find a small subset of the original features that can be used in place of the original feature set with the aim of significantly improving efficiency (in terms of storage and time) while not hurting effectiveness much. In practice, it turns out that feature selection techniques often *improve* effectiveness instead of reducing it. The reason for this is that some of the features eliminated during feature selection may be noisy or inaccurate, and therefore hinder the ability of the classification model to learn a good model.

Information gain is one of the most widely used feature selection criteria for text classification applications. Information gain is based on information theory principles. As its name implies, it measures how much information about the class labels is gained when we observe the value of some feature. Let us return to the spam classification example in Figure 9.1. Observing the value of the feature "cheap" provides us quite a bit of information with regard to the class labels. If "cheap" occurs, then it is very likely that the label is "spam", and if "cheap" does not occur, then it is very likely that the label is "not spam". In information theory, *entropy* is the expected information contained in some distribution, such as the class distribution $P(c)$. Therefore, the information gain of some feature f measures how the entropy of $P(c)$ changes after we observe f. Assuming a multiple-Bernoulli event space, it is computed as follows:

$$IG(w) = H(C) - H(C|w)$$
$$= -\sum_{c \in \mathcal{C}} P(c) \log P(c) + \sum_{w \in \{0,1\}} P(w) \sum_{c \in \mathcal{C}} P(c|w) \log P(c|w)$$

where $H(C)$ is the entropy of $P(c)$ and $H(C|w)$ is known as the *conditional entropy*. As an illustrative example, we compute the information gain for the term "cheap" from our spam classification example:

$$
\begin{aligned}
IG(cheap) = & -P(spam) \log P(spam) - P(\overline{spam}) \log P(\overline{spam}) + \\
& P(cheap) P(spam|cheap) \log P(spam|cheap) + \\
& P(cheap) P(\overline{spam}|cheap) \log P(\overline{spam}|cheap) + \\
& P(\overline{cheap}) P(spam|\overline{cheap}) \log P(spam|\overline{cheap}) + \\
& P(\overline{cheap}) P(\overline{spam}|\overline{cheap}) \log P(\overline{spam}|\overline{cheap}) \\
= & -\frac{3}{10} \log \frac{3}{10} - \frac{7}{10} \log \frac{7}{10} + \frac{4}{10} \cdot \frac{3}{4} \log \frac{3}{4} \\
& + \frac{4}{10} \cdot \frac{1}{4} \log \frac{1}{4} + \frac{6}{10} \cdot \frac{0}{6} \log \frac{0}{6} + \frac{6}{10} \cdot \frac{6}{6} \log \frac{6}{6} \\
= & \; 0.2749
\end{aligned}
$$

where $P(\overline{cheap})$ is shorthand for $P(cheap = 0)$, $P(\overline{spam})$ means $P(C = \text{not spam})$, and it is assumed that $0 \log 0 = 0$. The corresponding information gains for "buy", "banking", "dinner", and "the" are $0.0008, 0.0434, 0.3612$, and 0.0, respectively. Therefore, according to the information gain, "dinner" is the most informative word, since it is a perfect predictor of "not spam" according to the training set. On the opposite side of the spectrum, "the" is the worst predictor, since it appears in every document and therefore has no discriminative power.

Similar information gain measures can be derived for other event spaces, such as the multinomial event space. There are many different ways to use the information gain to actually select features. However, the most common thing to do is to select the K features with the largest information gain and train a model using only those features. It is also possible to select a percentage of all features or use a threshold.

Although many other feature selection criteria exist, information gain tends to be a good general-purpose feature selection criteria, especially for text-based classification problems. We provide pointers to several other feature selection techniques in the "References and Further Reading" section at the end of this chapter.

9.1.5 Spam, Sentiment, and Online Advertising

Although ranking functions are a very critical part of any search engine, classification and categorization techniques also play an important role in various search-related tasks. In this section, we describe several real-world text classification applications. These applications are *spam detection*, *sentiment classification*, and *online advertisement classification*.

Spam, spam, spam

Classification techniques can be used to help detect and eliminate various types of spam. Spam is broadly defined to be any content that is generated for malevolent purposes,[7] such as unsolicited advertisements, deceptively increasing the ranking of a web page, or spreading a virus. One important characteristic of spam is that it tends to have little, if any, useful content. This definition of spam is very subjective, because what may be useful to one person may not be useful to another. For this reason, it is often difficult to come up with an objective definition of spam.

There are many types of spam, including email spam, advertisement spam, blog spam, and web page spam. Spammers use different techniques for different types of spam. Therefore, there is no one single spam classification technique that works for all types of spam. Instead, very specialized spam classifiers are built for the different types of spam, each taking into account domain-specific information. Much has been written about email spam, and filtering programs such as Spam-Assassin[8] are in common use. Figure 9.7 shows the SpamAssassin output for an example email. SpamAssassin computes a score for the email that is compared to a threshold (default value 5.0) to determine whether it is spam. The score is based on a combination of features, one of the most important of which is the output of a Bayes classifier. In this case, the URL contained in the body of the email was on a blacklist, the timestamp on the email is later than the time it was received, and the Bayes classifier gives the email a 40–60% chance of being in the class "spam" based on the words in the message. These three features did not, however, give the email a score over 5, so it was not classified as spam (which is a mistake).

---

[7] The etymology of the word spam, with respect to computer abuse, is quite interesting. The meaning is believed to have been derived from a 1970 Monty Python skit set in a restaurant where everything on the menu has spam (the meat product) in it. A chorus of Vikings begins singing a song that goes, "Spam, spam, spam, spam, ..." on and on, therefore tying the word spam to repetitive, annoying behavior.

[8] http://spamassassin.apache.org/

```
To: ...
From: ...
Subject: non profit debt
X-Spam-Checked: This message probably not SPAM
X-Spam-Score: 3.853, Required: 5
X-Spam-Level: *** (3.853)
X-Spam-Tests: BAYES_50,DATE_IN_FUTURE_06_12,URIBL_BLACK
X-Spam-Report-rig: ---- Start SpamAssassin (v2.6xx-cscf) results
        2.0 URIBL_BLACK        Contains an URL listed in the URIBL blacklist
                    [URIs: bad-debtyh.net.cn]
        1.9 DATE_IN_FUTURE_06_12   Date: is 6 to 12 hours after Received: date
        0.0 BAYES_50           BODY: Bayesian spam probability is 40 to 60%
                    [score: 0.4857]


Say good bye to debt
Acceptable Unsecured Debt includes All Major Credit Cards, No-collateral
Bank Loans, Personal Loans,
Medical Bills etc.
http://www.bad-debtyh.net.cn
```

Fig. 9.7. Example output of SpamAssassin email spam filter

Since this book focuses on search engines, we will devote our attention to web page spam, which is one of the most difficult and widespread types of spam. Detecting web page spam is a difficult task, because spammers are becoming increasingly sophisticated. It seems sometimes that the spammers themselves have advanced degrees in information retrieval! There are many different ways that spammers target web pages. Gyöngyi and Garcia-Molina (2005) proposed a web spam taxonomy that attempts to categorize the different web page spam techniques that are often used to artificially increase the ranking of a page. The two top-level categories of the taxonomy are *link spam* and *term spam*.

With link spam, spammers use various techniques to artificially increase the link-based scores of their web pages. In particular, search engines often use measures such as inlink count and PageRank, which are based entirely on the link structure of the Web, for measuring the importance of a web page. However, these techniques are susceptible to spam. One popular and easy link spam technique involves posting links to the target web page on blogs or unmoderated message boards. Another way for a website to artificially increase its link-based score is to join a link exchange network. Link exchange networks are large networks of websites that all connect to each other, thereby increasing the number of links coming into the site. Another link spam technique is called link farming. Link farms are similar to exchange networks, except the spammer himself buys a large number of domains, creates a large number of sites, and then links them all together. There are various other approaches, but these account for a large fraction of link spam. A number of alternatives to PageRank have been proposed recently that attempt to dampen the potential effect of link spam, including HostTrust (Gyöngyi et al., 2004) and SpamRank (Benczúr et al., 2005).

The other top-level category of spam is term spam. Term spam attempts to modify the textual representation of the document in order to make it more likely to be retrieved for certain queries or keywords. As with link-based scores, term-based scores are also susceptible to spam. Most of the widely used retrieval models, including BM25 and language modeling, make use of some formulation that involves term frequency and document frequency. Therefore, by increasing the term frequency of target terms, these models can easily be tricked into retrieving non-relevant documents. Furthermore, most web ranking functions match text in the incoming anchor text and the URL. Modifying the URL to match a given term or phrase is easy. However, modifying the incoming anchor text requires more effort, but can easily be done using link exchanges and link farms. Another technique, called *dumping*, fills documents with many unrelated words (often an entire dictionary). This results in the document being retrieved for just about any query, since it contains almost every combination of query terms. Therefore, this acts as a recall enhancing measure. This can be combined with the other spamming techniques, such as repetition, in order to have high precision as well as high recall. *Phrase stitching* (combining words and sentences from various sources) and *weaving* (adding spam terms into a valid source such as a news story) are other techniques for generating artificial content. All of these types of term spam should be considered when developing a ranking function designed to prevent spam.

Figure 9.8 shows an example of a web page containing spam. The page contains both term spam with repetition of important words and link spam where related spam sites are mentioned.

As should be apparent by now, there is an overwhelming number of types of spam. Here, we simply focused on web page spam and did not even start to consider the other types of spam. Indeed, it would be easy to write an entire book on subjects related to spam. However, before we end our spam discussion, we will describe just one of the many different ways that classification has been used to tackle the problem of detecting web page spam.

Website:

BETTING NFL FOOTBALL PRO FOOTBALL SPORTSBOOKS NFL FOOTBALL LINE ONLINE NFL SPORTSBOOKS NFL

Players Super Book

When It Comes To Secure NFL Betting And Finding The Best Football Lines Players Super Book Is The Best Option! Sign Up And Ask For 30 % In Bonuses.

MVP Sportsbook

Football Betting Has Never been so easy and secure! MVP Sportsbook has all the NFL odds you are looking for. Sign Up Now and ask for up to

30 % in Cash bonuses.

Term spam:

pro football sportsbooks nfl football line online nfl sportsbooks nfl football gambling odds online pro nfl betting pro nfl gambling online nfl football spreads offshore football gambling online nfl gamblibg spreads online football gambling line online nfl betting nfl sportsbook online online nfl betting spreads betting nfl football online online football wagering online gambling online gambling football online nfl football betting odds offshore football sportsbook online nfl football gambling ...

Link spam:

MVP Sportsbook Football Gambling Beverly Hills Football Sportsbook
Players SB Football Wagering   Popular Poker Football Odds
Virtual Bookmaker Football Lines   V Wager Football Spreads
Bogarts Casino Football Point Spreads   Gecko Casino Online Football Betting
Jackpot Hour Online Football Gambling   MVP Casino Online Football Wagering
Toucan Casino NFL Betting   Popular Poker NFL Gambling
All Tracks NFL Wagering   Bet Jockey NFL Odds
Live Horse Betting NFL Lines MVP Racebook NFL Point Spreads
Popular Poker NFL Spreads   Bogarts Poker NFL Sportsbook ...

Fig. 9.8. Example of web page spam, showing the main page and some of the associated term and link spam

Ntoulas et al. (2006) propose a method for detecting web page spam using content (textual) analysis. The method extracts a large number of features from each web page and uses these features in a classifier. Some of the features include the number of words on the page, number of words in the title, average length of the words, amount of incoming anchor text, and the fraction of visible text. These features attempt to capture very basic characteristics of a web page's text. Another feature used is the compressibility of the page, which measures how much the page can be reduced in size using a compression algorithm. It turns out that pages that can be compressed more are much more likely to be spam, since pages that contain many repeated terms and phrases are easier to compress. This has also been shown to be effective for detecting email spam. The authors also use as features the fraction of terms drawn from globally popular words[9] and the fraction of globally popular words appearing on the page. These features attempt to capture whether or not the page has been filled with popular terms that are highly likely to match a query term. The last two features are based on n-gram likelihoods. Experiments show that pages that contain very rare and very common n-grams are more likely to be spam than those pages that contain n-grams of average likelihood. All of these features were used with a *decision tree* learning algorithm, which is another type of supervised classification algorithm, and shown to achieve classification accuracy well above 90%. The same features could easily be used in a Naïve Bayes or Support Vector Machine classifier.

Sentiment

As we described in Chapter 6, there are three primary types of web queries. The models described in Chapter 7 focus primarily on informational and navigational queries. Transactional queries, the third type, present many different challenges. If a user queries for a product name, then the search engine should display a variety of information that goes beyond the standard ranked list of topically relevant results. For example, if the user is interested in purchasing the product, then links to online shopping sites can be provided to help the user complete her purchase. It may also be possible that the user already owns the product and is searching for accessories or enhancements. The search engine could then derive revenue from the query by displaying advertisements for related accessories and services.

---

[9] The list of "globally popular" words in this experiment was simply the N most frequent words in the test corpus.

Another possible scenario, and the one that we focus on in detail here, is that the user is researching the product in order to determine whether he should purchase it. In this case, it would be valuable to retrieve information such as product specifications, product reviews, and blog postings about the product. In order to reduce the amount of information that the user needs to read through, it would be preferable to have the system automatically aggregate all of the reviews and blog posts in order to present a condensed, summarized view.

There are a number of steps involved with building such a system, each of which involves some form of classification. First, when crawling and indexing sites, the system has to automatically classify whether or not a web page contains a review or if it is a blog posting expressing an opinion about a product. The task of identifying opinionated text, as opposed to factual text, is called *opinion detection*. After a collection of reviews and blog postings has been populated, another classifier must be used to extract product names and their corresponding reviews. This is the *information extraction* task. For each review identified for a given product, yet another classifier must be used to determine the *sentiment* of the page. Typically, the sentiment of a page is either "negative" or "positive", although the classifier may choose to assign a numeric score as well, such as "two stars" or "four stars". Finally, all of the data, including the sentiment, must be aggregated and presented to the user in some meaningful way. Figure 9.9 shows part of an automatically generated product review from a web service. This sentiment-based summary of various aspects of the product, such as "ease of use", "size", and "software", is generated from individual user reviews.

Rather than go into the details of all of these different classifiers, we will focus our attention on how sentiment classifiers work. As with our previous examples, let us consider how a person would identify the sentiment of some piece of text. For a majority of cases, we use vocabulary clues in order to determine the sentiment. For example, a positive digital camera review would likely contain words such as "great", "nice", and "amazing". On the other hand, negative reviews would contain words such as "awful", "terrible", and "bad". This suggests one possible solution to the problem, where we build two lists. The first list will contain words that are indicative of positive sentiment, and another list will contain words indicative of negative sentiment. Then, given a piece of text, we could simply count the number of positive words and the number of negative words. If there are more positive words, then assign the text a positive sentiment label. Otherwise, label it as having negative sentiment. Even though this approach is perfectly reasonable, it turns out that people are not very good at creating lists of words that indicate pos-

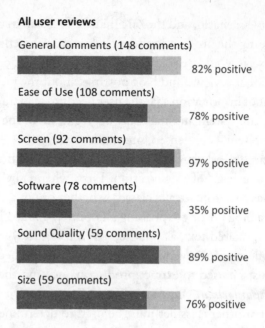

Fig. 9.9. Example product review incorporating sentiment

itive and negative sentiment. This is largely due to the fact that human language is ambiguous and largely dependent on context. For example, the text "the digital camera lacks the amazing picture quality promised" would likely be classified as having positive sentiment because it contains two positive words ("amazing" and "quality") and only one negative word ("lacks").

Pang et al. (2002) proposed using machine learning techniques for sentiment classification. Various classifiers were explored, including Naïve Bayes, Support Vector Machines, and *maximum entropy*, which is another popular classification technique. The features used in the classifiers were unigrams, bigrams, part-of-speech tags, adjectives, and the position of a term within a piece of text. The authors report that an SVM classifier using only unigram features exhibited the best performance, resulting in more accurate results than a classifier trained using all of the features. In addition, it was observed that the multiple-Bernoulli event space outperformed the multinomial event space for this particular task. This is likely caused by the fact that most sentiment-related terms occur only once in any piece of text, and therefore term frequency adds very little to the model. Interestingly, the machine learning models were significantly more accurate than the baseline model that used human-generated word lists. The SVM classifier with unigrams had an accuracy of over 80%, whereas the baseline model had an accuracy of only around 60%.

Classifying advertisements

As described in Chapter 6, *sponsored search* and *content match* are two different advertising models widely used by commercial search engines. The former matches advertisements to queries, whereas the latter matches advertisements to web pages. Both sponsored search and content match use a *pay per click* pricing model, which means that advertisers must pay the search engine only if a user clicks on the advertisement. A user may click on an advertisement for a number of reasons. Clearly, if the advertisement is "topically relevant," which is the standard notion of relevance discussed in the rest of this book, then the user may click on it. However, this is not the only reason why a user may click. If a user searches for "tropical fish", she may click on advertisements for pet stores, local aquariums, or even scuba diving lessons. It is less likely, however, that she would click on advertisements for fishing, fish restaurants, or mercury poisoning. The reason for this is that the concept "tropical fish" has a certain semantic scope that limits the type of advertisements a user may find interesting.

Although it is possible to use standard information retrieval techniques such as query expansion or query reformulation analysis to find these semantic matches for advertising, it is also possible to use a classifier that maps queries (and web pages) into semantic classes. Broder et al. (2007) propose a simple yet effective technique for classifying textual items, such as queries and web pages, into a semantic hierarchy. The hierarchy was manually constructed and consists of over 6,000 nodes, where each node represents a single semantic class. As one moves deeper down the hierarchy, the classes become more specific. Human judges manually placed thousands of *queries* with commercial intent into the hierarchy based on each query's intended semantic meaning.

Given such a hierarchy and thousands of labeled instances, there are many possible ways to classify unseen queries or web pages. For example, one could learn a Naïve Bayes model or use SVMs. Since there are over 6,000 classes, however, there could be data sparsity issues, with certain classes having very few labeled instances associated with them. A bigger problem, however, would be the efficiency of this approach. Both Naïve Bayes and SVMs would be very slow to classify an item into one of 6,000 possible classes. Since queries must be classified in real time, this is not an option. Instead, Broder et al. propose using cosine similarity with $tf.idf$

weighting to match queries (or web pages) to semantic classes. That is, they frame the classification problem as a *retrieval* problem, where the query is the query (or web page) to be classified and the document set consists of 6,000 "documents", one for each semantic class. For example, for the semantic class "Sports", the "document" for it would consists of all of the queries labeled as "Sports". These "documents" are stored in an inverted index, which allows for efficient retrieval for an incoming query (or web page). This can be viewed as an example of a nearest neighbor classifier.

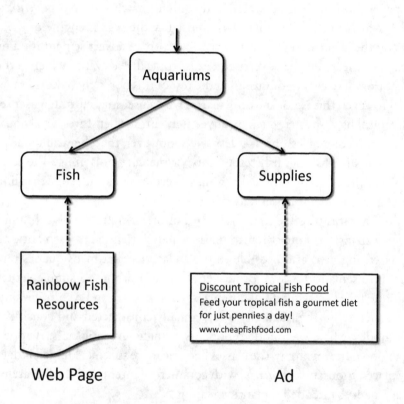

Fig. 9.10. Example semantic class match between a web page about rainbow fish (a type of tropical fish) and an advertisement for tropical fish food. The nodes "Aquariums", "Fish", and "Supplies" are example nodes within a semantic hierarchy. The web page is classified as "Aquariums - Fish" and the ad is classified as "Supplies - Fish". Here, "Aquariums" is the least common ancestor. Although the web page and ad do not share any terms in common, they can be matched because of their semantic similarity.

To use such a classifier in practice, one would have to preclassify every advertisement in the advertising inventory. Then, when a new query (or web page) arrives, it is classified. There are a number of ways to use the semantic classes to improve matching. Obviously, if the semantic class of a query exactly matches the semantic class of an advertisement, it should be given a high score. However, there are other cases where two things may be very closely related, even though they do not have exactly the same semantic class. Therefore, Broder et al. propose a way of measuring the distance between two semantic classes within the hierarchy based on the inverse of the *least common ancestor* of the two nodes in the hierarchy. A common ancestor is a node in the hierarchy that you must pass through in order to reach both nodes. The least common ancestor is the one with the maximum depth in the hierarchy. The distance is 0 if the two nodes are the same and very large if the the least common ancestor is the root node. Figure 9.10 shows an example of how a web page can be semantically matched to an advertisement using the hierarchy. In the figure, the least common ancestor of the web page and ad classes is "Aquariums", which is one node up the hierarchy. Therefore, this match would be given a lower score than if both the web page and ad were classified into the same node in the hierarchy. The full advertisement score can be computed by combining this distance based on the hierarchy with the standard cosine similarity score. In this way, advertisements are ranked in terms of both topical relevance and semantic relevance.

9.2 Clustering

Clustering algorithms provide a different approach to organizing data. Unlike the classification algorithms covered in this chapter, clustering algorithms are based on *unsupervised* learning, which means that they do not require any training data. Clustering algorithms take a set of unlabeled instances and group (cluster) them together. One problem with clustering is that it is often an ill-defined problem. Classification has very clear objectives. However, the notion of a good clustering is often defined very subjectively.

In order to gain more perspective on the issues involved with clustering, let us examine how we, as humans, cluster items. Suppose, once again, that you are at a grocery store and are asked to cluster all of the fresh produce (fruits and vegetables). How would you proceed? Before you began, you would have to decide what criteria you would use for clustering. For example, you could group the items by their color, their shape, their vitamin C content, their price, or some meaningful combination of these factors. As with classification, the clustering criteria largely depend on *how the items are represented*. Input instances are assumed to be a feature vector that represents some object, such as a document (or a fruit). If you are interested in clustering according to some property, it is important to make sure that property is represented in the feature vector.

After the clustering criteria have been determined, you would have to determine how you would assign items to clusters. Suppose that you decided to cluster the produce according to color and you have created a red cluster (red grapes, red apples) and a yellow cluster (bananas, butternut squash). What do you do if you come across an orange? Do you create a new orange cluster, or do you assign it to the red or yellow cluster? These are important questions that clustering algorithms must address as well. These questions come in the form of *how many clusters to use* and *how to assign items to clusters*.

Finally, after you have assigned all of the produce to clusters, how do you quantify how well you did? That is, you must *evaluate* the clustering. This is often very difficult, although there have been several automatic techniques proposed.

In this example, we have described clusters as being defined by some fixed set of properties, such as the "red" cluster. This is, in fact, a very specific form of cluster, called *monothetic*. We discussed monothetic classes or clusters in Chapter 6, and mentioned that most clustering algorithms instead produce *polythetic* clusters, where members of a cluster share many properties, but there is no single defining property. In other words, membership in a cluster is typically based on the *similarity* of the feature vectors that represent the objects. This means that a crucial part of defining the clustering algorithm is specifying the similarity measure that is used. The classification and clustering literature often refers to a *distance measure*, rather than a similarity measure, and we use that terminology in the following discussion. Any similarity measure, which typically has a value S from 0 to 1, can be converted into a distance measure by using $1 - S$. Many similarity and distance measures have been studied by information retrieval and machine learning researchers, from very simple measures such as Dice's coefficient (mentioned in Chapter 6) to more complex probabilistic measures.

The reader should keep these factors in mind while reading this section, as they will be recurring themes throughout. The remainder of this section describes three clustering algorithms based on different approaches, discusses evaluation issues, and briefly describes clustering applications.

9.2.1 Hierarchical and K-Means Clustering

We will now describe two different clustering algorithms that start with some initial clustering of the data and then iteratively try to improve the clustering by optimizing some objective function. The main difference between the algorithms is the objective function. As we will show, different objective functions lead to different types of clusters. Therefore, there is no one "best" clustering algorithm. The choice of algorithm largely depends on properties of the data set and task.

Throughout the remainder of this section, we assume that our goal is to cluster some set of N instances (which could be web pages, for example), represented as feature vectors, into K clusters, where K is a constant that is fixed *a priori*.

Hierarchical clustering

Hierarchical clustering is a clustering methodology that builds clusters in a hierarchical fashion. This methodology gives rise to a number of different clustering algorithms. These algorithms are often "clustered" into two groups, depending on how the algorithm proceeds.

Divisive clustering algorithms begin with a single cluster that consists of all of the instances. During each iteration it chooses an existing cluster and divides it into two (or possibly more) clusters. This process is repeated until there are a total of K clusters. The output of the algorithm largely depends on how clusters are chosen and split.

Divisive clustering is a *top-down* approach. The other general type of hierarchical clustering algorithm is called *agglomerative clustering*, which is a *bottom-up* approach. Figures 9.11 and 9.12 illustrate the difference between the two types of algorithms. An agglomerative algorithm starts with each input as a separate cluster. That is, it begins with N clusters, each of which contains a single input. The algorithm then proceeds by joining two (or possibly more) existing clusters to form a new cluster. Therefore, the number of clusters decreases after each iteration. The algorithm terminates when there are K clusters. As with divisive clustering, the output of the algorithm is largely dependent on how clusters are chosen and joined.

The hierarchy generated by an agglomerative or divisive clustering algorithm can be conveniently visualized using a *dendrogram*.[10] A dendrogram graphically represents how a hierarchical clustering algorithm progresses. Figure 9.13 shows

---

[10] From the Greek word *dendron*, meaning "tree."

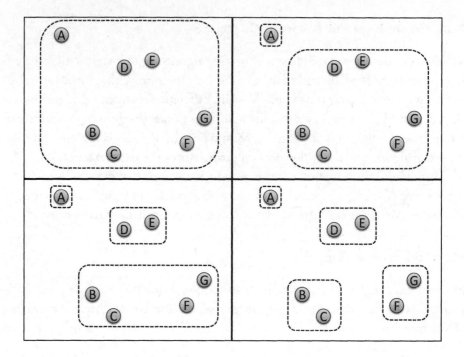

Fig. 9.11. Example of divisive clustering with $K = 4$. The clustering proceeds from left to right and top to bottom, resulting in four clusters.

the dendrogram that corresponds to generating the entire agglomerative clustering hierarchy for the points in Figure 9.12. In the dendrogram, points D and E are first combined to form a new cluster called H. Then, B and C are combined to form cluster I. This process is continued until a single cluster M is created, which consists of A, B, C, D, E, and F. In a dendrogram, the height at which instances combine is significant and represents the similarity (or distance) value at which the combination occurs. For example, the dendrogram shows that D and E are the most similar pair.

Algorithm 1 is a simple implementation of hierarchical agglomerative clustering.[11] The algorithm takes N vectors $X_1, \ldots, X_N$, representing the instances, and the desired number of clusters K as input. The array (vector) A is the assignment vector. It is used to keep track of which cluster each input is associated with. If $A[i] = j$, then it means that input X_i is in cluster j. The algorithm considers joining every pair of clusters. For each pair of clusters (C_i, C_j), a cost $C(C_i, C_j)$

---

[11] Often called *HAC* in the literature.

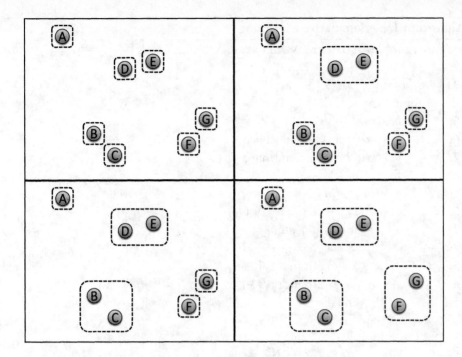

Fig. 9.12. Example of agglomerative clustering with $K = 4$. The clustering proceeds from left to right and top to bottom, resulting in four clusters.

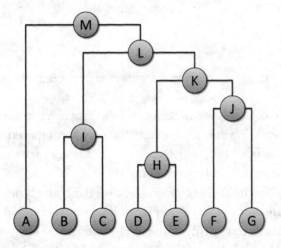

Fig. 9.13. Dendrogram that illustrates the agglomerative clustering of the points from Figure 9.12

Algorithm 1 Agglomerative Clustering

1: **procedure** AGGLOMERATIVECLUSTER$(X_1, \ldots, X_N, K)$
2:      $A[1], \ldots, A[N] \leftarrow 1, \ldots, N$
3:      $ids \leftarrow \{1, \ldots, N\}$
4:      **for** $c = N$ to K **do**
5:          $bestcost \leftarrow \infty$
6:          $bestcluster A \leftarrow$ undefined
7:          $bestcluster B \leftarrow$ undefined
8:          **for** $i \in ids$ **do**
9:              **for** $j \in ids - \{i\}$ **do**
10:                  $c_{i,j} \leftarrow COST(C_i, C_j)$
11:                  **if** $c_{i,j} < bestcost$ **then**
12:                      $bestcost \leftarrow c_{i,j}$
13:                      $bestcluster A \leftarrow i$
14:                      $bestcluster B \leftarrow j$
15:                  **end if**
16:              **end for**
17:          **end for**
18:          $ids \leftarrow ids - \{bestCluster A\}$
19:          **for** $i = 1$ to N **do**
20:              **if** $A[i]$ is equal to $bestCluster A$ **then**
21:                  $A[i] \leftarrow bestCluster B$
22:              **end if**
23:          **end for**
24:      **end for**
25: **end procedure**

---

is computed. The cost is some measure of how expensive it would be to merge clusters C_i and C_j. We will return to how the cost is computed shortly. After all pairwise costs have been computed, the pair of clusters with the lowest cost are then merged. The algorithm proceeds until there are K clusters.

As shown by Algorithm 1, agglomerative clustering largely depends on the cost function. There are many different ways to define the cost function, each of which results in the final clusters having different characteristics. We now describe a few of the more popular choices and the intuition behind them.

Single linkage measures the cost between clusters C_i and C_j by computing the distance between every instance in cluster C_i and every one in C_j. The cost is then the *minimum* of these distances, which can be stated mathematically as:

$$COST(C_i, C_j) = \min\{dist(X_i, X_j)|X_i \in C_i, X_j \in C_j\}$$

where $dist$ is the distance between input X_i and X_j. It is typically computed using the Euclidean distance[12] between X_i and X_j, but many other distance measures have been used. Single linkage relies only on the minimum distance between the two clusters. It does not consider how far apart the remainder of the instances in the clusters are. For this reason, single linkage could result in very "long" or spread-out clusters, depending on the structure of the two clusters being combined.

Complete linkage is similar to single linkage. It begins by computing the distance between every instance in cluster C_i and C_j. However, rather than using the *minimum* distance as the cost, it uses the *maximum* distance. That is, the cost is:

$$COST(C_i, C_j) = \max\{dist(X_i, X_j)|X_i \in C_i, X_j \in C_j\}$$

Since the maximum distance is used as the cost, clusters tend to be more compact and less spread out than in single linkage.

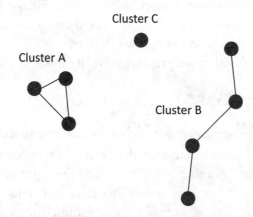

Fig. 9.14. Examples of clusters in a graph formed by connecting nodes representing instances. A link represents a distance between the two instances that is less than some threshold value.

To illustrate the difference between single-link and complete-link clusters, consider the graph shown in Figure 9.14. This graph is formed by representing in-

---

[12] The Euclidean distance between two vectors x and y is computed according to $\sqrt{\sum_i (x_i - y_i)^2}$ where the subscript i denotes the ith component of the vector.

stances (i.e., the X_is) as nodes and connecting nodes where $dist(X_i, X_j) < T$, where T is some threshold value. In this graph, clusters A, B, and C would all be single-link clusters. The single-link clusters are, in fact, the *connected components* of the graph, where every member of the cluster is connected to at least one other member. The complete-link clusters would be cluster A, the singleton cluster C, and the upper and lower pairs of instances from cluster B. The complete-link clusters are the *cliques* or maximal complete subgraphs of the graph, where every member of the cluster is connected to every other member.

Average linkage uses a cost that is a compromise between single linkage and complete linkage. As before, the distance between every pair of instances in C_i and C_j is computed. As the name implies, average linkage uses the *average* of all of the pairwise costs. Therefore, the cost is:

$$COST(C_i, C_j) = \frac{\sum_{X_i \in C_i, X_j \in C_j} dist(X_i, X_j)}{|C_i||C_j|}$$

where $|C_i|$ and $|C_j|$ are the number of instances in clusters C_i and C_j, respectively. The types of the clusters formed using average linkage depends largely on the structure of the clusters, since the cost is based on the average of the distances between every pair of instances in the two clusters.

Average group linkage is closely related to average linkage. The cost is computed according to:

$$COST(C_i, C_j) = dist(\mu_{C_i}, \mu_{C_j})$$

where $\mu_C = \frac{\sum_{X \in C} X}{|C|}$ is the *centroid* of cluster C_i. The centroid of a cluster is simply the average of all of the instances in the cluster. Notice that the centroid is also a vector with the same number of dimensions as the input instances. Therefore, average group linkage represents each cluster according to its centroid and measures the cost by the distance between the centroids. The clusters formed using average group linkage are similar to those formed using average linkage.

Figure 9.15 provides a visual summary of the four cost functions described up to this point. Specifically, it shows which pairs of instances (or centroids) are involved in computing the cost functions for the set of points used in Figures 9.11 and 9.12.

Ward's method is the final method that we describe. Unlike the previous costs, which are based on various notions of the distance between two clusters, Ward's method is based on the statistical property of *variance*. The variance of a set of numbers measures how spread out the numbers are. Ward's method attempts to

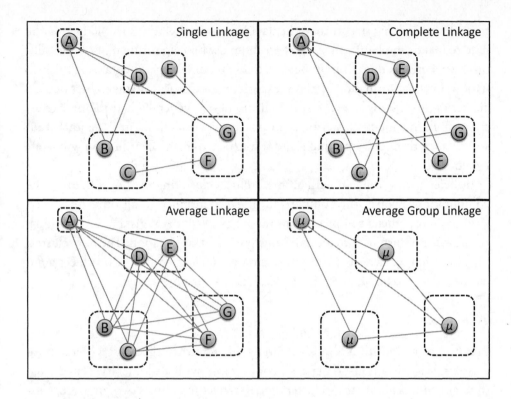

Fig. 9.15. Illustration of how various clustering cost functions are computed

minimize the sum of the variances of the clusters. This results in compact clusters with a minimal amount of spread around the cluster centroids. The cost, which is slightly more complicated to compute than the previous methods, is computed according to:

$$COST(C_i, C_j) = \sum_{k \neq i,j} \sum_{X \in C_k} (X - \mu_{C_k}) \cdot (X - \mu_{C_k}) +$$
$$\sum_{X \in C_i \cup C_j} (X - \mu_{C_i \cup C_j}) \cdot (X - \mu_{C_i \cup C_j})$$

where $C_i \cup C_j$ is the union of the instances in clusters C_i and C_j, and $\mu_{C_i \cup C_j}$ is the centroid of the cluster consisting of the instances in $C_i \cup C_j$. This cost measures what the intracluster variance would be if clusters i and j were joined.

So, which of the five agglomerative clustering techniques is the best? Once again the answer depends on the data set and task the algorithm is being applied to. If the underlying structure of the data is known, then this knowledge may be used to make a more informed decision about the best algorithm to use. Typically, however, determining the best method to use requires experimentation and evaluation. In the information retrieval experiments that have involved hierarchical clustering, for example, *average-link* clustering has generally had the best effectiveness. Even though clustering is an unsupervised method, in the end there is still no such thing as a free lunch, and some form of manual evaluation will likely be required.

Efficiency is a problem with all hierarchical clustering methods. Because the computation involves the comparison of every instance to all other instances, even the most efficient implementations are $O(N^2)$ for N instances. This limits the number of instances that can be clustered in an application. The next clustering algorithm we describe, K-means, is more efficient because it produces a *flat* clustering, or *partition*, of the instances, rather than a hierarchy.

K-means

The K-means algorithm is fundamentally different than the class of hierarchical clustering algorithms just described. For example, with agglomerative clustering, the algorithm begins with N clusters and iteratively combines two (or more) clusters together based on how costly it is to do so. As the algorithm proceeds, the number of clusters increases. Furthermore, the algorithm has the property that once instances X_i and X_j are in the same cluster as each other, there is no way for them to end up in different clusters as the algorithm proceeds.

With the K-means algorithm, the number of clusters never changes. The algorithm starts with K clusters and ends with K clusters. During each iteration of the K-means algorithm, each instance is either kept in the same cluster or assigned to a different cluster. This process is repeated until some stopping criteria is met.

The goal of the K-means algorithm is to find the cluster assignments, represented by the assignment vector $A[1], \ldots, A[N]$, that minimize the following cost function:

$$COST(A[1], \ldots, A[N]) = \sum_{k=1}^{K} \sum_{i:A[i]=k} dist(X_i, C_k)$$

where $dist(X_i, C_k)$ is the distance between instance X_i and class C_k. As with the various hierarchical clustering costs, this distance measure can be any reasonable measure, although it is typically assumed to be the following:

$$dist(X_i, C_k) = ||X_i - \mu_{C_k}||^2$$
$$= (X_i - \mu_{C_k}) \cdot (X_i - \mu_{C_k})$$

which is the Euclidean distance between X_i and μ_{C_k} squared. Here, as before, μ_{C_k} is the centroid of cluster C_k. Notice that this distance measure is very similar to the cost associated with Ward's method for agglomerative clustering. Therefore, the method attempts to find the clustering that minimizes the intracluster variance of the instances.

Alternatively, the cosine similarity between X_i and μ_{C_k} can be used as the distance measure. As described in Chapter 7, the cosine similarity measures the angle between two vectors. For some text applications, the cosine similarity measure has been shown to be more effective than the Euclidean distance. This specific form of K-means is often called *spherical K-means*.

One of the most naïve ways to solve this optimization problem is to try every possible combination of cluster assignments. However, for large data sets this is computationally intractable, because it requires computing an exponential number of costs. Rather than finding the *globally* optimal solution, the K-means algorithm finds an approximate, heuristic solution that iteratively tries to minimize the cost. This solution returned by the algorithm is not guaranteed to be the global optimal. In fact, it is not even guaranteed to be locally optimal. Despite its heuristic nature, the algorithm tends to work very well in practice.

Algorithm 2 lists the pseudocode for one possible K-means implementation. The algorithm begins by initializing the assignment of instances to clusters. This can be done either randomly or by using some knowledge of the data to make a more informed decision. An iteration of the algorithm then proceeds as follows. Each instance is assigned to the cluster that it is closest to, in terms of the distance measure $dist(X_i, C_k)$. The variable $change$ keeps track of whether any of the instances changed clusters during the current iteration. If some have changed, then the algorithm proceeds. If none have changed, then the algorithm ends. Another reasonable stopping criterion is to run the algorithm for some fixed number of iterations.

In practice, K-means clustering tends to converge very quickly to a solution. Even though it is not guaranteed to find the optimal solution, the solutions returned are often optimal or close to optimal. When compared to hierarchical clustering, K-means is more efficient. Specifically, since KN distance computations

---

Algorithm 2 K-Means Clustering

1: **procedure** KMEANSCLUSTER$(X_1, \ldots, X_N, K)$
2:     $A[1], \ldots, A[N] \leftarrow$ initial cluster assignment
3:     **repeat**
4:         $change \leftarrow false$
5:         **for** $i = 1$ to N **do**
6:             $\hat{k} \leftarrow \arg\min_k dist(X_i, C_k)$
7:             **if** $A[i]$ **is not equal** $\hat{k}$ **then**
8:                 $A[i] \leftarrow \hat{k}$
9:                 $change \leftarrow true$
10:             **end if**
11:         **end for**
12:     **until** $change$ **is equal to** $false$ **return** $A[1], \ldots, A[N]$
13: **end procedure**

---

are done in every iteration and the number of iterations is small, implementations of K-means are $\mathcal{O}(KN)$ rather than the $\mathcal{O}(N^2)$ complexity of hierarchical methods. Although the clusters produced by K-means depend on the starting points chosen (the initial clusters) and the ordering of the input data, K-means generally produces clusters of similar quality to hierarchical methods. Therefore, K-means is a good choice for an all-purpose clustering algorithm for a wide range of search engine–related tasks, especially for large data sets.

9.2.2 K Nearest Neighbor Clustering

Even though hierarchical and K-means clustering are different from an algorithmic point of view, one thing that they have in common is the fact that both algorithms place every input into exactly one cluster, which means that clusters do not overlap.[13] Therefore, these algorithms *partition* the input instances into K partitions (clusters). However, for certain tasks, it may be useful to allow clusters to overlap. One very simple way of producing overlapping clusters is called K *nearest neighbor clustering*. It is important to note that the K here is very different from the K in K-means clustering, as will soon become very apparent.

---

[13] Note that this is true for hierarchical clusters at a given level of the dendrogram (i.e., at a given similarity or distance value). Clusters from different levels of the dendrogram do overlap.

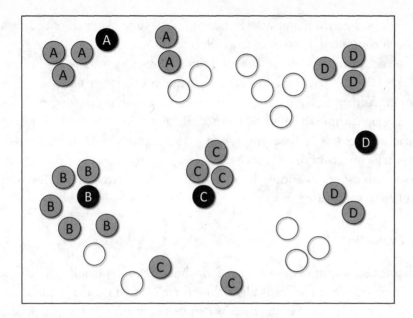

Fig. 9.16. Example of overlapping clustering using nearest neighbor clustering with $K =$ 5. The overlapping clusters for the black points (A, B, C, and D) are shown. The five nearest neighbors for each black point are shaded gray and labeled accordingly.

In K nearest neighbor clustering, a cluster is formed around every input instance. For input instance x, the K points that are nearest to x according to some distance metric and x itself form a cluster. Figure 9.16 shows several examples of nearest neighbor clusters with $K = 5$ formed for the points $A, B, C,$ and D. Although the figure only shows clusters around four input instances, in reality there would be one cluster per input instance, resulting in N clusters.

As Figure 9.16 illustrates, the algorithm often fails to find meaningful clusters. In sparse areas of the input space, such as around D, the points assigned to cluster D are rather far away and probably should not be placed in the same cluster as D. However, in denser areas of the input space, such as around B, the clusters are better defined, even though some related inputs may be missed because K is not large enough. Applications that use K nearest neighbor clustering tend to emphasize finding a small number of closely related instances in the K nearest neighbors (i.e., precision) over finding all the closely related instances (recall).

K nearest neighbor clustering can be rather expensive, since it requires computing distances between every pair of input instances. If we assume that computing the distance between two input instances takes constant time with respect to K and N, then this computation takes $\mathcal{O}(N^2)$ time. After all of the distances have been computed, it takes at most $\mathcal{O}(N^2)$ time to find the K nearest neighbors for each point. Therefore, the total time complexity for K nearest neighbor clustering is $\mathcal{O}(N^2)$, which is the same as hierarchical clustering.

For certain applications, K nearest neighbor clustering is the best choice of clustering algorithm. The method is especially useful for tasks with very dense input spaces where it is useful or important to find a number of related items for every input. Examples of these tasks include language model smoothing, document score smoothing, and pseudo-relevance feedback. We describe how clustering can be applied to smoothing shortly.

9.2.3 Evaluation

Evaluating the output of a clustering algorithm can be challenging. Since clustering is an unsupervised learning algorithm, there is often little or no labeled data to use for the purpose of evaluation. When there is no labeled training data, it is sometimes possible to use an objective function, such as the objective function being minimized by the clustering algorithm, in order to evaluate the quality of the clusters produced. This is a chicken and egg problem, however, since the evaluation metric is defined by the algorithm and vice versa.

If some labeled data exists, then it is possible to use slightly modified versions of standard information retrieval metrics, such as precision and recall, to evaluate the quality of the clustering. Clustering algorithms assign each input instance to a cluster identifier. The cluster identifiers are arbitrary and have no explicit meaning. For example, if we were to cluster a set of emails into two clusters, some of the emails would be assigned to cluster identifier 1, while the rest would be assigned to cluster 2. Not only do the cluster identifiers have no meaning, but the clusters may not have a meaningful interpretation. For example, one would hope that one of the clusters would correspond to "spam" emails and the other to "non-spam" emails, but this will not necessarily be the case. Therefore, care must be taken when defining measures of precision and recall.

One common procedure of measuring precision is as follows. First, the algorithm clusters the input instances into $K = |\mathcal{C}|$ clusters. Then, for each cluster C_i, we define MaxClass(C_i) to be the (human-assigned) class label associated with the most instances in C_i. Since MaxClass(C_i) is associated with more of the instances in C_i than any other class label, it is assumed that it is the *true* label for cluster C_i. Therefore, the precision for cluster C_i is the fraction of instances in the cluster with label MaxClass(C_i). This measure is often microaveraged across instances, which results in the following measure of precision:

$$ClusterPrecision = \frac{\sum_{i=1}^{K} |\text{MaxClass}(C_i)|}{N}$$

where $|\text{MaxClass}(C_i)|$ is the total number of instances in cluster C_i with the label MaxClass(C_i). This measure has the intuitive property that if each cluster corresponds to exactly one class label and every member of a cluster has the same label, then the measure is 1.

In many search applications, clustering is only one of the technologies that are being used. Typically, the output of a clustering algorithm is used as part of some complex end-to-end system. In these cases, it is important to analyze and evaluate how the clustering algorithm affects the entire end-to-end system. For example, if clustering is used as a subcomponent of a web search engine in order to improve ranking, then the clustering algorithm can be evaluated and tuned by measuring the impact on the effectiveness of the ranking. This can be difficult, as end-to-end systems are often complex and challenging to understand, and many factors will impact the ranking.

9.2.4 How to Choose K

Thus far, we have largely ignored how to choose K. In hierarchical and K-means clustering, K represents the number of clusters. In K nearest neighbors smoothing, K represents the number of nearest neighbors used. Although these two things are fundamentally different, it turns out that both are equally challenging to set properly in a fully automated way. The problem of choosing K is one of the most challenging issues involved with clustering, since there is really no good solution. No magical formula exists that will predict the optimal number of clusters to use in every possible situation. Instead, the best choice of K largely depends on the task and data set being considered. Therefore, K is most often chosen experimentally.

In some cases, the application will dictate the number of clusters to use. This, however, is rare. Most of the time, the application offers no clues as to the best choice of K. In fact, even the range of values for K to try might not be obvious. Should 2 clusters be used? 10? 100? 1,000? There is no better way of getting an understanding of the best setting for K than running experiments that evaluate the quality of the resulting clusters for various values of K.

With hierarchical clustering, it is possible to create the entire hierarchy of clusters and then use some decision mechanism to decide what level of the hiearchy to use for the clustering. In most situations, however, the number of clusters has to be manually chosen, even with hierarchical clustering.

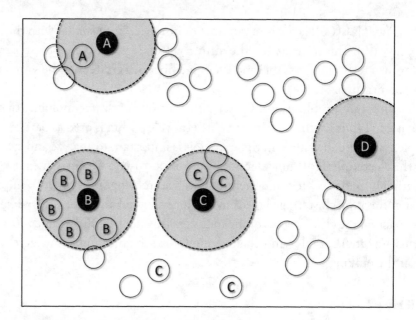

Fig. 9.17. Example of overlapping clustering using Parzen windows. The clusters for the black points (A, B, C, and D) are shown. The shaded circles indicate the windows used to determine cluster membership. The neighbors for each black point are shaded gray and labeled accordingly.

When forming K nearest neighbor clusters, it is possible to use an adaptive value for K. That is, for instances in very dense regions, it may be useful to choose a large K, since the neighbors are likely to be related. Similarly, in very sparse areas, it may be best to choose only a very small number of nearest neighbors, since moving too far away may result in unrelated neighbors being included. This idea is closely related to *Parzen windows*,[14] which are a variant of K nearest neighbors used for classification. With Parzen windows, the number of nearest neighbors is not fixed. Instead, all of the neighbors within a fixed distance ("window") of an instance are considered its nearest neighbors. In this way, instances in dense

---

[14] Named after Emanuel Parzen, an American statistician.

areas will have many nearest neighbors, and those in sparse areas will have few. Figure 9.17 shows the same set of points from Figure 9.16, but clustered using a Parzen window approach. We see that fewer outliers get assigned to incorrect clusters for points in sparse areas of the space (e.g., point C), whereas points in denser regions have more neighbors assigned to them (e.g., B). However, the clusters formed are not perfect. The quality of the clusters now depends on the size of the window. Therefore, although this technique eliminates the need to choose K, it introduces the need to choose the window size, which can be an equally challenging problem.

9.2.5 Clustering and Search

A number of issues with clustering algorithms have resulted in them being less widely used in practice than classification algorithms. These issues include the computational costs, as well as the difficulty of interpreting and evaluating the clusters. Clustering has been used in a number of search engines for organizing the results, as we discussed in section 6.3.3. There are very few results for a search compared to the size of the document collection, so the efficiency of clustering is less of a problem. Clustering is also able to discover structure in the result set for arbitrary queries that would not be possible with a classification algorithm.

Topic modeling, which we discussed in section 7.6.2, can also be viewed as an application of clustering with the goal of improving the ranking effectiveness of the search engine. In fact, most of the information retrieval research involving clustering has focused on this goal. The basis for this research is the well-known *cluster hypothesis*. As originally stated by van Rijsbergen (1979), the cluster hypothesis is:

> *Closely associated documents tend to be relevant to the same requests.*

Note that this hypothesis doesn't actually mention clusters. However, "closely associated" or similar documents will generally be in the same cluster. So the hypothesis is usually interpreted as saying that documents in the same cluster tend to be relevant to the same queries.

Two different tests have been used to verify whether the cluster hypothesis holds for a given collection of documents. The first compares the distribution of similarity scores for pairs of relevant documents (for a set of queries) to the distribution for pairs consisting of a non-relevant and a relevant document. If the cluster hypothesis holds, we might expect to see a separation between these two distributions. On some smaller corpora, such as the CACM corpus mentioned in Chapter 8, this is indeed the case. If there were a number of clusters of relevant documents, however, which were not similar to each other, then this test may fail to show any separation. To address this potential problem, Voorhees (1985) proposed a test based on the assumption that if the cluster hypothesis holds, relevant documents would have high *local precision*, even if they were scattered in many clusters. Local precision simply measures the number of relevant documents found in the top five nearest neighbors for each relevant document.

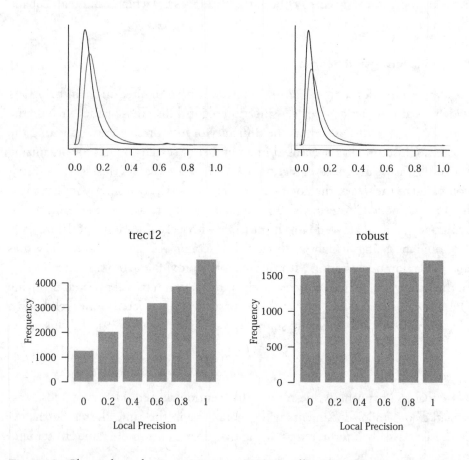

Fig. 9.18. Cluster hypothesis tests on two TREC collections. The top two compare the distributions of similarity values between relevant-relevant and relevant-nonrelevant pairs (light gray) of documents. The bottom two show the local precision of the relevant documents.

Figure 9.18 shows the results of these tests used on two TREC collections. These collections have similar types of documents, including large numbers of news stories. The 250 queries for the robust collection are known to be harder in terms of the typical MAP values obtained than the 150 queries used for trec12. The tests on the top row of the figure show that for both collections there is poor separation between the distributions of similarity values. The tests on the lower row, however, show that relevant documents in the trec12 collection have high local precision. The local precision is lower in the robust collection, which means that relevant documents tend to be more isolated and, consequently, harder to retrieve.

Given that the cluster hypothesis holds, at least for some collections and queries, the next question is how to exploit this in a retrieval model. There are, in fact, a number of ways of doing this. The first approach, known as *cluster-based retrieval*, ranks *clusters* instead of individual documents in response to a query. If there were K clusters $C_1 \dots C_K$, for example, we could rank clusters using the query likelihood retrieval model. This means that we rank clusters by $P(Q|C_j)$, where Q is the query, and:

$$P(Q|C_j) = \prod_{i=1}^{n} P(q_i|C_j)$$

The probabilities $P(q_i|C_j)$ are estimated using a smoothed unigram language model based on the frequencies of words in the cluster, as described for documents in Chapter 7. After the clusters have been ranked, documents within each cluster could be individually ranked for presentation in a result list. The intuition behind this ranking method is that a cluster language model should provide better estimates of the important word probabilities than document-based estimates. In fact, a relevant document with no terms in common with the query could potentially be retrieved if it were a member of a highly ranked cluster with other relevant documents.

Rather than using this two-stage process, the cluster language model can be directly incorporated into the estimation of the *document* language model as follows:

$$P(w|D) = (1 - \lambda - \delta)\frac{f_{w,D}}{|D|} + \delta\frac{f_{w,C_j}}{|C_j|} + \lambda\frac{f_{w,Coll}}{|Coll|}$$

where λ and δ are parameters, $f_{w,D}$ is the word frequency in the document D, f_{w,C_j} is the word frequency in the cluster C_j that contains D, and $f_{w,Coll}$ is the word frequency in the collection $Coll$. The second term, which comes from the cluster language model, increases the probability estimates for words that occur frequently in the cluster and are likely to be related to the topic of the document. In other words, the cluster language model makes the document more similar to other members of the cluster. This document language model with cluster-based smoothing can be used directly by the query likelihood retrieval model to rank documents as described in section 7.3.1.

The document language model can be further generalized to the case where the document D is a member of multiple overlapping clusters, as follows:

$$P(w|D) = (1 - \lambda - \delta)\frac{f_{w,D}}{|D|} + \delta \sum_{C_j} \frac{f_{w,C_j}}{|C_j|} P(D|C_j) + \lambda \frac{f_{w,Coll}}{|Coll|}$$

In this case, the second term in the document language model probability estimate for a word w is the weighted sum of the probabilities from the cluster language models for all clusters. The weight ($P(D|C_j)$) is the probability of the document being a member of cluster C_j. We can also make the simplifying assumption that $P(D|C_j)$ is uniform for those clusters that contain D, and zero otherwise.

Retrieval experiments have shown that retrieving clusters can yield small but variable improvements in effectiveness. Smoothing the document language model with cluster-based estimates, on the other hand, provides significant and consistent benefits. In practice, however, the expense of generating clusters has meant that cluster-based techniques have not been deployed as part of the ranking algorithm in operational search engines. However, promising results have recently been obtained using *query-specific clustering*, where clusters are constructed only from the top-ranked (e.g., 50) documents (Liu & Croft, 2008; Kurland, 2008). These clusters, which can be used for either cluster-based retrieval or document smoothing, can obviously be generated much more efficiently.

References and Further Reading

Classification and clustering have been thoroughly investigated in the research areas of statistics, pattern recognition, and machine learning. The books by Duda et al. (2000) and Hastie et al. (2001) describe a wide range of classification and clustering techniques and provide more details about the mathematical foundations the techniques are built upon. These books also provide good overviews of other useful machine learning techniques that can be applied to various search engine tasks.

For a more detailed treatment of Naïve Bayes classification for text classification, see McCallum and Nigam (1998). C. J. C. Burges (1998) gives a very detailed tutorial on SVMs that covers all of the basic concepts and theory. However, the subject matter is not light and requires a certain level of mathematical sophistication to fully understand. In addition, Joachims (2002a) is an entire book describing various uses of SVMs for text classification.

Van Rijsbergen (1979) provides a review of earlier research on clustering in information retrieval, and describes the cluster hypothesis and cluster-based retrieval. Diaz (2005) proposed an alternative interpretation of the cluster hypothesis by assuming that closely related documents should have similar *scores*, given the same query. Using this assumption, Diaz developed a framework for smoothing retrieval scores using properties of K nearest neighbor clusters. Language modeling smoothing using K-means clustering was examined in Liu and Croft (2004). Another language modeling smoothing technique based on overlapping K nearest neighbor clusters was proposed in Kurland and Lee (2004).

There are various useful software packages available for text classification. The Mallet software toolkit[15] provides implementations of various machine learning algorithms, including Naïve Bayes, maximum entropy, boosting, Winnow, and conditional random fields. It also provides support for parsing and tokenizing text into features. Another popular software package is SVMLight,[16] which is an SVM implementation that supports all of the kernels described in this chapter. Clustering methods are included in a number of packages available on the Web.

---

[15] http://mallet.cs.umass.edu/

[16] http://svmlight.joachims.org/

Exercises

9.1. Provide an example of how people use clustering in their everyday lives. What are the features that they use to represent the objects? What is the similarity measure? How do they evaluate the outcome?

9.2. Assume we want to do classification using a very fine-grained ontology, such as one describing all the families of human languages. Suppose that, before training, we decide to collapse all of the labels corresponding to Asian languages into a single "Asian languages" label. Discuss the negative consequences of this decision.

9.3. Suppose that we were to estimate $P(d|c)$ according to:

$$P(d|c) = \frac{N_{d,c}}{N_c}$$

where $N_{d,c}$ is the number of times document d is assigned to class c in the training set, and N_c is the number of instances assigned class label c in the training set. This is analogous to the way that $P(c)$ is estimated. Why can this estimate not be used in practice?

9.4. For some classification data set, compute estimates for $P(w|c)$ for all words w using both the multiple-Bernoulli and multinomial models. Compare the multiple-Bernoulli estimates with the multinomial estimates. How do they differ? Do the estimates diverge more for certain types of terms?

9.5. Explain why the solution to the original SVM formulation $w = \arg\max_w \frac{2}{||w||}$ is equivalent to the alternative formulation $w = \arg\min_w \frac{1}{2}||w||^2$.

9.6. Compare the accuracy of a one versus all SVM classifier and a one versus one SVM classifier on a multiclass classification data set. Discuss any differences observed in terms of the efficiency and effectiveness of the two approaches.

9.7. Under what conditions will the microaverage equal the macroaverage?

9.8. Cluster the following set of two-dimensional instances into three clusters using each of the five agglomerative clustering methods:

$(-4, -2), (-3, -2), (-2, -2), (-1, -2), (1, -1), (1, 1), (2, 3), (3, 2), (3, 4), (4, 3)$

Discuss the differences in the clusters across methods. Which methods produce the same clusters? How do these clusters compare to how you would manually cluster the points?

9.9. Use K-means and spherical K-means to cluster the data points in Exercise 9.8. How do the clusterings differ?

9.10. Nearest neighbor clusters are not symmetric, in the sense that if instance A is one of instance B's nearest neighbors, the reverse is not necessarily true. Explain how this can happen with a diagram.

9.11. The K nearest neighbors of a document could be represented by links to those documents. Describe two ways this representation could be used in a search application.

9.12. Can the *ClusterPrecision* evaluation metric ever be equal to zero? If so, provide an example. If not, explain why.

9.13. Test the cluster hypothesis on the CACM collection using both methods shown in Figure 9.18. What do you conclude from these tests?

10

Social Search

> "You will be assimilated."
>
> Borg Collective, *Star Trek: First Contact*

10.1 What Is Social Search?

In this chapter we will describe *social search*, which is rapidly emerging as a key search paradigm on the Web. As its name implies, social search deals with search within a social environment. This can be defined as an environment where a *community* of users *actively participate* in the search process. We interpret this definition of social search very broadly to include any application involving activities such as defining individual user profiles and interests, interacting with other users, and modifying the representations of the objects being searched. The active role of users in social search applications is in stark contrast to the standard search paradigms and models, which typically treat every user the same way and restrict interactions to query formulation.

Users may interact with each other online in a variety of ways. For example, users may visit a social media site,[1] which have recently gained a great deal of popularity. Examples of these sites include Digg (websites), Twitter (status messages), Flickr (pictures), YouTube (videos), Del.icio.us (bookmarks), and CiteU-Like (research papers). Social networking sites, such as MySpace, Facebook, and LinkedIn, allow friends, colleagues, and people with similar interests to interact with each other in various ways. More traditional examples of online social interactions include email, instant messenger, massively multiplayer online games (MMOGs), forums, and blogs.

---

[1] Social media sites are often collectively referred to as Web 2.0, as opposed to the classical notion of the Web ("Web 1.0"), which consists of non-interactive HTML documents.

As we see, the online world is a very social environment that is rich with users interacting with each other in various forms. These social interactions provide new and unique data resources for search systems to exploit, as well as a myriad of privacy issues. Most of the web search approaches we described in Chapter 7 only consider features of the documents or the link structure of the Web. In socially rich environments, however, we also have a plethora of user interaction data available that can help enhance the overall user experience in new and interesting ways.

It would be possible to write an entire book on online social interactions and search within such environments. The focus of this chapter is to highlight and describe a few aspects of social search that are particularly interesting from a search engine and information retrieval perspective.

The first topic we cover is *user tags*. Many social media websites allow users to assign tags to items. For example, a video-sharing website may allow users to not only assign tags to their own videos, but also to videos created by other people. An underwater video, for example, may have the tags "swimming", "underwater", "tropic", and "fish". Some sites allow multi-term tags, such as "tropical fish", but others allow only single-term tags. As we will describe, user tags are a form of *manual indexing*, where the content of an object is represented by manually assigned terms. There are many interesting search tasks related to user tags, such as searching for items using tags, automatically suggesting tags, and visualizing clusters of tags.

The second topic covered here is *searching within communities*, which describes online communities and how users search within such environments. Online communities are virtual groups of users that share common interests and interact socially in various ways in an online environment. For example, a sports fan who enjoys the outdoors and photography may be a member of baseball, hiking, and digital camera communities. Interactions in these communities range from passive activities (reading web pages) to those that are more active (writing in blogs and forums). These communities are virtual and *ad hoc*, meaning that there is typically no formal mechanism for joining one, and consequently people are implicitly rather than explicitly members of a community. Therefore, being able to automatically determine which communities exist in an online environment, and which users are members of each, can be valuable for a number of search-related tasks. One such task that we will describe is community-based question answering, whereby a user posts a question to an online system and members of his own community, or the community most related to his question, provide answers to the question. Such a search task is much more social, interactive, and focused than standard web search.

The next topics we describe are *filtering* and *recommender systems*. It may be considered somewhat unusual to include these in a chapter on social search, because they are not typical "Web 2.0" applications. Both types of systems, however, rely on representations of individual users called *profiles*, and for that reason fit into our broad definition. Both systems also combine elements of document retrieval and classification. In standard search tasks, systems return documents in response to many different queries. These queries typically correspond to short-term information needs. In filtering, there is a fixed query (the profile) that represents some long-term information need. The search system monitors incoming documents and retrieves only those documents that are relevant to the information need. Many online news websites provide document filtering functionality. For example, CNN provides an alerts service, which allows users to specify various topics of interest, such as "tropical storms", or more general topics, such as sports or politics. When a new story matches a user's profile, the system alerts the user, typically via email. In this way, the user does not need to continually search for articles of interest. Instead, the search system is tasked with finding relevant documents that match the user's long-term information needs. Recommender systems are similar to document filtering systems, except the goal is to predict how a user would rate some item, rather than retrieving relevant documents. For example, Amazon.com employs a recommender system that attempts to predict how much a user would like certain items, such as books, movies, or music. Recommender systems are social search algorithms because predictions are estimated based on ratings given by similar users, thereby implicitly linking people to a community of users with related interests.

The final two topics covered in this chapter, *peer-to-peer (P2P)* search and *metasearch*, deal with architectures for social search. Peer-to-peer search is the task of querying a community of "nodes" for a given information need. Nodes can be individuals, organizations, or search engines. When a user issues a query, it is passed through the P2P network and run on one or more nodes, and then results are returned. This type of search can be fully distributed across a large network of nodes. Metasearch is a special case of P2P search where all of the nodes are search engines. Metasearch engines run queries against a number of search engines, collect the results, and then merge the results. The goal of metasearch engines is to provide better coverage and accuracy than a single search engine.

Finally, we note that *personalization* is another area that could be regarded as part of social search, because it covers a range of techniques for improving search by representing individual user preferences and interests. Since most of these techniques provide context for the query, however, they were discussed as part of query refinement in section 6.2.5.

10.2 User Tags and Manual Indexing

Before electronic search systems became available at libraries, patrons had to rely on card catalogs for finding books. As their name implies, card catalogs are large collections (catalogs) of cards. Each card contains information about a particular author, title, or subject. A person interested in a specific author, title, or subject would go to the appropriate catalog and attempt to find cards describing relevant books. The card catalogs, therefore, act as indexes to the information in a library.

Card catalogs existed long before computers did, which means that these cards were constructed manually. Given a book, a person had to extract the author, title, and subject headings of the book so that the various catalogs could be built. This process is known as *manual indexing*. Given that it is impractical to manually index the huge collections of digital media available today, search engines use *automatic indexing* techniques to assign identifiers (terms, phrases, features) to documents during index construction. Since this process is automatic, the quality and accuracy of the indexing can be much lower than that of manual indexing. The advantages of automatic indexing, however, are that it is *exhaustive*, in the sense that every word in the document is indexed and nothing is left out, and *consistent*, whereas people can make mistakes indexing or have certain biases in how they index. Search evaluations that have compared manual to automatic indexing have found that automatic indexing is at least as effective and often much better than manual indexing. These studies have also shown, however, that the two forms of indexing complement each other, and that the most effective searches use both.

As a compromise between manually indexing every item (library catalogs) and automatically indexing every item (search engines), social media sites provide users with the opportunity to manually *tag* items. Each tag is typically a single word that describes the item. For example, an image of a tiger may be assigned the tags "tiger", "zoo", "big", and "cat". By allowing users to assign tags, some items end up with tags, and others do not. Of course, to make every item searchable, it is likely that every item is automatically indexed. Therefore, some items will contain both automatic and manual identifiers. As we will show later in this section, this results in unique challenges for retrieval models and ranking functions.

Social media tagging, like card catalog generation, is called *manual tagging*. This clash in naming is rather unfortunate, because the two types of indexing are actually quite different. Card catalogs are manually generated by experts who choose keywords, categories, and other descriptors from a *controlled vocabulary* (fixed ontology). This ensures that the descriptors are more or less standardized. On the other hand, social media tagging is done by end users who may or may not be experts. There is little-to-no quality control done on the user tags. Furthermore, there is no fixed vocabulary from which users choose tags. Instead, user tags form their own descriptions of the important concepts and relationships in a domain. User-generated ontologies (or taxonomies) are known as *folksonomies*. Therefore, a folksonomy can be interpreted as a dynamic, community-influenced ontology.

There has been a great deal of research and interest invested in developing a semantically tagged version of the Web, which is often called the *semantic web*. The goal of the semantic web is to semantically tag web content in such a way that it becomes possible to find, organize, and share information more easily. For example, a news article could be tagged with metadata, such as the title, subject, description, publisher, date, and language. However, in order for the semantic web to materialize and yield significant improvements in relevance, a standardized, fixed ontology of metadata tags must be developed and used consistently across a large number of web pages. Given the growing popularity of social media sites that are based on flexible, user-driven folksonomies, compared to the small number of semantic web sites that are based on rigid, predefined ontologies, it seems as though users, in general, are more open to tagging data with a relatively unrestricted set of tags that are meaningful to them and that reflect the specific context of the application.

Given that users are typically allowed to tag items in any way that they wish, there are many different types of tags. For example, Golder and Huberman (2006) described seven different categories of tags. Z. Xu et al. (2006) proposed a simplified set of five tag categories, which consists of the following:

1. Content-based tags. Tags describing the content of an item. Examples: "car", "woman", and "sky".
2. Context-based tags. Tags that describe the context of an item. Examples: "New York City" or "Empire State Building".

3. Attribute tags. Tags that describe implicit attributes of the item. Examples: "Nikon" (type of camera), "black and white" (type of movie), or "homepage" (type of web page).

4. Subjective tags. Tags that subjectively describe an item. Examples: "pretty", "amazing", and "awesome".

5. Organizational tags. Tags that help organize items. Examples: "todo", "my pictures", and "readme".

As we see, tags can be applied to many different types of items, ranging from web pages to videos, and used for many different purposes beyond just tagging the content. Therefore, tags and online collaborative tagging environments can be very useful tools for users in terms of searching, organizing, sharing, and discovering new information. It is likely that tags are here to stay and will become even more widely used in the future. Therefore, it is important to understand the various issues surrounding them and how they are used within search engines today.

In the remainder of this section, we will describe how tags can be used for search, how new tags for an item can be inferred from existing tags, and how sets of tags can be visualized and presented to the user.

10.2.1 Searching Tags

Since this is a book about search engines, the first tag-related task that we discuss is searching a collection of collaboratively tagged items. One unique property of tags is that they are almost exclusively textual keywords that are used to describe textual or non-textual items. Therefore, tags can provide a textual dimension to items that do not explicitly have a simple textual representation, such as images or videos. These textual representations of non-textual items can be very useful for searching. We can apply many of the retrieval strategies described in Chapter 7 to the problem. Despite the fact that searching within tagged collections can be mapped to a text search problem, tags present certain challenges that are not present when dealing with standard document or web retrieval.

The first challenge, and by far the most pervasive, is the fact that tags are very sparse representations of very complex items. Perhaps the simplest way to search a set of tagged items is to use a Boolean retrieval model. For example, given the query "fish bowl", one could run the query "fish AND bowl", which would only return items that are tagged with both "fish" and "bowl", or "fish OR bowl", which would return items that are tagged with either "fish" or "bowl". Conjunctive (AND) queries are likely to produce high-quality results, but may miss many relevant items. Thus, the approach would have high precision but low recall. At the opposite end of the spectrum, the disjunctive (OR) queries will match many more relevant items, but at the cost of precision.

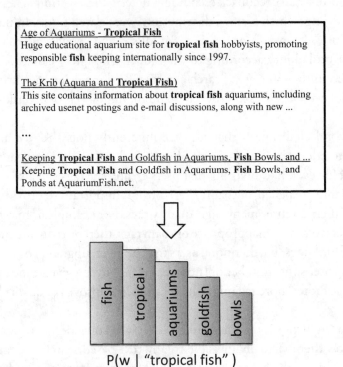

<u>Age of Aquariums</u> - **Tropical Fish**
Huge educational aquarium site for **tropical fish** hobbyists, promoting responsible **fish** keeping internationally since 1997.

<u>The Krib (Aquaria and **Tropical Fish**)</u>
This site contains information about **tropical fish** aquariums, including archived usenet postings and e-mail discussions, along with new ...

...

Keeping **Tropical Fish** and Goldfish in Aquariums, **Fish** Bowls, and ...
Keeping **Tropical Fish** and Goldfish in Aquariums, **Fish** Bowls, and Ponds at AquariumFish.net.

P(w | "tropical fish")

Fig. 10.1. Search results used to enrich a tag representation. In this example, the tag being expanded is "tropical fish". The query "tropical fish" is run against a search engine, and the snippets returned are then used to generate a distribution over related terms.

Of course, it is highly desirable to achieve both high precision and high recall. However, doing so is very challenging. Consider the query "aquariums" and a picture of a fish bowl that is tagged with "tropical fish" and "goldfish". Most retrieval models, including Boolean retrieval, will not be able to find this item, because there is no overlap between the query terms and the tag terms. This problem, which was described in Chapter 6 in the context of advertising, is known as the *vocabulary mismatch* problem. There are various ways to overcome this problem, including simple things such as stemming. Other approaches attempt to enrich the sparse tag (or query) representation by performing a form of pseudo-relevance feedback. Figure 10.1 illustrates how web search results may be used to enrich a tag representation. In the example, the tag "tropical fish" is run as a query against a search engine. The snippets returned are then processed using any of the standard pseudo-relevance feedback techniques described in section 7.3.2, such as relevance modeling, which forms a distribution over related terms. In this example, the terms "fish", "tropical", "aquariums", "goldfish", and "bowls" are the terms with the highest probability according to the model. The query can also, optionally, be expanded in the same way. Search can then be done using the enriched query and/or tag representations in order to maintain high levels of precision as well as recall.

The second challenge is that tags are inherently noisy. As we have shown, tags can provide useful information about items and help improve the quality of search. However, like anything that users create, the tags can also be off topic, inappropriate, misspelled, or spam. Therefore it is important to provide proper incentives to users to enter many high-quality tags. For example, it may be possible to allow users to report inappropriate or spam tags, thereby reducing the incentive to produce junk tags. Furthermore, users may be given upgraded or privileged access if they enter some number of (non-spam) tags over a given time period. This incentive promotes more tagging, which can help improve tag quality and coverage.

The final challenge is that many items in a given collection may not be tagged, which makes them virtually invisible to any text-based search system. For such items, it would be valuable to automatically infer the missing tags and use the tags for improving search recall. We devote the next section to diving deeper into the details of this problem.

10.2.2 Inferring Missing Tags

As we just described, items that have no tags pose a challenge to a search system. Although precision is obviously a very important metric for many tag-related search tasks, recall may also be important in some cases. In such cases, it is important to automatically infer a set of tags for items that have no manual tags assigned to them.

Let us first consider the case when the items in our collection are textual, such as books, news articles, research papers, or web pages. In these cases, it is possible to infer tags based solely on the textual representation of the item. One simple approach would involve computing some weight for every term that occurs in the text and then choosing the K terms with the highest weight as the inferred tags. There are various measures of term importance, including a $tf.idf$-based weight, such as:

$$wt(w) = \log(f_{w,D} + 1) \log(\frac{N}{df_w})$$

where $f_{w,d}$ is the number of times term w occurs in item D, N is the total number of items, and df_w is the number of items that term w occurs in. Other term importance measures may take advantage of document structure. For example, terms that occur in the title of an item may be given more weight.

It is also possible to treat the problem of inferring tags as a classification problem, as was recently proposed by Heymann, Ramage, and Garcia-Molina (2008). Given a fixed ontology or folksonomy of tags, the goal is to train a binary classifier for each tag. Each of these classifiers takes an item as input and predicts whether the associated tag should be applied to the item. This approach requires training one classifier for every tag, which can be a cumbersome task and requires a large amount of training data. Fortunately, however, training data for this task is virtually free since users are continuously tagging (manually labeling) items! Therefore, it is possible to use all of the existing tag/item pairs as training data to train the classifiers. Heymann et al. use an SVM classifier to predict web page tags. They compute a number of features, including $tf.idf$ weights for terms in the page text and anchor text, as well as a number of link-based features. Results show that high precision and recall can be achieved by using the textual features alone, especially for tags that occur many times in the collection. A similar classification approach can be applied to other types of items, such as images or videos. The challenge when dealing with non-textual items is extracting useful features from the items.

The two approaches we described for inferring missing tags choose tags for items independently of the other tags that were assigned. This may result in very relevant, yet very redundant, tags being assigned to some item. For example, a picture of children may have the tags "child", "children", "kid", "kids", "boy", "boys", "girl", "girls"—all of which would be relevant, but as you see, are rather redundant. Therefore, it is important to choose a set of tags that are both relevant and non-redundant. This is known as the *novelty* problem.

Carbonell and Goldstein (1998) describe the *Maximal Marginal Relevance* (MMR) technique, which addresses the problem of selecting a diverse set of items. Rather than choosing tags independently of each other, MMR chooses tags iteratively, adding one tag to the item at a time. Given an item i and the current set of tags for the item T_i, the MMR technique chooses the next tag according to the tag t that maximizes:

$$MMR(t; T_i) = \left(\lambda Sim_{item}(t, i) - (1 - \lambda) \max_{t \in T_i} Sim_{tag}(t_i, t) \right)$$

where Sim_{item} is a function that measures that similarity between a tag t and item i (such as those measures described in this section), Sim_{tag} measures the similarity between two tags (such as the measures described in section 10.2.1), and λ is a tunable parameter that can be used to trade off between relevance ($\lambda = 1$) and novelty ($\lambda = 0$). Therefore, a tag that is very relevant to the item and not very similar to any of the other tags will have a large MMR score. Iteratively choosing tags in this way helps eliminate the production of largely redundant sets of tags, which is useful not only when presenting the inferred tags to the user, but also from the perspective of using the inferred tags for search, since a diverse set of tags should help further improve recall.

10.2.3 Browsing and Tag Clouds

As we have shown, tags can be used for searching a set of collaboratively tagged items. However, tags can also be used to help users browse, explore, and discover new items in a large collection of items. There are several different ways that tags can be used to aid browsing. For example, when a user is viewing a given item, all of the item's tags may be displayed. The user may then click on one of the tags and be shown a list of results of items that also have that tag. The user may then repeat this process, repeatedly choosing an item and then clicking on one of the tags. This allows users to browse through the collection of items by following a chain of related tags.

Such browsing behavior is very focused and does not really allow the user to explore a large range of the items in the collection. For example, if a user starts on a picture of a tropical fish, it would likely take many clicks for the user to end up viewing an image of an information retrieval textbook. Of course, this may be desirable, especially if the user is only interested in things closely related to tropical fish.

One way of providing the user with a more global view of the collection is to allow the user to view the most popular tags. These may be the most popular tags for the entire site or for a particular group or category of items. Tag popularity may be measured in various ways, but is commonly computed as the number of times the tag has been applied to some item. Displaying the popular tags allows the user to begin her browsing and exploration of the collection using one of these tags as a starting point.

animals architecture art australia autumn baby band barcelona beach berlin birthday black blackandwhite blue california cameraphone canada canon car cat chicago china christmas church city clouds color concert day dog england europe family festival film florida flower flowers food france friends fun garden germany girl graffiti green halloween hawaii holiday home house india ireland italy japan july kids lake landscape light live london macro me mexico music nature new newyork night nikon nyc ocean paris park party people portrait red river rock sanfrancisco scotland sea seattle show sky snow spain spring street summer sunset taiwan texas thailand tokyo toronto travel tree trees trip uk usa vacation washington water wedding

Fig. 10.2. Example of a tag cloud in the form of a weighted list. The tags are in alphabetical order and weighted according to some criteria, such as popularity.

Thus far we have described ways that tags may aid users with browsing. One of the most important aspects of browsing is displaying a set of tags to a user in a visually appealing and meaningful manner. For example, consider displaying the 50 most popular tags to the user. The simplest way to do so is to just display the tags in a list or table, possibly in alphabetical or sorted order according to popularity. Besides not being very visually appealing, this display also does not allow the user to quickly observe all of the pertinent information. When visualizing tags, it is useful to show the list of tags in alphabetical order, so that users may quickly scan through the list or find the tags they are looking for. It is also beneficial to portray the popularity or importance of a given tag. There are many ways to visualize this information, but one of the most widely used techniques is called *tag clouds*. In a tag cloud, the display size of a given tag is proportional to its popularity or importance. Tags may be arranged in a random order within a "cloud" or alphabetically. Figure 10.2 shows an example of a tag cloud where the tags are listed alphabetically. Such a representation is also called a weighted list. Based on this tag cloud, the user can easily see that the tags "wedding", "party", and "birthday" are all very popular. Therefore, tag clouds provide a convenient, visually appealing way of representing a set of tags.

10.3 Searching with Communities

10.3.1 What Is a Community?

The collaborative tagging environments that we just described are filled with implicit social interactions. By analyzing the tags that users submit or search for, it is possible to discover groups of users with related interests. For example, ice hockey fans are likely to tag pictures of their favorite ice hockey players, tag their favorite ice hockey web pages, search for ice hockey–related tags, and so on. Tagging is just one example of how interactions in an online environment can be used to infer relationships between entities (e.g., people). Groups of entities that interact in an online environment and that share common goals, traits, or interests are an *online community*. This definition is not all that different from the traditional definition of community. In fact, online communities are actually very similar to traditional communities and share many of the same social dynamics. The primary difference between our definition and that of a traditional community is that an online community can be made up of users, organizations, web pages, or just about any other meaningful online entity.

Let us return to our example of users who tag and search for ice hockey–related items. It is easy to see that ice hockey fans form an online community. Members of the community do many other things other than tag and search. For example, they also post to blogs, newsgroups, and other forums. They may also send instant messages and emails to other members of the community about their ice hockey experiences. Furthermore, they may buy and sell ice hockey–related items online, through sites such as eBay. Hence, there are many ways that a user may participate in a community. It is important to note, however, that his membership in the community is implicit. Another important thing to notice is that users are very likely to have a number of hobbies or interests, and may be members of more than one online community. Therefore, in order to improve the overall user experience, it can be useful for search engines and other online sites to automatically determine the communities associated with a given user.

Some online communities consist of non-human entities. For example, a set of web pages that are all on the same topic form an online community that is often called a *web community*. These pages form a community since they share similar traits (i.e., they are all about the same topic). Since web pages are created by users, web communities share many of the same characteristics as communities of users. Automatically identifying web communities can be useful for improving search.

The remainder of this section covers several aspects of online communities that are useful from a search engine perspective. We first describe several effective methods for automatically finding online communities. We then discuss community-based question answering, where people ask questions and receive answers from other members of the community. Finally, we cover collaborative searching, which is a search paradigm that involves a group of users searching together.

10.3.2 Finding Communities

The first task that we describe is how to automatically find online communities. As we mentioned before, online communities are implicitly defined by interactions among a set of entities with common traits. This definition is rather vague and makes it difficult to design general-purpose algorithms for finding every possible type of online community. Instead, several algorithms have been developed that can effectively find special types of communities that have certain assumed characteristics. We will describe several such algorithms now.

Most of the algorithms used for finding communities take as input a set of entities, such as users or web pages, information about each entity, and details about how the entities interact or are related to each other. This can be conveniently represented as a graph, where each entity is a node in the graph, and interactions (or relationships) between the entities are denoted by edges. Graphs can be either directed or undirected. The edges in directed graphs have directional arrows that indicate the source node and destination node of the edge. Edges in undirected graphs do not have directional arrows and therefore have no notion of source and destination. Directed edges are useful for representing non-symmetric or causal relationships between two entities. Undirected edges are useful for representing symmetric relationships or for simply indicating that two entities are related in some way.

Using this representation, it is easy to define two criteria for finding communities within the graph. First, the set of entities (nodes) must be similar to each other according to some similarity measure. Second, the set of entities should interact with each other more than they interact with other entities. The first requirement makes sure that the entities actually share the same traits, whereas the second ensures that the entities interact in a meaningful way with each other, thereby making them a community rather than a set of users with the same traits who never interact with each other.

The first algorithm that we describe is the HITS algorithm, which was briefly discussed in Chapter 4 in the context of PageRank. The HITS algorithm is similar to PageRank, except that it is query-dependent, whereas PageRank is usually query-independent. You may be wondering what HITS has to do with finding communities, since it was originally proposed as a method for improving web search. Both PageRank and HITS, however, are part of a family of general, powerful algorithms known as *link analysis* algorithms. These algorithms can be applied to many different types of data sets that can be represented as directed graphs.

Given a graph of entities, we must first identify a subset of the entities that may possibly be members of the community. We call these entities the *candidate entities*. For example, if we wish to find the ice hockey online community, then we must query each node in the graph and find all of the nodes (users) that are interested in ice hockey. This can be accomplished by, for example, finding all users of a system who have searched for anything hockey-related. This ensures that the first criteria, which states that entities should be similar to each other, is satisfied. Another example is the task of finding the "fractal art" web community. Here, we could search the Web for the query "fractal art" and consider only those entities (web pages) that match the query. Again, this ensures that all of the pages are topically similar to each other. This first step finds sets of similar items, but fails to identify the sets of entities that actively participate, via various interactions, within the community, which is the second criteria that we identified as being important.

Given the candidate entities, the HITS algorithm can be used to find the "core" of the community. The HITS algorithm takes a graph G with node set V and edge set E as input. For finding communities, the vertex set V consists of the candidate entities, and the edge set E consists of all of the edges between candidate entities. For each of the candidate entities (nodes) p in the graph, HITS computes an authority score ($A(p)$) and a hub score ($H(p)$). It is assumed that good hubs are those that point to good authorities and that good authorities are those that are pointed to by good hubs. Notice the circularity in these definitions. This means that the authority score depends on the hub score, which in turn depends on the authority score. Given a set of authority and hub scores, the HITS algorithm updates the scores according to the following equations:

Algorithm 3 HITS

1: **procedure** HITS$(G = (V, E), K)$
2:      $A_0(p) \leftarrow 1 \, \forall p \in V$
3:      $H_0(p) \leftarrow 1 \, \forall p \in V$
4:      **for** $i = 1$ to K **do**
5:          $A_i(p) \leftarrow 0 \, \forall p \in V$
6:          $H_i(p) \leftarrow 0 \, \forall p \in V$
7:          $Z_A \leftarrow 0$
8:          $Z_H \leftarrow 0$
9:          **for** $p \in V$ **do**
10:              **for** $q \in V$ **do**
11:                  **if** $(p, q) \in E$ **then**
12:                      $H_i(p) \leftarrow H_i(p) + A_{i-1}(q)$
13:                      $Z_H \leftarrow Z_H + A_{i-1}(q)$
14:                  **end if**
15:                  **if** $(q, p) \in E$ **then**
16:                      $A_i(p) \leftarrow A_i(p) + H_{i-1}(q)$
17:                      $Z_A \leftarrow Z_A + H_{i-1}(q)$
18:                  **end if**
19:              **end for**
20:          **end for**
21:          **for** $p \in V$ **do**
22:              $A_i(p) \leftarrow \frac{A_i(p)}{Z_A}$
23:              $H_i(p) \leftarrow \frac{H_i(p)}{Z_H}$
24:          **end for**
25:      **end for**
26:      **return** A_K, H_K
27: **end procedure**

$$A(p) = \sum_{q \to p} H(q)$$

$$H(p) = \sum_{p \to q} A(q)$$

where $p \to q$ indicates that an edge exists between entity p (source) and entity q (destination). As the equations indicate, $A(p)$ is the sum of the hub scores of the entities that point at p, and $H(p)$ is the sum of the authority scores pointed at by p. Thus, to be a strong authority, an entity must have many incoming edges, all with relatively moderate hub scores, or have very few incoming links that have very large hub scores. Similarly, to be a good hub, an entity must have many outgoing edges to less authoritative pages, or few outgoing edges to very highly authoritative pages.

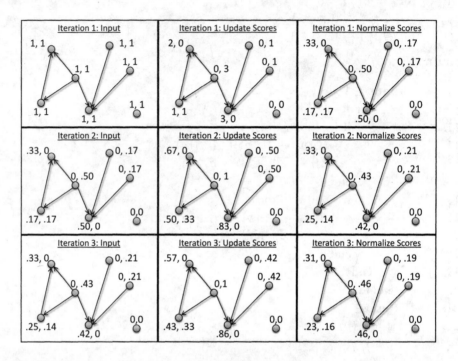

Fig. 10.3. Illustration of the HITS algorithm. Each row corresponds to a single iteration of the algorithm and each column corresponds to a specific step of the algorithm.

An iterative version of HITS is given in Algorithm 3. The algorithm begins by initializing all hub and authority scores to 1. The algorithm then updates the hub and authority scores according to the equations we just showed. Then, the hub scores are normalized so that the sum of the scores is 1. The same is also done for the authority scores. The entire process is then repeated on the normalized scores for a fixed number of iterations, denoted by K. The algorithm is guaranteed to converge and typically does so after a small number of iterations. Figure 10.3 shows an example of the HITS algorithm applied to a graph with seven nodes and six edges. The algorithm is carried out for three iterations. Notice that the nodes with many incoming edges tend to have higher authority scores, and those with more outgoing edges tend to have larger hub scores. Another characteristic of the HITS algorithm is that nodes that are not connected to any other nodes will always have hub and authority scores of 0.

Once the hub and authority scores have been computed, the entities can be ranked according to their authority score. This list will contain the most authoritative entities within the community. Such entities are likely to be the "leaders" or form the "core" of the community, based on their interactions with other members of the community. For example, if this algorithm were applied to the computer science researcher citation graph to find the information retrieval research community, the most authoritative authors would be those that are cited many times by prolific authors. These would arguably be the luminaries in the field and those authors that form the core of the research community. When finding web communities on the web graph, the algorithm will return pages that are linked to by a large number of reputable web pages.

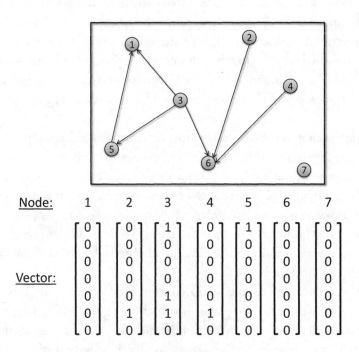

Fig. 10.4. Example of how nodes within a directed graph can be represented as vectors. For a given node p, its vector representation has component q set to 1 if $p \rightarrow q$.

Clustering algorithms, such as the ones described in Chapter 9, may also be used for finding online communities. These algorithms easily adapt to the problem, since community finding is an inherently unsupervised learning problem. Both agglomerative clustering and K-means can be used for finding communities. Both of these clustering algorithms require a function that measures the distance between two clusters. As we discussed in Chapter 9, the Euclidean distance is often used. However, it is not immediately clear how to apply the Euclidean distance to nodes in a (directed or undirected) graph. One simple way is to represent each node (entity) in the graph as a vector that has $|V|$ components—one for every node in the graph. For some node p, component q of its vector representation is set to 1 if $p \rightarrow q$, and 0 otherwise. This results in each node being represented by the nodes it points to. Figure 10.4 shows how the nodes of a graph are represented this way. Each vector may optionally be normalized. Using this representation, it is possible to use the Euclidean distance and directly apply agglomerative clustering or K-means to the problem. A high similarity according to the Euclidean distance will occur when two entities have edges directed toward many of the same entities. For example, returning to the problem of finding the information retrieval research community, two authors would be considered very similar if they tended to cite the same set of authors. It is realistic to assume that most members of the information retrieval research community tend to cite many of the same authors, especially those that would be given a large authority score by HITS.

Evaluating the effectiveness of community-finding algorithms is typically more difficult than evaluating traditional clustering tasks, since it is unclear how to determine whether some entity should be part of a given community. In fact, it is likely that if a group of people were asked to manually identify online communities, there would be many disagreements due to the vague definition of a community. Therefore, it is impossible to say whether HITS or agglomerative clustering is better at finding communities. The best choice largely depends on the task and data set for the application.

Now that you have seen several ways of automatically finding online communities, you may be wondering how this information can be put to practical use. There are many different things that can be done after a set of communities has been identified. For example, if a user has been identified as part of the information retrieval research community, then when the user visits a web page, targeted content may be displayed to the user that caters to her specific interests. Search engines could use the community information as additional contextual information for improving the relevance of search results, by retrieving results that are also topically related to the community or communities associated with the user. Online community information can also be used in other ways, including enhanced browsing, identifying experts, website recommendation, and possibly even suggesting who may be a compatible date for you!

10.3.3 Community-Based Question Answering

In the last section, we described how to automatically find online communities. In this section, we describe how such communities can be used effectively to help answer complex information needs that would be difficult to answer using conventional search engines. For example, consider a person who is interested in learning about potential interactions between a medicine he was just prescribed and an herbal tea he often drinks. He could use a search engine and spend hours entering various queries, looking at search results, and trying to find useful information on the subject. The difficulty with using this approach is that no single page may exist that completely satisfies the person's information need. Now, suppose that the person could ask his question directly to a large group of other people, several of whom are pharmacists or herbal experts. He would be much more likely to get an answer. This search scenario, where a person submits a question to a community consisting of both experts and non-experts in a wide range of topics, each of whom can opt to answer the question, is called *community-based question answering* (CQA). These systems harness the power of human knowledge in order to satisfy a broad range of information needs. Several popular commercial systems of this type exist today, including Yahoo! Answers and Naver, a Korean search portal.

There are both pros and cons to CQA systems. The pros include users being able to get answers to complex or obscure information needs; the chance to see multiple, possibly differing opinions about a topic; and the chance to interact with other users who may share common interests, problems, and goals. The cons include the possibility of receiving no answer at all to a question, having to wait (possibly days) for an answer, and receiving answers that are incorrect, misleading, offensive, or spam.

As we just mentioned, many of the answers that people submit are of low quality. It turns out, however, that the old computer programming adage of "garbage in, garbage out" also applies to questions. Studies have shown that low-quality answers are often given to low-quality questions. Indeed, there are a wide range of questions that users can, and do, ask. Table 10.1 shows a small sample of questions submitted to Yahoo! Answers. Some of the questions in the table are well-formed

What part of Mexico gets the most tropical storms?
How do you pronounce the french words, coeur and miel?
GED test?
Why do I have to pay this fine?
What is Schrödinger's cat?
What's this song?
Hi...can u ppl tell me sumthing abt death dreams??
What are the engagement and wedding traditions in Egypt?
Fun things to do in LA?
What lessons from the Tao Te Ching do you apply to your everyday life?
Foci of a hyperbola?
What should I do today?
Why was iTunes deleted from my computer?
Heather Locklear?
Do people in the Australian Defense Force (RAAF) pay less tax than civilians?
Whats a psp xmb?
If C(-3, y) and D(1, 7) lie upon a line whose slope is 2, find the value of y.?
Why does love make us so irrational?
Am I in love?
What are some technologies that are revolutionizing business?

Table 10.1. Example questions submitted to Yahoo! Answers

and grammatically correct, whereas others are not. In addition, some of the questions have simple, straightforward answers, but many others do not.

Besides allowing users to ask and answer questions, CQA services also provide users with the ability to search the archive of previously asked questions and the corresponding answers. This search functionality serves two purposes. First, if a user finds that a similar question has been asked in the past, then they may not need to ask the question and wait for responses. Second, search engines may augment traditional search results with hits from the question and answer database. For example, if a user enters the query "schrödingers cat", the search engine may choose to return answers to "What is Schrödinger's cat?" (which appears in Table 10.1) in addition to the other, more standard set of ranked web pages.

Therefore, given a query,[2] it is important to be able to automatically find potential answers in the question and answer database. There are several possible

---

[2] For the remainder of our discussion, we use the term "query" to refer to a question or a search query.

ways to search this database. New queries can be matched against the archived questions alone, the archived answers alone, or questions and answers combined. Studies have shown that it is better to match queries against the archived questions rather than answers, since generally it is easier to find related questions (which are likely to have relevant answers) than it is to match queries directly to answers.

Matching queries to questions can be achieved using any of the retrieval models described in Chapter 7, such as language modeling or BM25. However, traditional retrieval models are likely to miss many relevant questions because of the vocabulary mismatch problem. Here, vocabulary mismatch is caused by the fact that there are many different ways to ask the same question. For example, suppose we had the query "who is the leader of india?". Related questions are "who is the prime minister of india?", "who is the current head of the indian government?", and so on. Notice that the only terms in common among any two of these questions are "who", "is", "the", "of", and "india". Blindly applying any standard retrieval model would retrieve non-related questions such as "who is the finance minister of india?" and "who is the tallest person in all of india?". Stopword removal in this case does not help much. Instead, better matches can be achieved by generalizing the notion of "leader" to include other concepts, such as "prime minister", "head", and "government".

In section 6.4, we described cross-language retrieval, where a user queries in a source language (e.g., English) and documents are retrieved in a target language (e.g., French). Most of the retrieval methods developed for cross-language retrieval are based on machine translation techniques, which require learning translation probabilities of the form $P(s|t)$, where s is a word in the source language and t is a word in the target language. Translation models can also be used to help overcome the vocabulary mismatch problem within a single language. This is achieved by estimating $P(t|t')$, where t and t' are both words in the same language. This probability can be interpreted as the probability that word t is used in place of t'. Returning to our example, it is likely that $P(\text{leader}|\text{minister})$ and $P(\text{leader}|\text{government})$ would have non-zero values, and therefore result in more relevant questions being retrieved. We will now describe two translation-based models that have been used for finding related questions and answers in an archive.

The first model was proposed by Berger and Lafferty (1999). It is similar to the query likelihood model described in section 7.3.1, except it allows query terms to be "translated" from other terms. Given a query, related questions[3] are ranked according to:

$$P(Q|A) = \prod_{w \in Q} \sum_{t \in \mathcal{V}} P(w|t) P(t|A)$$

where Q is the query, A is a related question in the archive, $\mathcal{V}$ is the vocabulary, $P(w|t)$ are the translation probabilities, and $P(t|D)$ is the smoothed probability of generating t given document D (see section 7.3.1 for more details). Therefore, we see that the model allows query term w to be translated from other terms t that may occur in the question. One of the primary issues with this model is that there is no guarantee the question will be related to the query; since every term is translated independently, the question with the highest score may be a good term-for-term translation of the query, but not a good *overall* translation.

The second model, developed by Xue et al. (2008), is an extension of Berger's model that attempts to overcome this issue by allowing matches of the original query terms to be given more weight than matches of translated terms. Under this model, questions (or answers) are ranked using the following formula:

$$P(Q|A) = \prod_{w \in Q} \frac{(1 - \beta) f_{w,A} + \beta \sum_{t \in \mathcal{V}} P(w|t) f_{t,A} + \mu \frac{c_w}{|C|}}{|A| + \mu}$$

where β is a parameter between 0 and 1 that controls the influence of the translation probabilities, and μ is the Dirichlet smoothing parameter. Notice that when $\beta = 0$, this model is equivalent to the original query likelihood model, with no influence from the translation model. As β approaches 1, the translation model begins to have more impact on the ranking and becomes more similar to Berger's model.

Ranking using these models can be computationally expensive, since each involves a sum over the entire vocabulary, which can be very large. Query processing speeds can be significantly improved by considering only a small number of translations per query term. For example, if the five most likely translations of each query term are used, the number of terms in the summation will be reduced from $\mathcal{V}$ to 5.

The one major issue that has been ignored thus far is how to compute the translation probabilities. In cross-language retrieval, translation probabilities can be

---

[3] The discussion focuses on question retrieval, but the same models can be used to retrieve archived answers. As we said, question retrieval is generally more effective.

everest	xp	search
everest	xp	search
mountain	window	google
tallest	install	information
29,035	drive	internet
highest	computer	website
mt	version	web
ft	click	list
measure	pc	free
feet	program	info
mount	microsoft	page

Table 10.2. Translations automatically learned from a set of question and answer pairs. The 10 most likely translations for the terms "everest", "xp", and "search" are given.

automatically learned using a parallel corpus. Translation probabilities are estimated from pairs of documents of the form $\{(D_1^s, D_1^t), \ldots, (D_N^s, D_N^t)\}$, where D_i^s is document i written in the source language and D_i^t is document i written in the target language. However, the notion of a parallel corpus becomes hazy when dealing with *intra*language translations. A variety of approaches have been used for estimating translation probabilities within the same language. For finding related questions, one of the most successful approaches makes the assumption that question/answer pairs form a parallel corpus from which translation probabilities can be estimated. That is, translation probabilities are estimated from archived pairs of the form $\{(Q_1, A_1), \ldots, (Q_N, A_N)\}$, where Q_i is question i and A_i is answer i. Example translations estimated from a real question and answer database using this approach are shown in Table 10.2. Pointers to algorithms for estimating translation probabilities given a parallel corpus are given in the "References and Further Reading" section at the end of this chapter.

In this section, we assumed that people in a community would provide answers to questions, and an archive of questions and answers would be created by this process. As we mentioned in Chapter 1, it is also possible to design *question answering* systems that find answers for a more limited range of questions in the text of large document corpora. We describe these systems in more detail in Chapter 11.

10.3.4 Collaborative Searching

The final community-based search task that we consider is *collaborative searching*. As the name suggests, collaborative searching involves a group of users with a common goal searching together in a collaborative setting. There are many situations where collaborative searching can be useful. For example, consider a group of students working together on a world history report. In order to complete the report, the students must do background research on the report topic. Traditionally, the students would split the topic into various subtopics, assign each group member one of the subtopics, and then each student would search the Web or an online library catalog, independently of the other students, for information and resources on their specific subtopic. In the end, the students would have to combine all of the information from the various subtopics to form a coherent report. Each student would learn a great deal about his or her particular subtopic, and no single student would have a thorough understanding of all of the material in the report. Clearly, every student would end up learning a great deal more if the research process were more collaborative. A collaborative search system would allow the students to search the Web and other resources together, so that every member of the group could contribute and understand every subtopic of the report. Collaborative search can also be useful within companies, where colleagues must collect information about various aspects of a particular project. Last, but certainly not least, recreational searchers may find collaborative search systems particularly useful. Suppose you and your friends are planning a party. A collaborative search system would help everyone coordinate information-gathering tasks, such as finding recipes, choosing decorations, selecting music, deciding on invitations, etc.

There are two common types of collaborative search scenarios, depending on where the search participants are physically located with respect to each other. The first scenario, known as *co-located* collaborative search, occurs when all of the search participants are in the same location, such as the same office or same library, sitting in front of the same computer. The other scenario, known as *remote* collaborative searching, occurs when the search participants are physically located in different locations. The participants may be in different offices within the same building, different buildings within the same city, or even in completely different countries across the globe. Figure 10.5 provides a schematic for these scenarios. Both situations present different challenges, and the systems developed for each have different requirements in terms of how they support search. To illustrate this, we briefly describe two examples of collaborative search systems.

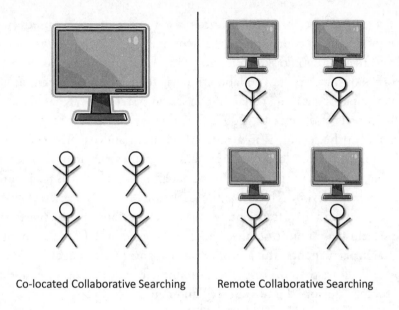

Co-located Collaborative Searching | Remote Collaborative Searching

Fig. 10.5. Overview of the two common collaborative search scenarios. On the left is co-located collaborative search, which involves multiple participants in the same location at the same time. On the right is remote collaborative search, where participants are in different locations and not necessarily all online and searching at the same time.

The CoSearch system developed by Amershi and Morris (2008) is a co-located collaborative search system. The system has a primary display, keyboard, and mouse that is controlled by the person called the "driver", who leads the search task. Additional participants, called "observers", each have a mouse or a Bluetooth-enabled[4] mobile phone. The driver begins the session by submitting a query to a search engine. The search results are displayed on the primary display and on the display of any user with a mobile phone. Observers may click on search results, which adds the corresponding page into a shared "page queue." This allows every participant to recommend which page should be navigated to next in a convenient, centralized manner, rather than giving total control to the driver. In addition to the page queue, there is also a "query queue," where participants submit new queries. The query queue provides everyone with a list of potentially useful queries to explore next, and provides the driver with a set of options generated

---

[4] Bluetooth is the name of a short-range wireless technology that allows for communication between devices, such as laptops, printers, PDAs, and mobile phones.

collectively by the group. The CoSearch system provides many useful ways for a group of people to collaboratively search together, since it allows everyone to work toward a common task, while at the same time preserving the important division of labor that is part of collaboration, via the use of multiple input devices.

An example of a remote collaborative search system is SearchTogether, developed by Morris and Horvitz (2007b). In this system, it is assumed that every participant in the session is in a different location and has his own computer. Furthermore, unlike co-located search, which assumes that all of the participants are present during the entire search session, remote search makes no assumptions about whether everyone is online at the same time. Therefore, whereas co-located search sessions tend to be transient, remote search sessions can be persistent. Users of the system may submit queries, which are logged and shared with all of the other search participants. This allows all participants to see what others are searching for, and allows them to resubmit or refine the queries. Users can add ratings (e.g., "thumbs up" or "thumbs down") and comments to pages that are viewed during the search process, which will be aggregated and made available to other participants. In addition, a participant may explicitly recommend a given page to another participant, which will then show up in her recommended pages list. Therefore, the SearchTogether system provides most of the functionality of the CoSearch system, except it is adapted to the specific needs of remote collaboration. One particular advantage of a persistent search session is that new participants, who were not previously part of the search process, can quickly be brought up to speed by browsing the query history, page ratings, comments, and recommendations.

As we have outlined, collaborative search systems provide users with a unique set of tools to effectively collaborate with each other during a co-located or remote search session. Despite the promise of such systems, very few commercial collaborative search systems exist today. However, such systems are beginning to gain considerable attention in the research community. Given this, and the increasingly collaborative nature of the online experience, it may be only a matter of time before collaborative search systems become more widely available.

10.4 Filtering and Recommending

10.4.1 Document Filtering

As we mentioned previously, one part of social search applications is representing individual users' interests and preferences. One of the earliest applications that focused on user profiles was document filtering. Document filtering, often simply referred to as *filtering*, is an alternative to the standard ad hoc search paradigm. In ad hoc search, users typically enter many different queries over time, while the document collection stays relatively static. In filtering, the user's information need stays the same, but the document collection itself is dynamic, with new documents arriving periodically. The goal of filtering, then, is to identify (filter) the relevant new documents and send them to the user. Filtering, as described in Chapter 3, is a *push* application.

Filtering is also an example of a supervised learning task, where the profile plays the part of the training data and the incoming documents are the test items that need to be classified as "relevant" or "not relevant." However, unlike a spam detection model, which would take thousands of labeled emails as input, a filtering system profile may only consist of a single query, making the learning task even more challenging. For this reason, filtering systems typically use more specialized techniques than general classification techniques in order to overcome the lack of training data.

Although they are not as widely used as standard web search engines, there are many examples of real-world document filtering systems. For example, many news sites offer filtering services. These services include alerting users when there is breaking news, when an article is published in a certain new category (e.g., sports or politics), or when an article is published about a certain topic, which is typically specified using one or more keywords (e.g., "terrorism" or "global warming"). The alerts come in the form of emails, SMS (text messages), or even personalized news feeds, thereby allowing the user to keep up with topics of interest without having to continually check the news site for updates or enter numerous queries to the site's search engine. Therefore, filtering provides a way of personalizing the search experience by maintaining a number of long-term information needs.

Document filtering systems have two key components. First, the user's long-term information needs must be accurately represented. This is done by constructing a *profile* for every information need. Second, given a document that has just arrived in the system, a decision mechanism must be devised for identifying which are the relevant profiles for that document. This decision mechanism must not only be efficient, especially since there are likely to be thousands of profiles, but it must also be highly accurate. The filtering system should not miss relevant documents and, perhaps even more importantly, should not be continually alerting users about non-relevant documents. In the remainder of this section, we describe the details of these two components.

Profiles

In web search, users typically enter a very short query. The search engine then faces the daunting challenge of determining the user's underlying information need from this very sparse piece of information. There are numerous reasons why most search engines today expect information needs to be specified as short keyword queries. However, one of the primary reasons is that users do not want to (or do not have the time to) type in long, complex queries for each and every one of their information needs. Many simple, non-persistent information needs can often be satisfied using a short query to a search engine. Filtering systems, on the other hand, cater to long-term information needs. Therefore, users may be more willing to spend more time specifying their information need in greater detail in order to ensure highly relevant results over an extended period of time. The representation of a user's long-term information need is often called a *filtering profile* or just a *profile*.

What actually makes up a filtering profile is quite general and depends on the particular domain of interest. Profiles may be as simple as a Boolean or keyword query. Profiles may also contain documents that are known to be relevant or non-relevant to the user's information need. Furthermore, they may contain other items, such as social tags and related named entities. Finally, profiles may also have one or more relational constraints, such as "published before 1990", "price in the $10–$25 range", and so on. Whereas the other constraints described act as soft filters, relational constraints of this form act as hard filters that must be satisfied in order for a document to be retrieved.

Although there are many different ways to represent a profile, the underlying filtering model typically dictates the actual representation. Filtering models are very similar to the retrieval models described in Chapter 7. In fact, many of the widely used filtering models are simply retrieval models where the profile takes the place of the query. There are two common types of filtering models. The first are *static* models. Here, static refers to the fact that the user's profile does not change over time, and therefore the same model can always be applied. The second are *adaptive* models, where the user's profile is constantly changing over time. This scenario requires the filtering model to be dynamic over time as new information is incorporated into the profile.

Static filtering models

As we just described, *static filtering models* work under the assumption that the filtering profile remains static over time. In some ways, this makes the filtering process easier, but in other ways it makes it less robust. All of the popular static filtering models are derived from the standard retrieval models described in Chapter 7. However, unlike web search, filtering systems do not return a ranked list of documents for each profile. Instead, when a new document enters the system, the filtering system must decide whether or not it is relevant with respect to each profile. Figure 10.6 illustrates how a static filtering system works. As new documents arrive, they are compared to each profile. Arrows from a document to a profile indicate that the document was deemed relevant to the profile and returned to the user.

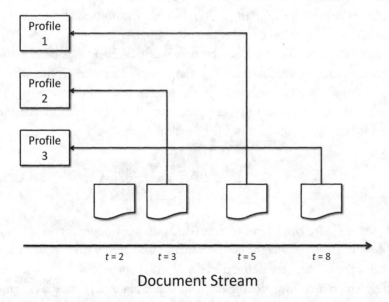

Fig. 10.6. Example of a static filtering system. Documents arrive over time and are compared against each profile. Arrows from documents to profiles indicate the document matches the profile and is retrieved.

In the most simple case, a Boolean retrieval model can be used. Here, the filtering profile would simply consist of a Boolean query, and a new document would be retrieved for the profile only if it satisfied the query. The Boolean model, despite its simplicity, can be used effectively for document filtering, especially where precision is important. In fact, many web-based filtering systems make use of a Boolean retrieval model.

One of the biggest drawbacks of the Boolean model is the low level of recall. Depending on the filtering domain, users may prefer to have good coverage over very high precision results. There are various possible solutions to this problem, including using the vector space model, the probabilistic model, BM25, or language modeling. All of these models can be extended for use with filtering by specifying a profile using a keyword query or a set of documents. Directly applying these models to filtering, however, is not trivial, since each of them returns a score, not a "retrieve" or "do not retrieve" answer as in the case of the Boolean model. One of the most widely used techniques for overcoming this problem is to use a score threshold to determine whether to retrieve a document. That is, only documents with a similarity score above the threshold will be retrieved. Such a threshold would have to be tuned in order to achieve good effectiveness. Many complex issues arise when applying a global score threshold, such as ensuring that scores are comparable across profiles and over time.

As a concrete example, we describe how static filtering can be done within the language modeling framework for retrieval. Given a static profile, which may consist of a single keyword query, multiple queries, a set of documents, or some combination of these, we must first estimate a profile language model denoted by P. There are many ways to do this. One possibility is:

$$ P(w|P) = \frac{(1-\lambda)}{\sum_{i=1}^{K} \alpha_i} \sum_{i=1}^{K} \alpha_i \frac{f_{w,T_i}}{|T_i|} + \lambda \frac{c_w}{|C|} $$

where $T_1, \ldots, T_k$ are the pieces of text (e.g., queries, documents) that make up the profile, and α_i is the weight (importance) associated with text T_i. The other variables and parameters are defined in detail in Chapter 7.

Then, given an incoming document, a document language model (D) must be estimated. We again follow the discussion in Chapter 7 and estimate D using the following:

$$ P(w|D) = (1-\lambda) \frac{f_{w,D}}{|D|} + \lambda \frac{c_w}{|C|} $$

Documents can then be ranked according to the negative KL-divergence between the profile language model (P) and the document language model (D) as follows:

$$-KL(P||D) = \sum_{w \in V} P(w|P) \log P(w|D) - \sum_{w \in V} P(w|P) \log P(w|P)$$

Document D is then delivered to profile P if $-KL(P||D) \geq t$, where t is some relevance threshold.

Document filtering can also be treated as a machine learning problem. At its core, filtering is a classification task that often has a very small amount of training data (i.e., the profile). The task is then to build a binary classifier that determines whether an incoming document is relevant to the profile. However, training data would be necessary in order to properly learn such a model. For this task, the training data comes in the form of binary relevance judgments over profile/document pairs. Any of the classification techniques described in Chapter 9 can be used. Suppose that a Support Vector Machine with a linear kernel is used; the scoring function would then have the following form:

$$s(P; D) = w \cdot f(P, D) = w_1 f_1(P, D) + w_2 f_2(P, D) + \ldots + w_d f_d(P, D)$$

where $w_1, \ldots, w_d$ are the set of weights learned during the SVM training process, and $f_1(P, D), \ldots, f_d(P, D)$ are the set of features extracted from the profile/document pair. Many of the features that have been successfully applied to text classification, such as unigrams and bigrams, can also be applied to filtering. Given a large amount of training data, it is likely that a machine learning approach will outperform the simple language modeling approach just described. However, when there is little or no training data, the language modeling approach is a good choice.

Adaptive filtering models

Static filtering profiles are assumed not to change over time. In such a setting, a user would be able to create a profile, but could not update it to better reflect his information need. The only option would be to delete the profile and create a new one that would hopefully produce better results. This type of system is rigid and not very robust.

Adaptive filtering is an alternative filtering technique that allows for dynamic profiles. This technique provides a mechanism for updating the profile over time.

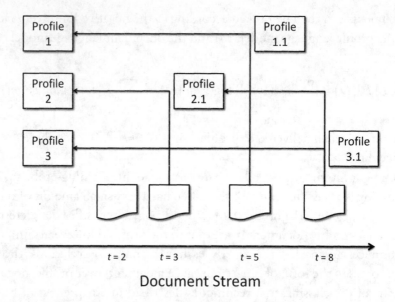

Fig. 10.7. Example of an adaptive filtering system. Documents arrive over time and are compared against each profile. Arrows from documents to profiles indicate the document matches the profile and is retrieved. Unlike static filtering, where profiles are static over time, profiles are updated dynamically (e.g., when a new match occurs).

Profiles may be either updated using input from the user or done automatically based on user behavior, such as click or browsing patterns. There are various reasons why it may be useful to update a profile as time goes on. For example, users may want to fine-tune their information need in order to find more specific types of information. Therefore, adaptive filtering techniques are more robust than static filtering techniques and are designed to adapt to find more relevant documents over the life span of a profile. Figure 10.7 shows an example adaptive filtering system for the same set of profiles and incoming documents from Figure 10.6. Unlike the static filtering case, when a document is delivered to a profile, the user provides feedback about the document, and the profile is then updated and used for matching future incoming documents.

As Figure 10.7 suggests, one of the most common ways to adapt a profile is in response to user feedback. User feedback may come in various forms, each of which can be used in different ways to update the user profile. In order to provide a concrete example of how profiles can be adapted in response to user feedback, we consider the case where users provide *relevance feedback* (see Chapter 6) on documents. That is, for some set of documents, such as the set of documents retrieved for a given profile, the user explicitly states whether or not the document is relevant to the profile. Given the relevance feedback information, there are a number of ways to update the profile. As before, how the profile is represented and subsequently updated largely depends on the underlying retrieval model that is being used.

As described in Chapter 7, the Rocchio algorithm can be used to perform relevance feedback in the vector space model. Therefore, if profiles are represented as vectors in a vector space model, Rocchio's algorithm can be applied to update the profiles when the user provides relevance feedback information. Given a profile P, a set of non-relevant feedback documents (denoted $Nonrel$), and a set of relevant feedback documents (denoted Rel), the adapted profile P' is computed as follows:

$$P' = \alpha.P + \beta.\frac{1}{|Rel|} \sum_{D_i \in Rel} D_i - \gamma.\frac{1}{|Nonrel|} \sum_{D_i \in Nonrel} D_i$$

where D_i is the vector representing document i, and α, β, and γ are parameters that control how to trade off the weighting between the initial profile, the relevant documents, and the non-relevant documents.

Chapter 7 also described how *relevance models* can be used with language modeling for pseudo-relevance feedback. However, relevance models can also be used for true relevance feedback as follows:

$$P(w|P) = \frac{1}{|Rel|} \sum_{D_i \in Rel} \sum_{D \in \mathcal{C}} P(w|D)P(D_i|D)$$

$$\approx \frac{1}{|Rel|} \sum_{D_i \in Rel} P(w|D_i)$$

where $\mathcal{C}$ is the set of documents in the collection, Rel is the set of documents that have been judged relevant, D_i is document i, and $P(D_i|D)$ is the probability that document D_i is generated from document D's language model. The approximation ($\approx$) can be made because D_i is a document, and $P(D_i|D)$ is going to be 1 or very close to 1 when $D_i = D$ and nearly 0 for most other documents. Therefore, the probability of w in the profile is simply the average probability of w in the language models of the relevant documents. Unlike the Rocchio algorithm, the non-relevant documents are not considered.

If a classification technique, such as one of those described in Chapter 9, is used for filtering, then an *online learning* algorithm can be used to adapt the classification model as new user feedback arrives. Online learning algorithms update model parameters, such as the hyperplane w in SVMs, by considering only one new item or a batch of new items. These algorithms are different from standard supervised learning algorithms because they do not have a "memory." That is, once an input has been used for training, it is discarded and cannot be explicitly used in the future to update the model parameters. Only the new training inputs are used for training. The details of online learning methods are beyond the scope of this book. However, several references are given in the "References and Further Reading" section at the end of this chapter.

Model	Profile Representation	Profile Updating
Boolean	Boolean Expression	N/A
Vector Space	Vector	Rocchio
Language Modeling	Probability Distribution	Relevance Modeling
Classification	Model Parameters	Online Learning

Table 10.3. Summary of static and adaptive filtering models. For each, the profile representation and profile updating algorithm are given.

Both static and adaptive filtering, therefore, can be considered special cases of many of the retrieval models and techniques described in Chapters 6, 7, and 9. Table 10.3 summarizes the various filtering models, including how profiles are represented and updated. In practice, the vector space model and language modeling have been shown to be effective and easy to implement, both for static and adaptive filtering. The classification models are likely to be more robust in highly dynamic environments. However, as with all classification techniques, the model requires training data to learn an effective model.

Fast filtering with millions of profiles

In a full-scale production system, there may be thousands or possibly even millions of profiles that must be matched against incoming documents. Fortunately, standard information retrieval indexing and query evaluation strategies can be applied to perform this matching efficiently. In most situations, profiles are represented as a set of keywords or a set of feature values, which allows each profile to be indexed using the strategies discussed in Chapter 5. Scalable indexing infrastructures can easily handle millions, or possibly even billions, of profiles. Then, once the profiles are indexed, an incoming document can be transformed into a "query", which again is represented as either a set of terms or a set of features. The "query" is then run against the index of profiles, retrieving a ranked list of profiles. The document is then delivered to only those profiles whose score, with respect to the "query", is above the relevance threshold previously discussed.

Evaluation

Many of the evaluation metrics described in Chapter 8 can be used to evaluate filtering systems. However, it is important to choose appropriate metrics, because filtering differs in a number of ways from standard search tasks, such as news or web search. One of the most important differences is the fact that filtering systems do not produce a ranking of documents for each profile. Instead, relevant documents are simply delivered to the profile as they arrive. Therefore, measures such as precision at rank k and mean average precision are not appropriate for the task. Instead, set-based measures are typically used.

	Relevant	Non-Relevant
Retrieved	TP	FP
Not retrieved	FN	TN

Table 10.4. Contingency table for the possible outcomes of a filtering system. Here, TP (true positive) is the number of relevant documents retrieved, FN (false negative) is the number of relevant documents not retrieved, FP (false positive) is the number of non-relevant documents retrieved, and TN (true negative) is the number of non-relevant documents not retrieved.

Table 10.4, which is similar to Table 8.3 in Chapter 8, shows all of the possibilities for an incoming document with respect to some profile. A document may be either relevant or non-relevant, as indicated by the column headings. Furthermore, a document may be either retrieved or not retrieved by the filtering system, as indicated by the row headings. All of the filtering evaluation metrics described here can be formulated in terms of the cells in this table.

The simplest way to evaluate a filtering system is using the classical evaluation measures of precision and recall, which correspond to $\frac{TP}{TP+FP}$ and $\frac{TP}{TP+FN}$, respectively. The F measure, which is the harmonic mean of precision and recall, is also commonly used. Typically, these measures are computed for each profile in the system and then averaged together.[5]

It is possible to define a more general evaluation metric that combines each of the four cells in Table 10.4 in the following way:

$$U = \alpha \cdot TP + \beta \cdot TN + \delta \cdot FP + \gamma \cdot FN$$

where the coefficients α, β, δ, and γ can be set in different ways to achieve different trade-offs between the various components of the measure. One setting of the coefficients that has been widely used in filtering experiments is $\alpha = 2$, $\beta = 0$, $\delta = -1$, and $\gamma = 0$. This results in true positives (relevant retrieved documents) being given weight 2 and false negatives (relevant documents that were not retrieved) being penalized by a factor of 1. Of course, different coefficients can be chosen based on the actual costs of the underlying task.

10.4.2 Collaborative Filtering

Static and adaptive filtering are not social tasks, in that profiles are assumed to be independent of each other. If we now consider the complex relationships that exist between profiles, additional useful information can be obtained. For example, suppose that we have an adaptive filtering system with two profiles, which we call profile A (corresponding to user A) and profile B (corresponding to user B). If both user A and B judged a large number of the same documents to be relevant and/or non-relevant to their respective profiles, then we can infer that the two profiles are similar to each other. We can then use this information to improve the relevance of the matches to both user A and B. For example, if user A judged a document to be relevant to profile A, then it is likely that the document will also be relevant to profile B, and so it should probably be retrieved, even if the score assigned to it by the adaptive filtering system is below the predetermined threshold. Such a system is social, in the sense that a document is returned to the user based on both the document's topical relevance to the profile and any judgments or feedback that users with similar profiles have given about the document.

Filtering that considers the relationship between profiles (or between users) and uses this information to improve how incoming items are matched to profiles (or users) is called *collaborative filtering*. Collaborative filtering is often used as a component of *recommender systems*. Recommender systems use collaborative

---

[5] Recall that this type of averaging is known as *macroaveraging*.

filtering algorithms to recommend items (such as books or movies) to users. Many major commercial websites, such as Amazon.com and Netflix, make heavy use of recommender systems to provide users with a list of recommended products in the hopes that the user will see something she may like but may not have known about, and consequently make a purchase. Therefore, such systems can be valuable both to the end users, who are likely to see relevant products, including some that they may not have considered before, and to search engine companies, who can use such systems to increase revenue.

In the remainder of this section, we focus on collaborative filtering algorithms for recommender systems. It is important to note that these algorithms differ from static and adaptive filtering algorithms in a number of ways. First, when collaborative filtering algorithms are used for making recommendations, they typically associate a single profile with each user. That is, the user is the profile. Second, static and adaptive filtering systems would make a binary decision (retrieve or do not retrieve) for each incoming document, but collaborative filtering algorithms for recommender systems provide *ratings* for items. These ratings may be 0 (relevant) and 1 (non-relevant) or more complex, such as ratings on a scale of 1 through 5. Finally, collaborative filtering algorithms for recommender systems provide a rating for every incoming item, as well as every item in the database for which the current user has not explicitly provided a judgment. On the other hand, static and adaptive filtering algorithms only decide whether or not to send incoming documents to users and never retrospectively examine older documents to determine whether they should be retrieved.

Figure 10.8 represents a virtual space of users, where users with similar preferences and tastes are close to each other. The dialog boxes drawn above each user's head denote their preference for some item, such as a movie about tropical fish. Those users who have not rated the movie have question marks in their dialog boxes. It is the job of the collaborative filtering algorithm to predict as accurately as possible what rating these users would give to the movie.

Collaborative filtering is conceptually simple, but the details can be difficult to get correct. For example, one must decide how to represent users and how to measure the similarity between them. After similar users have been identified, the user ratings must be combined in some way. Another important issue concerns how collaborative filtering and, in particular, recommender systems should be evaluated. We will address these issues in the remainder of this section while describing the details of two collaborative filtering algorithms that have been used successfully in recommender systems.

Fig. 10.8. A set of users within a recommender system. Users and their ratings for some item are given. Users with question marks above their heads have not yet rated the item. It is the goal of the recommender system to fill in these question marks.

Rating with user clusters

In both of the algorithms that follow, we assume that we have a set of users $\mathcal{U}$ and a set of items $\mathcal{I}$. Furthermore, $r_u(i)$ is user u's rating of item i, and $\hat{r}_u(i)$ is our system's prediction for user u's rating for item i. Note that $r_u(i)$ is typically undefined when user u has not provided a rating for item i, although, as we will describe later, this does not need to be the case. Therefore, the general collaborative filtering task is to compute $\hat{r}_u(i)$ for every user/item pair that does not have an explicit rating. We assume that the only input we are given is the explicit ratings $r_u(i)$, which will be used for making predictions. Furthermore, for simplicity, we will assume that ratings are integers in the range of 1 through M, although most of the algorithms described will work equally well for continuous ratings.

One simple approach is to first apply one of the clustering algorithms described in Chapter 9 to the set of users. Typically, users are represented by their rating vectors $r_u = [r_u(i_1) \ldots r_u(i_{|\mathcal{U}|})]$. However, since not all users judge all items, not every entry of the vector r_u may be defined, which makes it challenging to compute distance measures, such as cosine similarity. Therefore, the distance measures must be modified to account for the missing values. The simplest way to do this is to fill in all of the missing ratings with some value, such as 0. Another possibility is to fill in the missing values with the user's average rating, denoted by $\bar{r}_u$, or the item's average rating.

One of the common similarity measures used for clustering users is the *correlation* measure, which is computed as follows:

$$\frac{\sum_{i \in I_u \cap I_{u'}} (r_u(i) - \hat{r}_u) \cdot (r_{u'}(i) - \hat{r}_{u'})}{\sqrt{\sum_{i \in I_u \cap I_{u'}} (r_u(i) - \hat{r}_u)^2 \sum_{i \in I_u \cap I_{u'}} (r_{u'}(i) - \hat{r}_{u'})^2}}$$

where I_u and $I_{u'}$ are the sets of items that users u and u' judged, respectively, which means that the summations are only over the set of items that both user u and u' judged. Correlation takes on values in the range –1 to 1, with 1 being achieved when two users have identical ratings for the same set of items, and –1 being achieved when two users rate items exactly the opposite of each other.

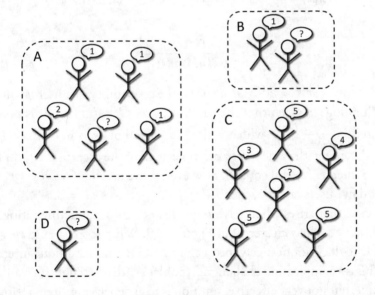

Fig. 10.9. Illustration of collaborative filtering using clustering. Groups of similar users are outlined with dashed lines. Users and their ratings for some item are given. In each group, there is a single user who has not judged the item. For these users, the unjudged item is assigned an automatic rating based on the ratings of similar users.

In Figure 10.9, we provide a hypothetical clustering of the users, denoted by dashed boundaries. After users have been clustered, any user within a cluster that has not judged some item could be assigned the average rating for the item among other users in the cluster. For example, the user who has not judged the tropical fish movie in cluster A would be assigned a rating of 1.25, which is the average of the ratings given to the movie by the four other users in cluster A. This can be stated mathematically as:

$$\hat{r}_u(i) = \frac{1}{|Cluster(u)|} \sum_{u' \in Cluster(u)} r_{u'}(i)$$

where $Cluster(u)$ represents the cluster that user u belongs to.

Averaging the ratings of a group of users is one simple way of aggregating the ratings within a cluster. Another possible approach is to use the expected rating of the item, given the ratings of the other users within the cluster, which is calculated as:

$$\hat{r}_u(i) = \sum_{x=1}^{M} x \cdot P(r_u(i) = x | C = Cluster(u))$$

$$= \sum_{x=1}^{M} x \cdot \frac{|u' : r_{u'}(i) = x|}{|Cluster(u)|}$$

where $P(r_u(i) = x | C = Cluster(u))$ is the probability that user u will rate the item with rating m, given that they are in cluster $Cluster(u)$. This probability is estimated as $\frac{|u':r_{u'}(i)=x|}{|Cluster(u)|}$, which is the proportion of users in $Cluster(u)$ who have rated item i with value x. For example, if all of the users in $Cluster(u)$ rate the item 5, then $\hat{r}_u(i)$ will equal 5. However, if five users in $Cluster(u)$ rate the item 1 and five users rate it 5, then $\hat{r}_u(i) = 1 \cdot \frac{5}{10} + 5 \cdot \frac{5}{10} = 3$.

One issue that arises when relying on clustering for predicting ratings is very sparse clusters, such as cluster D in Figure 10.9. What score should be assigned to a user who does not fit nicely into a cluster and has rather unique interests and tastes? This is a complex and challenging problem with no straightforward answer. One simple, but not very effective, solution is to assign average item ratings to every unrated item for the user. Unfortunately, this explicitly assumes that "unique" users are average, which is actually unlikely to be true.

Rating with nearest neighbors

An alternative strategy to using clusters is to use nearest neighbors for predicting user ratings. This approach makes use of the K nearest neighbors clustering technique described in Chapter 9. To predict ratings for user u, we first find the K

users who are closest to the user according to some similarity measure. Once we have found the nearest neighbors, we will use the ratings (and similarities) of the neighbors for prediction as follows:

$$\hat{r}_u(i) = \overline{r}_u + \frac{1}{\sum_{u' \in \mathcal{N}(u)} sim(u, u')} \sum_{u' \in \mathcal{N}(u)} sim(u, u')(r_{u'}(i) - \overline{r}_{u'})$$

where $sim(u, u')$ is the similarity of user u and u', and $\mathcal{N}(u)$ is the set of u's nearest neighbors. This algorithm predicts user u's rating of item i by first including the user's average item rating ($\overline{r}_u$). Then, for every user u' in u's nearest neighborhood, $r_{u'}(i) - \overline{r}_{u'}$ is weighted by $sim(u, u')$ and added into the predicted value. You may wonder why $r_{u'}(i) - \overline{r}_{u'}$ is used instead of $r_{u'}(i)$. The difference is used because ratings are relative. Certain users may very rarely rate any item with 1, whereas other users may never rate an item below 3. Therefore, it is best to measure ratings relative to a given user's average rating for the purpose of prediction.

Although the approaches using clusters and nearest neighbors are similar in nature, the nearest-neighbors approach tends to be more robust with respect to noise. Furthermore, when using nearest neighbors, there is no need to choose a clustering cost function, only a similarity function, thereby simplifying things. Empirical results suggest that predicting ratings using nearest neighbors and the correlation similarity measure tends to outperform the various clustering approaches across a range of data sets. Based on this evidence, the nearest neighbor approach, using the correlation similarity function, is a good choice for a wide range of practical collaborative filtering tasks.

Evaluation

Collaborative filtering recommender systems can be evaluated in a number of ways. Standard information retrieval metrics, such as those described in Chapter 8, can be used, including accuracy, precision, recall, and the F measure.

However, standard information retrieval measures are very strict, since they require the system to predict exactly the correct value. Consider the case when the actual user rating is 4 and system A predicts 3 and system B predicts 1. The accuracy of both system A and B is zero, since they both failed to get exactly the right answer. However, system A is much closer to the correct answer than system B. For this reason, a number of evaluation metrics that consider the difference between the actual and predicted ratings have been used. One such measure is *absolute error*, which is computed as:

$$ABS = \frac{1}{|\mathcal{U}||\mathcal{I}|} \sum_{u \in \mathcal{U}} \sum_{i \in \mathcal{I}} |\hat{r}_u(i) - r_u(i)|$$

where the sums are over the set of user/item pairs for which predictions have been made. The other measure is called *mean squared error*, which can be calculated as:

$$MSE = \frac{1}{|\mathcal{U}||\mathcal{I}|} \sum_{u \in \mathcal{U}} \sum_{i \in \mathcal{I}} (\hat{r}_u(i) - r_u(i))^2$$

The biggest difference between absolute error and mean squared error is that mean squared error penalizes incorrect predictions more heavily, since the penalty is squared.

These are the most commonly used evaluation metrics for collaborative filtering recommender systems. So, in the end, which measure should you use? Unfortunately, that is not something we can easily answer. As we have repeated many times throughout the course of this book, the proper evaluation measure depends a great deal on the underlying task.

10.5 Peer-to-Peer and Metasearch

10.5.1 Distributed Search

We have described social search applications that involve networks or communities of people, but a number of tools for finding and sharing information are implemented using communities of "nodes," where each node can store and search information, and communicate with other nodes. The simplest form of this type of distributed search environment is a *metasearch engine*, where each node is a complete web search engine and the results from a relatively small number of different search engines are combined with the aim of improving the effectiveness of the ranking. A *peer-to-peer* (P2P) search application, on the other hand, typically has a large number of nodes, each with a relatively small amount of information and only limited knowledge about other nodes.

In contrast to search applications that use only a single document collection, all distributed search[6] applications must carry out three additional, important functions:

---

[6] Often called *distributed information retrieval* or *federated search*.

- *Resource representation*: Generating a description of the information resource (i.e., the documents) stored at a node.
- *Resource selection*: Selecting one or more resources to search based on their descriptions.
- *Result merging*: Merging the ranked result lists from the searches carried out at the nodes containing the selected information resources.

These functions are carried out by designated nodes that depend on the architecture of the application. The simplest assumption is that there will be one special node that provides the directory services of selection and merging, and every other node is responsible for providing its own representation. For a metasearch application with the architecture shown in Figure 10.10, the resource representation and selection functions are trivial. Rather than selecting which search engines to use for a particular query, the query will instead be broadcast by the metasearch engine to *all* engines being used by the application. For each search engine, this is done using the application programming interface (API) and transforming the query into the appropriate format for the engine. This transformation is generally very simple since most search engine query languages are similar.

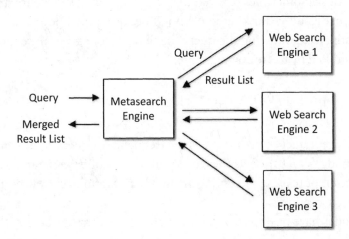

Fig. 10.10. Metasearch engine architecture. The query is broadcast to multiple web search engines and result lists are merged.

More generally, in a distributed search environment, each node can be represented by the probabilities of occurrence of the words in the documents stored at that node. This is the unigram *language model* that was used to represent documents in Chapter 7. In this case, there is only one language model representing *all* the documents at that node, and the probabilities are estimated using word frequencies summed over the documents. In other words, the documents stored at that node are treated as one large document to estimate the language model. This representation is compact, and has been shown to perform well in distributed retrieval experiments. In some applications, nodes may not be actively cooperating in the distributed search protocol (process) and, in that case, only provide a search API. A language model description of the contents of those nodes can still be generated by *query-based sampling*. This involves generating a series of queries to retrieve a sample of documents from the node, which are used to estimate the language model. Different strategies have been used for selecting query terms, but even queries based on random selection from the terms in retrieved documents have been shown to generate an accurate language model.

Resource selection in a general distributed search application involves first ranking the nodes using their representations, and then selecting the top k ranked nodes, or all nodes that score above some threshold value. Since we are representing the nodes using a language model, the natural ranking algorithm to use is *query likelihood*. This is sometimes referred to in the distributed search literature as the KL-divergence resource ranking algorithm, since query likelihood is a special case of KL-divergence. Following the query likelihood score given in section 7.3.1, a node N is ranked by the following score:

$$\log P(Q|N) = \sum_{i=1}^{n} \log \frac{f_{q_i,N} + \mu P(q_i|C)}{|N| + \mu}$$

where there are n query terms, $f_{q_i,N}$ is the frequency of query term q_i in the documents at node N, $P(q_i|C)$ is the background probability estimated using some large collection of text C, and $|N|$ is the number of term occurrences in the documents stored at node N.

After nodes have been selected, local searches are carried out at each of those nodes. The results of these searches must be merged to produce a single ranking. If the same retrieval model (e.g., query likelihood) and the same global statistics (e.g., the background model) are used for each local search, the merge can be based directly on the local scores. If different global statistics are used in each node, such as calculating *idf* weights using only the documents at that node, then the local scores can be recalculated by sharing these statistics before merging. If different retrieval models are used, or if global statistics cannot be shared, then the scores must be *normalized* before merging. A common heuristic approach to score normalization is to use the score from the resource ranking of the node that returned a document d, R_d, to modify the local document score, S_d, as follows:

$$S'_d = S_d(\alpha + (1 - \alpha)R'_d)$$

where α is a constant, and R'_d is the resource ranking score normalized with respect to other resource scores. One way of normalizing the resource score is to calculate the minimum and maximum possible scores for a given query, R_{min} and R_{max}, and then:

$$R'_d = (R_d - R_{min})/(R_{max} - R_{min})$$

It is also possible to learn a score-normalizing function by comparing scores from a sample document collection to the local scores (Si & Callan, 2003).

Result merging in a metasearch application is somewhat different than general distributed search. The two main characteristics of metasearch are that document scores from local searches generally are not available, and local searches are often done over collections with very similar content. A metasearch engine that uses multiple web search engines, for example, is essentially using different retrieval models on the same collection (the Web). In this case, local searches produce ranked lists that have high *overlap* in terms of the documents that are retrieved. Effective methods of combining ranked result lists have been developed specifically for this situation. The most well-studied methods can be described by the following formula, giving the modified score for a document, S'_d, as a function of the scores $S_{d,i}$ produced by the ith search engine:

$$S'_d = n_d^\gamma \sum_{i=1}^{k} S_{d,i}$$

where n_d is the number of search engines that returned document d in the result list, $\gamma = (-1, 0, 1)$, and there are k search engines that returned results. When $\gamma = -1$, the modified score is the average of the local search scores; when $\gamma = 0$, the modified score is the sum of the local scores; and when $\gamma = 1$, the modified score is the sum of the local scores weighted by the number of search engines that returned document d. The last variation is known as *CombMNZ* (combine and multiply by the number of non-zero results) and has been shown to be effective in many search engine combination experiments.

In a typical metasearch application, scores are not available, and document ranks are used instead. In this case, the CombMNZ formula with scores based on ranks can be used. This means, for example, that if m documents are retrieved in a result list, the score for a document at rank r would be $(m - r + 1)/m$. This rank-based CombMNZ produces a merged ranking with reasonable effectiveness, although it is worse than a score-based combination. More effective rank-based combinations can be achieved with techniques based on voting procedures (Montague & Aslam, 2002).

In general, distributed search on non-overlapping collections can be comparable in effectiveness to searching a single collection that is the union of all the distributed collections. Of course, in most applications it would not be possible to build such a collection, but it does serve as a useful effectiveness benchmark. Experiments with TREC collections indicate that when average precision at rank 10 or 20 is used as the effectiveness measure, a distributed search that selected only 5–10 collections out of 200 was at least as effective as a centralized search, and sometimes was more effective (Powell et al., 2000). On the other hand, in a P2P testbed where the collection was distributed between 2,500 nodes and only 1% of these nodes were selected, the average precision at rank 10 was 25% lower than a centralized search (Lu & Callan, 2006).

Metasearch, which combines different searches on the same or very similar collections, generally improves retrieval effectiveness compared to a single search. TREC experiments with metasearch have shown improvements of 5–20% in mean average precision (depending on the query set used) for combinations using four different search engines, compared to the results from the single best search engine (Montague & Aslam, 2002).

10.5.2 P2P Networks

P2P networks are used in a range of applications involving communities of users, although they were popularized through file-sharing applications for music and video, such as KaZaA and BearShare. Search in file-sharing applications is generally restricted to finding files with a specified title or some other attribute, such as the artist for music files. In other words, they support simple exact-match retrieval (see Chapter 7). A number of different network architectures or *overlays*[7]

---

[7] A network overlay describes the logical connections between nodes implemented on top of the underlying physical network, which is usually the Internet.

have been developed to support this type of search. Figure 10.11 shows three of these architectures.

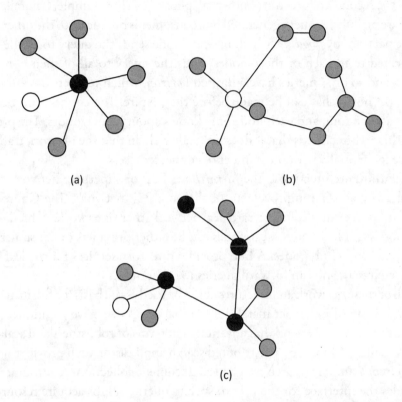

Fig. 10.11. Network architectures for distributed search: (a) central hub; (b) pure P2P; and (c) hierarchical P2P. Dark circles are hub or superpeer nodes, gray circles are provider nodes, and white circles are consumer nodes.

Each node in a P2P network can act as a client, a server, or both. Clients (information *consumers*) issue queries to initiate search. Servers (information *providers*) respond to queries with files (if they have a match) and may also route queries to other nodes. Servers that maintain information about the contents of other nodes provide a directory service and are called *hubs*. The architectures in Figure 10.11 differ primarily in how they route queries to providers. In the first architecture, which was the basis of the pioneering Napster file-sharing application, there is a single central hub that provides directory services. Consumers send queries to the hub, which routes them to nodes that contain the matching files. Although this architecture is efficient, it is also susceptible to failures or attacks that affect the central hub.

In the second architecture, known as "pure" P2P (for example, Gnutella 0.4[8]), there are no hubs. A query generated by a consumer is broadcast to the other nodes in the network by *flooding*, which means a node sends the query to all the nodes connected to it, each of those nodes sends the query to all of their connected nodes, and so on. Queries have a limited *horizon*, which restricts the number of network "hops" that can be made before they expire. The connections between nodes are random, and each node only knows about its neighbors. The problem with this architecture is that it does not scale well, in that the network traffic can grow exponentially with the number of connected users.

The third architecture is the *hierarchical* P2P or superpeer network, which was developed as an improvement of the pure P2P network. The Gnutella 0.6 standard is an example. In a hierarchical network, there is a two-level hierarchy of hub nodes and leaf nodes. Leaf nodes can be either providers or consumers, and connect only to hub nodes. A hub provides directory services for the leaf nodes connected to it, and can forward queries to other hubs.

All of these network architectures could be used as the basis for full distributed search instead of just exact match for file sharing. As we have mentioned, however, a hierarchical network has advantages in terms of robustness and scalability (Lu & Callan, 2006). For a distributed search application, each provider node in the network supports search over a local document collection. A consumer node provides the interface for the user to specify queries. Hubs acquire resource descriptions for neighboring hubs and providers, which they use to provide resource selection and result merging services. Specifically, resource descriptions for *neighborhoods* are used to route queries more efficiently than flooding, and resource descriptions for providers are used to rank the local document collections. Instead of selecting a fixed number of the top-ranked providers, in the P2P system each hub must be able to decide how many providers to use to respond to the query.

Neighborhood resource descriptions are an important part of the query routing process. A neighborhood of a hub H_i in the direction of a hub H_j is the set of hubs that a query can reach in a fixed number of hops. Figure 10.12 shows an example of a hub with three neighborhoods generated by a maximum of three hops. The advantage of this definition of neighborhoods is that the information about

---

[8] This means it is version 0.4 of the Gnutella standard. See http://en.wikipedia.org/wiki/Gnutella.

the providers that can be reached by traveling several hops beyond the immediate neighbors improves the effectiveness of query routing.

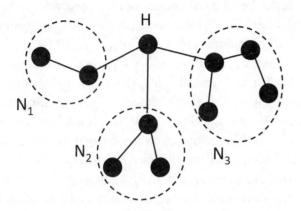

Fig. 10.12. Neighborhoods (N_i) of a hub node (H) in a hierarchical P2P network

The resource description for a hub is the aggregation of the resource descriptions of the providers that are connected to it. In other words, it is a language model recording probabilities of occurrences of words. A neighborhood resource description is the aggregation of the hub descriptions in the neighborhood, but a hub's contribution is reduced based on the number of hops to the hub. In other words, the closest neighbor hubs contribute the most to the neighborhood description.

Retrieval experiments with distributed search implemented on a hierarchical P2P network show that effectiveness is comparable to searching using a centralized hub, which is the architecture we assumed in the last section. More specifically, using neighborhood and provider descriptions to select about 1% of the 2,500 nodes in a P2P testbed produced the same average precision as selecting 1% of the nodes using a centralized hub, with about one-third of the message traffic of a query-flooding protocol (Lu & Callan, 2006).

Another popular architecture for file-sharing systems that we have not mentioned is a *structured* network. These networks associate each data item with a key and distribute keys to nodes using a *distributed hash table* (DHT). Distributed hash tables can support only exact match searching, but since they are used in a number of applications, we describe briefly how they can be used to locate a file.

In a DHT, all keys and nodes are represented as m-bit numbers or identifiers. The name of a file is converted to a key using a hash function. The key and the associated file are stored at one or more nodes whose identifiers are "close" in value to the key. The definition of distance between keys depends on the specific DHT algorithm. In the Chord DHT, for example, the distance is the numeric difference between the two m-bit numbers (Balakrishnan et al., 2003).

To find a file, a query containing the key value of the file name is submitted to any node. Both storing and retrieving files relies on a node being able to forward requests to a node whose identifier is "closer" to the key. This guarantees that the request will eventually find the closest node. In Chord, keys are treated as points on a circle, and if k_1 and k_2 are the identifiers for two "adjacent" nodes, the node with identifier k_2 is responsible for all keys that fall between k_1 and k_2. Each node maintains a routing table containing the IP addresses of a node halfway around the key "circle" from the node's identifier, a node a quarter of the way around, a node an eighth of the way, etc. A node forwards a request for key k to the node from this table with the highest identifier not exceeding k. The structure of the routing table ensures that the node responsible for k can be found in $\mathcal{O}(log N)$ hops for N nodes.

References and Further Reading

Social search is growing in popularity amongst information retrieval researchers. In particular, there has been an increased interest in social tagging and collaborative online environments over the past few years. It is likely that this interest will continue to grow, given the amount of research and exploration of new applications that remains to be done.

The subject of the relative effectiveness of manual and automatic indexing has been discussed for many years in information retrieval, and dates back to the original Cranfield studies (Cleverdon, 1970). A number of papers, such as Rajashekar and Croft (1995), have shown the advantages of automatic indexing relative to manual indexing, and also that effectiveness improves when the two representations are combined. Several researchers have looked at the usefulness of tags and other types of metadata for improving search effectiveness. Research by Heymann, Koutrika, and Garcia-Molina (2008) showed that social media tags, such as those from deli.cio.us, are not useful for improving search, mainly due to poor coverage and the fact that most of the tags are already present as anchor text. Hawking and Zobel (2007) report similar results for other types of metadata, and discuss the implications for the semantic web.

Both Sahami and Heilman (2006) and Metzler et al. (2007) proposed similar techniques for matching short segments of text by expanding the representations to use web search results. Although these methods were evaluated in the context of query similarity, they can easily be applied to measuring the similarity between tags.

Tag clouds similar to Figure 10.2 can be generated by software available on the Web, such as Wordle.[9]

More details of the HITS algorithm described in this section for finding communities can be found in Gibson et al. (1998). Furthermore, Hopcroft et al. (2003) describe various agglomerative clustering approaches. Other work related to finding online communities includes that of Flake et al. (2000), which describes how a variety of community-finding approaches can be implemented efficiently. In addition, Borgs et al. (2004) looks at the problem of identifying community structure within newsgroups, while Almeida and Almeida (2004) propose a community-aware search engine. Finally, Leuski and Lavrenko (2006) describe how clustering and language modeling can be used to analyze the behavior and interactions of users in a virtual world.

---

[9] http://www.wordle.net/

Jeon et al. (2005) described the approach of question ranking for community-based question answering. Xue et al. (2008) extended this work with more effective estimation methods for the translation probabilities and showed that combining the archived questions and answers produced better rankings. The problem of answer quality and its effect on CQA is addressed in Jeon et al. (2006). Agichtein et al. (2008) incorporate more features into a prediction of question and answer quality, and show that features derived from the community graph of people who ask and answer questions are very important.

The concept of community-based question answering had its origins in *digital reference* services (Lankes, 2004). There are other search tasks, beyond community-based question answering, in which users search for human-generated answers to questions. Several of these have been explored within the information retrieval community. Finding answers to questions in FAQs[10] has been the subject of a number of papers. Burke et al. (1997) and Berger et al. (2000), for example, both attempt to overcome the vocabulary mismatch problem in FAQ retrieval by considering synonyms and translations. Jijkoun and de Rijke (2005) describe retrieval from FAQ data derived from the Web, and Riezler et al. (2007) describe a translation-based model for web FAQ retrieval. *Forums* are another source of questions and answers. Cong et al. (2008) describe how question-answer pairs can be extracted from forum threads to support CQA services.

There are a number of collaborative search systems beyond those we described, including CIRE (Romano et al., 1999) and S^3 (Morris & Horvitz, 2007a). Morris (2008) provides a good survey of how practitioners actually use collaborative web search systems. Pickens et al. (2008) evaluate algorithms for iterative merging of ranked lists to support collaborative search.

Belkin and Croft (1992) provide a perspective on the connection between ad hoc retrieval and document filtering. Y. Zhang and Callan (2001) describe an effective method for automatically setting filtering thresholds. The work by Schapire et al. (1998) describes how *boosting*, an advanced machine learning technique, and Rocchio's algorithm can be applied to filtering. Finally, Allan (1996) showed how incremental feedback, which is akin to online learning, can be used to improve filtering effectiveness. Although not covered in this chapter, a research area within information retrieval called *topic detection and tracking* has largely focused on topical filtering (tracking) of news articles. See Allan (2002) for an overview of research on the topic.

---

[10] FAQ is an abbreviation of Frequently Asked Questions.

For a more complete treatment of collaborative filtering algorithms described in this chapter, see Breese et al. (1998). Furthermore, Herlocker et al. (2004) detail the many aspects involved with evaluating collaborative filtering systems.

Callan (2000) gives an excellent overview of research in distributed search. A more recent paper by Si and Callan (2004) compares the effectiveness of techniques for resource selection. A different approach to query-based sampling for generating resource descriptions, called query probing, is described by Ipeirotis and Gravano (2004). This work is focused on providing access to *deep Web* databases, which are databases that are accessible through the Web, but only through a search interface.

There are many papers describing techniques for combining the output of multiple search engines or retrieval models. Croft (2000) gives an overview of much of this research, and Montague and Aslam (2002) provide pointers to more recent work.

A general overview of P2P search and more details of how distributed search is implemented in a hierarchical network can be found in Lu and Callan (2006, 2007).

Exercises

10.1. Describe how social media tags are similar to anchor text. How are they different?

10.2. Implement two algorithms for measuring the similarity between two tags. The first algorithm should use a standard retrieval model, such as language modeling. The second algorithm should use the Web or another resource to expand the tag representation. Evaluate the effectiveness of the two algorithms on a set of 10–25 tags. Describe the algorithms, evaluation metrics, tag set, and results.

10.3. Compute five iterations of HITS (see Algorithm 3) and PageRank (see Figure 4.11) on the graph in Figure 10.3. Discuss how the PageRank scores compare to the hub and authority scores produced by HITS.

10.4. Describe two examples of online communities that were not already discussed in this chapter. How can the community-finding algorithms presented in this chapter be used to detect each?

10.5. Find a community-based question answering site on the Web and ask two questions, one that is low-quality and one that is high-quality. Describe the answer quality of each question.

10.6. List the basic operations an indexer must support to handle the following tasks: 1) static filtering, 2) adaptive filtering, and 3) collaborative filtering.

10.7. Find two examples of document filtering systems on the Web. How do they build a profile for your information need? Is the system static or adaptive?

10.8. Implement the nearest neighbor–based collaborative filtering algorithm. Using a publicly available collaborative filtering data set, compare the effectiveness, in terms of mean squared error, of the Euclidean distance and correlation similarity.

10.9. Both the clustering and nearest neighbor–based collaborative filtering algorithms described in this chapter make predictions based on user/user similarity. Formulate both algorithms in terms of item/item similarity. How can the distance between two items be measured?

10.10. Form a group of 2–5 people and use a publicly available collaborative search system. Describe your experience, including the pros and cons of using such a system.

10.11. Suggest how the maximum and minimum resource ranking scores, R_{max} and R_{min}, could be estimated for a given query.

10.12. Use the rank-based version of CombMNZ to combine the results of two search engines for a sample set of queries. Evaluate the combined ranking and compare its effectiveness to the two individual result lists.

10.13. Choose your favorite file-sharing application and find out how it works. Describe it and compare it to the P2P networks mentioned in this chapter.

10.14. In a P2P network with *small-world* properties, any two nodes are likely to be connected by a small number of hops. These networks are characterized by a node having *local* connections to nodes that are "close" and a few *long-range* connections to distant nodes, where distance can be measured by content similarity or some other attribute, such as latency. Do you think Gnutella 0.4 or 0.6 would have content-based small-world properties? What about a structured network based on Chord?

11

Beyond Bag of Words

> "It means the future is here, and all bets are off."
>
> Agent Mulder, *The X-Files*

11.1 Overview

The term "bag of words" is used to refer to a simple representation of text that is used in retrieval and classification models. In this representation, a document is considered to be an unordered collection of words with no relationships, either syntactic or statistical, between them.[1] Many of the retrieval models discussed in Chapter 7, such as the query likelihood model, the BM25 model, and even the vector space model, are based on a bag of words representation. From a linguistic point of view, the bag of words representation is extremely limited. No one could read a sorted bag of words representation and get the same meaning as normal text. The sorted version of the last sentence, for example, is "a and as bag could get meaning no normal of one read representation same sorted text the words".

Despite its obvious limitations, the bag of words representation has been very successful in retrieval experiments compared to more complex representations of text content. Incorporating even simple phrases and word proximity into a word-based representation, which would seem to have obvious benefits, took many years of research before retrieval models were developed that had significant and consistent effectiveness benefits. Search applications, however, have evolved beyond the stage where a bag of words representation of documents and queries would be adequate. For these applications, representations and ranking based on many different features are required. Features derived from the bag of words are still important, but linguistic, structural, metadata, and non-textual content features can also be used effectively in retrieval models such as the inference network

---

[1] In mathematics, a bag is like a set, but duplicates (i.e., multiple occurrences of a word) are allowed.

or the ranking SVM. We start this chapter by examining the general properties of a feature-based retrieval model.

In previous chapters we have discussed a number of representation features and how they can be used in ranking. In this chapter, we look at four aspects of representation in more detail and describe how they could affect the future development of search engines. Bag of words models assume there is no relationship between words, so we first look at how term dependencies can be captured and used in a linear feature-based model. Document structure is ignored in a bag of words representation, but we have seen how it can be important in web search. The second aspect of representation we look at is how the structured representations used in a database system could be used in a search engine. In a bag of words representation, queries are treated the same as documents. In question-answering applications, however, the syntactic structure of the query can be particularly important. The third aspect of representation we look at is how query structure is used to answer questions. Finally, bags of words are based on words, and there are many applications, such as image search or music search, where the features used to represent the objects that are retrieved may not be words. The fourth aspect of representation we look at is what these non-text features could be, and how they are used in ranking.

In the final section of this chapter, we indulge in some mild (not wild) speculation about the future of search.

11.2 Feature-Based Retrieval Models

We described *feature-based retrieval models* briefly in Chapter 7, and provide more detail here because of their growing importance as the basis for modern search engines.

For a set of documents $\mathcal{D}$ and a set of queries $\mathcal{Q}$, we can define a scoring or ranking function $S_\Lambda(D; Q)$ parameterized by Λ, which is a vector of parameters. Given a query Q_i, the scoring function $S_\Lambda(D; Q_i)$ is computed for each $D \in \mathcal{D}$, and documents are then ranked in descending order according to their scores. For *linear* feature-based models, we restrict the scoring function to those with the form:

$$S_\Lambda(D; Q) = \sum_j \lambda_j \cdot f_j(D, Q) + Z$$

where $f_j(D, Q)$ is a feature function that maps query/document pairs to real values, and Z is a constant that does not depend on D (but may depend on Λ

or Q). The feature functions correspond to the *features* that we have previously mentioned. Although some models permit non-linear combinations of features, the scoring functions that have been used in research and applications to date are based on linear combinations. For this reason, we focus here on linear feature-based models. Note that this ranking function is a generalization of the abstract ranking model that we described in Chapter 5.

In addition to defining the form of the scoring function, we also need to specify the method for finding the best values for the parameters. To do this, we need a set of training data $\mathcal{T}$ and an evaluation function $E(\mathcal{R}_\Lambda; \mathcal{T})$, where $\mathcal{R}_\Lambda$ is the set of rankings produced by the scoring function for all the queries. The evaluation function produces real-valued output given the set of ranked lists and the training data. Note that E is only required to consider the document *rankings* and not the document scores. This is a standard characteristic of the evaluation measures described in Chapter 8, such as mean average precision, precision at 10, or NDCG.

The goal of a linear feature-based retrieval model is to find a parameter setting Λ that maximizes the evaluation metric E for the training data. Formally, this can be stated as:

$$\widehat{\Lambda} = \arg\max_\Lambda E(\mathcal{R}_\Lambda; \mathcal{T})$$

where $\mathcal{R}_\Lambda$ are the rankings produced by the linear scoring function $\sum_j \lambda_j \cdot f_j(D, Q) + Z$.

For a small number of features, the optimal parameter values can be found by a brute-force search over the entire space of possible values. For larger numbers of features, an optimization procedure, such as that provided by the Ranking SVM model, is needed. The key advantages of the linear feature-based models compared to other retrieval models are the ease with which new features can be added to the model, and efficient procedures for optimizing effectiveness given training data. It is these advantages that make linear feature-based models the ideal framework for incorporating the range of representation features we discuss in this chapter.

A relatively small number of features have been used as the basis of the retrieval models described in Chapter 7 that focus on topical relevance. These include:

- *Term occurrence*: whether or not a term occurs within a document
- *Term frequency*: number of times a term occurs within a document
- *Inverse document frequency*: inverse of the proportion of documents that contain a given term
- *Document length*: number of terms in a document

- *Term proximity*: occurrence patterns of terms within a document (the most common way of incorporating term dependency)

The Galago query language (and the inference network model it is based on) provides a means of specifying a range of features and scoring documents based on a weighted linear combination of these features. Galago is more general in that it also supports the definition and combination of arbitrary features using the #feature operator. For example, using this operator, it is possible to have a feature based on the BM25 term-weighting function as part of the scoring function. Galago, like the inference network model, does not specify a particular optimization method for finding the best parameter values (i.e., the feature weights).

11.3 Term Dependence Models

In Chapter 4, we discussed the potential importance of relationships between words that are part of phrases. In Chapter 5, we showed how term proximity information can be incorporated into indexes. Chapter 6 described techniques for measuring the association between words, and Chapter 7 showed how term relationships can be expressed in the Galago query language. Exploiting the relationships between words is clearly an important part of building an effective search engine, especially for applications such as web search that have large numbers of documents containing all or most of the query words. Retrieval models that make use of term relationships are often called *term dependence models* because they do not assume that words occur independently of each other. More generally, term dependence information can be incorporated into a number of features that are used as part of the ranking algorithm.

The Galago implementation of web search described in section 7.5 is based on a specific linear feature-based model known as the *Markov Random Field* (MRF) model (Metzler & Croft, 2005b). This model, in addition to allowing arbitrary features, explicitly represents dependencies between terms. Although a number of term dependence models have been proposed, we describe the MRF model because it has produced significant effectiveness benefits in both document ranking and in the related process of pseudo-relevance feedback (Metzler & Croft, 2007a).

The MRF model works by first constructing a graph that consists of a document node and one node per query term. These nodes represent random variables within a Markov random field, which is a general way of modeling a joint distribution. Thus, in the MRF model, the joint distribution over the document random variable and query term random variables is being modeled. Markov random fields are typically represented as graphs, by what is known as a *graphical model*. In particular, MRFs are undirected graphical models, which means the edges in the graph are undirected. The inference network model described in Chapter 7 was an example of a directed graphical model.

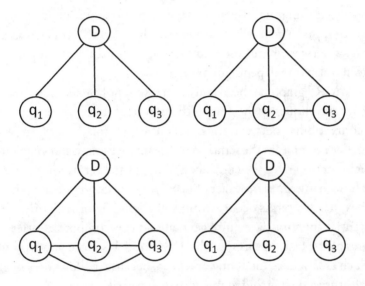

Fig. 11.1. Example Markov Random Field model assumptions, including full independence (top left), sequential dependence (top right), full dependence (bottom left), and general dependence (bottom right)

The MRF models dependencies between random variables by drawing an edge between them. Since the importance of query terms depends on the document, the document node is always connected to every query term node. It is straightforward to model query term dependencies by drawing edges between the query term nodes. There are several possible ways to determine which query term nodes to draw an edge between. These different cases are summarized in Figure 11.1. In the simplest case, no edges are drawn between the query terms. This corresponds to the *full independence* assumption, where no dependencies exist between the query terms. This is analogous to a unigram language model or any of the bag of words models described in Chapter 7. Another possibility is to draw edges between adjacent query terms. This is known as the *sequential dependence* assumption. Here it is assumed that adjacent terms are dependent on each other, but not on terms that are farther away. This type of assumption is similar to a bigram language model. Another possible assumption is that all terms are somehow dependent on all other terms. This is known as the *full dependence* assumption. The final possibility is that edges are drawn between the query terms in some meaningful way, such as automatically or manually identifying terms that are dependent on each other. This is referred to as *general dependence*. In practice, however, it has been shown that using the sequential dependence assumption is the best option. In fact, all attempts to manually or automatically determine which terms to model dependencies between have come up short against using the simple assumption that adjacent terms are dependent on each other.

After the MRF graph has been constructed, a set of *potential functions* must be defined over the cliques of the graph. The potential functions are meant to measure the compatibility between the observed values for the random variables in the clique. For example, in the sequential dependence graph shown in Figure 11.1, a potential function over the clique consisting of the terms q_1, q_2, and D might compute how many times the exact phrase "$q_1\ q_2$" occurs in document D, or how many times the two terms occur within some window of each other. Therefore, these potential functions are quite general and can compute a variety of different features of the text. In this way, the MRF model is more powerful than other models, such as language modeling or BM25, because it allows dependencies and arbitrary features to be included in a straightforward manner.

By constructing queries that have a particular form, the Galago search engine can be used to emulate one of the instantiations of the MRF model that has been very effective in TREC experiments. This approach was also used in section 7.5. For example, given the query *president abraham lincoln*, the full independence MRF model is computed using the following query:

#combine(president abraham lincoln)

Notice that this is the most basic formulation possible and does not consider any dependencies between terms. The sequential dependence MRF model can be computed by issuing the following query:

#weight(0.8 #combine(president abraham lincoln)
        0.1 #combine(#od:1(president abraham)
                #od:1(abraham lincoln)
        0.1 #combine(#uw:8(president abraham)
                #uw:8(abraham lincoln)

This query formulation consists of three parts, each of which corresponds to a specific feature type used within the MRF model. The first part scores the contribution of matching individual terms. The second part scores the contribution of matching subphrases within the query. This gives higher weight to documents that match "president abraham" and "abraham lincoln" as exact phrases. Notice that these phrases only consist of adjacent pairs of query terms, because the sequential dependence model only models dependencies between adjacent query terms. The first part of the formulation scores the contribution of matching unordered windows of adjacent query terms. In particular, if the terms "president" and "abraham" occur within a window of eight terms of each other in any order, then the document's score will be boosted. Notice that each component is weighted, with the individual term component having weight 0.8 and the exact phrase and unordered window components being weighted 0.1. These weights, which were derived empirically, show the relative importance of matching individual terms versus matching phrase and proximity features within text. The individual terms are by far the most important things to match, although the other features play an important role.

The algorithm for converting a plain text query Q to a sequential dependence MRF query in Galago is very simple. The first component (for individual terms) is simply #combine(Q). The second component puts every adjacent pair of query terms in a #od:1 operator, and then combines all such operators with a #combine. The third and final component puts every adjacent pair of query terms into a #uw:8 operator, and again combines them with a #combine operator. The three components are then given weights 0.8, 0.1, and 0.1, as described earlier, and combined within a #weight operator.

Finally, the full dependence MRF model is much more complex, since many more dependencies are modeled. However, we show the full dependence MRF model query for the sake of completeness here:

```
#weight(0.8 #combine(president abraham lincoln)
        0.1 #combine(#od:1(president abraham)
                     #od:1(abraham lincoln)
                     #od:1(president abraham lincoln))
        0.1 #combine(#uw:8(president abraham)
                     #uw:8(abraham lincoln)
                     #uw:8(president lincoln)
                     #uw:12(president abraham lincoln)))
```

It is important to note that the #combine operator used in all of the examples here could easily be replaced with the #feature operator in order to compute the individual term, exact phrase, and unordered phrase features differently. For example, one could implement BM25 weighting using #feature and compute a dependence model based on it instead of Galago's default weighting.

The MRF model can also be used to model dependencies in pseudo-relevance feedback, which is an important technique for query expansion that we described in section 7.3.2. Figure 11.2 compares a graphical model representation of the relevance model technique used for pseudo-relevance feedback with the MRF approach, which is known as *latent concept expansion*.[2] The relevance model graph (the top one) represents a bag of words, or unigram, model where words occur independently of each other, given a particular document. Pseudo-relevance feedback uses a set of highly ranked documents to estimate the probability of expansion words (the question marks) given the query words. The words with the highest probability are added to the query.

In the lower latent concept expansion graph, there are dependencies represented between query words and expansion words. The process of pseudo-relevance feedback is still the same, in that highly ranked documents are used to estimate the probabilities for possible expansion words, but the dependencies will change the way that those probabilities are estimated and generally produce better results. By modeling dependencies between the expansion words, the latent concept expansion model can produce multiword phrases as expansion terms rather than only words. As an example, Table 11.1 shows the top-ranked one- and two-word concepts produced by the latent concept expansion model for the query "hubble telescope achievements".

To summarize, the MRF model, which is a linear feature-based retrieval model, is an effective method of incorporating features based on term dependence in the scoring function used to rank documents. Latent concept expansion supports pseudo-relevance feedback in the MRF framework. Latent concept expansion can be viewed as a "feature expansion" technique, in that it enriches the original feature set by including new features based on the expanded query.

---

[2] Latent, or hidden, concepts are words or phrases that users have in mind but do not mention explicitly when they express a query.

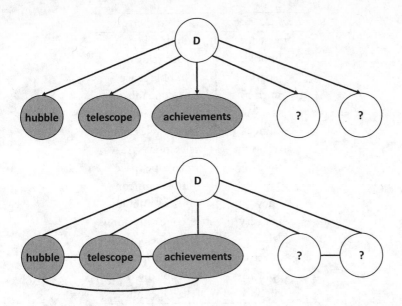

Fig. 11.2. Graphical model representations of the relevance model technique (top) and latent concept expansion (bottom) used for pseudo-relevance feedback with the query "hubble telescope achievements"

11.4 Structure Revisited

The goal of having a common platform for dealing with both structured and unstructured data is a long-standing one, going back to the 1960s. A number of approaches have been suggested, both from the database and information retrieval perspective, but the motivation for finding a solution or solutions that work has grown tremendously since the advent of very large-scale web databases. Areas that were once the exclusive concerns of information retrieval, such as statistical inference and ranking, have now become important topics for database researchers, and both communities have a common interest in providing efficient indexing and optimization techniques for web-scale data. Exploiting document structure is a critical part of web search, and combining different sources of evidence effectively is an important part of many database applications. There are many possibilities for integration, such as extending a database model to more effectively deal with probabilities, extending an information retrieval model to handle more complex structures and multiple relations, or developing a unified model and sys-

1-word concepts	2-word concepts
telescope	hubble telescope
hubble	space telescope
space	hubble space
mirror	telescope mirror
NASA	telescope hubble
launch	mirror telescope
astronomy	telescope NASA
shuttle	telescope space
test	hubble mirror
new	NASA hubble
discovery	telescope astronomy
time	telescope optical
universe	hubble optical
optical	telescope discovery
light	telescope shuttle

Table 11.1. Most likely one- and two-word concepts produced using latent concept expansion with the top 25 documents retrieved for the query "hubble telescope achievements" on the TREC ROBUST collection

tem. Applications such as web search, e-commerce, and data mining provide the testbeds where these systems are being evaluated and compared.

In Chapter 7, we showed how document structure can be handled in the Galago query language. From a conventional database perspective, there are major problems with using Galago to represent and query data. Using relational database terminology, there is no schema,[3] no means of defining the data type of attributes, and no joins between relations.[4] Instead, as described in Chapter 7, a document is represented as a (possibly nested) set of contexts defined by tag pairs. Documents are stored in a simple database with only primary-key access, where the primary key is the document identifier. The query language supports the definition and combination of search features based on the structure and contents of the documents. Different document types with different contexts can be incorporated

---

[3] A schema is a description of the logical structure of the database, which in this case would be the names of the relations (tables) and the attributes in each relation.

[4] A join connects tuples (rows) from two different relations based on one or more common attributes. An example would be to connect product information with vendor information based on the product number attribute.

into a single Galago database. Each document is indexed only by the contexts it contains. Although there is no way of defining the data type of contexts, operators associated with a specific data type could be defined and applied to particular contexts. For example, a date range operator could be applied to a context that contains the creation date for a document.

Although this is very different from the functionality of a full relational database system, in many applications involving search engines this additional functionality is not needed. The BigTable storage system described in Chapter 3, for example, does not have data types or joins. Additionally, it has only a very simple specification of tuple and attribute names. Systems such as BigTable focus on providing data persistence and reliable access to data in an environment where many components can fail, and scalable performance using distributed computing resources. Access to the data is provided through a simple API that allows client applications to read, write, or delete values. Figure 11.3 summarizes the functions provided by the search engine and the database system in applications such as web search or e-commerce. Note that the indexes created by the search engine are not stored in the database system.

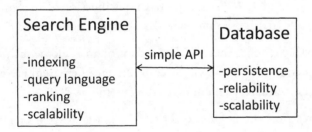

Fig. 11.3. Functions provided by a search engine interacting with a simple database system

11.4.1 XML Retrieval

XML is an important standard for both exchanging data between applications and encoding documents. To support this more data-oriented view, the database community has defined languages for describing the structure of XML data (*XML Schema*), and querying and manipulating that data (*XQuery* and *XPath*). XQuery is a query language that is similar to the database language SQL, with the major difference that it must handle the hierarchical structure of XML data instead of the simpler tabular structure of relational data. XPath is a subset of XQuery that is used to specify the search constraints for a single type of XML data or document. XPath, for example, could be used in an XML movie database to find the movies that were directed by a particular person and were released in a particular year. XQuery could be used to combine information about movies with information about actors, assuming that the XML movie database contained both movie and actor "documents." An example would be to find movies starring actors who were born in Australia.

Complex database query languages, such as XQuery, that focus on the structure of data and combining data are generally less useful in text search applications. The extent to which structure is useful in queries for databases of XML documents has been studied in the INEX project.[5] This project has taken a similar approach to TREC for search evaluation. This means that a number of XML search tasks have been defined, and appropriate test collections constructed for evaluating those tasks. One type of query used in these evaluations is the *content-and-structure* (CAS) query. These queries contain a description of a topic and explicit references to the XML structure. CAS queries are specified using a simplified version of XPath called *NEXI*.[6] The two important constructs in this query language are *paths* and *path filters*. A path is a specification of an element (or node) in the XML tree structure. Some examples of path specifications in NEXI are:

//A//B - any B element[7] that is a descendant of an A element in the XML tree. A descendant element will be contained in the parent element.
//A/* - any descendant element of an A element.

A path filter restricts the results to those that satisfy textual or numerical constraints. Some examples are:

//A[about(.//B,"topic")] - A elements that contain a B element that is about "topic". The **about** predicate is not defined, but is implemented using some type of retrieval model. .//B is a *relative* path.
//A[.//B = 777] - A elements that contain a B element with value equal to 777.

---

[5] INitiative for the Evaluation of XML Retrieval, http://inex.is.informatik.uni-duisburg.de/.

[6] Narrowed Extended XPath (Trotman & Sigurbjörnsson, 2004).

[7] This means an element that has a start tag <B> and an end tag </B>.

The database used in the earlier INEX experiments consisted of technical articles from computer science publications. The following are examples of some of the CAS queries:

//article[.//fm/yr < 2000]//sec[about(.,"search engines")]
- find articles published before 2000 (fm is the front matter of the article) that contain sections discussing the topic "search engines".

//article[about(.//st,+comparison) AND about (.//bib,"machine learning")]
- find articles with a section title containing the word "comparison" and with a bibliography that mentions "machine learning".

//*[about(.//fgc, corba architecture) AND about(.//p, figure
corba architecture)]
- find any elements that contain a figure caption about "corba architecure" and a paragraph mentioning "figure corba architecture".

Although these queries seem reasonable, INEX experiments and previous research indicate that people do not use structural cues in their queries or, if they are forced to, generally will use them incorrectly. There is essentially no evidence that structure in user queries improves search effectiveness. For this reason, the INEX project has increasingly focused on content-only queries, which are the same as the queries we have been discussing throughout this book, and on techniques for automatically ranking XML elements rather than documents.

To summarize, structure is an important part of defining features for effective ranking, but not for user queries. In applications such as web search, relatively simple user queries are transformed into queries that involve many features, including features based on document structure. The Galago query language is an example of a language that can be used to specify the features that are used for ranking, and user queries can be transformed into Galago queries. Most of the structural cues that can be specified in NEXI can be incorporated into features using Galago.

Database systems are used in many search applications. The requirements for these applications, however, are different than those for typical database applications, such as banking. This has led to the development of storage systems that are simple from a database schema and query language perspective, but are also efficient, reliable, and scalable.

11.4.2 Entity Search

In addition to exploiting the existing structure in documents, it is also possible to create structure by analyzing the document contents. In Chapter 4, we described information extraction techniques that can be used to identify entities in text such as people, organizations, and locations. *Entity search* uses this structure to provide a ranked list of entities in response to a query instead of a list of documents. To do this, a representation for each entity is generated based on the words that occur near the entity in the document texts. The simplest approach to building these representations is to create "pseudo-documents" by accumulating all words that occur within a specified text window (e.g., 20 words) for each occurrence of an entity. For example, if the organization entity "california institute of technology" occurred 65 times in a corpus, every word within 20 words of those 65 occurrences would be accumulated into the pseudo-document representation. This is the approach used in the early research on entity search, such as Conrad and Utt (1994). These large word-based representations can be stored in a search engine and then used to rank entities in response to a query.

Figure 11.4 shows an example of entity retrieval given in the Conrad paper. The top-ranked organizations for this query will have co-occurred with words such as "biomedical" a number of times in the corpus.

Query:
　　　biomedical research and technology

Top Ranked Results:

　　　minneapolis research
　　　signs inc.
　　　syntex
　　　california institute of technology
　　　massachusetts institute of technology
　　　therapeutic products

Fig. 11.4. Example of an entity search for organizations using the TREC *Wall Street Journal* 1987 Collection

The approach of building representations from words that occur in the context or locality of a target word or phrase (sometimes called *context vectors*) has been used to automatically build a thesaurus that retrieves words and phrases for query expansion (Jing & Croft, 1994). Interestingly, it has also been used by cognitive scientists as the basis for a model of semantic memory (Lund & Burgess, 1996).

Much of the recent research on entity search has focused on methods for finding people who have expertise in a particular area or topic. This task, known as *expert search*, has been studied for some time but has been evaluated more thoroughly since it became part of a TREC track in 2005. The main contribution of this research has been the development of probabilistic retrieval models for entities (or experts) based on the language modeling approach (Balog et al., 2006). In general, given a set of documents D and a query q, we can rank candidate entities e by the joint distribution $P(e, q)$ of entities and query terms. We can represent this distribution as:

$$P(e, q) = \sum_{d \in D} P(e, q|d) P(d)$$

If we focus on the $P(e, q|d)$ term, the problem of entity ranking can be decomposed into two components:

$$P(e, q|d) = P(q|e, d) P(e|d)$$

where the $P(e|d)$ component corresponds to finding documents that provide information about an entity, and the $P(q|e, d)$ component involves ranking entities in those documents with respect to a query. Different ways of estimating these probabilities result in different entity ranking algorithms. If we assume that words and entities are independent given a document, then $P(e, q|d) = P(q|d) P(e|d)$, and the two components could be computed separately by using q and e as queries for probabilistic retrieval. This assumption, however, ignores the relationship between words and entities that appear in the same document (which is captured in the context vector approach) and consequently the effectiveness of the method suffers. Instead, we can estimate the strength of association between e and q using the proximity of co-occurrence of the query words and the entities in a document. One way to do this, assuming a query consisting of a single term and a single entity occurrence in a document, is to estimate $P(q|e, d)$ as:

$$P(q|e, d) = \frac{1}{Z} \sum_{i=1}^{N} \delta_d(i, q) k(q, e)$$

where δ_d is an indicator function that is 1 when the term at position i in d is q and 0 otherwise, k is a proximity-kernel function, $Z = \sum_{i=1}^{N} k(q, e)$ is a normalizing constant, and N is the length of the document.

If the query has multiple terms, we can compute the ranking score as follows:

$$P(e, q) \stackrel{rank}{=} \prod_{q_i \in q} \left\{ \sum_{d \in D} P(q_i|e, d) P(e|d) \right\}$$

Petkova and Croft (2007) showed that the most effective kernel function is the Gaussian kernel, which is shown in Table 9.1 and, in this case, is

$$\exp -||q - e||^2 / 2\sigma^2$$

where $q - e$ is the distance in words between the query q and the entity e. This paper also showed that, for expert search, accurate named entity recognition does not have a large effect on performance and that using a simple Galago query such as #od:2(<first name> <last name>) works well for estimating $P(e|d)$ for people entities.

11.5 Longer Questions, Better Answers

In nearly all visions of the future that we see in movies or on television, the search engine, disguised as a computer system such as HAL 9000 in *2001: A Space Odyssey* or the Computer in the *Star Trek* series, has evolved into a human-like assistant that can answer complex questions about any subject. Although web search engines provide access to a huge range of information, we are still a long way from achieving the capabilities of these intelligent assistants. One obvious difference is that queries to web search engines are generally formulated as a small number of keywords, rather than as actual questions expressed in natural language. In Chapter 10, we described how people who use community-based question answering systems describe their information needs in sentences, or even paragraphs, because they know that other people will read them and give better responses if the problem is described well. In contrast, the same long queries will generally produce very poor responses or nothing at all from a web search engine. People are forced to translate their problem into one or more appropriate keywords to get a reasonable result list. A long-term goal of information retrieval research is to develop retrieval models that produce accurate results from a longer, more specific query.

The task of *question answering*, which we mentioned briefly in Chapter 1 and again in Chapter 10, involves providing a specific answer to a user's query, rather than a ranked list of documents. This task has a long history in the fields of natural language processing and artificial intelligence. Early question answering systems relied on detailed representations in logic of small, very specific domains such as baseball, lunar rocks, or toy blocks. More recently, the focus has shifted to an information retrieval perspective where the task involves identifying or extracting answers found in large corpora of text.

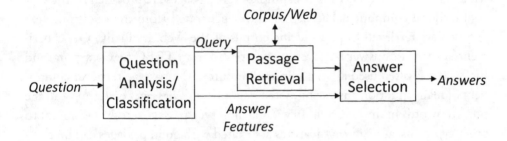

Fig. 11.5. Question answering system architecture

Figure 11.5 shows the typical components of a question answering system that retrieves answers from a text corpus. The range of questions that is handled by such a system is usually limited to *fact-based* questions with simple, short answers, such as *who*, *where*, and *when* questions that have people's names, organization names, places, and dates as answers. The following questions are a sample from the TREC question answering (QA) track:[8]

Who invented the paper clip?
Where is the Valley of the Kings?
When was the last major eruption of Mt. St. Helens?

There are, of course, other types of fact-based questions that could be asked, and they can be asked in many different ways. The task of the question analysis and classification component of the system is to classify a question by the type of answer that is expected. For the TREC QA questions, one classification that is frequently used has 31 different major categories,[9] many of which correspond to

---

[8] The TREC QA questions were drawn from the query logs of a variety of search applications (Voorhees & Harman, 2005).

[9] This is the question classification created by BBN. This classification and others are discussed in Metzler and Croft (2005a).

named entities (see Chapter 4) that can be automatically identified in text. Table 11.2 gives an example of a TREC question for each of these categories. Question classification is a moderately difficult task, given the large variation in question formats. The question word *what*, for example, can be used for many different types of questions.

The information derived from question analysis and classification is used by the answer selection component to identify answers in candidate text passages, which are usually sentences. The candidate text passages are provided by the passage retrieval component based on a query generated from the question. Text passages are retrieved from a specific corpus or the Web. In TREC QA experiments, candidate answer passages were retrieved from TREC news corpora, and the Web was often used as an additional resource. The passage retrieval component of many question answering systems simply finds passages containing all the non-stopwords in the question. In general, however, passage retrieval is similar to other types of search, in that features associated with good passages can be combined to produce effective rankings. Many of these features will be based on the question analysis. Text passages containing named entities of the type associated with the question category as well as all the important question words should obviously be ranked higher.

For example, with the question "where is the valley of the kings", sentences containing text tagged as a location and the words "valley" and "kings" would be preferred. Some systems identify text patterns associated with likely answers for the question category, using either text mining techniques with the Web or predefined rules. Patterns such as <question-location> in <location>, where question-location is "valley of the kings" in this case, often may be found in answer passages. The presence of such a pattern should improve the ranking of a text passage. Another feature that has been shown to be useful for ranking passages is related words from a thesaurus such as *Wordnet*. For example, using Wordnet relations, words such as "fabricates", "constructs", and "makes" can be related to "manufactures" when considering passages for the question "who manufactures magic chef appliances". A linear feature-based retrieval model provides the appropriate framework for combining features associated with answer passages and learning effective weights.

The final selection of an answer from a text passage can potentially involve more linguistic analysis and inference than is used to rank the text passages. In most cases, however, users of a question answering system will want to see the context of an answer, or even multiple answers, in order to verify that it appears

Example Question	Question Category
What do you call a group of geese?	Animal
Who was Monet?	Biography
How many types of lemurs are there?	Cardinal
What is the effect of acid rain?	Cause/Effect
What is the street address of the White House?	Contact Info
Boxing Day is celebrated on what day?	Date
What is sake?	Definition
What is another name for nearsightedness?	Disease
What was the famous battle in 1836 between Texas and Mexico?	Event
What is the tallest building in Japan?	Facility
What type of bridge is the Golden Gate Bridge?	Facility Description
What is the most popular sport in Japan?	Game
What is the capital of Sri Lanka?	Geo-Political Entity
Name a Gaelic language.	Language
What is the world's highest peak?	Location
How much money does the Sultan of Brunei have?	Money
Jackson Pollock is of what nationality?	Nationality
Who manufactures Magic Chef appliances?	Organization
What kind of sports team is the Buffalo Sabres?	Org. Description
What color is yak milk?	Other
How much of an apple is water?	Percent
Who was the first Russian astronaut to walk in space?	Person
What is Australia's national flower?	Plant
What is the most heavily caffeinated soft drink?	Product
What does the Peugeot company manufacture?	Product Description
How far away is the moon?	Quantity
Why can't ostriches fly?	Reason
What metal has the highest melting point?	Substance
What time of day did Emperor Hirohito die?	Time
What does your spleen do?	Use
What is the best-selling book of all time?	Work of Art

Table 11.2. Example TREC QA questions and their corresponding question categories

to be correct or possibly to make a decision about which is the best answer. For example, a system might return "Egypt" as the answer to the Valley of the Kings question, but it would generally be more useful to return the passage "The Valley of the Kings is located on the West Bank of the Nile near Luxor in Egypt." From this perspective, we could view search engines as providing a spectrum of responses for different types of queries, from focused text passages to entire documents. Longer, more precise questions should produce more accurate, focused responses, and in the case of fact-oriented questions such as those shown in Table 11.2, this will generally be true.

The techniques used in question answering systems show how syntactic and semantic features can be used to obtain more accurate results for some queries, but they do not solve the more difficult challenges of information retrieval. A TREC query such as "Where have dams been removed and what has been the environmental impact?" looks similar to a fact-based question, but the answers need to be more comprehensive than a list of locations or a ranked list of sentences. On the other hand, using question answering techniques to identify the different text expressions for dam removal should be helpful in ranking answer passages or documents. Similarly, a TREC query such as "What is being done to increase mass transit use?", while clearly not a fact-based question, should also benefit from techniques that could recognize discussions about the use of mass transit. These potential benefits, however, have yet to be demonstrated in retrieval experiments, which indicates that there are significant technical issues involved in applying these techniques to large numbers of queries. Search engines currently rely on users learning, based on their experience, to submit queries such as "mass transit" instead of the more precise question.

11.6 Words, Pictures, and Music

Although information retrieval has traditionally focused on text, much of the information that people are looking for, particularly on the Web, is in the form of images, videos, or audio. Web search engines, as well as a number of other sites, provide searches specifically for images and video, and online music stores are a very popular way of finding music. All of these services are text-based, relying on titles, captions, user-supplied "tags," and other related text to create representations of non-text media for searching. This approach can be effective and is relatively straightforward to implement. In some cases, however, there may not be any associated text, or the text may not capture important aspects of the object being represented. Many of the videos stored at video-sharing sites do not have good textual descriptions, for example, and because there are so many of them, user tags do not solve this problem. Another example is that titles do not provide an appropriate description for searching music files to find a particular melody. For these situations, researchers have been developing *content-based retrieval* techniques for non-text media.

Some non-text media use words to convey information and can be converted into text. *Optical character recognition* (OCR) technology, for example, is used to convert scanned documents containing written or printed text into machine-readable text. *Speech recognition* technology[10] is used to convert recorded speech (or *spoken documents*) into text. Both OCR and speech recognition produce "noisy" text, meaning that the text has errors relative to the original printed text or speech transcript. Figure 11.6 shows two examples of the errors produced by OCR. In both cases, the OCR output was produced by off-the-shelf OCR software. The first example is based on a text passage created using a word processor, printed, copied multiple times (to reduce the quality), and finally scanned for OCR. The resulting output has some small errors, but in general the OCR error rate for high-quality printed text is low. The second example uses much lower quality[11] input that was created by scanning a photocopy of an old conference paper. In this case, the OCR output contains significant errors, with words such as "sponsorship" and "effectiveness" being virtually unreadable. Note that OCR errors occur at the character level. In other words, the errors are a result of confusion about individual characters and cause the output of incorrect characters.

Figure 11.7 shows the output of high-quality speech recognition software for a news broadcast. Most words are recognized correctly, but when the system encounters words that it has not seen before (known as *out-of-vocabulary*, or OOV, words), it makes some significant errors. Many of the OOV words come from personal or organization names, such as "Pinochet" in this example, and considerable research effort has gone into addressing this problem. Note that speech recognition errors tend to create new words in the output, such as "coastal fish" in the example, since the software attempts to find known words that best match the sound patterns as well as a language model. Both this type of error and the

---

[10] Sometimes referred to as ASR (Automatic Speech Recognition).

[11] By "quality" we mean image quality measured in terms of contrast, sharpness, clean background, etc.

Original:

The fishing supplier had many items in stock, including a large variety of tropical fish and aquariums of all sizes.

OCR:

The fishing supplier had many items in stock, including a large variety of tropical fish and aquariums ot aH sizes~

Original:

* This work was carried out under the sponsorship of National Science Foundation Grants NSF-GN-380 (Studies in Indexing Depth and Retrieval Effectiveness) and NSF-GN-432 (Requirements Study for Future Catalogs).

OCR:

This work was carried out under the sp011J!0rship 01 NatiolUl1 Setenee Foundation 0rant. NSF-0N-SB0 (Studl .. In Indexing Depth and Retrieval Eflccth"ene&&) and NSF-0N-432 (Requirements Study lor Future 'Catalogs)•

Fig. 11.6. Examples of OCR errors

character-level errors from OCR have the potential to reduce the effectiveness of search.

A number of evaluations with OCR and ASR data have been done at TREC and other forums. These studies indicate that retrieval effectiveness generally is not significantly impacted by OCR or ASR errors. The main reason for this is the large amount of redundancy in the collections that are used for these evaluations. For example, in ASR evaluations, there are often many relevant spoken documents that each contain many instances of the important words for a query. Even if some instances of words are not recognized, other instances may be. In addition, even if a query word is consistently not recognized, there are usually a number of other words in the query that can be used to estimate relevance. A similar situation occurs with OCR data, where some instances of a word in a scanned document may be of higher image quality than others, and thus will be recognized successfully. The only situation where OCR and ASR errors were shown to significantly reduce effectiveness was with short documents, which have little redundancy, and in environments with high error rates. Techniques such as character n-gram indexing and expansion with related terms can improve performance in these situations.

Transcript:
French prosecutors are investigating former Chilean strongman Augusto
Pinochet. The French justice minister may seek his extradition from
Britain. Three French families whose relatives disappeared in Chile
have filed a Complaint charging Pinochet with crimes against humanity.
The national court in Spain has ruled crimes committed by the
Pinochet regime fall under Spanish jurisdiction.

Speech recognizer output:
french prosecutors are investigating former chilean strongman of
coastal fish today the french justice minister may seek his
extradition from britain three french families whose relatives
disappeared until i have filed a complaint charging tenants say with
crimes against humanity the national court in spain has ruled crimes
committed by the tennessee with james all under spanish jurisdiction

Fig. 11.7. Examples of speech recognizer errors

In contrast to media that can be converted to noisy text, content-based retrieval of pictures[12] is a more challenging problem. The features that can be extracted from an image, such as color, texture, and shape, have little semantic content relative to words. For example, one of the common features used in image
retrieval applications is the *color histogram*. Color in images is represented using
a specific color model, such as RGB.[13] The RGB model represents colors as mixtures of red, blue, and green, typically with 256 values (8 bits) being used for each
component. A color histogram for an image can be created by first "quantizing"
the color values to reduce the number of possible "bins" in the histogram. If the
RGB values are quantized into 8 levels instead of 256 levels, for example, the number of possible color combinations is reduced from $256 \times 256 \times 256$ to $8 \times 8 \times 8 =$
512 values or bins. Then, for each pixel in the image, the bin corresponding to
the color value for that pixel is incremented by one. The resulting histogram can
be used to represent the images in a collection and also be indexed for fast retrieval. Given a new image as a query, the color histogram for that image would
be compared with the histograms from the image collection using some similarity
measure, and images would be ranked using the similarity values.

---

[12] Also known as *content-based image retrieval* (CBIR).

[13] Another common model is HSV (Hue, Saturation, and Value).

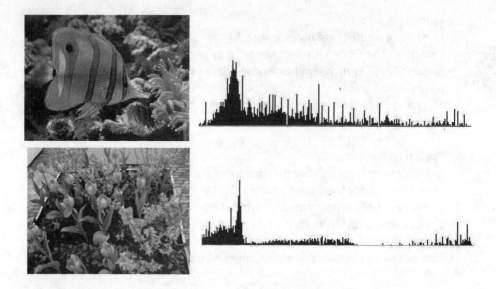

Fig. 11.8. Two images (a fish and a flower bed) with color histograms. The horizontal axis is hue value.

Figure 11.8 shows two example images and their color histograms. In this case, the histogram is based only on hue values (rather than RGB values), so the peaks in the histogram correspond to peaks in colors. Both the fish and the flowers are predominantly yellow, so both histograms have a similar peak in that area of the spectrum (on the left). The other smaller peaks are associated with greens and blues.

The color feature is useful for finding images with strong color similarity, such as pictures of sunsets, but two pictures with completely different content can be considered very similar based solely on their colors. The picture of the flowers in Figure 11.8, for example, may be ranked highly in comparison with the picture of the fish because of the similar peaks in the histograms. The ability to find semantically related images can be improved by combining color features with texture and shape features. Figure 11.9 shows two examples of image retrieval based on texture features (the cars and the trains), and one example of retrieval based on shape features (the trademarks). Texture is broadly defined as the spatial arrangement of gray levels in the image, and shape features describe the form of object boundaries and edges. The examples show that images with similar appearance can generally be found using these types of representations, although the second

Fig. 11.9. Three examples of content-based image retrieval. The collection for the first two consists of 1,560 images of cars, faces, apes, and other miscellaneous subjects. The last example is from a collection of 2,048 trademark images. In each case, the leftmost image is the query.

example makes it clear that similarity in terms of texture does not guarantee semantic similarity. In the case of text-based search, high-ranking documents that are not relevant can at least be easily understood by the user. With content-based image retrieval, a retrieval failure such as the picture of the ape in Figure 11.9 will be difficult to explain to a user who is looking for pictures of trains.

Retrieval experiments have shown that the most effective way of combining image features is with a probabilistic retrieval model. If images have text captions or user tags, these features can easily be incorporated into the ranking, as we have discussed previously. Video retrieval applications are similar to image retrieval, except that they may have even more features, such as closed caption text or text generated from speech recognition. The image component of a video is typically represented as a series of *key frame* images. To generate key frames, the video is first segmented into *shots* or scenes. A video shot can be defined as a continuous sequence of visually coherent frames, and boundaries can be detected by visual discontinuities, such a sharp decrease in the similarity of one frame to the next. Given the segmentation into shots, a single frame (picture) is selected as the key frame. This can be done simply by using the first frame in each shot, or by more sophisticated techniques based on visual similarity and motion analysis. Figure 11.10 shows an example of four key frames extracted from a video of a news conference.

Fig. 11.10. Key frames extracted from a TREC video clip

The image retrieval techniques we have discussed assume that the query is an image. In many applications, users would prefer to describe the images they are looking for with a text query. Words cannot be compared directly to features derived from the image. Recent research has shown, however, that given enough training data, a probabilistic retrieval model can learn to associate words or categories with image-based features and, in effect, automatically annotate images. There are actually two questions that we need to answer using this model:

- Given an image with no text annotation, how can we automatically assign meaningful keywords to that image?
- Given a text query $\{q_1, \ldots q_n\}$, how can we retrieve images that are relevant to the query?

The relevance model described in section 7.3.2 has been shown to be effective for this task. Instead of estimating the joint probability of observing a word w with the query words $P(w, q_1, \ldots q_n)$, the relevance model is used to estimate $P(w, i_1, \ldots i_m)$, where an image is assumed to be represented by a set of image terms $\{i_1, \ldots i_m\}$. The "vocabulary" of image terms in this approach is constrained by using image segmentation and clustering techniques to identify regions that are visually similar.[14] As an example, in one test corpus of 5,000 images, a vocabulary of 500 image terms was used to represent the images, with each image being described by 1–10 terms. The joint probabilities are estimated using a training set of images that have text annotations. This model can be used to answer both of the questions just mentioned. To retrieve images for a text query, a process similar to pseudo-relevance feedback would be followed:

---

[14] One such technique represents images as "blobs" (Carson et al., 1999).

1. Use the text query to rank images that do contain text annotations.
2. Estimate joint probabilities for the image vocabulary given the top-ranked images.
3. Rerank images using the query expanded with image terms to find images that do not have text annotations.

people, pool,   cars, formula,   clouds, jet,   fox, forest,
swimmers, water   tracks, wall   plane, sky   river, water

Fig. 11.11. Examples of automatic text annotation of images

Alternatively, the joint probability estimates from the training set can be used to assign keywords to images that do not have annotations. Figure 11.11 shows examples of images annotated using this approach. Most of the words used to describe the images are reasonable, although the annotation for the picture of the bear shows that significant errors can be made. Retrieval experiments using automatic annotation techniques have shown that this approach has promise and can increase the effectiveness of image and video retrieval in some applications. Significant questions remain about the type and size of text and image vocabularies that will be the most effective.

Music is a media that is even less associated with words than pictures. Pictures can at least be described by words, and automatic annotation techniques can be used to retrieve images using text queries. Apart from the title, composer, performer, and lyrics, however, it is very difficult to describe a piece of music using words. Music has a number of representations that are used for different purposes. Figure 11.12 shows three of these representations for "Fugue #10" composed by Bach. The first is the audio signal from a performance of the music. This is what is stored in a compressed form in MP3 files. The second is a MIDI[15] representation that provides a digital specification of "events" in the music, such as the pitch, intensity, duration, and tempo of musical notes. MIDI is the standard for

---

[15] Musical Instrument Digital Interface

communication between electronic instruments and computers. The third representation is conventional musical notation, which contains the most explicit information, especially for polyphonic music made up of multiple parts or voices.

Fig. 11.12. Three representations of Bach's "Fugue #10": audio, MIDI, and conventional music notation

A number of approaches have been developed for deriving index terms for searching from these basic representations. In the case of audio, one of the most successful has been the use of "signatures" created by hashing to represent the music. A signature could be created, for example, based on the peaks in a *spectrogram* of the audio in a time slice.[16] This type of indexing is the basis of services that can

---

[16] A spectrogram represents the energy or amplitude of each frequency in the audio signal at a given time.

identify music based on a short recording captured using a mobile phone (e.g., Wang, 2006).

Another popular approach to content-based retrieval of music is *query-by-humming*. In this type of system, a user literally sings, hums, or plays a tune, and a music collection is searched for similar melodies. This type of searching is based on music that has a single melody line (monophonic). The query is converted into a representation of a melody that consists of information such as the sequence of notes, relative pitches, and intervals between notes. The music in the collection must also be converted to the same type of representation, and this is most readily done using MIDI as the starting point. The query will be a very noisy representation of the relevant melody, so a number of retrieval models developed for text searching, such as n-gram matching and language models, have been adapted for this task (Dannenberg et al., 2007). Search techniques for polyphonic music based on probabilistic models have also been used for the retrieval of music scores represented in conventional music notation.

In summary, search techniques based on retrieval models for text have been developed for a large range of non-text media. In the case of scanned and spoken documents, retrieval effectiveness is similar to text documents because OCR and speech recognition tools generally have low error rates. Content-based retrieval of images and video shows promise, but search applications for these media must rely on associated text from sources such as captions and user tags to achieve good effectiveness. Music is difficult to describe in text, but effective music search applications have been developed because index terms that have a strong relationship to what users look for can be derived from the audio or MIDI representations.

11.7 One Search Fits All?

So what is the future of search? Certainly it does not look like we will build the omniscient assistant system anytime soon. On the other hand, as we discussed before, using that type of system as our goal makes it clear how much further we have to go from current search engines. Our knowledge and understanding of search and effectiveness are steadily increasing, despite the field being more than 40 years old. Interestingly, this has produced a variety of different search services, rather than a single search engine with more and more capability. At the home page for a popular web search engine, we find links to search engines for the Web, images, blogs, maps, academic papers, products, patents, news, books, financial information, videos, government documents, and photographs. In addition, there are links to tools for desktop search, enterprise search, and advertising search. Rather than being simply multiple instances of the same search engine, it is clear that many of these use somewhat different features, ranking algorithms, and interfaces. If we look at the research literature, an even greater range of applications, media, and approaches to search are being developed and evaluated. One safe prediction is that this expansion of new ideas will continue.

Despite the proliferation of customized search engines, there is also a growing consensus on the principles that underlie them. Researchers from information retrieval and related fields, such as machine learning and natural language processing, have developed similar approaches to representing text and modeling the process of retrieval. These approaches are rapidly being expanded to include structured data and non-text media. Research results based on new applications or data have consistently reinforced the view that probabilistic models of text and linear feature-based models for retrieval provide a powerful and effective framework for understanding search. Another prediction is that the sophistication of this underlying "theory" of search will continue to grow and provide steady improvements in effectiveness for a range of applications.

What impact will this "theory" have on search engines? If there is more agreement about how to represent text and other types of data, and more agreement about how to rank potential answers in response to questions, then the search tools that developers use will become more similar than they are currently. Open source search engines, web search engines, desktop search engines and enterprise search engines available today all use different term weighting, different features, different ranking algorithms, and different query languages. This is simply due to the fact that there is no consensus yet on the *right* way to do these things, but this will change. When there is more agreement on the underlying models, there will still be a variety of search tools available, but the choice between them will be based more on the efficiency of the implementation, the flexibility and adaptability for new applications, and the extent to which the tools implement the more sophisticated algorithms suggested by the models. This is analogous to what happened with database systems, where there have been multiple vendors and organizations providing tools based on the relational model since the 1980s.

Another aspect of search, which we have not devoted enough coverage to in this book, is the fundamental importance of the *interaction* between users and the search engine, and the impact of the user's *task* on this process. Information scientists in particular have focused on these issues and have contributed important insights to our understanding of how people find relevant information. As social search and social networking applications have grown, the study of interaction has also expanded to include interaction between users as well as between a user and a search engine. In the near future, we can expect to see theories and models of search that incorporate users and interaction in a more explicit way than current models. Fuhr (2008) is a recent example of this development.

A common vision of the future, supported by countless films and television series, assumes an interface based on a simple natural language input with multimedia output. Interaction in this interface is based on dialog. Despite, or because of, its simplicity, this seems like a reasonable long-term goal. In current search interfaces, queries are certainly simple but, as we have discussed, a considerable effort can go into formulating these simple queries in order to find the one that retrieves relevant information. In addition, there is very little dialog or interaction, and even simple ideas, such as relevance feedback, are not used. Even worse, the availability of many different search engines means that another decision (which search engine?) is added to the interaction.

Developers in search engine companies and researchers are studying techniques for improving interaction. Some interfaces put results from multiple types of search engines into a single results display. Simple examples of this include putting a map search engine result at the top of the result list when the query includes an address, or a link to an academic paper at the top when the query matches the title closely. It is clear, however, that interfaces in the future must continue to evolve in order to more actively incorporate users and their knowledge into the search process.

A final prediction is self-serving in the context of this book. Search, in all its forms, will continue to be of critical importance in future software applications. Training people to understand the principles, models, and evaluation techniques that underlie search engines is an important part of continuing to improve their effectiveness and efficiency. There are not enough courses that focus on this topic, but through this book and others like it, more people will know more about search.

References and Further Reading

Linear feature-based retrieval models are discussed in Metzler and Croft (2007b). This paper contains references to other models that were discussed in Chapter 7. Another recent paper discussing linear models is Gao et al. (2005).

Many term dependency models have been proposed in the information retrieval literature, although few have produced interesting results. van Rijsbergen (1979) presented one of the most-cited dependency models as an extension of the Bayesian classification approach to retrieval. In another early paper, Croft et al. (1991) showed that phrases and term proximity could potentially improve effectiveness by modeling them as dependencies in the inference net model. Gao et al. (2004) describe a dependence model that showed significant effectiveness benefits, especially for sequential dependencies (or n-grams). Other recent research with larger test collections have shown that term proximity information is an extremely useful feature.

From an information retrieval perspective, dealing with structure in data started in the 1970s with commercial search services such as MEDLINE and DIALOG that had Boolean field restrictions. In the 1970s and 1980s, a number of papers described the implementation of search engines using relational database systems (e.g., Crawford, 1981). Efficiency issues persisted with this approach until the 1990s, although object management systems were successfully used to support indexes (e.g., Brown et al., 1994). The 1990s were also the period when important work was done on developing probabilistic extensions of database models for search applications. Fuhr and his colleagues described a probabilistic relational algebra (Fuhr & Rölleke, 1997) and a probabilistic datalog system (Fuhr, 2000).

In the commercial world, text retrieval had become a standard function in database systems such as Oracle by the early 1990s, but the explosion of web data and the growth of text-based web applications later that decade made the ability to handle text effectively a critical part of most information systems. An interesting discussion of database and search engine integration from the database perspective can be found in Chaudhuri et al. (2005).

Another important line of research has been retrieval using structured and XML documents. Early work in this area dealt with office documents (Croft, Krovetz, & Turtle, 1990) and document markup (Croft et al., 1992). The XQuery query language for XML data is described in Chamberlin (2002). Kazai et al. (2003) describe the INEX project that evaluates retrieval methods for XML documents. Trotman and Lalmas (2006) describe the NEXI language.

In the area of question answering, Metzler and Croft (2005a) give an overview of techniques for question classification. Probabilistic approaches to question answering that have been shown to be effective include the maximum entropy model (Ittycheriah et al., 2001) and the translation model (Echihabi & Marcu, 2003). Both are very similar to the retrieval models described in Chapter 7.

Taghva et al. (1996) describe the first comprehensive set of experiments showing that OCR errors generally have little effect on retrieval effectiveness. Harding et al. (1997) show how n-grams can compensate for situations where there are significant OCR error rates.

The book by Coden et al. (2002) contains a collection of papers about spoken document retrieval. Singhal and Pereira (1999) describe an expansion technique for spoken documents that gave significant effectiveness improvements. The data and major results from the TREC spoken document track are described in Voorhees and Harman (2005).

Many papers have been published about content-based image retrieval. Flickner et al. (1995) describe QBIC, one of the first commercial systems to incorporate retrieval using color, texture, and shape features. The Photobook system (Pentland et al., 1996) also had a significant impact on other CBIR projects. Ravela and Manmatha (1997) describe one of the first texture-based retrieval techniques to be evaluated using an information retrieval approach. The SIFT (scale-invariant feature transform) algorithm (Lowe, 2004) is currently a popular method for representing images for search. Vasconcelos (2007) gives a recent overview of the field of CBIR.

In the area of content-based retrieval of music, most research is published in the International Conference on Music Information Retrieval (ISMIR).[17] Byrd and Crawford (2002) give a good overview of the research issues in this field. Midomi[18] is an example of searching music by "humming."

With regard to the information science perspective on search and interaction, Belkin has written a number of key papers, such as Koenemann and Belkin (1996) and Belkin (2008). The book by Ingwersen and Järvelin (2005) contains in-depth discussions of the role of interaction and context in search. Marchionini (2006) discusses similar issues with an emphasis on the search interface.

---

[17] http://www.ismir.net/

[18] http://www.midomi.com

Exercises

11.1. Can you find other "visions of the future" related to search engines on the Web or in books, films, or television? Describe these systems and any unique features they may have.

11.2. Does your favorite web search engine use a bag of words representation? How can you tell whether it does or doesn't?

11.3. Use the Galago #feature operator to create a ranking algorithm that uses both a BM25 feature and a query likelihood feature.

11.4. Show how the linear feature-based ranking function is related to the abstract ranking model from Chapter 5.

11.5. Write a program that converts textual queries to sequential dependence MRF queries in Galago, as described in the text. Run some queries against an index, and compare the quality of the results with and without term dependence. Which types of queries are the most improved using the dependence model? Which are hurt the most?

11.6. How many papers dealing with term dependency can you find in the SIGIR proceedings since 2000? List their citations.

11.7. Think of five queries where you are searching for documents structured using XML. The queries must involve structure and content features. Write the queries in English and in NEXI (explain the XML structure if it is not obvious). Do you think the structural part of the query will improve effectiveness? Give a detailed example.

11.8. Find out about the text search functionality of a database system (either commercial or open source). Describe it in as much detail as you can, including the query language. Compare this functionality to a search engine.

11.9. Find a demonstration of a question answering system running on the Web. Using a test set of questions, identify which types of questions work and which don't on this system. Report effectiveness using MRR or another measure.

11.10. Using the text-based image search for a web search engine, find examples of images that you think could be retrieved by similarity based on color. Use a tool such as Photoshop to generate color histogram values based on hue (or one of the

RGB channels) for your test images. Compare the histograms using some similarity measure (such as the normalized sum of the differences in the bin values). How well do these similarities match your visual perceptions?

11.11. Look at a sample of images or videos that have been tagged by users and separate the tags into three groups: those you think could eventually be done automatically by image processing and object recognition, those you think would not be possible to derive by image processing, and spam. Also decide which of the tags should be most useful for queries related to those images. Summarize your findings.

11.12. What features would you like to have to support indexing and retrieval of personal digital photographs and videos? Which of these features are available in off-the-shelf software? Which of the features are discussed in research papers?

11.13. Starting with two MP3 files of two versions of the same song (i.e., different artists), use tools available on the Web to analyze and compare them. You should be able to find tools to generate MIDI from the audio, spectrograms, etc. Can you find any similarities between these files that come from the melody? You could also try recording a song using a microphone and comparing the audio file created from the recording with the original.

References

AbdulJaleel, N., & Larkey, L. S. (2003). Statistical transliteration for English-Arabic cross language information retrieval. In *CIKM '03: Proceedings of the twelfth international conference on information and knowledge management* (pp. 139–146). ACM.

Agichtein, E., Brill, E., & Dumais, S. (2006). Improving web search ranking by incorporating user behavior information. In *SIGIR '06: Proceedings of the 29th annual international ACM SIGIR conference on research and development in information retrieval* (pp. 19–26). ACM.

Agichtein, E., Brill, E., Dumais, S., & Ragno, R. (2006). Learning user interaction models for predicting web search result preferences. In *SIGIR '06: Proceedings of the 29th annual international ACM SIGIR conference on research and development in information retrieval* (pp. 3–10). ACM.

Agichtein, E., Castillo, C., Donato, D., Gionis, A., & Mishne, G. (2008). Finding high-quality content in social media. In *WSDM '08: Proceedings of the international conference on web search and web data mining* (pp. 183–194). ACM.

Allan, J. (1996). Incremental relevance feedback for information filtering. In *SIGIR '96: Proceedings of the 19th annual international ACM SIGIR conference on research and development in information retrieval* (pp. 270–278). ACM.

Allan, J. (Ed.). (2002). *Topic detection and tracking: Event-based information organization*. Norwell, MA: Kluwer Academic Publishers.

Almeida, R. B., & Almeida, V. A. F. (2004). A community-aware search engine. In *WWW '04: Proceedings of the 13th international conference on World Wide Web* (pp. 413–421). ACM.

Amershi, S., & Morris, M. R. (2008). CoSearch: A system for co-located collaborative web search. In *CHI '08: Proceeding of the twenty-sixth annual SIGCHI conference on human factors in computing systems* (pp. 1,647–1,656). ACM.

Anagnostopoulos, A., Broder, A., & Carmel, D. (2005). Sampling search-engine results. In *WWW '05: Proceedings of the 14th international conference on World Wide Web* (pp. 245–256). ACM.

Anh, V. N., & Moffat, A. (2005). Simplified similarity scoring using term ranks. In *SIGIR '05: Proceedings of the 28th annual international ACM SIGIR conference on research and development in information retrieval* (pp. 226–233). ACM.

Anh, V. N., & Moffat, A. (2006). Pruned query evaluation using pre-computed impacts. In *SIGIR '06: Proceedings of the 29th annual international ACM SIGIR conference on research and development in information retrieval* (pp. 372–379). New York: ACM.

Baeza-Yates, R., & Ramakrishnan, R. (2008). Data challenges at Yahoo! In *EDBT '08: Proceedings of the 11th international conference on extending database technology* (pp. 652–655). ACM.

Baeza-Yates, R., & Ribeiro-Neto, B. A. (1999). *Modern information retrieval.* New York: ACM/Addison-Wesley.

Balakrishnan, H., Kaashoek, M. F., Karger, D., Morris, R., & Stoica, I. (2003). Looking up data in P2P systems. *Communications of the ACM*, 46(2), 43–48.

Balog, K., Azzopardi, L., & de Rijke, M. (2006). Formal models for expert finding in enterprise corpora. In *SIGIR '06: Proceedings of the 29th annual international ACM SIGIR conference on research and development in information retrieval* (pp. 43–50). ACM.

Barroso, L. A., Dean, J., & Hölzle, U. (2003). Web search for a planet: The Google cluster architecture. *IEEE Micro*, 23(2), 22–28.

Beeferman, D., & Berger, A. (2000). Agglomerative clustering of a search engine query log. In *Proceedings of the sixth ACM SIGKDD international conference on knowledge discovery and data mining* (pp. 407–416). ACM.

Belew, R. K. (2000). *Finding out about.* Cambridge, UK: Cambridge University Press.

Belkin, N. J. (2008). (Somewhat) grand challenges for information retrieval. *SIGIR Forum*, 42(1), 47–54.

Belkin, N. J., & Croft, W. B. (1992). Information filtering and information retrieval: Two sides of the same coin? *Communications of the ACM*, *35*(12), 29–38.

Belkin, N. J., Oddy, R. N., & Brooks, H. M. (1997). ASK for information retrieval: Part I.: background and theory. In *Readings in information retrieval* (pp. 299–304). San Francisco: Morgan Kaufmann. (Reprinted from *Journal of Documentation*, 1982, *38*, 61–71)

Benczúr, A., Csalogány, K., Sarlós, T., & Uher, M. (2005). Spamrank – fully automatic link spam detection. In *AIRWeb: 1st international workshop on adversarial information retrieval on the web* (pp. 25–38).

Berger, A., Caruana, R., Cohn, D., Freitag, D., & Mittal, V. (2000). Bridging the lexical chasm: Statistical approaches to answer-finding. In *SIGIR '00: Proceedings of the 23rd annual international ACM SIGIR conference on research and development in information retrieval* (pp. 192–199). ACM.

Berger, A., & Lafferty, J. (1999). Information retrieval as statistical translation. In *SIGIR '99: Proceedings of the 22nd annual international ACM SIGIR conference on research and development in information retrieval* (pp. 222–229). ACM.

Berger, A., & Mittal, V. O. (2000). Ocelot: a system for summarizing web pages. In *SIGIR '00: Proceedings of the 23rd annual international ACM SIGIR conference on research and development in information retrieval* (pp. 144–151). ACM.

Bergman, M. K. (2001). The deep web: Surfacing hidden value. *Journal of Electronic Publishing*, *7*(1).

Bernstein, Y., & Zobel, J. (2005). Redundant documents and search effectiveness. In *CIKM '05: Proceedings of the 14th ACM international conference on information and knowledge management* (pp. 736–743). ACM.

Bernstein, Y., & Zobel, J. (2006). Accurate discovery of co-derivative documents via duplicate text detection. *Information Systems*, *31*, 595–609.

Bikel, D. M., Miller, S., Schwartz, R., & Weischedel, R. (1997). Nymble: A high-performance learning name-finder. In *Proceedings of the fifth conference on applied natural language processing* (pp. 194–201). Morgan Kaufmann.

Bikel, D. M., Schwartz, R. L., & Weischedel, R. M. (1999). An algorithm that learns what's in a name. *Machine Learning*, *34*(1–3), 211–231.

Blei, D. M., Ng, A. Y., & Jordan, M. I. (2003). Latent Dirichlet allocation. *Journal of Machine Learning Research*, *3*, 993–1,022.

Borgs, C., Chayes, J., Mahdian, M., & Saberi, A. (2004). Exploring the community structure of newsgroups. In *KDD '04: Proceedings of the tenth ACM SIGKDD international conference on knowledge discovery and data mining* (pp. 783–787). ACM.

Breese, J., Heckerman, D., & Kadie, C. (1998). Empirical analysis of predictive algorithms for collaborative filtering. In *UAI '98: Proceedings of the uncertainty in artifical intelligence conference* (pp. 43–52).

Brill, E. (1994). Some advances in transformation-based part of speech tagging. In *AAAI '94: National conference on artificial intelligence* (pp. 722–727).

Brin, S., & Page, L. (1998). The anatomy of a large-scale hypertextual Web search engine. *Computer Networks and ISDN Systems, 30*(1–7), 107–117.

Broder, A. (2002). A taxonomy of web search. *SIGIR Forum, 36*(2), 3–10.

Broder, A., Fontoura, M., Josifovski, V., & Riedel, L. (2007). A semantic approach to contextual advertising. In *SIGIR '07: Proceedings of the 30th annual international ACM SIGIR conference on research and development in information retrieval* (pp. 559–566). ACM.

Broder, A., Fontura, M., Josifovski, V., Kumar, R., Motwani, R., Nabar, S., et al. (2006). Estimating corpus size via queries. In *CIKM '06: Proceedings of the 15th ACM international conference on information and knowledge management* (pp. 594–603). ACM.

Broder, A., Glassman, S. C., Manasse, M. S., & Zweig, G. (1997). Syntactic clustering of the Web. *Computer Networks and ISDN Systems, 29*(8–13), 1157–1166.

Brown, E. W., Callan, J., Croft, W. B., & Moss, J. E. B. (1994). Supporting full-text information retrieval with a persistent object store. In *EDBT '94: 4th international conference on extending database technology* (Vol. 779, pp. 365–378). Springer.

Buckley, C., & Voorhees, E. M. (2004). Retrieval evaluation with incomplete information. In *SIGIR '04: Proceedings of the 27th annual international ACM SIGIR conference on research and development in information retrieval* (pp. 25–32). ACM.

Burges, C., Shaked, T., Renshaw, E., Lazier, A., Deeds, M., Hamilton, N., et al. (2005). Learning to rank using gradient descent. In *ICML '05: Proceedings of the 22nd international conference on machine learning* (pp. 89–96). ACM.

Burges, C. J. C. (1998). A tutorial on support vector machines for pattern recognition. *Data Mining and Knowledge Discovery, 2*(2), 121–167.

Burke, R. D., Hammond, K. J., Kulyukin, V. A., Lytinen, S. L., Tomuro, N., & Schoenberg, S. (1997). *Question answering from frequently asked question files: Experiences with the FAQ finder system* (Tech. Rep.). Chicago, IL, USA.

Büttcher, S., & Clarke, C. L. A. (2007). Index compression is good, especially for random access. In *CIKM '07: Proceedings of the sixteenth ACM conference on information and knowledge management* (pp. 761–770). ACM.

Büttcher, S., Clarke, C. L. A., & Lushman, B. (2006). Hybrid index maintenance for growing text collections. In *SIGIR '06: Proceedings of the 29th annual international ACM SIGIR conference on research and development in information retrieval* (pp. 356–363). ACM.

Byrd, D., & Crawford, T. (2002). Problems of music information retrieval in the real world. *Information Processing and Management*, *38*(2), 249–272.

Callan, J. (2000). Distributed information retrieval. In *Advances in information retrieval: Recent research from the CIIR* (pp. 127–150). Norwell, MA: Kluwer Academic Publishers.

Callan, J., Croft, W. B., & Broglio, J. (1995). TREC and Tipster experiments with Inquery. *Information Processing and Management*, *31*(3), 327–343.

Callan, J., Croft, W. B., & Harding, S. M. (1992). The Inquery retrieval system. In *Proceedings of DEXA-92, 3rd international conference on database and expert systems applications* (pp. 78–83).

Cao, Y., Xu, J., Liu, T.-Y., Li, H., Huang, Y., & Hon, H.-W. (2006). Adapting ranking SVM to document retrieval. In *SIGIR '06: Proceedings of the 29th annual international ACM SIGIR conference on research and development in information retrieval* (pp. 186–193). ACM.

Carbonell, J., & Goldstein, J. (1998). The use of MMR, diversity-based reranking for reordering documents and producing summaries. In *SIGIR '98: Proceedings of the 21st annual international ACM SIGIR conference on research and development in information retrieval* (pp. 335–336). ACM.

Carson, C., Thomas, M., Belongie, S., Hellerstein, J. M., & Malik, J. (1999). Blobworld: A system for region-based image indexing and retrieval. In *VISUAL '99: Third international conference on visual information and information systems* (pp. 509–516). Springer.

Carterette, B., Allan, J., & Sitaraman, R. (2006). Minimal test collections for retrieval evaluation. In *SIGIR '06: Proceedings of the 29th annual international ACM SIGIR conference on research and development in information retrieval* (pp. 268–275). ACM.

Carterette, B., & Jones, R. (2007). Evaluating search engines by modeling the relationship between relevance and clicks. In *NIPS '07: Proceedings of the conference on neural information processing systems* (pp. 217–224). MIT Press.

Chakrabarti, S., van den Berg, M., & Dom, B. (1999). Focused crawling: A new approach to topic-specific web resource discovery. *Computer Networks*, *31*(11-16), 1,623–1,640.

Chamberlin, D. (2002). XQuery: An XML query language. *IBM Systems Journal*, *41*(4), 597–615.

Chang, F., Dean, J., Ghemawat, S., Hsieh, W. C., Wallach, D. A., Burrows, M., et al. (2006). Bigtable: a distributed storage system for structured data. In *OSDI '06: Proceedings of the 7th symposium on operating systems design and implementation* (pp. 205–218). USENIX Association.

Charikar, M. S. (2002). Similarity estimation techniques from rounding algorithms. In *STOC '02: Proceedings of the annual ACM symposium on theory of computing* (pp. 380–388). ACM.

Chaudhuri, S., Ramakrishnan, R., & Weikum, G. (2005). Integrating DB and IR technologies: What is the sound of one hand clapping? In *CIDR 2005: Second biennial conference on innovative data systems research* (pp. 1–12).

Chen, Y.-Y., Suel, T., & Markowetz, A. (2006). Efficient query processing in geographic web search engines. In *SIGMOD '06: Proceedings of the ACM SIGMOD international conference on management of data* (pp. 277–288). ACM.

Cho, J., & Garcia-Molina, H. (2002). Parallel crawlers. In *WWW 2002: Proceedings of the 11th annual international world wide web conference* (pp. 124–135). ACM.

Cho, J., & Garcia-Molina, H. (2003). Effective page refresh policies for web crawlers. *ACM Transactions on Database Systems*, *28*, 390–426.

Church, K. W. (1988). A stochastic parts program and noun phrase parser for unrestricted text. In *Proceedings of the second conference on applied natural language processing* (pp. 136–143). Association for Computational Linguistics.

Church, K. W., & Hanks, P. (1989). Word association norms, mutual information, and lexicography. In *Proceedings of the 27th annual meeting on Association for Computational Linguistics* (pp. 76–83). Association for Computational Linguistics.

Clarke, C. L., Agichtein, E., Dumais, S., & White, R. W. (2007). The influence of caption features on clickthrough patterns in web search. In *SIGIR '07: Proceedings of the 30th annual international ACM SIGIR conference on research and development in information retrieval* (pp. 135–142). ACM.

Cleverdon, C. (1970). Evaluation tests of information retrieval systems. *Journal of Documentation, 26*(1), 55–67.

Coden, A., Brown, E. W., & Srinivasan, S. (Eds.). (2002). *Information retrieval techniques for speech applications.* London: Springer-Verlag.

Cong, G., Wang, L., Lin, C.-Y., Song, Y.-I., & Sun, Y. (2008). Finding question-answer pairs from online forums. In *SIGIR '08: Proceedings of the 31st annual international ACM SIGIR conference on research and development in information retrieval* (pp. 467–474). ACM.

Conrad, J. G., & Utt, M. H. (1994). A system for discovering relationships by feature extraction from text databases. In *SIGIR '94: Proceedings of the 17th annual international ACM SIGIR conference on research and development in information retrieval* (pp. 260–270). Springer-Verlag.

Cooper, W. S. (1968). Expected search length: A single measure of retrieval effectiveness based on the weak ordering action of retrieval systems. *American Documentation, 19*(1), 30–41.

Cooper, W. S., Gey, F. C., & Dabney, D. P. (1992). Probabilistic retrieval based on staged logistic regression. In *SIGIR '92: Proceedings of the 15th annual international ACM SIGIR conference on research and development in information retrieval* (pp. 198–210). ACM.

Cowie, J., & Lehnert, W. (1996). Information extraction. *Communications of the ACM, 39*(1), 80–91.

Crawford, R. (1981). The relational model in information retrieval. *Journal of the American Society for Information Science, 32*(1), 51–64.

Croft, W. B. (2000). Combining approaches to information retrieval. In *Advances in information retrieval: Recent research from the CIIR* (pp. 1–36). Norwell, MA: Kluwer Academic Publishers.

Croft, W. B., Krovetz, R., & Turtle, H. (1990). Interactive retrieval of complex documents. *Information Processing and Management, 26*(5), 593–613.

Croft, W. B., & Lafferty, J. (2003). *Language modeling for information retrieval.* Norwell, MA: Kluwer Academic Publishers.

Croft, W. B., Smith, L. A., & Turtle, H. R. (1992). A loosely-coupled integration of a text retrieval system and an object-oriented database system. In *SIGIR '92: Proceedings of the 15th annual international ACM SIGIR conference on research and development in information retrieval* (pp. 223–232). ACM.

Croft, W. B., & Turtle, H. (1989). A retrieval model incorporating hypertext links. In *Hypertext '89: Proceedings of the second annual ACM conference on hypertext* (pp. 213–224). ACM.

Croft, W. B., Turtle, H. R., & Lewis, D. D. (1991). The use of phrases and structured queries in information retrieval. In *SIGIR '91: Proceedings of the 14th annual international ACM SIGIR conference on research and development in information retrieval* (pp. 32–45). ACM.

Cronen-Townsend, S., Zhou, Y., & Croft, W. B. (2006). Precision prediction based on ranked list coherence. *Information Retrieval*, *9*(6), 723–755.

Cucerzan, S., & Brill, E. (2004). Spelling correction as an iterative process that exploits the collective knowledge of web users. In D. Lin & D. Wu (Eds.), *Proceedings of EMNLP 2004* (pp. 293–300). Association for Computational Linguistics.

Cui, H., Wen, J.-R., Nie, J.-Y., & Ma, W.-Y. (2003). Query expansion by mining user logs. *IEEE Transactions on Knowledge and Data Engineering*, *15*(4), 829–839.

Dannenberg, R. B., Birmingham, W. P., Pardo, B., Hu, N., Meek, C., & Tzanetakis, G. (2007). A comparative evaluation of search techniques for query-by-humming using the MUSART testbed. *Journal of the American Society for Information Science and Technology*, *58*(5), 687–701.

Dean, J., & Ghemawat, S. (2008). MapReduce: simplified data processing on large clusters. *Communications of the ACM*, *51*(1), 107–113.

DeCandia, G., Hastorun, D., Jampani, M., Kakulapati, G., Lakshman, A., Pilchin, A., et al. (2007). Dynamo: Amazon's highly available key-value store. In *SOSP '07: Proceedings of the twenty-first ACM SIGOPS symposium on operating systems principles* (pp. 205–220). ACM.

Deerwester, S. C., Dumais, S. T., Landauer, T. K., Furnas, G. W., & Harshman, R. A. (1990). Indexing by Latent Semantic Analysis. *Journal of the American Society of Information Science*, *41*(6), 391–407.

Deutsch, P. (1996). *DEFLATE compressed data format specification version 1.3* (RFC No. 1951). Internet Engineering Task Force. Available from http://www.rfc-editor.org/rfc/rfc1951.txt

Diaz, F. (2005). Regularizing ad hoc retrieval scores. In *CIKM '05: Proceedings of the 14th ACM international conference on information and knowledge management* (pp. 672–679). ACM.

Duda, R. O., Hart, P. E., & Stork, D. G. (2000). *Pattern classification* (2nd ed.). Wiley-Interscience.

Dunlop, M. D., & van Rijsbergen, C. J. (1993). Hypermedia and free text retrieval. *Information Processing and Management*, 29(3), 287–298.

Echihabi, A., & Marcu, D. (2003). A noisy-channel approach to question answering. In *ACL '03: Proceedings of the 41st annual meeting on Association for Computational Linguistics* (pp. 16–23). Association for Computational Linguistics.

Efthimiadis, E. N. (1996). Query expansion. In M. E. Williams (Ed.), *Annual review of information systems and technology (ARIST)* (Vol. 31, pp. 121–187).

Elmasri, R., & Navathe, S. (2006). *Fundamentals of database systems* (5th ed.). Reading, MA: Addison-Wesley.

Fagin, R., Lotem, A., & Naor, M. (2003). Optimal aggregation algorithms for middleware. *Journal of Computer and Systems Sciences*, 66(4), 614–656.

Feng, J., Bhargava, H. K., & Pennock, D. M. (2007). Implementing sponsored search in web search engines: Computational evaluation of alternative mechanisms. *INFORMS Journal on Computing*, 19(1), 137–148.

Fetterly, D., Manasse, M., & Najork, M. (2003). On the evolution of clusters of near-duplicate web pages. In *LA-WEB '03: Proceedings of the first conference on Latin American Web Congress* (pp. 37–45). IEEE Computer Society.

Finn, A., Kushmerick, N., & Smyth, B. (2001). Fact or fiction: Content classification for digital libraries. In *DELOS workshop: Personalisation and recommender systems in digital libraries*.

Flake, G. W., Lawrence, S., & Giles, C. L. (2000). Efficient identification of web communities. In *KDD '00: Proceedings of the sixth ACM SIGKDD international conference on knowledge discovery and data mining* (pp. 150–160). ACM.

Flickner, M., Sawhney, H. S., Ashley, J., Huang, Q., Dom, B., Gorkani, M., et al. (1995). Query by image and video content: The QBIC system. *IEEE Computer*, 28(9), 23–32.

Fox, S., Karnawat, K., Mydland, M., Dumais, S., & White, T. (2005). Evaluating implicit measures to improve web search. *ACM Transactions on Information Systems*, 23(2), 147–168.

Fuhr, N. (2000). Probabilistic datalog: Implementing logical information retrieval for advanced applications. *Journal of the American Society for Information Science and Technology*, 51(2), 95–110.

Fuhr, N. (2008). A probability ranking principle for interactive information retrieval. *Information Retrieval*, *11*(3), 251–265.

Fuhr, N., & Buckley, C. (1991). A probabilistic learning approach for document indexing. *ACM Transactions on Information Systems*, *9*(3), 223–248.

Fuhr, N., & Rölleke, T. (1997). A probabilistic relational algebra for the integration of information retrieval and database systems. *ACM Transactions on Information Systems*, *15*(1), 32–66.

Fujii, H., & Croft, W. B. (1993). A comparison of indexing techniques for Japanese text retrieval. In *SIGIR '93: Proceedings of the 16th annual international ACM SIGIR conference on research and development in information retrieval* (pp. 237–246). ACM.

Gao, J., Nie, J.-Y., Wu, G., & Cao, G. (2004). Dependence language model for information retrieval. In *SIGIR '04: Proceedings of the 27th annual international ACM SIGIR conference on research and development in information retrieval* (pp. 170–177). ACM.

Gao, J., Qi, H., Xia, X., & Nie, J.-Y. (2005). Linear discriminant model for information retrieval. In *SIGIR '05: Proceedings of the 28th annual international ACM SIGIR conference on research and development in information retrieval* (pp. 290–297). ACM.

Garcia-Molina, H., Ullman, J. D., & Widom, J. D. (2008). *Database systems: The complete book*. Prentice Hall.

Gibson, D., Kleinberg, J., & Raghavan, P. (1998). Inferring web communities from link topology. In *HYPERTEXT '98: Proceedings of the ninth ACM conference on hypertext and hypermedia* (pp. 225–234). ACM.

Golder, S. A., & Huberman, B. A. (2006). Usage patterns of collaborative tagging systems. *Journal of Information Science*, *32*(2), 198–208.

Goldstein, J., Kantrowitz, M., Mittal, V., & Carbonell, J. (1999). Summarizing text documents: sentence selection and evaluation metrics. In *SIGIR '99: Proceedings of the 22nd annual international ACM SIGIR conference on research and development in information retrieval* (pp. 121–128). ACM.

Grefenstette, G. (1998). *Cross-language information retrieval*. Norwell, MA: Kluwer Academic Publishers.

Guo, J., Xu, G., Li, H., & Cheng, X. (2008). A unified and discriminative model for query refinement. In *SIGIR '08: Proceedings of the 31st annual international ACM SIGIR conference on research and development in information retrieval* (pp. 379–386). ACM.

Gupta, S., Kaiser, G., Neistadt, D., & Grimm, P. (2003). DOM-based content extraction of HTML documents. In *WWW '03: Proceedings of the 12th international conference on World Wide Web* (pp. 207–214). ACM.

Gyöngyi, Z., & Garcia-Molina, H. (2005). Web spam taxonomy. In *AIRWeb: 1st international workshop on adversarial information retrieval on the web* (pp. 39–47).

Gyöngyi, Z., Garcia-Molina, H., & Pedersen, J. (2004). Combating web spam with TrustRank. In *VLDB 2004: Proceedings of the thirtieth international conference on very large data bases* (pp. 576–587). Morgan Kaufmann.

Ha, L. Q., Sicilia-Garcia, E. I., Ming, J., & Smith, F. J. (2002). Extension of Zipf's law to words and phrases. In *Proceedings of the 19th international conference on computational linguistics* (pp. 1–6). Association for Computational Linguistics.

Harding, S. M., Croft, W. B., & Weir, C. (1997). Probabilistic retrieval of OCR degraded text using n-grams. In *ECDL '97: Proceedings of the first European conference on research and advanced technology for digital libraries* (pp. 345–359). Springer-Verlag.

Hastie, T., Tibshirani, R., & Friedman, J. (2001). *The elements of statistical learning: Data mining, inference, and prediction*. Springer.

Hatcher, E., & Gospodnetic, O. (2004). *Lucene in action*. Manning Publications.

Haveliwala, T. H. (2002). Topic-sensitive PageRank. In *WWW '02: Proceedings of the 11th international conference on World Wide Web* (pp. 517–526). ACM.

Hawking, D., & Zobel, J. (2007). Does topic metadata help with web search? *Journal of the American Society for Information Science and Technology*, *58*(5), 613–628.

He, B., Patel, M., Zhang, Z., & Chang, K. (2007). Accessing the deep web. *Communications of the ACM*, *50*(5), 94–101.

Heaps, H. (1978). *Information retrieval: Computational and theoretical aspects*. New York: Academic Press.

Hearst, M. A. (1999). User interfaces and visualization. In *Modern information retrieval* (pp. 257–324). ACM/Addison-Wesley.

Hearst, M. A. (2006). Clustering versus faceted categories for information exploration. *Communications of the ACM*, *49*(4), 59–61.

Hearst, M. A., & Pedersen, J. O. (1996). Reexamining the cluster hypothesis: scatter/gather on retrieval results. In *SIGIR '96: Proceedings of the 19th annual international ACM SIGIR conference on research and development in information retrieval* (pp. 76–84). ACM.

Henzinger, M. (2006). Finding near-duplicate web pages: A large-scale evaluation of algorithms. In *SIGIR '06: Proceedings of the 29th annual international ACM SIGIR conference on research and development in information retrieval* (pp. 284–291). ACM.

Herlocker, J. L., Konstan, J. A., Terveen, L. G., & Riedl, J. T. (2004). Evaluating collaborative filtering recommender systems. *ACM Transactions on Information Systems, 22*(1), 5–53.

Heymann, P., Koutrika, G., & Garcia-Molina, H. (2008). Can social bookmarking improve web search? In *WSDM '08: Proceedings of the international conference on web search and web data mining* (pp. 195–206). ACM.

Heymann, P., Ramage, D., & Garcia-Molina, H. (2008). Social tag prediction. In *SIGIR '08: Proceedings of the 31st annual international ACM SIGIR conference on research and development in information retrieval* (pp. 531–538). ACM.

Hiemstra, D. (1998). A linguistically motivated probabilistic model of information retrieval. In *ECDL '98: Proceedings of the second european conference on research and advanced technology for digital libraries* (pp. 569–584). Springer-Verlag.

Hoad, T., & Zobel, J. (2003). Methods for identifying versioned and plagiarised documents. *Journal of the American Society of Information Science and Technology, 54*(3), 203–215.

Hobbs, J., Douglas, R., Appelt, E., Bear, J., Israel, D., Kameyama, M., et al. (1997). Fastus: A cascaded finite-state transducer for extracting information from natural-language text. In *Finite state language processing* (chap. 13). Cambridge, MA: MIT Press.

Hofmann, T. (1999). Probabilistic latent semantic indexing. In *SIGIR '99: Proceedings of the 22nd annual international ACM SIGIR conference on research and development in information retrieval* (pp. 50–57). ACM.

Hopcroft, J., Khan, O., Kulis, B., & Selman, B. (2003). Natural communities in large linked networks. In *KDD '03: Proceedings of the ninth ACM SIGKDD international conference on knowledge discovery and data mining* (pp. 541–546). ACM.

Ingwersen, P., & Järvelin, K. (2005). *The turn: Integration of information seeking and retrieval in context*. Secaucus, NJ: Springer-Verlag.

Ipeirotis, P. G., & Gravano, L. (2004). When one sample is not enough: Improving text database selection using shrinkage. In *SIGMOD '04: Proceedings of the 2004 ACM SIGMOD international conference on management of data* (pp. 767–778). ACM.

Ittycheriah, A., Franz, M., Zhu, W.-J., Ratnaparkhi, A., & Mammone, R. J. (2001). Question answering using maximum entropy components. In *NAACL '01: Second meeting of the North American Chapter of the Association for Computational Linguistics on language technologies* (pp. 1–7). Association for Computational Linguistics.

Järvelin, K., & Kekäläinen, J. (2002). Cumulated gain-based evaluation of IR techniques. *ACM Transactions on Information Systems, 20*(4), 422–446.

Jeon, J., Croft, W. B., & Lee, J. H. (2005). Finding similar questions in large question and answer archives. In *CIKM '05: Proceedings of the 14th ACM international conference on information and knowledge management* (pp. 84–90). ACM.

Jeon, J., Croft, W. B., Lee, J. H., & Park, S. (2006). A framework to predict the quality of answers with non-textual features. In *SIGIR '06: Proceedings of the 29th annual international ACM SIGIR conference on research and development in information retrieval* (pp. 228–235). ACM.

Jijkoun, V., & de Rijke, M. (2005). Retrieving answers from frequently asked questions pages on the web. In *CIKM '05: Proceedings of the 14th ACM international conference on information and knowledge management* (pp. 76–83). ACM.

Jing, Y., & Croft, W. B. (1994). An association thesaurus for information retrieval. In *Proceedings of RIAO-94, 4th international conference "recherche d'information assistee par ordinateur"* (pp. 146–160).

Joachims, T. (2002a). *Learning to classify text using support vector machines: Methods, theory and algorithms.* Norwell, MA: Kluwer Academic Publishers.

Joachims, T. (2002b). Optimizing search engines using clickthrough data. In *KDD '02: Proceedings of the eighth ACM SIGKDD international conference on knowledge discovery and data mining* (pp. 133–142). ACM.

Joachims, T., Granka, L., Pan, B., Hembrooke, H., & Gay, G. (2005). Accurately interpreting clickthrough data as implicit feedback. In *SIGIR '05: Proceedings of the 28th annual international ACM SIGIR conference on research and development in information retrieval* (pp. 154–161). ACM.

Jones, R., Rey, B., Madani, O., & Greiner, W. (2006). Generating query substitutions. In *WWW '06: Proceedings of the 15th international conference on World Wide Web* (pp. 387–396). ACM.

Jurafsky, D., & Martin, J. H. (2006). *Speech and language processing* (2nd ed.). London: Prentice Hall.

Kazai, G., Gövert, N., Lalmas, M., & Fuhr, N. (2003). The INEX evaluation initiative. In H. Blanken, T. Grabs, H.-J. Schek, R. Schenkel, & G. Weikum (Eds.), *Intelligent XML retrieval* (pp. 279–293). Springer.

Kelly, D., & Teevan, J. (2003). Implicit feedback for inferring user preference: A bibliography. *SIGIR Forum, 32*(2).

Kleinberg, J. M. (1999). Authoritative sources in a hyperlinked environment. *Journal of the ACM, 46*(5), 604–632.

Knuth, D. E. (1998). *The art of computer programming: Sorting and searching* (2nd ed., Vol. 3). Redwood City, CA: Addison-Wesley Longman.

Koenemann, J., & Belkin, N. J. (1996). A case for interaction: a study of interactive information retrieval behavior and effectiveness. In *CHI '96: Proceedings of the SIGCHI conference on human factors in computing systems* (pp. 205–212). ACM.

Kraaij, W., Westerveld, T., & Hiemstra, D. (2002). The importance of prior probabilities for entry page search. In *SIGIR '02: Proceedings of the 25th annual international ACM SIGIR conference on research and development in information retrieval* (pp. 27–34). ACM.

Krovetz, R. (1993). Viewing morphology as an inference process. In *SIGIR '93: Proceedings of the 16th annual international ACM SIGIR conference on research and development in information retrieval* (pp. 191–202). ACM.

Kukich, K. (1992). Techniques for automatically correcting words in text. *ACM Computing Surveys, 24*(4), 377–439.

Kurland, O. (2008). The opposite of smoothing: A language model approach to ranking query-specific document clusters. In *SIGIR '08: Proceedings of the 31st annual international ACM SIGIR conference on research and development in information retrieval* (pp. 171–178). ACM.

Kurland, O., & Lee, L. (2004). Corpus structure, language models, and ad hoc information retrieval. In *SIGIR '04: Proceedings of the 27th annual international ACM SIGIR conference on research and development in information retrieval* (pp. 194–201). ACM.

Kurland, O., & Lee, L. (2005). Pagerank without hyperlinks: structural re-ranking using links induced by language models. In *SIGIR '05: Proceedings of the 28th annual international ACM SIGIR conference on research and development in information retrieval* (pp. 306–313). ACM.

Lafferty, J., & Zhai, C. (2001). Document language models, query models, and risk minimization for information retrieval. In *SIGIR '01: Proceedings of the 24th annual international ACM SIGIR conference on research and development in information retrieval* (pp. 111–119). ACM.

Lankes, R. D. (2004). The digital reference research agenda. *Journal of the American Society for Information Science and Technology, 55*(4), 301–311.

Larkey, L. S., Ballesteros, L., & Connell, M. E. (2002). Improving stemming for Arabic information retrieval: Light stemming and co-occurrence analysis. In *SIGIR '02: Proceedings of the 25th annual international ACM SIGIR conference on research and development in information retrieval* (pp. 275–282). ACM.

Lavrenko, V., & Croft, W. B. (2001). Relevance based language models. In *SIGIR '01: Proceedings of the 24th annual international ACM SIGIR conference on research and development in information retrieval* (pp. 120–127). ACM.

Lawrie, D. J., & Croft, W. B. (2003). Generating hierarchical summaries for web searches. In *SIGIR '03: Proceedings of the 26th annual international ACM SIGIR conference on research and development in information retrieval* (pp. 457–458). ACM.

Leouski, A., & Croft, W. (1996). *An evaluation of techniques for clustering search results* (Tech. Rep. Nos. IR–76). Department of Computer Science, University of Massachusetts Amherst.

Lester, N., Moffat, A., & Zobel, J. (2005). Fast on-line index construction by geometric partitioning. In *CIKM '05: Proceedings of the 14th ACM international conference on information and knowledge management* (pp. 776–783). New York: ACM.

Leuski, A., & Lavrenko, V. (2006). Tracking dragon-hunters with language models. In *CIKM '06: Proceedings of the 15th ACM international conference on information and knowledge management* (pp. 698–707). ACM.

Liu, X., & Croft, W. B. (2004). Cluster-based retrieval using language models. In *SIGIR '04: Proceedings of the 27th annual international ACM SIGIR conference on research and development in information retrieval* (pp. 186–193). ACM.

Liu, X., & Croft, W. B. (2008). Evaluating text representations for retrieval of the best group of documents. In *ECIR '08: Proceedings of the 30th European conference on information retrieval* (pp. 454–462). Springer.

Lowe, D. G. (2004). Distinctive image features from scale-invariant keypoints. *International Journal of Computer Vision, 60*(2), 91–110.

Lu, J., & Callan, J. (2006). Full-text federated search of text-based digital libraries in peer-to-peer networks. *Information Retrieval*, *9*(4), 477–498.

Lu, J., & Callan, J. (2007). Content-based peer-to-peer network overlay for full-text federated search. In *RIAO '07: Proceedings of the eighth RIAO conference*.

Luhn, H. P. (1958). The automatic creation of literature abstracts. *IBM Journal of Research and Development*, *2*(2), 159–165.

Lund, K., & Burgess, C. (1996). Producing high-dimensional semantic spaces from lexical co-occurrence. *Behavior Research Methods, Instrumentation, and Computers*, *28*(2), 203–208.

Manning, C. D., Raghavan, P., & Schütze, H. (2008). *Introduction to information retrieval*. New York: Cambridge University Press.

Manning, C. D., & Schütze, H. (1999). *Foundations of statistical natural language processing*. Cambridge, MA: The MIT Press.

Marchionini, G. (2006). Exploratory search: from finding to understanding. *Communications of the ACM*, *49*(4), 41–46.

McBryan, O. A. (1994). GENVL and WWWW: Tools for Taming the Web. In *WWW '94: Proceedings of the first international World Wide Web conference* (p. 15). CERN, Geneva.

McCallum, A. (2005). Information extraction: distilling structured data from unstructured text. *Queue*, *3*(9), 48–57.

McCallum, A., & Nigam, K. (1998). A comparison of event models for naive Bayes text classification. In *AAAI-98 workshop on learning for text categorization*.

Menczer, F., & Belew, R. K. (1998). Adaptive information agents in distributed textual environments. In *AGENTS '98: Proceedings of the second international conference on autonomous agents* (pp. 157–164). ACM.

Metzler, D., & Croft, W. B. (2004). Combining the language model and inference network approaches to retrieval. *Information Processing and Management*, *40*(5), 735–750.

Metzler, D., & Croft, W. B. (2005a). Analysis of statistical question classification for fact-based questions. *Information Retrieval*, *8*(3), 481–504.

Metzler, D., & Croft, W. B. (2005b). A Markov random field model for term dependencies. In *SIGIR '05: Proceedings of the 28th annual international ACM SIGIR conference on research and development in information retrieval* (pp. 472–479). ACM.

Metzler, D., & Croft, W. B. (2007a). Latent concept expansion using Markov random fields. In *SIGIR '07: Proceedings of the 30th annual international ACM SIGIR conference on research and development in information retrieval* (pp. 311–318). ACM.

Metzler, D., & Croft, W. B. (2007b). Linear feature-based models for information retrieval. *Information Retrieval, 10*(3), 257–274.

Metzler, D., Dumais, S. T., & Meek, C. (2007). Similarity measures for short segments of text. In *ECIR '07: Proceedings of the European conference on information retrieval* (pp. 16–27). Springer.

Metzler, D., Lavrenko, V., & Croft, W. B. (2004). Formal multiple-Bernoulli models for language modeling. In *SIGIR '04: Proceedings of the 27th annual international ACM SIGIR conference on research and development in information retrieval* (pp. 540–541). ACM.

Metzler, D., Strohman, T., & Croft, W. B. (2008). A statistical view of binned retrieval models. In *ECIR 2008: Proceedings of the 30th European conference on information retrieval* (pp. 175–186). Springer.

Metzler, D., Strohman, T., Turtle, H., & Croft, W. (2004). Indri at TREC 2004: Terabyte track. In *NIST special publication 500–261: Text REtrieval Conference proceedings (TREC 2004)*. National Institute of Standards and Technology.

Miller, D. R. H., Leek, T., & Schwartz, R. M. (1999). A Hidden Markov Model information retrieval system. In *SIGIR '99: Proceedings of the 22nd annual international ACM SIGIR conference on research and development in information retrieval* (pp. 214–221). ACM.

Mizzaro, S. (1997). Relevance: The whole history. *Journal of the American Society of Information Science, 48*(9), 810–832.

Moffat, A., Webber, W., & Zobel, J. (2007). Strategic system comparisons via targeted relevance judgments. In *SIGIR '07: Proceedings of the 30th annual international ACM SIGIR conference on research and development in information retrieval* (pp. 375–382). ACM.

Montague, M., & Aslam, J. A. (2002). Condorcet fusion for improved retrieval. In *CIKM '02: Proceedings of the eleventh international conference on information and knowledge management* (pp. 538–548). ACM.

Morris, M. R. (2008). A survey of collaborative web search practices. In *CHI '08: Proceeding of the twenty-sixth annual SIGCHI conference on human factors in computing systems* (pp. 1,657–1,660). ACM.

Morris, M. R., & Horvitz, E. (2007a). S^3: Storable, shareable search. In *Interact (1)* (pp. 120–123).

Morris, M. R., & Horvitz, E. (2007b). SearchTogether: an interface for collaborative web search. In *UIST '07: Proceedings of the 20th annual ACM symposium on user interface software and technology* (pp. 3–12). ACM.

Ntoulas, A., Najork, M., Manasse, M., & Fetterly, D. (2006). Detecting spam web pages through content analysis. In *WWW '06: Proceedings of the 15th international conference on World Wide Web* (pp. 83–92).

Ogilvie, P., & Callan, J. (2003). Combining document representations for known-item search. In *SIGIR '03: Proceedings of the 26th annual international ACM SIGIR conference on research and development in informaion retrieval* (pp. 143–150). ACM.

Pang, B., Lee, L., & Vaithyanathan, S. (2002). Thumbs up?: sentiment classification using machine learning techniques. In *EMNLP '02: Proceedings of the ACL-02 conference on empirical methods in natural language processing* (pp. 79–86). Association for Computational Linguistics.

Peng, F., Ahmed, N., Li, X., & Lu, Y. (2007). Context sensitive stemming for web search. In *SIGIR '07: Proceedings of the 30th annual international ACM SIGIR conference on research and development in information retrieval* (pp. 639–646). ACM.

Peng, F., Feng, F., & McCallum, A. (2004). Chinese segmentation and new word detection using conditional random fields. In *COLING '04: Proceedings of the 20th international conference on computational linguistics* (p. 562). Association for Computational Linguistics.

Pentland, A., Picard, R. W., & Sclaroff, S. (1996). Photobook: Content-based manipulation of image databases. *International Journal of Computer Vision*, *18*(3), 233–254.

Petkova, D., & Croft, W. B. (2007). Proximity-based document representation for named entity retrieval. In *CIKM '07: Proceedings of the sixteenth ACM conference on information and knowledge management* (pp. 731–740). ACM.

Pickens, J., Golovchinsky, G., Shah, C., Qvarfordt, P., & Back, M. (2008). Algorithmic mediation for collaborative exploratory search. In *SIGIR '08: Proceedings of the 31st annual international ACM SIGIR conference on research and development in information retrieval* (pp. 315–322). ACM.

Pinto, D., Branstein, M., Coleman, R., Croft, W. B., King, M., Li, W., et al. (2002). QuASM: a system for question answering using semi-structured data. In

JCDL '02: Proceedings of the 2nd ACM/IEEE-CS joint conference on digital libraries (pp. 46–55). ACM.

Ponte, J. M., & Croft, W. B. (1998). A language modeling approach to information retrieval. In *SIGIR '98: Proceedings of the 21st annual international ACM SIGIR conference on research and development in information retrieval* (pp. 275–281). ACM.

Porter, M. F. (1997). An algorithm for suffix stripping. In *Readings in information retrieval* (pp. 313–316). San Francisco: Morgan Kaufmann.

Powell, A. L., French, J. C., Callan, J., Connell, M., & Viles, C. L. (2000). The impact of database selection on distributed searching. In *SIGIR '00: Proceedings of the 23rd annual international ACM SIGIR conference on research and development in information retrieval* (pp. 232–239). ACM.

Pritchard-Schoch, T. (1993). WIN–WESTLAW goes natural. *Online, 17*(1), 101–103.

Rajashekar, T. B., & Croft, W. B. (1995). Combining automatic and manual index representations in probabilistic retrieval. *Journal of the American Society of Information Science, 46*(4), 272–283.

Ravela, S., & Manmatha, R. (1997). Image retrieval by appearance. In *SIGIR '97: Proceedings of the 20th annual international ACM SIGIR conference on research and development in information retrieval* (pp. 278–285). ACM.

Riezler, S., Vasserman, A., Tsochantaridis, I., Mittal, V., & Liu, Y. (2007). Statistical machine translation for query expansion in answer retrieval. In *Proceedings of the 45th annual meeting of the association of computational linguistics* (pp. 464–471). ACL.

Robertson, S. E. (1997). The probability ranking principle in IR. In *Readings in information retrieval* (pp. 281–286). Morgan Kaufmann. (Reprinted from *Journal of Documentation*, 1977, *33*, 294–304)

Robertson, S. E. (2004). Understanding inverse document frequency: On theoretical arguments for IDF. *Journal of Documentation, 60*, 503–520.

Robertson, S. E., & Walker, S. (1994). Some simple effective approximations to the 2-poisson model for probabilistic weighted retrieval. In *SIGIR '94: Proceedings of the 17th annual international ACM SIGIR conference on research and development in information retrieval* (pp. 232–241). Springer-Verlag.

Robertson, S. E., Zaragoza, H., & Taylor, M. (2004). Simple BM25 extension to multiple weighted fields. In *CIKM '04: Proceedings of the thirteenth ACM international conference on information and knowledge management* (pp. 42–49). ACM.

Rocchio, J. J. (1971). Relevance feedback in information retrieval. In G. Salton (Ed.), *The SMART retrieval system: Experiments in automatic document processing* (pp. 313–323). Englewood Cliffs, NJ: Prentice-Hall.

Romano, N. C., Roussinov, D., Nunamaker, J. F., & Chen, H. (1999). Collaborative information retrieval environment: Integration of information retrieval with group support systems. In *HICSS '99: Proceedings of the thirty-second annual Hawaii international conference on system sciences-volume 1* (pp. 1,053). IEEE Computer Society.

Sahami, M., & Heilman, T. D. (2006). A web-based kernel function for measuring the similarity of short text snippets. In *WWW '06: Proceedings of the 15th international conference on World Wide Web* (pp. 377–386). ACM.

Salton, G. (1968). *Automatic information organization and retrieval.* New York: McGraw-Hill.

Salton, G., & Buckley, C. (1988). Term-weighting approaches in automatic text retrieval. *Information Processing and Management, 24*(5), 513–523.

Salton, G., & McGill, M. J. (1983). *Introduction to modern information retrieval.* New York: McGraw-Hill.

Salton, G., Wong, A., & Yang, C. S. (1975). A vector space model for automatic indexing. *Communications of the ACM, 18*(11), 613–620.

Sanderson, M., & Zobel, J. (2005). Information retrieval system evaluation: effort, sensitivity, and reliability. In *SIGIR '05: Proceedings of the 28th annual international ACM SIGIR conference on research and development in information retrieval* (pp. 162–169). ACM.

Saracevic, T. (1975). Relevance: A review of and a framework for the thinking on the notion in information science. *Journal of the American Society for Information Science, 26*(6), 321–343.

Saraiva, P. C., de Moura, E. S., Ziviani, N., Meira, W., Fonseca, R., & Riberio-Neto, B. (2001). Rank-preserving two-level caching for scalable search engines. In *SIGIR '01: Proceedings of the 24th annual international ACM SIGIR conference on research and development in information retrieval* (pp. 51–58). New York: ACM.

Schapire, R. E., Singer, Y., & Singhal, A. (1998). Boosting and Rocchio applied to text filtering. In *SIGIR '98: Proceedings of the 21st annual international ACM SIGIR conference on research and development in information retrieval* (pp. 215–223). ACM.

Shannon, C. (1951). Prediction and entropy in printed English. *Bell System Technical Journal, 30*, 50–64.

Shannon, C., & Weaver, W. (1963). *A mathematical theory of communication.* Champaign, IL: University of Illinois Press.

Shneiderman, B., Byrd, D., & Croft, W. B. (1998). Sorting out searching: a user-interface framework for text searches. *Communications of the ACM, 41*(4), 95–98.

Si, L., & Callan, J. (2003). A semi-supervised learning method to merge search engine results. *ACM Transactions on Information Systems, 21*(4), 457–491.

Si, L., & Callan, J. (2004). Unified utility maximization framework for resource selection. In *CIKM '04: Proceedings of the eleventh international conference on information and knowledge management.* ACM.

Singhal, A., & Pereira, F. (1999). Document expansion for speech retrieval. In *SIGIR '99: Proceedings of the 22nd annual international ACM SIGIR conference on research and development in information retrieval* (pp. 34–41). ACM.

Smucker, M., Allan, J., & Carterette, B. (2007). A comparison of statistical significance tests for information retrieval evaluation. In *CIKM '07: Proceedings of the 14th ACM international conference on information and knowledge management.* ACM.

Song, F., & Croft, W. B. (1999). A general language model for information retrieval. In *CIKM '99: Proceedings of the eighth international conference on information and knowledge management* (pp. 316–321). ACM.

Song, R., Liu, H., Wen, J.-R., & Ma, W.-Y. (2004). Learning block importance models for web pages. In *WWW '04: Proceedings of the 13th international conference on World Wide Web* (pp. 203–211). ACM.

Sparck Jones, K., Walker, S., & Robertson, S. E. (2000). A probabilistic model of information retrieval: development and comparative experiments. *Information Processing and Management, 36*(6), 779–808.

Strohman, T. (2007). *Efficient processing of complex features for information retrieval.* Unpublished doctoral dissertation, University of Massachusetts Amherst.

Strohman, T., & Croft, W. B. (2006). Low latency index maintenance in Indri. In *OSIR 2006: Proceedings of the second international workshop on open source information retrieval* (pp. 7–11).

Strohman, T., Metzler, D., Turtle, H., & Croft, W. B. (2005). Indri: A language model-based search engine for complex queries. In *Proceedings of the international conference on intelligence analysis.*

Sun, J.-T., Shen, D., Zeng, H.-J., Yang, Q., Lu, Y., & Chen, Z. (2005). Web-page summarization using clickthrough data. In *SIGIR '05: Proceedings of the 28th annual international ACM SIGIR conference on research and development in information retrieval* (pp. 194–201). ACM.

Sutton, C., & McCallum, A. (2007). An introduction to conditional random fields for relational learning. In L. Getoor & B. Taskar (Eds.), *Introduction to statistical relational learning.* Cambridge, MA, USA: MIT Press.

Taghva, K., Borsack, J., & Condit, A. (1996). Evaluation of model-based retrieval effectiveness with OCR text. *ACM Transactions on Information Systems, 14*(1), 64–93.

Trotman, A., & Lalmas, M. (2006). Why structural hints in queries do not help XML-retrieval. In *SIGIR '06: Proceedings of the 29th annual international ACM SIGIR conference on research and development in information retrieval* (pp. 711–712). ACM.

Trotman, A., & Sigurbjörnsson, B. (2004). Narrowed Extended XPath I (NEXI). In *INEX workshop proceedings* (pp. 16–40). Springer.

Turpin, A., Tsegay, Y., & Hawking, D. (2007). Fast generation of result snippets in web search. In *SIGIR '07: Proceedings of the 30th annual international ACM SIGIR conference on research and development in information retrieval* (pp. 127–134). ACM.

Turtle, H. (1994). Natural language vs. Boolean query evaluation: a comparison of retrieval performance. In *SIGIR '94: Proceedings of the 17th annual international ACM SIGIR conference on research and development in information retrieval* (pp. 212–220). Springer-Verlag.

Turtle, H., & Croft, W. B. (1991). Evaluation of an inference network-based retrieval model. *ACM Transactions on Information Systems, 9*(3), 187–222.

Turtle, H., & Flood, J. (1995). Query evaluation: strategies and optimizations. *Information Processing and Management, 31*(6), 831–850.

Unicode Consortium. (2006). *The Unicode standard, version 5.0.* Addison-Wesley Professional.

van Rijsbergen, C. J. (1979). *Information retrieval* (2nd ed.). London: Butterworths.

Vasconcelos, N. (2007). From pixels to semantic spaces: Advances in content-based image retrieval. *Computer, 40*(7), 20–26.

Voorhees, E. M. (1985). The cluster hypothesis revisited. In *SIGIR '85: Proceedings of the 8th annual international ACM SIGIR conference on research and development in information retrieval* (pp. 188–196). ACM.

Voorhees, E. M., & Buckley, C. (2002). The effect of topic set size on retrieval experiment error. In *SIGIR '02: Proceedings of the 25th annual international ACM SIGIR conference on research and development in information retrieval* (pp. 316–323). ACM.

Voorhees, E. M., & Harman, D. (Eds.). (2005). *TREC: Experiment and evaluation in information retrieval*. Cambridge, MA: MIT Press.

Wang, A. (2006). The Shazam music recognition service. *Communications of the ACM, 49*(8), 44–48.

Wei, X., & Croft, W. B. (2006). LDA-based document models for ad-hoc retrieval. In *SIGIR '06: Proceedings of the 29th annual international ACM SIGIR conference on research and development in information retrieval* (pp. 178–185). ACM.

Wei, X., & Croft, W. B. (2007). Investigating retrieval performance with manually-built topic models. In *RIAO '07: Proceedings of the eighth RIAO conference.*

Welch, T. A. (1984). A technique for high-performance data compression. *Computer, 17,* 8–19.

Witten, I. H., Moffat, A., & Bell, T. C. (1999). *Managing Gigabytes: Compressing and indexing documents and images* (2nd ed.). San Francisco, CA, USA: Morgan Kaufmann.

Xia, F., Liu, T., Wang, J., Zhang, W., & Li, H. (2008). Listwise approach to learning to rank – theory and algorithm. In *ICML '08: Proceedings of the 25th annual international conference on machine learning* (pp. 1,192–1,199). Omnipress.

Xu, J., & Croft, W. B. (1998). Corpus-based stemming using cooccurrence of word variants. *ACM Transactions on Information Systems, 16*(1), 61–81.

Xu, J., & Croft, W. B. (2000). Improving the effectiveness of information retrieval with local context analysis. *ACM Transactions on Information Systems, 18*(1), 79–112.

Xu, Z., Fu, Y., Mao, J., & Su, D. (2006). Towards the semantic web: Collaborative tag suggestions. In *WWW 2006: Proceedings of the collaborative web tagging workshop.* Edinburgh, Scotland.

Xue, X., Jeon, J., & Croft, W. B. (2008). Retrieval models for question and answer archives. In *SIGIR '08: Proceedings of the 31st annual international ACM SIGIR conference on research and development in information retrieval* (pp. 475–482). ACM.

Yang, S., Zhu, H., Apostoli, A., & Cao, P. (2007). N-gram statistics in English and Chinese: Similarities and differences. In *ICSC '07: International conference on semantic computing* (pp. 454–460). IEEE Computer Society.

Yao, Y. (1995). Measuring retrieval effectiveness based on user preference of documents. *Journal of the American Society for Information Science, 46*(2), 133–145.

Yih, W., Goodman, J., & Carvalho, V. R. (2006). Finding advertising keywords on web pages. In *WWW '06: Proceedings of the 15th international conference on World Wide Web* (pp. 213–222). ACM.

Yu, S., Cai, D., Wen, J.-R., & Ma, W.-Y. (2003). Improving pseudo-relevance feedback in web information retrieval using web page segmentation. In *WWW '03: Proceedings of the 12th international conference on World Wide Web* (pp. 11–18). ACM.

Zamir, O., & Etzioni, O. (1999). Grouper: a dynamic clustering interface to web search results. *Computer Networks, 31*(11–16), 1,361–1,374.

Zeng, H.-J., He, Q.-C., Chen, Z., Ma, W.-Y., & Ma, J. (2004). Learning to cluster web search results. In *SIGIR '04: Proceedings of the 27th annual international ACM SIGIR conference on research and development in information retrieval* (pp. 210–217). ACM.

Zhai, C., & Lafferty, J. (2004). A study of smoothing methods for language models applied to information retrieval. *ACM Transactions on Information Systems, 22*(2), 179–214.

Zhang, V., Rey, B., Stipp, E., & Jones, R. (2006). Geomodification in query rewriting. In *GIR '06: Proceedings of the workshop on geographic information retrieval, ACM SIGIR 2006.*

Zhang, Y., & Callan, J. (2001). Maximum likelihood estimation for filtering thresholds. In *SIGIR '01: Proceedings of the 24th annual international ACM SIGIR conference on research and development in information retrieval* (pp. 294–302). ACM.

Zhou, Y., Xie, X., Wang, C., Gong, Y., & Ma, W.-Y. (2005). Hybrid index structures for location-based web search. In *CIKM '05: Proceedings of the 14th ACM international conference on information and knowledge management* (pp. 155–162). ACM.

Zobel, J. (1998). How reliable are the results of large-scale information retrieval experiments? In *SIGIR '98: Proceedings of the 21st annual international ACM SIGIR conference on research and development in information retrieval* (pp. 307–314). ACM.

Zobel, J., & Moffat, A. (2006). Inverted files for text search engines. *ACM Computing Surveys, 38*(2), 6.

Zobel, J., Moffat, A., & Ramamohanarao, K. (1996). Guidelines for presentation and comparison of indexing techniques. *ACM SIGMOD Record, 25*(3), 10–15.

Zobel, J., Moffat, A., & Ramamohanarao, K. (1998). Inverted files versus signature files for text indexing. *ACM Transactions on Database Systems, 23*(4), 453–490.

Zukowski, M., Héman, S., Nes, N., & Boncz, P. A. (2006). Super-scalar RAM-CPU cache compression. In *ICDE: International conference on data engineering* (p. 59). IEEE Computer Society.

Index